Understanding Anti-Americanism

Understanding
Anti-Americanism

ITS ORIGINS AND IMPACT
AT HOME AND ABROAD

Edited with an Introduction by

Paul Hollander

IVAN R. DEE

Chicago 2004

UNDERSTANDING ANTI-AMERICANISM. Copyright © 2004 by Paul Hollander. All rights reserved, including the right to reproduce this book or portions thereof in any form. For information, address: Ivan R. Dee, Publisher, 1332 North Halsted Street, Chicago 60622. Manufactured in the United States of America and printed on acid-free paper.

Library of Congress Cataloging-in-Publication Data:
Understanding anti-Americanism : its origins and impact at home and abroad / edited with an introduction by Paul Hollander.
    p. cm.
Includes bibliographical references.
ISBN 1-56663-564-0 (cloth : alk. paper) — ISBN 1-56663-616-7 (pbk : alk. paper)
    1. Anti-Americanism. 2. Anti-Americanism—History. 3. United States—Relations—Foreign countries. 4. Anti-Americanism—United States. 5. Public opinion—United States. I. Hollander, Paul, 1932–
    E840.U475 2004
    973.92—dc22

2004043849

Contents

Acknowledgments   vii

Introduction: The New Virulence and Popularity   3
PAUL HOLLANDER

PART I. ANTI-AMERICANISM ABROAD

1   The Philosophical Origins of Anti-Americanism
in Europe   45
JAMES CEASER

2   Sense of Superiority and Inferiority in French
Anti-Americanism   65
ANTHONY DANIELS

3   Recent Trends in British Anti-Americanism   84
MICHAEL MOSBACHER AND DIGBY ANDERSON

4   Affinity and Resentment: A Historical Sketch of
German Attitudes   105
MICHAEL FREUND

5   Anti-Americanism in the Middle East   124
PATRICK CLAWSON AND BARRY RUBIN

6   A Matter of Identity: The Anti-Americanism of
Latin American Intellectuals   144
MICHAEL RADU

7   Nicaraguan Anti-Americanism   165
DAVID BROOKS

8   Cuban Anti-Americanism: Historical, Popular,
and Official   190
MARK FALCOFF

9   Anti-Americanism in Post-Communist Russia   214
WALTER D. CONNOR

PART II. DOMESTIC DENUNCIATIONS

10   Anti-Americanism Then and Now   239
ROGER KIMBALL

11   The Rejection of American Society by the
Communist Left   258
HARVEY KLEHR AND JOHN EARL HAYNES

12   The Feminist Hostility Toward American Society   279
CATHY YOUNG

13   Peace Movements and the Adversary Culture   301
ADAM GARFINKLE

14   Moral Equivalence in Education: The Use of the
Holocaust in Discrediting American Society   322
SANDRA STOTSKY

15   Anti-Americanism and Popular Culture   347
BRUCE S. THORNTON

A Note on the Contributors   369

Acknowledgments

THE GENEROUS ASSISTANCE of the Bradley Foundation has been essential in the making of this book. I thank the National Association of Scholars for administering the Bradley Foundation grant. The Historical Research Foundation also provided prompt help in covering some of the expenses associated with producing this volume.

Jeffrey Beemer, a graduate student in sociology at the University of Massachusetts, Amherst, helped with many practical matters related to the use of computers, email, and data transmission.

Two conferences I attended (the second of which I organized), while unrelated to the book at hand, provided stimulation and insight into the phenomenon this book examines. The first was organized by *The New Criterion* and took place in Tunbridge Wells, England in October 2002; the second, funded by Liberty Fund in Savannah, Georgia, in March 2003. Only a handful of the contributors attended either of them.

I am grateful to all the contributors and especially to those who delivered their chapters on time.

P. H.

Northhampton, Massachusetts
February 2004

Understanding Anti-Americanism

PAUL HOLLANDER

Introduction: The New
Virulence and Popularity

*E*vents of the last few years, and 9/11 in particular, have made
the understanding of anti-Americanism a far more compelling
task than it used to be, although the phenomenon has been with
us for a long time. Its first incarnation, European anti-Americanism, has deep roots, and its stereotypes spread over much of the
world. As Simon Schama observed recently, "By the end of the
nineteenth century, the stereotype of the ugly American—vora-
cious, preachy, mercenary, and bombastically chauvinist—was
firmly in place in Europe." A series of famous visitors created or
confirmed "the stereotypes of cultural inferiority and boorish materialism," replete with images of America as "a strapping child-
monster whose runaway physical growth would never be matched
by moral or cultural maturity."[1] Such notions proved remarkably
tenacious and in recent decades have become more widespread
and venomous. The recent writings of Jean Baudrillard, the French
philosopher said to be "one of France's leading intellectuals,"[2]
echo these sentiments; they center on the idea of a profound, unbridgeable gap of understanding between America and Europe,
Americans and Europeans.

Baudrillard's views of American society and culture are in
many ways prototypical, at any rate of the cultural variety of
anti-Americanism. They also exemplify the protean character of
these beliefs as he projects upon America highly contradictory attributes. Thus America is at once "the only remaining primitive

society," a cultural "desert," *and* the embodiment of "radical modernity . . . the original version of modernity . . . it cultivates no origin or mythical authenticity; it has no past and no founding truth . . . it lives in a perpetual present . . ."; "The U.S. is utopia achieved"—but twenty pages later it is "anti-utopia . . . achieved: the anti-utopia of unreason . . . the neutralization of all values, the death of culture." He also writes:

> The confrontation between America and Europe reveals not so much a rapprochement as . . . an unbridgeable rift. There isn't just a gap between us but a whole chasm of modernity. . . . We are a desperately long way behind the stupidity and the mutational character, the naive extravagance and the social, racial, moral, morphological, and architectural eccentricity of their society. . . . The transcendental, historical Weltanschaung of Europe will always be beyond the Americans. . . . America is a world completely rotten with wealth, power, senility, indifference, puritanism and mental hygiene, poverty and waste, technological futility and aimless violence . . . the only country where quantity can be extolled without compunction.

Elsewhere Baudrillard writes, "Here, everything human is artificial. Furnace Creek [in Death Valley] is a synthetic, air-conditioned oasis"—as if the absence of air-conditioning in such a place would have been more authentic and thus preferable. Inauthenticity is *the* major blemish, the cardinal sin: ". . . it is Disneyland that is authentic here! The cinema and TV are America's reality! The freeways, the Safeways, the skylines, speed and deserts—these are America, not the galleries, churches and culture. . . ."

Baudrillard's peculiar misconceptions, preconceptions, projections, and stunning ignorance of matters American (trivial or profound) are further illustrated by such observations as: "The country is without hope. Even its garbage is clean [more inauthenticity!], its trade is lubricated, its traffic pacified . . . life is so liquid [?]. . . the bodies and the cars so fluid, the hair so blond, and the soft technologies so luxuriant that a European dreams of death and murder, of suicide motels, of orgies and cannibalism to counteract the perfection of the ocean . . . of that insane ease of life, to counteract the hyperreality [?] of everything here." Who besides the befuddled writer of these lines would have such "dreams"?

The main thrust of this muddled message appears to be that America is unnatural and inauthentic and that Americans lead lives of dehumanizing ease and comfort. While in one breath Baudrillard bemoans the primitive disorderliness and chaos of American life, elsewhere an exaggerated (and imaginary) orderliness and neatness stimulate his contempt. One final quote captures his fantasies and morbid fascination:

> What is arresting here is . . . both the absence of architecture in the cities . . . and the dizzying absence of emotion and character in the faces and bodies. Handsome, fluid, supple or cool, or grotesquely obese, probably less as a result of compulsive bulimia than a general incoherence [!], which results in a casualness about the body, or language, food, or the city: a loose network of individual, successive functions, a hypertrophied cell tissue proliferating in all directions. Thus the only tissue of the city is that of the freeways . . . the extraordinary spectacle of these thousands of cars moving . . . coming from nowhere, going nowhere . . . ceaselessly unrolling . . . without objectives . . .[3]

While dwelling on the "incoherence" of American life and even holding it responsible for obesity, Baudrillard is serenely unaware of his own incoherence. It would also be interesting, among other things, to learn how French expressways and traffic are more purposeful and authentic than their American counterparts.

It is precisely this emphasis (such as Baudrillard's) on the unbridgeable differences between cultures and groups of people that becomes the foundation and point of departure for the rise of hostile predisposition and generalization that is at the core of anti-Americanism and other forms of negative stereotyping.

Over a decade ago I noted with surprise how little serious scholarly writing there was about this phenomenon.[4] This book then, it must be said, fills a genuine need. Up-to-date, comprehensive analyses of anti-Americanism barely exist, especially the kind that examine comparatively its origins and manifestations in different parts of the world. And while anti-Americanism abroad has become increasingly difficult to ignore, few studies address the domestic variety and the connections and convergences between the foreign and domestic versions. This in part is due to semantic reasons: domestic anti-Americanism, more often than not, has other designations, including alienation, political estrangement, the adversary or counter culture, the culture of repudiation,[5] or the rejection of American society. In addition the term "anti-Americanism" in its domestic context has a bad flavor because of its historical association with right-wing political activities and beliefs during the early years of the cold war.

Yet anti-Americanism abroad and the reflexive disparagement of American society at home have much in common and nurture one another (as will be shown later), even when they spring from different sources. At least one important difference may be noted here. Anti-Americanism abroad tends to concentrate, more often than not, on tangible and widely shared grievances such as American economic policies, unfair trade practices, overbearing political dominance, American military presence, insults to national pride, the subversion of cultural traditions by American mass entertainments, rapacious energy policies, and so forth. By contrast, rejection and hostility at home have a more personal quality associated with what Robert Hughes has called "the culture of complaint" (the title of his 1993 book). The latter reflects the inclination, if not determination, to hold the social order responsible for a wide range of personal discontents and problems. I am not suggesting here that these claims are necessarily rooted in a neurotic disposition of unhappy individuals and should therefore be dismissed, but that they often involve (unlike those abroad) a determined, self-conscious effort to connect the personal to the social realm in the spirit of the well-known radical feminist assertion that "the personal is political." These complaints and denunciations often originate in the murkier depths of personal discontents and in the refusal to come to terms with the imperfections and conflicts of social existence and human nature.

In American society, increasingly saturated with a belief in the overwhelming social-environmental determination of personal lives and fortunes, it takes little effort or imagination to see a close connection between intimate personal problems and frustrations and the larger social world. Such "discoveries" often result in assigning responsibility for the personal problems to the social realm. The increasingly widespread cults and claims of victimhood and victimization are also associated with and depend heavily on such a socially deterministic view of personal problems and opportunities.

Another apparent difference between the two types of anti-Americanism is that the domestic version often seems to be more anguished and animated by a peculiarly intense bitterness and the conviction that the entity rejected is a unique incarnation of unspeakable evil. I am not suggesting that such attributions and projections cannot be found among the voices abroad but rather that they are more typical of internal, domestic hostility. The likely reason for this difference may be found in the psychodynamic of hate that springs from disappointment over unrealized and unrealistically high expectations originally directed at American society and its various institutions. Such deep disappointment is characteristic of many domestic critics.

The recognition that both varieties of anti-Americanism—foreign and domestic—are widespread and consequential is central to the conceptual foundation of this book.

It is another premise of this undertaking that a proper understanding of anti-Americanism can only be achieved by balancing two apparently incompatible perspectives or propositions. The first avers that anti-Americanism is a direct and rational response to the evident misdeeds of the United States abroad and its shortcomings and inequities at home. In other words, it is a set of attitudes created and stimulated by U.S. actions and policies and by the character of American social institutions, policies, and the defects and injustices thereof, even by the behavior of individual Americans, especially those abroad in some official capacity. The latter was the focus and the message of the popular 1958 novel, *The Ugly American*, which had twenty printings, was made into a popular movie, and in 1999 was reissued for the fourth time. It remains "required reading in dozens of courses of American history and culture." The novel "present[ed] Americans as bumbling, disdainful, incompetent and corrupt as they go about making enemies" abroad. William Lederer, its co-author, still believes that hostility to America is the result of the mistakes of U.S. foreign policy, of "greed and power. . . . We're still fighting poor, hungry, angry people with bombs and tanks when what they would really respond to is food and water, good roads, health care, and a little respect for their religion and culture."[6] He was not asked by the interviewer how the gratification of these needs would change the minds and attitudes of the well-educated, middle-class terrorists and suicide bombers prominent in recent times.

Stanley Hoffmann, a political scientist at Harvard University, has expressed a similar point of view:

> The anti-Americanism on the rise throughout the world is not just hostility toward the most powerful nation, or based on the old clichés of the left and the right; nor is it only envy or hatred of our values. It is, more often than not, a resentment of double standards and double talk, of crass ignorance and arrogance, of wrong assumptions and dubious policies.[7]

That is to say, anti-Americanism is a readily understandable response to the many wrongs the United States embodies and commits. If this explanation were correct, the reason for producing this book would be greatly diminished. There would be little to explain since it is not hard to grasp why people respond unfavorably to a morally repellent entity, an aggressive global power that is also riddled with domestic injustices and irrational and inhumane social institutions and practices. Anti-Americanism that responds to such self-evidently unattractive attributes would require little discussion. By the same token, one may also ask why anyone would seek lengthy and complex explanations for the rejection of phenomena such as slavery, Nazism, cannibalism, or the incest taboo. We wish to explore and feel the need to explain only what is both puzzling and wrong, in particular the victimization of the innocent. We wish to know why Jews have been subjected to murderous hatreds for millennia, why racism prevailed for centuries in the United States and elsewhere, why so many ethnic groups hate one another. Few would suggest that the qualities or behavior of Jews, blacks, or Gypsies explain, let alone justify, the treatment inflicted on them over time.

When anti-Americanism is seen as an entirely plausible and justified response to the nature of American society and U.S. foreign policy, it stimulates neither reflection nor research. This probably explains the dearth of studies of anti-Americanism since many of those qualified to undertake them consider the phenomenon normal and justified, rather than something in need of examination and deeper understanding.

In the second and conflicting view, anti-Americanism is a largely groundless, irrational predisposition[8] (similar to racism, sexism, or anti-Semitism), an expression of a deeply rooted scapegoating impulse, a disposition more closely related to the problems, frustrations, and deficiencies of those entertaining and articulating it—be they individuals, groups, nations, political parties, or movements—than to the real attributes of American foreign policy, society, or culture. As summed up by one commentator: "It is not that America went wrong here and there; it is that it is wrong root and branch. The conviction at the heart of those who engage in [anti-Americanism] is really quite simple: . . . America is an unmitigated evil . . . [and] is responsible for the evils of the rest of the world."[9] In the French context, as articulated by Philippe Roger, a French historian, this attitude has been described as "a kind of generalized anti-Americanism, not simply opposition to war in Iraq, [which] does exist, but . . . 'a routine of resentment . . .' rather than a critique of United States policy. . ."[10]

It is the conviction of unique depravity, evil, or corruption—a "profound and blanket dislike of anything the United States does at any time . . . a permanent, irrational, and often visceral distrust":[11]—that animates the detractors of the United States who qualify for the designation of "anti-American." They can be readily distinguished from critics unmoved and unmotivated by similar beliefs while perfectly willing to fault specific aspects of American society or U.S. foreign policy. As Todd Gitlin puts it: "Anti-Americanism is an emotion masquerading as an analysis. . . . When hatred of foreign policies ignites into hatred of an

entire people and their civilization, then thinking is dead and de-
monology lives. . . ." In the view of these anti-Americans, "American culture is like the AIDS virus: infectious, self-transforming
and lethal. . . . America and its works amount to nothing but un-
bridled wickedness. . . ."[12]

Anti-Americanism is further recognizable by the inclination to
equate the United States or its specific policies with some far
greater and unquestionable evil, by the urge to impose a moral
equivalence between the United States and entities such as Nazi
Germany, the Soviet Union, or Arab terrorists. (Sandra Stotsky's
essay in this volume provides a revealing illustration of this pro-
clivity in the use of the Holocaust in American high schools as a
device for the delegitimation of American society.)

Much of the profound aversion to America has been produced
by the belief that great opportunities have been squandered, with
a resounding failure to live up to splendid ideals.[13] The bitterness
generated by such frustrated, often youthful idealism was particularly clear and widespread in the 1960s. Bruce Thornton (a contributor to this volume) finds at the root of these high
expectations the American belief in progress and a certain romanticism: "Nowhere in the West has this optimism, this faith in a
progressive improving knowledge, been more tenaciously clung to
than in the United States. . . . The American character saw its spiritual, economic, and political possibilities as unlimited as the land
stretching westward. . . ." Romanticism (here and elsewhere)
stimulated "an adversarial stance toward a corrupt world" as well
as an "obsession with man's emotional life and the intensity and
value of feeling. . . . This obsession with one's subjective experience promotes a radical individualism, pitting the sensitive soul
against the strictures of a philistine, insensitive, and grasping social order"—a disposition that assumed mass proportions in and
after the 1960s.

Interestingly and originally, Thornton also argues that this romanticism has been given new support by a commercialized mass
culture:

All these expressions of Romantic sensibility—individualism,
nature-love, primacy of feeling, and the obsession with . . . sex-

ual passion—are alive and flourishing. . . . Two historical developments explain why.

. . . The most important was the creation of consumer capitalism, an economic system that depends on the creation of new products to gratify not needs but wants conjured up . . . by the new technology of mass advertising. The creation of wants in turn depends on fostering dissatisfaction with reality, an obsession with the self and its pleasures, and a distrust of traditional values and authority. . . .

A debased and trivialized Romanticism is thus today kept alive in advertising and popular culture, the vehicle both for engendering a dissatisfaction with everyday life when compared to exotic idealized worlds of the ad or movie, and for promising the means for gratifying, through a product, the desire for a more highly charged and intense life.

These trends intensified and spread in the 1960s, the period of "that great outburst of Romantic idealism among the children of privilege." Hence, "nourished by consumerism and the institutionalized sixties-style idealization of the irrational, Romanticism is alive and well. . . ."[14] And, one may add, it continues to supply themes and motives for the strongly felt rejection of existing social institutions and practices.

This second view of the nature of anti-Americanism requires a more thorough exploration and explanation. After all, notwithstanding the critiques and denunciations heaped upon the United States, millions of people from every corner of the globe continue to seek admission to this much vilified country. Global anti-Americanism has, in recent decades, also proved highly compatible with the popularity of American fashions, entertainments, and mass culture throughout the world. As Edward Rothstein has written: "Popular culture has become the standard-bearer for modernity. . . . American popular culture offers a powerful promise. Luxuriant and prurient passions are partially satisfied; desires for autonomy are offered fulfillment; material pleasures and possibilities become palpable. Choices are freely made. Who can resist such a siren song?"[15] The proximity between attraction, ambivalence, and rejection has also been noted by Ivan Klíma, the Czech writer and friend of America:

> Freedom . . . tends to be viewed in different ways. For some it represents freedom of spirit and independence from authority, for others it signifies vice and spiritual and moral depravity. Freedom can indeed have paradoxical consequences. One of them is the unbridled cult of entertainment, which increasingly nowadays seems to be the supreme social value: witness the astronomical sums paid to hockey and basketball players, pop singers, and film and TV stars. And the tide of violence, horror, and perversion, catering for the basest instincts, which streams every day from the gutter press and from film and television screens seems to me not so much an expression of freedom as a manifestation of moral decline. . . .[16]

The two views of anti-Americanism cannot be easily reconciled. It bears repeating that anti-Americanism is a deep-seated, emotional predisposition that perceives the United States as an unmitigated and uniquely evil entity and the source of all, or most, other evils in the world. Being critical of specific American institutions, policies, leaders, or cultural trends does not constitute the same mind-set. The problem of keeping the two attitudes apart intensifies when justified criticism of specific U.S. policies or attributes combines with or culminates in undifferentiated, diffuse, and empirically untenable hostility. In other words, even some of the most envenomed and embittered vilifiers of this society may be right about certain particulars of their indictment without justifying the overall conclusions they draw from them.

Another idea that animates this book, and one I have expressed before,[17] is that the deepest and broadest source of anti-Americanism, one that unites its proponents abroad and within the United States, is the aversion to (or, at best, ambivalence about) modernity, which the United States most strikingly represents. For those abroad, modernization, Westernization, and Americanization are inseparable; for those at home, the critical terminology regarding the bitter fruits of modernity is different, but many basic apprehensions are similar.

Fouad Ajami has written about the profound ambivalence that modernity inspires in different parts of the world:

> To come bearing modernism to those who want it but who rail against it at the same time, to represent and embody so much of what the world yearns for and fears, that is the American burden. . . . To the Europeans . . . the United States is unduly religious, almost embarrassingly so, its culture suffused with sacred symbolism. In the Islamic world, the burden is precisely the opposite. There, the United States scandalizes the devout. . . .[18]

Several aspects of modernity are indeed problematic and difficult to bear: the loss or decline of taken-for-granted beliefs that used to hold traditional societies together and make individual lives meaningful; the threats to a stable and well-defined sense of identity (perhaps the most strongly felt problem of modernity); the decline of community, the impersonality, isolation and anonymity of the individual associated with urban life and the growth of social and geographic mobility; the bureaucratization of life and the sense of losing control over one's destiny; the much lamented impact of continued urbanization (and suburbanization) and industrialization, and their destruction of the natural environment; the many evident misuses and misapplications of science and technology; the unintended ethical and aesthetic problems of belonging to a consumer society; the well-known social problems of modern mass societies, including crime, juvenile delinquency, family disintegration, escapist behavior (foremost among them drug and alcohol abuse), the vacuousness of mass culture and entertainment and their influence, the difficulties of old people less and less integrated into society—the list is long and could be continued.[19]

All such problematic phenomena are prominent in American society and are spreading elsewhere. Some are aggravated by peculiarly American attributes, such as an intense competitiveness, an excessive individualism, and unrealistically high expectations of the possibilities for self-fulfillment and the reconciliation of numerous conflicting values and desires.[20]

What is often not fully recognized is that the undesirable products or by-products of modernity (or Americanization) are the unintended consequences of the pursuit and attainment of goals widely shared even among the most unrelenting critics of America. They include personal and group freedoms, self-determination, achievement orientation, social and geographic mobility, a high standard of living (inseparable from high levels of productivity created by science and technology), and material-economic as well as social and political security.

Anti-Americanism abroad as well as at home is often an angry and anguished response to all these aspects of modernity. But not all of its many sources are directly related to modernity; specific local, social, and historical conditions may also account for it, as the chapters on different countries and regions in the first part of this book make clear.

Among the less specific sources of anti-Americanism we must also note a romantic as well as Marxist anti-capitalism; the nationalism of weaker or declining nations; the personal and cultural problems peculiar to intellectuals; the specter or standardization and homogenization associated with the spread of American mass culture; and resentment over losing in economic competition. It is of particular importance that at the present time virtually any widely shared grievance can lately become a source of anti-Americanism since all such grievances are easier to bear if some familiar and prominent entity may plausibly be held responsible for them.

THE INTENSIFICATION OF ANTI-AMERICANISM
IN RECENT TIMES

Both the friends and detractors of the United States, at home and abroad, agree that anti-Americanism has increased since the early 1990s following the collapse of the Soviet Union, and even more dramatically and unexpectedly since the attack on the World Trade Center on September 11, 2001. As one *New York Times* columnist saw it:

> One of the things that we Americans are finally waking up to since Sept. 11 is the degree to which we are disliked and resented around the world. Travel from Argentina to Japan, Russia to Senegal and you run into huge numbers of people who snarl

about America appointing itself the world's policeman, squandering the world's oil or undermining global treaties and institutions. We are accused of inflicting Big Macs, Microsoft Windows and Julia Roberts on the helpless masses.[21]

The intensification of anti-Americanism has fostered a variety of expressions, including acts of violence of which 9/11, was the most destructive and spectacular. It must, however, be recalled that numerous other lethal attacks were carried out before that date. The U.S. embassy in Beirut, Lebanon, was bombed in 1983, killing 63 employees, and that same year a bomb destroyed the U.S. Marine barracks in Beirut, killing 241. In 1988 the Pan Am flight over Scotland was brought down by terrorists, killing 259 passengers. In 1993 CIA employees were killed outside the CIA headquarters in Langley, Virginia, and in the same year the first attack on the World Trade Center in New York was carried out. In 1996 the Khobar Towers in Dharan, Saudi Arabia, housing military personnel were bombed with more than a dozen victims. In 1998 U.S. embassies in Nairobi and Dar es Salaam in East Africa were attacked with more than 300 killed. In 2000 the *USS Cole* was attacked at Yemen. In 2002 a reporter for the *Wall Street Journal* was kidnaped and murdered in Pakistan. Over the last three decades of the past century many other lethal attacks on American civilians and military and diplomatic personnel have occurred.[22] There have also been numerous aborted attempts, such as that of the "shoe bomber" seeking to bring down an airliner in 2002, and others targeting airliners as well as the Los Angeles airport.

A corresponding abundance of nonviolent expressions of anti-Americanism may be readily found in opinion polls around the world, in huge rallies and demonstrations, in the increasingly bitter rhetoric of media pundits at home and abroad, in UN debates and resolutions, and in innumerable unrecorded private conversations.

Even a pure and exceptionally destructive hate crime committed against the United States, as on 9/11, stimulated an outpouring of impassioned rhetorical attacks on the United States and its foreign and domestic policies. As one writer put it, the events following 9/11 "have increased the visceral loathing not of terrorism

or of Islamist fundamentalism but of President George Bush."[23]
Jean Bethke Elshtain noted: "Confronted with an aggressive foe
preaching hatred of any and all things Western, many [in the West]
have responded with a disturbing strain of self-loathing."[24]

Hostile critics quickly concluded that the "root cause" of the
visceral hatred of the United States and the violence it inspired
was none other than the United States itself. This being the case,
the violence was fully "understandable." As Jean Baudrillard
wrote: "It was the system itself which created the objective conditions for this brutal retaliation. . . ." More obscurely he added:
"Terrorism is the act that restores an irreducible singularity to the
heart of a system of generalized exchange."[25]

Five factors seem to account for the recent rise of anti-
Americanism:

1) The fall of Soviet communism, which eliminated the second
superpower; today the United States can plausibly be seen as the
only important global force shaping events around the world. Under these conditions it is understandable that Washington attracts
blame and is held responsible for a wide variety of worldwide political, economic, or cultural problems. As one Russian politician
recently said: "There was the Soviet Union and the balance of
pressures. Now, with this having disappeared . . . the United States
simply fell forward for lack of an opponent, and you became responsible for everything. . . . Now the United States has to fill the
entire space, they are responsible for everything—and therefore
they are to blame for everything."[26]

2) American assertions of military power always intensify anti-
Americanism and the associated political activism. In the last few
years there have been several such assertions, beginning with
Kosovo and continuing with the war against terror in Afghanistan
and against the Sadam Hussein regime.

All such military actions recall, for the critics, Vietnam and
the powerful anti-war movement it inspired as well as the atten-
dant radicalization of the political landscape. Present-day peace
activists hope for a similar, renewed radicalization and have
sought to reintroduce a broad political protest agenda unrelated to
war. (This topic is explored later in Adam Garfinkle's essay.)

The main source of strong disapproval of the American asser-tion of military power is rooted in the basic negative predisposi-tion sketched above. If the United States is perceived as a uniquely evil and destructive entity, these qualities are threateningly mul-tiplied when it uses military force to overwhelm its adversaries. A militarily triumphant American state is hard to behold among those who long for its demise. At the same time those abroad who oppose the United States attract the sympathy of adversarial groups at home and abroad who are impelled to give such regimes or movements at least the benefit of doubt.

Anti-terrorist measures at home—a domestic exercise of power—elicit corresponding apprehension and complaints and provide an ideal opportunity for domestic critics to conjure up im-ages of a new reign of domestic repression. In the *New York Times* one observer wrote recently:

> Three times in the last few weeks I have been told—by a novel-ist, an art historian and a professor of classics at Harvard . . . that the erosion of civil liberties under the Bush administration con-stitutes an early stage, or at least a precursor, to the kind of fas-cism Hitler brought to Germany. . . . One of the nation's leading scholars of international law suggested . . . that Bush's advisers were probably plotting to suspend the elections of 2004.[27]

The writer also noted the similarity between such (somewhat wishful) apprehensions and those more widespread in the 1960s, when apocalyptic fantasies of an imminent fascist takeover were rampant. Then they served to confirm the worst fears (and hopes) of the critics, who believed that from the crucible of such repres-sion a sweeping revolutionary transformation would emerge.

At the same it has also been suggested (by Barry Rubin, a con-tributor to this volume) that it was "the perceived softness [of the United States] in recent years that has encouraged anti-Americans to act on their belief. After the United States failed to respond ag-gressively to many terrorist attacks. . . .[28]

3) Another important source of renewed anti-Americanism both at home and abroad has been the personality and policies of the current president, George Bush permeated as it is with a

macho, cowboy image, aggressiveness, simplemindedness, and taken-for-granted loyalties devalued by the critics. He is correctly seen as possessed of a strong, reflexive patriotism and is undoubtedly pro-business; he is not an environmentalist and is disinterested in energy conservation. His critics also believe that he is generally unqualified to be president and gained this office through questionable legal-political manipulations.

Negative sentiments about President Bush abroad have been reflected in the findings of a poll by the *Sunday Times* of London in which "equal numbers called Saddam and Mr Bush the 'greatest threat to world peace'."[29] Similar animosity was revealed in a global attitude survey in which the question was asked (of those with an unfavorable view of the United States), "What is the problem with the U.S.?" In France and Germany almost three-quarters of the respondents said "mostly Bush," as did two-thirds of Italians and close to two-thirds of the British. Majorities in largely Muslim countries also blame Bush for whatever they consider wrong with the United States.[30]

4) "Globalization" is the fourth source of the growing animosity, though it is, for the most part, little more than a new expression of venerable anti-capitalist sentiments and attitudes. But globalization also results in the faster spread of modernity with its mixed blessings. At last the technological advances make it easier to share and communicate anti-American sentiments and policies. As Roger Scruton has pointed out:

> Globalization . . . in the eyes of its critics . . . means the loss of sovereignty, together with large-scale social, economic and aesthetic disruption. It also means an invasion of images that evoke outrage and disgust as much as envy. . . . The spectacle of Western freedom and Western prosperity going hand in hand with Western decadence and the crumbling of Western loyalties, is bound to provoke, in those who envy the one and despise the other, a seething desire to punish.[31]

Baudrillard managed to link globalization to 9/11. He wrote: "The violence of globalization also involves architecture, and hence the violent protest against it also involves the destruction of that architecture. . . . The horror for the 4,000 victims of dying in those towers was inseparable from the horror of living in them—the horror of living and working in sarcophagi of concrete and steel." In other words, blowing up the towers was in part an aesthetic protest against oppressive architecture, "a kind of perfect crime against form" created by globalization. Baudrillard moreover intuited that working in them (nobody "lived" in them) was as horrible as dying in them.[32] Norman Mailer too considered the World Trade Center towers "an architectural monstrosity" symbolizing "everything wrong in America."[33]

The major component of anti-Americanism associated with globalization is the belief that big corporations (capitalism) are in the process of extending their influence and power around the world, and that the United States, as the major capitalist country, plays a prime role in this undesirable process.

There is nothing new in this proposition except the terminology: the term "multinationals," widely used in the '70s and '80s, has been largely abandoned. Now, as in the past, capitalism (multinationals) is blamed for exploiting the poor in the third world, for environmental damages, and for encroachment on the autonomy of smaller or poorer states.

5) The most important recent contribution to anti-Americanism has been made by the combination of Arab-Islamic fundamentalist religious beliefs and the actions they have inspired, adding a new dimension of ruthlessness and violence to the phenomenon. Arab-Islamic terrorists have been responsible for most of the new anti-American and anti-Western violence in every corner of the world, from New York City to Bali. Roger Scruton has written:

> . . . The principal target of al Qa'eda, as of the late Ayatollah Khomeini, is neither Western civilization, nor Christianity, nor global capitalism . . . it is the United States. . . . In an uncanny way, the Islamists have identified the core component of the system they wish to destroy. . . . The attacks on America were a response to the world's most successful attempt at nation building

which projects its power, its freedom and its detritus so effectively around the globe.[34]

There is a qualitative difference between these attitudes and actions and the other, older kinds of anti-Americanism: "the [new] hatred is unconditional,"[35] and, one might add, murderous. A new dimension has also been added by the convergence of anti-American and anti-Israeli (and anti-Semitic) attitudes and actions.

Never before has anti-American (and anti-Israeli) violence been so explicitly linked to otherwordly rewards. As an Arab suicide bomber candidate explained: ". . . by pressing the detonator, you can immediately open the door to Paradise—it is the shortest path to Heaven. . . ." In a training video for the suicide bombers, the trainer asks the candidates: "Are you ready? Tomorrow you will be in Paradise." An Iman affiliated with Hamas pointed out "that the first drop of blood shed by a martyr during jihad washes away his sins instantaneously. On the Day of Judgment, he will face no reckoning. On the Day of Resurrection, he can intercede for seventy of his nearest and dearest to enter Heaven; and he will have at his disposal seventy-two houris, the beautiful virgins of Paradise."

The "spiritual leader" of Hamas, Sheikh Ahmed Yassin, has further explained: ". . . these rewards are not in themselves the goal of the martyr. The only aim is to win Allah's satisfaction. That can be done in the simplest and speediest manner by dying in the cause of Allah."

As to the specific preparations for the suicide mission (a member of Hamas explained): "We focus his attention on Paradise, on being in the presence of Allah, on meeting the Prophet Muhammad, on interceding for his loved ones, so that they too can be saved from the agonies of Hell. . . ." After the mission is accomplished,

> The bomber's family and the sponsoring organization celebrate his martyrdom with festivities, as if it were a wedding. Hundreds of guests congregate at the house to offer congratulations. The hosts serve the juices and sweets that the young man specified in his will. Often, the mother will ululate in joy over the honor that Allah has bestowed upon her family.[36]

The suicide bombers quoted here were engaging Israel, but similar expectations and ideas motivate those intent on killing Americans:

For Osama bin Laden 2001 marks the resumption of the war for religious dominance of the world that began in the seventh century. . . . Khomeini's designation of the United States as 'the Great Satan' was telling. In the Koran, Satan is described as 'the insidious tempter who whispers in the ears of men.' . . . And for members of Al Qaeda it is the seduction of America that represents the greatest threat to the kind of Islam they wish to impose on their fellow Muslims."[37]

Much of this represents an exceptionally intense religious protest against the modernity that is spearheaded and symbolized by the United States. As Jeffrey Herf has described it:

Today's Islamic fundamentalist fanatics are convinced that they possess absolute Truth. . . . They believe that force and terror are necessary to establish a utopia in place of the current decadent and corrupt world. . . . Terrorists . . . believe that they are in a possession of absolute truths and thus have the right and obligation to kill those who disagree and stand in their way. . . . [They] are persons with an ideological rationale that facilitates murdering the innocent with a clear conscience fueled by self-righteous indignation.[38]

Besides its murderousness, Arab-Islamic anti-Americanism also differs from the other varieties by its close connection with anti-Semitism and anti-Israeli militance. As Robert Wistrich has observed, ". . . The jihad to liberate Muslims across the world from oppression and injustice is simultaneously anti-American and anti-Jewish." The shared hatred of America and Israel is not only a product of the close political and economic ties between these two countries. It also flows from their jointly representing the "threatening forces of modernity such as secularism, capitalism, liberalism, and moral lassitude. . . . Uncle Sam, so to speak, has coalesced with Shylock into a terrifying specter of globalization that threatens to swamp the world of Islam."[39]

Contrary to much conventional, politically correct wisdom, this type of virulent hatred of America is not the product of the poverty, backwardness, and political repression prevalent in most Arab countries. As Michael Radu (another contributor to this volume) has pointed out:

> . . . Nothing in the background of Western-born or based Muslim terrorists supports the widespread fantasy that Islamic terrorism can somehow be explained by injustice, poverty, or discrimination. On the contrary, terrorism on the scale of the September 11 attacks *requires* elaborate coordination by multilingual, adaptable and highly educated people. . . . At bottom, therefore, international fundamentalist Islamic terrorism is not a social or economic but rather a cultural phenomenon. . . . Each and every person associated . . . with Al Qaeda in Europe, the Middle East, and North America is university educated and of middle-class or higher status. The jihad has resonance with them not because of their poverty or the injustices they suffered but because of their resentment of the cultural invasion of the West.[40]

True, the Palestinian suicide bombers in Israel and the West Bank are often the products of refugee camps and the financial benefits reaped by their families following their "martyrdom" have also been a motivating factor. But the religious motivation has been decisive in the suicide missions of all such volunteers. No secular terrorist group in recent times (and there have been many) has shown any interest in combining its acts of violence with suicide.

Arab anti-Americanism has also been stimulated (or tolerated) by repressive and corrupt Arab governments, which use it to divert attention from the reprehensible conditions that prevail in these countries. As Bernard Lewis has noted:

> Almost the entire Muslim world is affected by poverty and tyranny. Both of these problems are attributed, especially by those with an interest in diverting attention from themselves, to America—the first to American economic dominance and exploitation, now thinly disguised as 'globalization,' the second to America's support for the many so-called Muslim tyrants. . . .[41]

Anti-Americanism as official government policy, and as a diversion from domestic problems and especially economic difficulties, is not limited to the Arab world. Of the remaining Communist states, Cuba relies on it most extensively (as shown in the chapter herein by Mark Falcoff).

Finally it is also worth noting the affinities between Islamic-fundamentalist and Western radical-leftist anti-Americanism. As Martin Peretz has argued, there has been a fusion of "radical Islam with a global revolutionary, anti-Western perspective that echoes the anti-imperialism of the older Arab and European new left and even today's anti-globalization movement. . . . Like the anti-imperialist new left, Al Qaeda envisages revolution globally, with the United States as the principal adversary."[42]

DOMESTIC TRENDS

While domestic anti-Americanism often complements similar sentiments and attitudes abroad, the connections between the domestic and foreign denunciations of America are by no means clear-cut, especially as a mass phenomenon. Doubtless, critics abroad seize on the accusations produced by domestic critics, and domestic critics in turn eagerly point to hostility abroad, and to the alleged misdeeds of the United States around the world, as further justifications for their own beliefs.

Anti-Americanism abroad has far more to do with specific conditions in given countries and regions than with the levels of domestic rejection prevailing in American society. By the same token, the increase of anti-Americanism abroad, as in the last few years, was not preceded or accompanied by a corresponding rise in domestic denunciations.

The repudiation of America within the United States—part of the belief system of an influential minority—has been firmly established and entrenched since the late 1960s and does not depend on confirmation or stimulation from abroad, welcome as they might be. On the other hand, it is important to note that there has been a deep division between Americans who used 9/11 to reaffirm their aversion to American society and those in the majority for whom it rekindled old-fashioned patriotic sentiments.[43]

For those predisposed to a harsh view of the character of American society and U.S. foreign policy, 9/11 became a new opportunity for reaffirming these sentiments, which often originated in the 1960s or in conventional Marxist critiques of America. Among these critics the moral indignation (if any) occasioned by the terrorist attacks was greatly overshadowed by readily available indignation focused on the policies and actions of the United States. There was little emotional energy left for the condemnation of the terrorists. Gore Vidal seized the occasion to observe that "the USA is the most corrupt political system on the earth." He suggested that the highest American authorities knew about the impending attacks but chose not to warn against them in order to gain a pretext for invading Afghanistan, an invasion "that would allow Union Oil of California to lay its pipeline for the profit of, among others, the Cheney-Bush junta."[44] Noam Chomsky, who has been proposing for some time that the United States is the foremost terrorist state, suggested that the American bombing of the pharmaceutical plant in the Sudan was a far more hideous act then the attacks on 9/11[45] which provided an excuse for trying to "destroy the hunger-stricken country of Afghanistan."[46] The late Edward Said, the acclaimed literary scholar, declared in an Egyptian publication that the United States was a genocidal power with "a history of reducing whole peoples, countries, and even continents to ruin by nothing short of holocaust."[47] Eric Foner, professor of history at Columbia University, could not decide "which is more frightening: the horror that engulfed New York City or the apocalyptic rhetoric emanating daily from the White House."[48] Oliver Stone, the filmmaker, called 9/11 "a revolt" and equated the Palestinians celebrating it on the streets with the public rejoicings occasioned by the French and Russian Revolutions.[49] Terry Eagelton, the literary scholar, was convinced that "They [the Bush administration] will use the crisis as an excuse to trample on our civil liberties."[50] John Berger, the critic and novelist, wrote (in his introduction to a venomously anti-American volume by the Indian writer Arundhati Roy) that the U.S. attack on the Taliban in Afghanistan was "an act of terror against the people of the world" and equated the 19 hijackers (of 9/11) who "gave their lives" with the 353 firemen who perished in the disaster. He was among those persuaded that 9/11 was "the direct result of trying to impose everywhere the new world economic order . . . which insists that man's supreme task is to make profit."[51] The same events somehow led Ralph Nader to the conclusion that "there is an escalation of corporate takeover of the United States. The ground and soil are ripe for a revolt by the American people."[52] Katha Pollit of the *Nation* told her daughter (who wanted to fly an American flag out of their window after 9/11) that "The flag stands for jingoism and vengeance and war."[53]

Susan Sontag was far more enraged by "our robotic President" and the public figures supporting him than by the terrorists, whose actions she considered "a consequence of specific American alliances and actions. . . ."[54] Norman Mailer noted that "Everything wrong with America led to the point where the country built that tower of Babel which consequently had to be destroyed." As to the war with Iraq, he proposed that it was intended "a stepping stone to taking over the rest of the world."[55] Elsewhere he proposed that the Iraq war was a reflection of the compulsive pursuit of manhood, designed to alleviate "the ongoing malaise of the white American male," that is to say, "we went to war because we very much needed a successful war as a species of psychic rejuvenation"[56]—an interesting attribution (or projection) coming from a person whose personal life and work has been preoccupied with the attainment of true masculinity. In a follow-up, Mailer could not resist conjuring up the specter of fascism (as many of his generation and kindred spirits did in the 1960s): "At present the specter of fascism settling upon us remains just that . . . a specter, but will we escape it if we are struck by economic miseries?"[57]

Barbara Foley, a professor of English at Rutgers University, warned her students, "Be aware that whatever its proximate cause, the ultimate cause [of the 9/11 attacks] is the fascism of U.S. [sic] foreign policy . . ."[58] Members of the Middle East Studies Association also reached the conclusion that the United States bore the primary responsibility for the terrorist attacks (which they refused to call "terrorist."[59] A speaker at a Green party conference proposed that "The World Trade Center Disaster is a globalized version of the Columbine High School Disaster. When you bully people long enough they are going to strike back."[60] Professor Thomas Laqueur of Berkeley suggested (like Chomsky) that "on the scale of evil the New York bombings are sadly not so extraordinary and our government has been responsible for many that are probably worse."[61] Robert Paul Churchill, a professor of philosophy at George Washington University, pointed out that "What the terrorists despised and sought to defeat was our arrogance, our gluttonous way of life, our miserliness toward the poor and starving; the exportation of a soulless pop culture . . . and a domineering attitude that insists on having our own way no matter what the cost to others." Steven Hook, a professor of political science at Kent State University, wrote:

> Even the staunchest defenders of the United States are forced to confront the inescapable reality that the conduct of the United States as a global superpower has spawned hatred and resentment that has and will again express itself in acts of wholesale violence. The nation's conduct in a wide variety of settings is exposed to heightened scrutiny. The atomic bombings of Hiroshima and Nagasaki, U.S. support for Cold War dictators in Chile and the Philippines, the lethal miscalculations of the Johnson and Nixon administrations in Vietnam, and the intimate relationship between Western oil interests and Persian Gulf autocrats . . .

were among the U.S. sins he recommended to reflect upon as part of a post-9/11 "national soul-searching."[62]

Last but not least was Nicholas De Genova, a professor of anthropology at Columbia University in New York, who at a teach-in expressed hopes "to see 'a million Mogadishus," refering to the killings of American soldiers in Somalia in 1993 whose bodies were dragged through the street to the delectation of the crowds. He also "called for the defeat of United States forces in Iraq and said the only true heroes are those who help defeat the American military."[63]

Similar attitudes were displayed by theologians and representatives of mainline churches. Mark Taylor, a theologian at Princeton, seized the opportunity to suggest shifting attention to the "organized terror experienced by ever larger world communities today as a result of U.S.-led, sponsored, or supported activities in its so-called 'war on terrorism.'" He believed that the World Trade Center had been attacked because it was a "symbol of today's wealth and trade," as if that were a reasonable enough justification. Tony Compolo, an evangelical minister (and one of the spiritual advisers of former President Clinton), thought the Crusades provided adequate explanation and justification for 9/11. All these self-flagellating clerics routinely invoked poverty as the all-purpose "root cause" of indiscriminate terror.[64] It is noteworthy (as Jean Bethke Elshtain points out) that these representatives of organized religion were among the many commentators inclined to ignore or dismiss the part played by religious beliefs and motives in these outbursts of political violence.

Such is a small sampling of the domestic outpouring of undisguised hostility toward the United States in the wake of 9/11.

As many of the sources of these quotations suggest, higher education remains a major and truly institutionalized source of domestic denunciations of American society. In addition to the social sciences and humanities in general the field of American Studies in particular has become a source and repository of extremely negative sentiments toward this society. Alan Wolfe has observed, after surveying major texts used in this specialty, that "scholars in the field . . . have developed a hatred for America so visceral that it makes one wonder why they bother studying America at all." These studies have come to represent a "chorus of denunciation" increasingly shaped by a combination of identity politics and postmodernism.[65]

Another field of study, and a further indicator of anti-American trends, is the recently created "Whiteness Studies." Its apparent goal is to immerse (white) students in feelings of collective guilt about their conscious or unconscious racism and their "white privilege," and to persuade them that the pervasive and profound racism of American society is virtually ineradicable. As a critic of this new undertaking has noted, "Black studies celebrates blackness. Chicano studies celebrate Chicanos, women's studies celebrate women, and white studies attacks white people as evil." At least thirty institutions, including Princeton University and UCLA, teach such courses of study.[66] The animating spirit of this undertaking is hardly original: the charge of incorrigible and ubiquitous racism (and the adamant denial that any significant progress has been made to overcome it) has for decades been tirelessly asserted and remains a major foundation of the attempted moral delegitimation of American society.

TRENDS ABROAD

The vehement anti-Americanism of Harold Pinter, the famous British playwright, provides an instructive illustration of the converging sentiments of many foreign and domestic critics, and ranks him with the likes of Chomsky, Said, and Vidal. All of them share an exceptionally intense hatred and contempt for the United States, and the conviction that it represents an unparalleled threat to mankind and to all cherished human values. Pinter begins his contribution to a recent symposium entitled "What We Think of America" by insisting that NATO aircraft, as a matter of policy, killed civilians during the Kosovo war. He moves on to propose that the American prison system "can accurately be described as a vast gulag" and suggests that the United States has been responsible, in recent times, for the death of hundreds of thousands of people around the world who "died because . . . they dared to question the status quo, the endless plateau of poverty, disease, degradation, and oppression which is their birthright." Morever,

> The United States has in fact—since the end of the Second World War . . . exercised a sustained, systematic, remorseless, and quite cynical manipulation of power worldwide, while masquerading as a force for universal good. . . . Arrogant, indifferent, contemptuous of International Law, both dismissive and manipulative of the United Nations, this is now the most dangerous power the world has ever known—the authentic 'rogue state' . . . of colossal military and economic might. . . . The 'rogue state' has . . . confirmed that it is a fully-fledged, award-winning, gold-plated monster. It has effectively declared war on the world. It knows only one language—bombs and death.[67]

More recently Pinter has reaffirmed, while addressing peace marchers in London, that the United States is "a monster out of control."[68]

A similar message from abroad comes from Carlos Fuentes, the well-known Mexican writer. Comparing the United States to past totalitarian systems, and to Nazism in particular, he writes:

> Hitler and Stalin made the mistake . . . of demanding personal homage superior to those deserved by their own nations: to exalt the name. Washington's circle of power is infinitely more capable. It shields itself within the Nation and gives it a total and exclusive ecumenical value. . . . Just as Hitler advanced in the name of the German Volk and Stalin in the name of the Proletariat, Bush claims to act in the name of the people of the United States. . . . Such a declaration locates us, once more, before the 'great lie' that Hitler so astutely evoked. . . .

Clarifying his remarks, Fuentes later wrote: "I don't compare Bush with Hitler and Stalin to equate them, but to distinguish them. The Nazi and Soviet dictators faced other powerful states. Today's U.S. president governs a country with no external counterforce . . . neither Hitler nor Stalin had the military power Bush has. Next to Bush, Hitler and Stalin were but petty officers."[69] In short, the United States—ruled by mendacious, unscrupulous leaders and possessing unprecedented military might—is far more dangerous than Nazi Germany or the Soviet Union under Stalin used to be. This is the core idea that haunts the anti-American imagination: the monster state led by immoral or morally enfeebled leaders presiding over vast power they misuse, an imagery that combines the fear of technology with the distrust of a social-political system seen as profoundly and menacingly different from all others.

For a third example of a veteran and voluble detractor of America, consider Günter Grass, the distinguished German writer. In the early 1980s he insisted that "the United States was disqualified from making moral judgements about anything." More recently the war with Iraq led him to observe:

> . . . We are witnessing the moral decline of the world's only superpower. . . . It is not just foreigners who cringe as this ideal [the

ideal America, that is] . . . now a caricature of itself. There are many Americans who . . . are horrified by the betrayal of their founding values and by the hubris of those holding the reins of power. I stand with them. . . .[70]

While the feelings and convictions of influential intellectuals abroad are important for understanding the nature of anti-Americanism, trends in pubic opinion must also be given attention.

The Pew Research Center's survey of global opinions has found that

since 2000, favorability ratings for the U.S. have fallen in 19 of the 27 countries where trend benchmarks are available. While criticism of America is on the rise, however, a reserve of goodwill . . . still remains. . . . The U.S. and its citizens continue to be rated positively by majorities in 35 of the 42 countries. . . . True dislike, if not hatred, is concentrated in Muslim nations of the Middle East and in Central Asia. . . .

Opinions about the U.S., however, are complicated and contradictory. People around the world embrace things American and, at the same time, decry U.S. influence on their societies. . . . U.S. global influence is simultaneously embraced and rejected by world publics. America is nearly universally admired for its technological achievements, and people in most countries say they enjoy U.S. movies and television programs. Yet . . . the spread of U.S. ideas and customs is disliked by majorities in almost every country included in this survey.[71]

Also of interest among the findings of the Pew survey is that during the period when animosity toward the United States has increased, a general discontent with domestic conditions in many parts of the world has also grown. Publics in the countries surveyed were dissatisfied with their own countries and especially their economies. These findings lend support to the suggestion that a good deal of anti-Americanism results from the desire to identify a plausible source for a wide range of grievances and frustrations, and that locating such blame is in itself satisfying.

In evaluating the Pew surveys it should be noted that they do not differentiate between the views of elite and nonelite groups. Clearly some elite groups in many parts of the world are far more hostile toward the United States and American culture than is the average citizen. Intellectuals almost everywhere are among them, and in Muslim countries the clergy. This proposition is also supported, at least indirectly, by another finding of the Pew survey, that "in general there is limited evidence to support the widely held view that poverty fuels discontent with the United States."[72]

French anti-Americanism has been expressed, among other ways, in the best-selling status of a remarkable book by Thierry Meyssan, which claims that "the Pentagon was struck not by an airplane but by a truck bomb planted by rogue U.S. military officers." The book also proposes that bin Laden was a CIA "stooge" and that 9/11 was carried out by agents of the military-industrial complex to justify dramatic increases in defense spending and the invasion of Afghanistan.[73]

More sophisticated French anti-American sentiments have been summed up by Regis Debray, a French intellectual who has migrated from the radical to a more moderate left, and whose career has included involvement with Latin American guerillas as well as advising President Mitterand. As Debray saw it, "The United States compensates for its shortsightedness . . . with an altogether biblical self-assurance in its transcendent destiny. Puritan America is hostage to a sacred morality; it regards itself as the predestined repository of Good, with a mission to strike down Evil . . . it pursues a politics that is at bottom theological. . . ." Like his fellow countryman Baudrillard, Debray too contrasts American foolishness and "arrogance" with the greater wisdom of Europe.[74]

German anti-Americanism has been sturdy and widespread and especially prominent among the younger generations. In a recent poll, 61 percent of Germans under thirty considered President Bush equally dangerous to Saddam Hussein or more so, but only 48 percent of those sixty or over shared these views. Many young Germans nurtured and validated their anti-American sentiments and stereotypes with the film *Bowling for Columbine*, Michael Moore's denunciation of American society and culture.[75]

South Korean anti-Americanism has certain attributes in common with its German counterpart—one might say that South Korea too has had much to thank the United States for but has developed a strong nationalistic reaction to such dependence or indebtedness. Both countries accommodate large numbers of American troops and military bases. Manifestations of South Korean anti-Americanism range from angry and violent demonstrations at U.S. military bases and the U.S. embassy, to "a pop star smashing [during a recent music award show] a model of an American tank on live television, drawing a rousing cheer," to popular South Korean films in which Americans are demonized, replacing North Koreans who had earlier been treated in this manner.[76]

Muslim anti-Americanism has been assiduously nurtured by large numbers of religious schools (*madrassa*) ("assembly lines for jihad") in various Arab countries, including Pakistan, ostensibly an ally of the United States. As a teacher in one such institution put it, "We prepare them for the jihad, mentally." In these schools, "what the students hear . . . is a drumbeat of American injustice, cruelty and closed-mindedness. . . ." In one of them the "teachers explained that even though the Jews flew the planes into the towers, it was Allah's will. Allah, the teachers said, put the idea in the minds of Jews." Following the attack, students celebrated, "stabbing the fingers on one hand into the palm of the other, to simulate a plane stabbing into a building."[77] Reportedly even "members of the Pakistani elite have turned against the United States" and believe that the United States used nuclear weapons in Afghanistan, and that the planes which struck on 9/11 "were flown by remote control . . . part of an American or Israeli conspiracy to defame Islam."[78]

Virulent strains of anti-Americanism are evident not only in Arab countries but also among the Muslim-Arab populations of Western Europe. In France, for example, when news of 9/11 "reached the [housing] projects, young men streamed onto the . . . courtyards . . . to clap, whistle, cheer, and shout in Arabic, 'God is great!'"[79] In Denmark too, "Muslims took to the streets to celebrate the terrorist attacks." According to one observer, "Many Western Europeans, from the man on the street to the cop on the corner, from the politician in the parliament to the immigration official at the border, have long considered it their obligation to turn a blind eye to the more disturbing aspects of the immigrant Muslim reality. . ."[80] The latter include expressions of plain and simple anti-Semitism that has increasingly converged with anti-Israeli and anti-American sentiments.

Anti-Americanism abroad, the characteristic volatile mixture of aversion, ambivalence, and morbid fascination (as well as "worldwide resentment") have also been captured by a recent exhibition at the Whitney Museum of Art in New York entitled "The American Effect: Global Perspectives on the United States, 1990–2003."[81]

THE ORIGIN AND ORGANIZATION OF THIS BOOK

Having written a book on anti-Americanism a decade before 9/11, I wanted to reexamine the phenomenon that has found increasingly violent expression. A revised edition of my book was not feasible for various practical reasons. Moreover I was not ready to undertake a prolonged, in-depth examination of anti-Americanism in different regions of the world. An edited volume, consisting of contributions by authors familiar with the particulars of the phenomenon in different parts of the world, was the alternative.

The selection of particular countries or regions was partly determined by the prominence of anti-Americanism in a given area and partly by the availability of contributors to deal with different areas. While it was impossible to cover the phenomenon in every major region of the world, the three major areas of resurgent (or steady) anti-Americanism are well represented: Arab–Middle Eastern, Latin American, and Western European.

I shall not attempt to summarize the diverse contributions of the different authors; they speak for themselves. Those about the global manifestations of anti-Americanism in Part I provide a wealth of information and insight about the influence of particular historical, social, and cultural conditions in various countries or regions and their connections with the broader currents underlying the phenomenon. The essays in Part II examine specific

American institutions and movements (the American Communist movement, feminism, education, popular culture and mass
media, the peace movements) which reflect a shared alienation
from and rejection of American society and culture.

Taken together these essays support, with varying degree of
emphasis and explicitness, the idea that anti-Americanism stems
from four major sources. The most general is the human need for
scapegoating; the second is the sole superpower status of the
United States that makes it exceedingly well suited to meet these
needs as both the richest and strongest nation in the world; the
third is the justified identification of the United States with
modernity and its problems; and, last but not least, the identifiable, specific errors and mistakes of American foreign policy and
the flaws of its domestic institutions and social arrangements.

A PERSONAL NOTE

I am not a native-born American but an immigrant. My views of
American society are thus bound to be different both from those
who were born and raised in the United States and those who assess this country from afar. I was born and grew up in Hungary,
where I left after the defeat of the revolution in 1956. England took
me in as a refugee and student; I attended college in London. I
came to the United States in 1959 at age twenty-seven to attend
graduate school; I stayed and became a citizen.

After my arrival in 1959 I experienced (and expressed) some of
the same negative feelings about Amerian society and culture that
animate many social critics here and abroad. These feelings were
grounded for the most part in matters cultural and social. I was,
for example, shocked and dismayed by the ignorance of the college
students I first encountered as a teaching assistant at the University of Illinois in Champaign. (Decades later I did not find such ignorance greatly diminished among the undergraduates at the
University of Massachusetts at Amherst, where I taught for thirty-
two years.)

I was also discouraged by what struck me as the superficial
friendliness of Americans, which seemed to be based on an opti-

mistic belief in the interchangeability of individuals and the promiscuous blending of "business and pleasure." I spotted inauthenticity, as have other critics. I found, and continue to find, American popular culture and mass entertainment mindless and a poor influence on all who consume them (especially the young), but I recognize that mass culture is not something imposed upon the masses thirsting for a higher variety. I found and continue to find much of advertising obtrusive and fraudulent. Of late I have been distressed and irritated by the widespread preference of my fellow citizens for SUVs and what this seems to signify: conspicuous consumption, status seeking, an element of aggression, an excessive anti-social individualism and indifference to energy saving and the natural environment.

All along I have had reservations about the often-lauded openness of American culture and about what I once described as

> The spectacle of a moral, ethical, aesthetic free-for-all (the most recent expression of which is a somewhat mindless veneration of "diversity"), the rapid changes in moral fashions, the determined and self-conscious quest for self-expression, self-realization. . . . The unqualified "openness to change" (a self-evident virtue within American culture) that inspires incomprehension or apprehension in those who are not products of this society and is frequently associated with suggestibility, instability, inability to discriminate, and moral confusion—all of which are indeed abundant in American society.[82]

More than once I have thought that had I been born in the United States, I might have joined the adversary culture. But since I was not, I have, I believe, acquired a sounder comparative perspective for judging American society and its political system, their strengths and weaknesses. As a non-native American I understand *both* the critics disturbed by many attributes of this society *and* perceive the groundlessness of their sweeping indictments.

Domestic anti-Americanism is an integral part of this culture, a product—however distorted, perverse, and exaggerated—of an American idealism, of high expectations disappointed. It is also a product of knowing little history and of the world outside the

United States. There is much in American culture I continue to find uncongenial or outright distressing, some of it closely linked to its idealism, which, regrettably, also entails the profoundly mistaken belief that all good things, all things highly valued, are compatible. They are not. Love of the environment and self-sufficiency in energy production are not compatible with gas-guzzling SUVs. Belief in the rights and autonomy of individuals is not compatible with identity politics, with mandated racial preferences and the encouragement of group pride. Aspiring to limitless self-realization and fulfillment is not compatible with harmonious life in a closely knit community. The freedom to move around endlessly is not compatible with being rooted in a sustaining community. There is endless tension between freedom and security, security and adventure, equality and excellence, the mandates of egalitarianism and achievement orientation.[83] We cannot admire excellence and disparage "elitism," encourage gifted children and abolish "tracking" as discriminatory.

Daniel Boorstin's remarks about the expectations of Americans, made almost half a century ago, remain all too well founded:

> We expect too much of the world. . . . We expect our two-week vacation to be romantic, exotic, cheap, and effortless. We expect a faraway atmosphere if we go to a nearby place; and we expect everything to be relaxing, sanitary, and Americanized if we go to a faraway place. . . . We expect anything and everything. We expect the contradictory and the impossible. We expect compact cars which are spacious; luxury cars which are economical. We expect to be rich and charitable, powerful and merciful, active and reflective, kind and competitive. . . . We expect to eat and stay thin, to be constantly on the move and ever more neighborly. . . .[84]

For those not raised in American society, such expectations suggest that Americans are on a treadmill of illusory gratifications and recurring frustrations. This is not to say that life is better in societies governed by low expectations—they have different problems.

Domestic anti-Americanism often is a reflection of unhappiness with life in a largely secular, excessively individualistic society, which—while it provides a wide range of choices and options—offers little help to its members in finding meaning and guiding values in their lives. The openness, freedom, and moral-ethical free-for-all that is characteristic of American culture can become troubling and burdensome. I suspect that such moral relativism and moral uncertainty are the most compelling sources of anti-Americanism both abroad and at home, entangled as they often are with scapegoating, envy, resentment, simpleminded anti-capitalism, mindless utopianism, and the expectation that a social system can be created and sustained that is free of the perennial conflict among human aspirations and values.

In the final analysis, understanding anti-Americanism requires not merely a renewed effort to grasp the deep and widespread ambivalence evoked by the costs and benefits of modernity, but more generally an understanding of the irreconcilability of many human values and desires that becomes more apparent with the progress of modernization.

While the essays in this book make clear that anti-Americanism may arise out of a multitude of circumstances—aggrieved nationalism, offended group interest, attempts to distract attention from bankrupt policies, anti-capitalism, the loss of traditions, the vulgarities of mass culture, the erosion of community, etc.—whatever its sources, it often acquires a dynamic of its own that springs from the needs of human beings to explain and reduce the responsibility for pain and misfortune in their lives.

NOTES

1. Simon Schama, "The Unloved American," *New Yorker*, March 10, 2003, pp. 34, 37. Henri Astier has also noted that "the 19th century introduced another enduring misconception: the United States as a cultural desert and a land without history." *Times Literary Supplement*, January 10, 2002, p. 4.

2. He was said to have been "politically radicalized" by Sartre. Evidently Sartre also succeeded in passing on to him his profound detestation of American society. Mike Gane, *Baudrillard Live*, London, 1993, pp. 1, 2.

3. Jean Baudrillard, *America*, London/New York, 1988, pp. 7, 23, 66, 73, 76, 77, 78, 81, 87, 97, 99, 104, 121–122, 125.

4. I made that observation in the book I wrote entitled *Anti-Americanism: Critiques at Home and Abroad*, New York, 1992; see also its updated edition, *Anti-Americanism: Irrational and Rational*, New Brunswick, N.J., 1995. A major work on the historical origins of anti-Americanism in Europe is James W. Ceaser, *Reconstructing America: The Symbol of America in Modern Thought*, New Haven, 1997. A recent addition to the literature is Jean-Francois Revel, *Anti-Americanism*, San Francisco, 2003, a somewhat sketchy and discursive treatment of the subject largely confined to the French setting. An exceptionally illuminating analysis is of recent anti-Americanism and its links with anti-Israeli sentiments may be found in Josef Joffe: "The Demons of Europe," *Commentary*, January 2004.

Older books related to the topic include Arnold Beichman's *Nine Lies About America*, New York, 1972, which examines the domestic critiques prevalent in the 1960s. A short monograph to be noted is Stephen Haseler, *The Varieties of Anti-Americanism: Reflex and Response*, Washington, D.C., 1985. Another slim and inevitably somewhat dated volume is Thomas Perry Thornton, ed., *Anti-Americanism: Origins and Context*, special issue of *The Annals*, May 1988.

There are more studies of anti-Americanism in particular settings, such as Carlos Rangel, *The Latin Americans: Their Love-Hate Relationship with the United States*, New York, 1977; Alvin Z. Rubinstein and Donald E. Smith, eds., *Anti-Americanism in the Third World: Implications for U.S. Foreign Policy*, New York, 1985; Rob Kroes et al., eds., *Anti-Americanism in Europe*, Amsterdam, 1986; Richard F. Kuisel, *Seducing the French: The Dilemma of Americanization*, Berkeley, Calif., 1993; J. L. Granatstein, *Yankee Go Home? Canadians and Anti-Americanism*, Toronto, 1996; Dan Diner, *America in the Eyes of Germans: An Essay on Anti-Americanism*, Princeton, 1966.

5. "The culture of repudiation" was a phrase coined by Roger Scruton in his *The West and the Rest*, Wilmington, Del., 2002.

6. Yvonne Daily, "The Persistence of the Ugly American," *New York Times Magazine*, December 2, 2001, p. 22.

7. Stanley Hoffman, "America Goes Backward," *New York Review of Books*, June 12, 2003, p. 80.

8. A fine recent example of such an irrational disposition was reported from a Mexican city and occasioned by the disappearance of young girls: "According to opinion polls, most Mexicans believe that the girls are murdered so that their organs can be extracted for transplants for wealthy patients in the United States. None of the recognizable remains found so far have been missing internal organs, but this theory has great symbolic weight." Alma Guillermoprieto, "A Hundred Women," *New Yorker*, September 29, 2003, p. 86. To be sure, this idea could also have anti-Mexican implications if it were assumed that the murders were committed by Mexican criminals to satisfy the demands of the American market for such body parts.

Such stories were already circulating in Mexico in 1990 as well as in other parts of Latin America and elsewhere. See Hollander, *Anti-Americanism*, cited, p. 363.

9. Lee Harris, "The Intellectual Origins of America-Bashing," *Policy Review*, January 2003, pp. 3, 4.

10. Adam Gopnik, "The Anti-Anti-Americans," *New Yorker*, September 1, 2002, p. 321.

11. Victor Davis Hanson, "I Love Iraq, Bomb Texas," *Commentary*, December 2002, p. 43, 47.

12. Todd Gitlin, "Anti-Anti-Americanism," *Dissent*, Winter 2003, pp. 103, 104.

13. Again, as Schama observed, "for most European travelers extravagant idealization was followed by equally unbalanced disenchantment," cited, p. 35. Such disenchantment has been far more common among idealistic Americans, products of a society and culture that has been inculcating high expectations from its earliest days.

14. Bruce Thornton, *Plagues of the Mind: The New Epidemic of False Knowledge*, Wilmington, Del. 1999, pp. 9, 19, 20–21, 23–24, 25.

15. Edward Rothstein: "Damning (Yet Desiring) Mickey and the Big Mac," *New York Times*, Arts & Ideas, March 2, 2002, p. A19.

16. Ivan Klima in "What We Think of America," *Granta*, March 2002, p. 52.

17. In the volume entitled *Anti-Americanism* cited above and in an op-ed entitled "Why Don't They Like Us?" *New York Times*, July 3, 1992, and more recently in "The Politics of Envy," *New Criterion*, November 2002.

18. Fouad Ajami, "The Falseness of Anti-Americanism," *Foreign Policy*, Sept./Oct. 2003, p. 58.

19. A concise and revealing analysis of these problems may be found in Peter Berger, *Facing Up to Modernity*, New York, 1977.

20. A fine summary of such "extravagant expectations" may be found in Daniel J. Boorstin, *The Image*, New York, 1961.

21. Nicholas D. Kristof,"Why Do They Hate Us?" *New York Times*, January 15, 2002, editorial page.

22. For a detailed chronological account of all such attacks, see Barry Rubin and Judith Colp Rubin, eds., *Anti-American Terrorism and the Middle East: A Documentary Reader*, New York, 2002, pp. 351–366.

23. James Traub, "Weimar Whiners," *New York Times Magazine*, June 1, 2003, p. 11. For further discussions of the expressions of hostility toward American society which followed 9/11, see Paul Hollander, "Anti-Americanism Revisited," *Weekly Standard*, October 22, 2001; also by the same author, "It Is a Crime That Some Don't See This as Hate" (original title: "Anti-Americanism and a World Class Hate Crime"), *Washington Post*, October 28, 2001; "Anti-Americanism: Murderous and Rhetorical," *Partisan Review*, No. 1, 2002; and "Loving Peace and Detesting America," *National Review Online*, March 24, 2003.

24. Jean Bethke Elshtain, *Just War Against Terror*, New York, 2003, p. 145–146.

25. Jean Baudrillard, *The Spirit of Terrorism*, London, 2002, p. 9.

26. David Remnick, "Post-Imperial Blues," *New Yorker*, October 13, 2003, p. 89.

27. Traub, "Weimar Whiners."

28. Barry Rubin "The Real Roots of Arab Anti-Americanism," *Foreign Affairs*, December 2002, p. 83.

29. Quoted in Nicholas D. Kristof: "Loss, Before Bullets Fly," *New York Times*, March 7, 2002, p. A27.

30. *What the World Thinks in 2002*, Pew Global Survey, Pew Research Center, Washington, D.C., p. 22.

31. Roger Scruton, *The West and the Rest*, Wilmington, Del., 2002, pp. 83, 132.

32. Baudrillard, *Spirit of Terrorism*, pp. 45, 46.

33. See *New Republic,* November 26, 2001, p. 4.

34. Scruton, *West and the Rest,* pp. 134, 156.

35. Ian Buruma and Avishai Margalit, "Occidentalism," *New York Review of Books,* January 17, 2002, p. 7.

36. Nasra Hassan, "An Arsenal of Believers," *New Yorker,* November 19, 2002, pp. 36, 37, 39, 40, 41. See also Jeffrey Goldberg, "In the Party of God," *New Yorker,* October 14 & 21, 2002.

37. Bernard Lewis, "The Revolt of Islam," *New Yorker,* November 19, 2001, p. 63.

38. Jeffrey Herf, "What Is Old and What Is New in the Terrorism of Islamic Fundamentalism?" *Partisan Review,* No. 1, 2002, pp. 25, 26.

39. Robert S. Wistrich, "The Old-New Anti-Semitism," *National Interest,* Summer 2002, pp. 68, 69.

40. Michael Radu, "Terrorism After the Cold War: Trends and Challenges," *Orbis,* Spring 2002, p. 286.

41. Bernard Lewis, "The Revolt of Islam," *New Yorker,* November 19, 2001, p. 57.

42. Martin Peretz, "World War," *New Republic,* October 7, 2002, p. 42.

43. A Pew Research Center poll taken in August 2002 found that 92 percent agreed "completely" or "mostly" with the statement "I am very patriotic." Janny Scott, "The Changing Face of Patriotism," *Week in Review, New York Times,* July 6, 2003. To be sure, there are harsh critics of America who consider themselves patriotic, hence approval of the statement does not necessarily shed light on the proportion of deeply alienated, hostile critics. In the same survey, when asked, "How proud are you to be an American?" 69 percent were "extremely proud"—a better measure of patriotism conventionally defined. By contrast, breast-beating critics often aver being ashamed to be American as they decry the evils the country stands for in their eyes.

44. "Author Vidal Blames U.S. for Conflict," *Boston Globe,* November 24, 2001; and Vidal in *The Observer,* October 27, 2002, quoted in the *New Republic,* November 11, 2002, p. 9.

45. Quoted in David Horowitz, *The Ayatollah of American Hate,* Los Angeles, 2001, p. 7.

46. Quoted in the *New Republic,* December 10, 2001, p. 9

47. Quoted in the *Weekly Standard,* October 8, 2001, p. 35.

48. *London Review of Books,* October 4, 2001, pp. 21–22.

49. "Voices of Reason? Not in Hollywood," *Boston Globe,* October 23, 2001.

50. Quoted in Tony Judt, "America and the War," *New York Review of Books,* November 15, 2001, p. 4.

51. Quoted in Ian Buruma, "The Anti-American," *New Republic,* April 29, 2002, p. 25.

52. Quoted in the *New Republic,* November 19, 2001, p. 10.

53. Katha Pollit, "Put Out the Flags," *The Nation,* October 8, 2001, p. 7.

54. "The Talk of the Town," *New Yorker,* September 24, 2001, p. 32.

55. Quoted in the *New Republic,* November 26, 2001, p. 8, and on March 31, 2003, p. 8.

56. Norman Mailer, "The White Man Unburdened," *New York Review of Books,* July 17, 2003, p. 4.

57. "Response to Ronald Tiersky" in the *New York Review of Books*, August 14, 2003, p. 42.

58. Quoted in the *New Criterion* October 2001, p. 2.

59. Quoted in the *New Republic*, December 3, 2001, pp. 15, 17.

60. *Progressive Review*, October 29, 2001.

61. Quoted in Judt, *New York Review of Books*, cited, p. 4.

62. *Prentice Hall Authors Speak Out: September 11 and Beyond* (pamphlet) Upper Saddle River, N.J., 2002, pp. 25, 47.

63. Tamar Lewin, "At Columbia, Call for Death of U.S. Forces is Denounced," *New York Times*, March, 29, 2003.

64. Quoted in Elshtain, *Just War*, pp. 82–83; see also pp. 117–118.

65. Alan Wolfe, "The Difference Between Criticism and Hatred. Anti-American Studies," *New Republic*, February 10, 2003, pp. 26, 30.

66. Darryl Fears, "Hue and Cry on 'Whiteness Studies,'" *Washington Post*, June 20, 2002, p. A12.

67. Harold Pinter in *Granta*, London, March, 2002, pp. 66–69. For broader trends in British anti-Americanism see Geoffrey Wheatcroft: "Smiley's (Anti-American) People" *New York Times, Week in Review*, January 1, 2004.

68. Schama, "Unloved American," p. 39.

69. Quoted in *New Republic*, October 28, 2002, p. 8.

70. Quoted in John Vinocur, "European Intellectuals and American Power," *New York Times Magazine*, April 29, 1984, p. 73; Günter Grass, "The U.S. Betrays Its Core Values," *Daily Hampshire Gazette*, Northampton, Mass., April 12–13, 2002.

71. *What the World Thinks in 2002*, pp. 1, 5.

72. Ibid., p. 56.

73. Quoted in Max Berley, "Plot Development," *New Republic*, April 22, 2002, p. 16.

74. Regis Debray, "The French Lesson," op-ed, *New York Times*, February 23, 2002.

75. Nina Bernstein, "Young Germans Ask: Thanks for What?" *Weekly News, New York Times*, March 9, 2002, p. 3.

76. Howard W. French with Don Kirk, "American Policies and Presence Are Under Fire in South Korea . . .," *New York Times*, December 8, 2002, p. 10, and James Brooke, "When American Villains Thwart Lovesick Koreans," *Week in Review, New York Times*, October 12, 2003, p. 12.

77. Rick Bragg, "Shaping Young Islamic Hearts and Hatreds," *New York Times*, October 14, 2001, p. B10.

78. David Rohde, "Turning Away from U.S., Pakistan's Elite Gravitate Toward Islamic Religious Parties," *New York Times*, October 13, 2002, p. 6.

79. Chris Hedges, "In Suburban Squalor Near Paris, Echoes of Jihad," *New York Times*, October 16, 2001.

80. Bruce Bawer, "Tolerating Intolerance: The Challenge of Fundamentalist Islam in Western Europe," *Partisan Review*, No. 3, 2002, pp. 346, 347.

81. Gary Shteyngart, "The Whole World is Watching," *New York Times*, July 13, 2003, p. 26. See also Frank Rich, "Ground Zero or Bust," *Art & Leisure, New York Times*, July 13, 2002.

82. Hollander, *Anti-Americanism*, cited, pp. 404–405.

83. An attempt to reconcile such conflicting desires has been made by the stratum of population that David Brooks has called the Bobos, that is to say, bourgeois bohemians. See his *Bobos in Paradise: The New Upper Class and How They Got There*, New York, 2000.

84. Boorstin, pp. 3–4.

PART I

Anti-Americanism Abroad

1

JAMES CEASER

The Philosophical Origins of Anti-Americanism in Europe

Only one opinion or ideology in the world today has a truly global reach. It is anti-Americanism. If not in every country, then certainly on every continent, large contingents of intellectuals, backed by significant numbers in the political class, organize their political thinking on the basis of anti-Americanism. It is prominent not only in nations that Americans count as hostile but in countries that have traditionally been considered its friends and allies. The authors of a massive Pew Institute Survey on public opinion in thirty-five nations recently observed that "while attitudes toward the United States are most negative in the Middle East/Conflict Area, ironically, criticisms of U.S. policies and ideals such as American-style democracy and business practices are also highly prevalent among the publics of traditional allies."[1] The only curious aspect of this statement is the claim of "irony," for anti-Americanism has long been a major element of opinion in other Western nations. What Jean François Revel said of the French intellectual climate could easily apply to the thinking in many other European countries: "If you remove anti-Americanism, nothing remains of French political thought today, either on the Left or on the Right."[2] Perhaps the only new development is that, with the cessation of the Communist threat after 1991, major political leaders in these nations have openly begun to court anti-American sentiment as an electoral strategy.

Anti-Americanism has both a "natural" and a theoretical source. The natural source derives from the dominant strategic position of the United States today. America is the only nation that has the capacity to project significant force far from its own borders, and it has showed its willingness to use that force for purposes it deems important, even without support from international bodies. It has always been the fate of the world's major power to be regarded with suspicion. There is no need for global surveys to confirm the strong opposition to Rome in the ancient world, especially among the Greeks, who—very much like the Europeans today—had secret contempt for the pragmatic power from the West that had dislodged them from their position of world preeminence. As for attitudes toward Great Britain in the nineteenth century, Americans need only consult the views of many of their own political leaders of that era, who spent much of their time lambasting the British for their arrogance and imperial excesses.

Americans often express bewilderment at being branded an "empire" and react with utter incredulity when they hear claims, such as those of the editor of *Le Monde Diplomatique*, Ignacio Ramonet, that "America subjugates the world like no other empire has done in the history of humanity."[3] Americans are doubtless justified in protesting this label, as an empire in a strict sense refers to a force that occupies and rules its subordinates. Indeed, if America were a veritable empire, it is doubtful whether it would tolerate the most excessive anti-American tirades, not to mention the regular opposition votes at the United Nations. But Americans would be deluding themselves if they believed that the milder form of leadership America exercises immunizes the United States from expressions of hostility. It is enough that America has the status of the world's primary power, and that others do not, to provoke envy and resentment.

There is a psychological aspect to this situation as well. People seem to possess a deep-seated impulse to believe that an identifiable entity (be it a person, a god, or a nation) is responsible for what occurs and that nothing happens by accident or fate. America, which has been designated as the world's "hyperpower," also serves the function of being the universal talisman. The philosopher Jean Baudrillard spoke for many when he described world reaction to the attacks on the United States of September 11, 2001: "How we have dreamt of this event, how all the world without exception dreamt of this event, for no one can avoid dreaming of the destruction of a power that has become hegemonic. . . . It is they who acted, but we who wanted the deed."[4]

Nor should Americans expect too much from others' gratitude. Gratitude is a sentiment that has clear limits in the relations among nations. George Washington famously warned in his Farewell Address of the danger of developing "an habitual fondness" for another nation, which can make a country a "slave . . . to its affection" and can "lead it astray from its duty and its interest."[5] It is true, of course, that many Eastern Europeans, recalling America's recent strong opposition to Soviet domination, remain deeply appreciative of the U.S. position in the cold war. But memories of American steadfastness during this period are bound to fade as time goes on, and there are indications that this process is already under way. It is also true that some in Western Europe still feel a genuine debt to America's assistance in the liberation of World War II. But most political leaders mention gratitude almost as an obligatory ritual, and many probably now resent the exercise. Gratitude, after all, is an emotion filled with ambiguity. It is a painful reminder either of past weakness or of defeat. Outside of Europe, the large amounts of aid given by the United States to Turkey, Jordan, and Egypt may have created ties of interest, but they have not generated much popular gratitude.

Yet if anti-Americanism were based just on this "natural" foundation, not only would it be less virulent than it is, but there would be nothing special about it. What differentiates anti-Americanism from the usual opposition to a dominant world power and gives it its exceptional character is its other source. America has become a symbol for something to be despised on philosophical grounds. Anti-Americanism rests on the singular idea that something associated with the United States, something at the core of American life, is deeply wrong and threatening to the rest of the world. Over a half-century ago the novelist Henry de Montherlant put the following statement in the mouth of one of his characters (a journalist): "One nation that manages to lower intelligence, morality, human quality on nearly all the surface of the earth, such a thing has never been seen before in the existence of the planet. I accuse the United States of being in a permanent state of crime against humankind."[6] America in this view represents all that is grotesque, obscene, monstrous, stultifying, stunted, leveling, deadening, deracinating, deforming, rootless, and—always in quotation marks—"free."

This view of America is an intellectual construction built up over a period of more than two centuries by some of the best-known theoretical minds of the West. It has been designed so as to be impervious to refutation by facts. The concern of these thinkers has rarely been with the actual qualities of the American people or the American political system but with a set of ideas related to a critique of modernity. The identification of America with an abstract idea is evident from the development of the neologisms "Americanization" or "Americanism," which are treated nowadays as ordinary terms of intellectual discourse. (By contrast, no one speaks of Venezuelanization or New Zealandism.) "Americanization," for example, is a synonym for the all-powerful social scientific concept of "globalization," differing only in its slightly more sinister connotation. One need only observe an "anti-globalization" rally today to see that the movement is chiefly a protest against "Americanization," with special animus directed against American (mass) culture's hegemony, symbolized by McDonald's, Disney, and Microsoft. As two analysts recently claimed in a book entitled *Dangereuse Amérique* (America the Dangerous), "America has colonized others' minds, even more than their territories."[7] The charge of American domination of others' minds and thoughts would seem particularly hard to square with the globalization of the ideology of anti-Americanism, which has been chiefly a creation of non-American nations.

Anti-Americanism, then, derives its explosive character from being a mix of "natural" and theoretical sources. This peculiar combination allows a philosophical discourse to invade the political realm in a manner akin to how theological discourse has often been employed in the political world. Anti-Americanism is the political religion of modern times.

Because the theoretical aspect of anti-Americanism derives from Western philosophy, one might think that its influence would be limited to those nations where that philosophy is deeply rooted. And it is perfectly true that anti-Americanism originated in Europe in the eighteenth and nineteenth centuries. But it is an error to suppose that anti-Americanism has remained confined to its birthplace. On the contrary, over the last century theoretical anti-Americanism has spread over much of the globe, helping, for example, to shape opinion in pre–World War II Japan, where many in the elite had studied German philosophy, and to influence thinking in Latin American and African countries today, where French thought carries so much weight. Western philosophy's influence has been enormous in the Islamic and Arab world as well. Well before the attacks of September 11, 2001, Bernard Lewis had traced Muslim views of America to "intellectual influences coming from Europe," especially German philosophy, "which enjoyed a considerable vogue among Arab and some other Muslim intellectuals in the thirties and early forties."[8] Recent accounts of the intellectual origins of contemporary radical Islamic movements by Paul Berman and Waller R. Newell have only added support to this argument by showing that the views of Islamic intellectual leaders about the West and America have been drawn in large measure from various currents of Western thought.[9] It is to this source that we owe the innumerable fatwahs and the countless jihads that have been pronounced against America. What has been attributed to a "clash of civilizations" has often been a phase of internecine intellectual warfare within philosophy, conducted with the assistance of mercenary forces recruited from other cultures.

The philosophical source of anti-Americanism has also meant that it has enjoyed considerable resonance within the United States, for America has a large intellectual class that takes part in the great theoretical discussions of the West. American thinkers, who are often the objects of this peculiar antipathy, often join with their accusers in the strange disorder known as BAIS (Battered American Intellectual Syndrome). Except for their lack of original- ity, the American intellectuals who suffer from this disorder would probably be among the greatest progenitors of anti-Americanism. As it is, they have had to be content to be its most generous con- sumers, continually fawning over European thinkers who have made the showering of contempt on America a central theme of their academic work. One of America's own famous philosophers, Richard Rorty, has courageously pleaded with American intellec- tuals to shed their "semi-conscious anti-Americanism . . . and for- get about Baudrillard's account of America as Disneyland. . . ."[10]

The hostile concept of America developed in several strata, each of which has influenced those that succeeded it. The initial stratum, which can be connected to the modern concept, was the product of romanticism. America became embroiled, almost as an afterthought, in the reactions to the French Revolution. To many critics, the American Revolution was seen as a precursor of the French Revolution. The two were conflated as products of modern rationalism, bolstering the claim that political societies could be established on the basis of abstract and universal principles. Con- servative romantics responded that nothing created or fashioned under the guidance of universal principles or with the assistance of rational science—nothing, to use *The Federalist*'s words, con- structed chiefly by "reflection and choice"—was solid or could long endure.[11] The early conservative Joseph de Maistre went so far as to deny the existence of "man" or "humankind," as referred to in the Declaration of Independence's assertion that "all men are created equal." According to Maistre, "There is no such thing in this world as man; I have seen in my life French, Italians, and Rus- sians . . . but as for man, I declare that I have never met one in my life; if he exists, it is entirely without my knowledge."[12] Not only was the Declaration based on flawed premises, but so too was the Constitution: "All that is new in [America's] constitution, all that results from common deliberation," Maistre warned, "is the most fragile thing in the world: one could not bring together more symptoms of weakness and decay."[13] Instead of human reason and rational deliberation, romantic thinkers placed their confidence in the organic growth of distinct and separate communities; they put their trust in history.

By the early nineteenth century, after the French Revolution had failed, the United States was the only society based on an Enlightenment conception of nature, and therefore became the primary target of many romantic thinkers. By surviving and prospering, the United States had refuted the charges of the inherent fragility of societies founded with the aid of reason. The romantics accordingly changed tactics and began to emphasize that America's continued existence was at the cost of everything deep or profound. Nothing constructed on the thin soil of Enlightenment principles could sustain a genuine culture. The poet Nikolaus Lenau, sometimes referred to as the "German Byron," provided the classic summary of the anti-American thought of the romantics: "With the expression *Bodenlosigkeit* [rootlessness] I think I am able to indicate the general character of all American institutions; what we call Fatherland is here only a property insurance scheme." In other words, there was no real community in America, no real *volk*. America's culture "had in no sense come up organically from within." There was only a dull materialism: "The American knows nothing; he seeks nothing but money; he has no ideas." Then came Lenau's haunting image of America: "the true land of the end, the outer edge of man."[14]

Even America's vaunted freedom was seen by many romantics as an illusion. American society was the very picture of a deadening conformity. The great romantic poet Heinrich Heine gave expression to this sentiment: "Sometimes it comes to my mind/To sail to America/To that pig-pen of Freedom/Inhabited by boors living in equality." America, as Heine put it in his prose writing, was a "gigantic prison of freedom," where the "most extensive of all tyrannies, that of the masses, exercises its crude authority."[15]

Opposition to America also came from those who favored the French Revolution and saw America as an unworthy and regressive rival. During the early years of the revolution, some of its proponents had already launched this critique. America, they claimed, was flawed because of its particular understanding of nature, which was too skewed toward the idea of the individual and toward self-interest. American principles failed to stress, as the French Revolution did, the higher and nobler qualities of virtue and fraternity. According to Condorcet, the American founders were tainted by "the prejudices that they imbibed in their youth"; the French Revolution was grounded on principles that were "purer, more precise, and more profound than those that guided the Americans."[16] This attack from the left only grew sharper in the nineteenth century, as revolutionaries now targeted not only the old monarchies but the new kind of liberalism associated with the United States. The problem with the American system—to use a term of opprobrium made famous by Rousseau and later picked up by Marx—was that it was "bourgeois." The leftist attack on America was now based in part on a new kind of historical rationalism ("scientific history") that claimed to know that American principles were but phases in the forward movement of history, which would end in the more advanced stage of communism. But this claim of scientific history was always supported by a romantic underpinning that faulted America for being a society that did not provide for a deeper and more rewarding communal existence. America was capitalist, or, as is said by many soft Marxist critics today, it is "ultra-liberal."

The next stratum in the construction of anti-Americanism emerged during the era of mass industrialization in the late nineteenth and early twentieth centuries. America was seen as the source of the techniques of mass production and of the methods and the mentality that supported the new modes of production and distribution. Friedrich Nietzsche was an early exponent of this view, arguing that America sought the reduction of everything to the calculable in an effort to dominate and get rich: "The breathless haste with which they [the Americans] work—the distinctive vice of the new world—is already beginning ferociously to infect old Europe and is spreading a spiritual emptiness [Geistlosigkeit] over the continent." Long in advance of Hollywood movies or rap music, the spread of American culture was likened to a disease. Its progress in Europe seemed ineluctable. "The faith of the Americans is becoming the faith of the European as well," Nietzsche warned.[17]

It was Nietzsche's disciples, however, who transformed the idea of America into an abstract category. Arthur Moeller Van den Bruck, best known for having popularized the phrase "The Third Reich," proposed the concept of *Amerikanertum* (Americanness), which was to be "not geographically but spiritually understood." Americanness marked "the decisive step by which we make our way from a dependence on the earth to the use of the earth, the step that mechanizes and electrifies inanimate material and makes the elements of the world into agencies of human use." It embraced a mentality of dominance, use, and exploitation on an ever-expanding scale, or what came to be called the mentality of "technologism" (*die Technik*): "In America, everything is a block, pragmatism, and the national Taylor system."[18] Another author, Paul Dehns, entitled an article, significantly, "The Americanization of the World." Americanization was defined here in the "economic sense" as the "modernization of methods of industry, exchange, and agriculture, as well as all areas of practical life," and in a wider and more general sense as the "uninterrupted, exclusive and relentless striving after gain, riches and influence."[19]

It would be difficult to understate how deeply this current of anti-American thinking penetrated philosophy and social science in the early part of the twentieth century. The works of two thinkers, who were far better known in their own time than today, illustrate this point: Theodor Lessing (a philosopher) and Richard Müller Freienfels (a psychologist). Lessing, who might be described as a left-wing follower of Nietzsche, published in 1914 a well-received book entitled *Europe and Asia*, which contrasted the cultures and mentalities of people from these two continents.[20] The book enjoyed enough success that Lessing was able to bring out four subsequent editions. On each occasion he added more about a continent he had all but omitted in the original work: America. In the end, and in light of the momentous events of World War I, Lessing felt the need to refocus the entire work: "The contrast with which this work deals [between Europe and Asia] is no longer real or practical. . . . In reality the entire earth

has been for some time becoming one great America." For a philosophical mind, the harshness of his treatment of America seems
almost to defy belief, although he was doing no more really than
summarizing the essence of existing theoretical views of the
United States. After comparing everyday life in America to existence in one of the lowest circles of Dante's *Inferno*, Lessing
moved to a more abstract account of the principle of American society: "The law of her being is called production; her life is utility.
Her faith is the faith in success and in the rule of efficiency. She
symbolizes the subjugation of nature by man and especially of
man by man. . . ." Lessing then shifted to the unnatural character
of American life, where everything appeared to him misshapen
and deformed, in the direction of the gargantuan: "As grapefruits,
strawberries, pineapples, grapes, chrysanthemums, roses, vegeta-
bles, and corn have all been grown too far over their natural sizes,
thus destroying the loveliness and natural goodness of things of
the earth, so also has America produced the most beautiful girls
and women and the healthiest and most vigorous of youngsters
and men—the first without souls, the other without dreams."[21]
Americans are aliens posing as humans, almost as in a scenario
from *Night of the Living Dead*.

   This same view worked its way into social science, in the studies of psychology of Richard Müller Freienfels, whom John Dewey
considered a leading social scientist of the day. One of Freienfels's
major works was *Geheimnisse der Seele* (Mysteries of the Soul),
published in 1927, which offered a general history of human psychological development.[22] One of the main chapters is entitled
"The Americanization of the Soul," which treats "the problem of
that Americanism which we shall endeavor to understand as a
transformation of the life of the soul in general." Freienfels makes
clear that he is discussing "Americanism" rather than America itself. Americanism is an "abstraction" that is "determining the expression of the twentieth century all the world over."

   Americanism is found more in America, but it is not limited
to the United States. Its decisive characteristic is a flattening of
the soul and a loss of depth. The cause lies in a "mathematization
of life" and a "mechanization of life": "Mass and quantity are be-

coming decisive, and they leave no room for quality. . . . From the standpoint of any non-American, it means a psychological wilderness, an empty and superficial world." Americanism is clearly the great malady of our age. It is threatening to spread everywhere: "Even in Europe the American, or rather the Americanistic spirit, is becoming more and more prevalent, while . . . depth and individuality and refined intelligence are disappearing."[23] Parts of Freienfels's argument strikingly parallel the analysis of America and modernity found in one the most widely studied philosophic works of the 1960s, Herbert Marcuse's *One-Dimensional Man*.

The next stratum in the construction of anti-Americanism— and the one that still most powerfully influences modern discourse on America—was the creation of two renowned German thinkers, Ernst Jünger and Martin Heidegger. These two established the framework for contemporary anti-Americanism by transforming the theme of technologism into a fully theoretical or metaphysical view. Technologism is a force that Western thought created but that now governs and determines how man lives and thinks. "America" in this thought emerges as the symbol of technologism, but a symbol in a negative sense, as technologism utterly uncontrolled. In different ways these authors suggest a choice or an alternative, not against technologism per se but against the American variant.

Jünger's essay on "Total Mobilization" (1930) and then his classic book *The Worker* (1932) were milestones in the elaboration of the argument of technologism. They were, as Heidegger reported, the source for his own famous reflections on the subject. Jünger spoke of all the great modern movements—fascism, bolshevism, Americanism—as those designed to deploy the totality of society's resources to achieve an objective. "Progress," or victory at any rate, could be secured only in this way. Modernity was based on "total mobilization": "Esteem for quantity is increasing: quantity of assent, quantity of public opinion has become the decisive factor in politics." Despite its claims of freedom, America no less than the others was a mass society that had found its own way to total mobilization. There was no genuine freedom left in the modern world: "Even the dream of freedom is disappearing as if under a pincer's iron grasp; the movements of uniformly molded masses trapped in the snare set by the world-spirit comprise a great and fearful spectacle."[24] A terrible beauty was born. America was no more the symbol of this new tyranny than bolshevism, although Jünger in one of his literary works, *The Adventuresome Heart* (1930), revealed a special horror of America when, in contemplating American city life and commercialism, he was reminded of "my old doubts of whether Americans are really human."[25] Jünger was the cool and calm observer of this modernity, which he accepted as an unalterable reality. Still, he suggested a third way between the other two—a German way—that might "bring victory of the soul over the machine." His portrayal of Americanism was in part a call to action on behalf of a different alternative.

Like some of his predecessors, Martin Heidegger offered a technical or philosophical definition of the concept of Americanism, apart, as it were, from the United States. Americanism, he wrote, is "the still unfolding and not yet full or completed essence of the emerging monstrousness of modern times."[26] But Heidegger in this case clearly was less interested in definitions than in fashioning a symbol—something more vivid and human than "technologism." In a word—and the word was Heidegger's—America was "*katestrophenhaft*," the site of catastrophe.[27]

In one his earliest and perhaps best known passages on America, Heidegger in 1935 echoed the prevalent view of Europe being in a "middle" position between Americanism and bolshevism:

> Europe . . . lies today in a great pincer, squeezed between Russia on the one side and America on the other. From a metaphysical point of view, Russia and America are the same, with the same dreary technological frenzy and the same unrestricted organization of the average man.[28]

Even though European thinkers, as the originators of modern science, were largely responsible for this development, Europe, with its pull of tradition, had managed to stop well short of its full implementation. It was in America and Russia that the idea of quantity divorced from quality had taken over and grown, as Heidegger put it, "into a boundless et cetera of indifference and always the sameness." The result in both countries was "an active onslaught that destroys all rank and every world creating impulse. . . . This is the onslaught of what we call the demonic, in the sense of destructive evil."[29]

America and the Soviet Union comprised the axis of evil. But America, in Heidegger's view, represented the greater and more significant threat, as "Bolshevism is only a variant of Americanism." In a kind of overture to the left after World War II, Heidegger spoke of entering into a "dialogue" with Marxism, which was possible because of its sensitivity to the general idea of history.[30] A similar encounter with Americanism was out of the question, as America was without a genuine sense of history. Americanism was "the most dangerous form of boundlessness, because it appears in a middle class way of life mixed with Christianity, and all this in an atmosphere that lacks completely any sense of history." When the United States declared war on Germany, Heidegger wrote: "We know today that the Anglo Saxon world of Americanism is resolved to destroy Europe. . . . The entry of America into this world war is not an entry into history, but is already the last American act of American absence of historical sense."[31]

In creating this symbol of America, Heidegger managed to include within it many of the problems or maladies of modern times, from the rise of instantaneous global communication, to an indifference to the environment, to the reduction of culture to a commodity for consumption. He was especially interested in consumerism, which he thought was emblematic of the spirit of his age: "Consumption for the sake of consumption is the sole procedure that distinctively characterizes the history of a world that has become an unworld. . . . Being today means being replaceable."[32] America was the home of this way of thinking; it was the very embodiment of the reign of the ersatz, encouraging the absorption of the unique and authentic into the uniform and the standard. Heidegger cited a passage from the German poet Rainer Maria Rilke:

> Now is emerging from out of America pure undifferentiated things, mere things of appearance, sham articles. . . . A house in

the American understanding, an American apple or an American
vine has nothing in common with the house, the fruit, or the
grape that had been adopted in the hopes and thoughts of our
forefathers.[33]

Following Nietzsche, Heidegger depicted America as an inva-
sive force taking over the soul of Europe, sapping it of its depth
and spirit: "The surrender of the German essence to Americanism
has already gone so far as on occasion to produce the disastrous effect that Germany actually feels herself ashamed that her people
were once considered to be 'the people of poetry and thought.'"[34]
Europe was almost dead, almost Americanized, but not quite. Europe by its consciousness of the problem might still put itself in
the position of being ready to receive what Heidegger called "the
Happening"; but it would be able to do so only if it were able to
summon the interior strength to reject Americanism and "push it
back to the other hemisphere."[35] The path to salvation, if there
was one, lay in anti-Americanism.

Heidegger's political views are commonly deplored today on
account of his early and open support of Nazism. Because of this
connection, many like to suppose that his influence on subsequent political thought (as distinct from general intellectual
thought) in Europe has been meager. Yet nothing could be farther
from the truth. Heidegger's major ideas were sufficiently protean
that with a bit of tinkering they could easily be adopted by the left,
which they were. Following the war, Heidegger's thought, shorn of
its national socialism but fortified in its anti-Americanism, was
embraced by many on the left, often without attribution. In the
writings of numerous thinkers like Jean-Paul Sartre, "Heideggeri-
anism" was married to communism, and this odd coupling became the core of the intellectual left for the next generation.

The Heideggarian view of America (interwoven with Marxist
elements) became the dominant view of America in the period
that followed. Communist parties, for their own obvious purposes, seized on the weapon of anti-Americanism and employed it
with such regularity that many came to think it was a creation of

communism that would vanish if ever communism should cease. The collapse of communism has served, on the contrary, to reveal the true depth and strength of anti-Americanism. Uncoupled from communism, which gave it a certain strength but also placed limits on its appeal, anti-Americanism has worked its way more than ever before into the mainstream of intellectual thought. Only one of the infamous Heideggerian pincers now remains to threaten Europe and the world. If Europe once found identity in being in "the middle" (or as a "third force"), many argue today that it must find its identity in becoming a "pole of opposition" to America (and the leader of a "second force").

Variants of the Heideggarian view of America have become part of the great themes of modern (or postmodern) philosophical thought. One of the most influential treatments is that of the philosopher Alexandre Kojève, who is best known for his revival of the idea of "the end of history." Kojève's account of history is presented in a spirit of "cool" observation and detachment, offering no judgments. Yet the picture of the end of history is nothing if not amusing. It is characterized by "the disappearance of man." Although a biological creature in the form of man will continue to exist, man properly speaking—an agent who acts on the world and struggles to create something new—will cease to exist. Man will be replaced by "an animal of the species of Homo sapiens" that will engage in some activities analogous to those of humans. It will practice a kind of art but in the way that "spiders weave their webs"; it will construct edifices, but after the fashion of "birds building their nests"; it will engage in discussion in the manner of the "discourse of bees"; and it will perform music but with noises that resemble those of "frogs and cicadas."[36] In 1947 Kojève considered the end of history and the disappearance of man in the perspective of a future possibility. But after taking a trip to America a few years later he concluded that the "end of History in the Hegelian-Marxist sense was not something yet to come, but is already present." Its outline was visible in America: "The American way of life is the type of life proper to the post-historic period, and the presence today of the United States in the World prefigures the

future 'eternal present' of humanity in its entirety. Thus the return of man to an animal nature appeared no longer as a possibility to come, but as a certitude already present."[37]
    The picture of life at the end of history is sketched by Jean
Baudrillard in the form of a travel log of America.[38] The work is
meant to describe America as it is, without judgment, and the
mere fact that Baudrillard characterizes Americans as fat, dumb,
primitive, and uncultured is surely no reason to think that he is
anti-American! On the contrary, he claims that he is utterly
charmed by the "inspired banality" of America, whereas Europeans suffer from possessing the "art of thinking about things, of
analyzing them, and of reflecting on them," and as a result can get
nothing done. Americans get everything done. America is history's
final stop, "utopia achieved": "America is the original version of
modernity . . . and Americans make up the ideal material for an
analysis of all the variants possible of the modern world." Americans are happily ahistorical, living without "a past or a founding
truth," which allows them to adapt perfectly to the modern world
of signs and simulacra, as one finds in Disneyland. The "distinctly
American miracle" is that of the "obscene," or tastelessness,
which allows Americans to progress without qualms by con-
structing things like suburbs. America is a happy mass society
"where the quantitative is exalted without apology."[39]
    Over time Baudrillard has moved from an ironic and conde-
scending contemplation of America to a more openly contemptuous
and vitriolic anti-Americanism. Events seemed to have pushed him
from his ironic perch and led him to take positions that are more
conventionally anti-American. During the first Gulf War in 1991, he
hoped for the defeat of America, less for any simple strategic reason
than for a deeper philosophical or metaphysical reason. His postmodernism now assumed the form of arguing that America and its
technological way of thought are premised on the idea of controlling, ordering, homogenizing, and dominating. It eliminates "the
other." America is a vast despotism that practices a "consensual in-
tegrism (of Enlightenment, of rights of man, . . . of sentimental humanism) that is just as ferocious as that of any tribal region or
primitive society."[40] The deepest source of barbarism is America.

The 1999 Kosovo War, fought by America and the NATO allies, became another occasion for voicing this anti-American argument. In this case the opponents not only attacked America but also America's control or alleged hegemony of Europe. The compliance of Europe in this venture became proof of the spread of the American malady to the old continent. This view was best expressed by Regis Debray, who spent his early career fomenting Third World revolutions with Che Guevara. According to Debray, all of Europe had been "deprogrammed" to adopt American ways of thinking. A mind became Americanized when "the notion of time is replaced by that of space, when historical thinking is replaced by technological calculation, and political thinking by moralistic thinking." America found its purest expression in a media-saturated world. "With CNN, all the planet becomes America." The Kosovo situation, for all it revealed about the crisis of Europe, represented an opportunity. A NATO failure would force Europeans to realize the extent to which they had become "as uncultured and shortsighted as their leader."[41] Kosovo offered the chance to rescue the European mind from Americanism and, to use Heidegger's phrase, "push America back to the other hemisphere." Others followed Debray's lead, equating the evil of an American-led NATO with that of Milosevic. According to the Parisian philosopher Daniel Bensaid, "The barbarism of ethnic cleansing is not a barbarism of 'another age,' opposed by the unified force of the absolute good of 'civilization.' Milosevic and NATO are twin contemporary forms of modern barbarism."[42]

Some of the harshest expressions of anti-Americanism have been heard recently in the buildup and aftermath of the second Gulf War in 2003. Large parts of the world joined together in opposition to the American-led effort to oust Saddam Hussein. Part of this opposition derived from the "natural" source of anti-Americanism that seeks to thwart the world's dominant power; another part of the criticism was not anti-American at all but came from those who believed that this war was a strategic mistake. But much of the opposition drew upon the symbolic America and demonstrated just how far theoretical anti-Americanism has penetrated into the political realm. The political religion of anti-Americanism is now confirmed as a one of the great facts of our time and one with which political leaders will be compelled to deal in the years ahead.

In a well-known and farsighted passage, Edward Gibbon, author of the *Decline and Fall of the Roman Empire*, raised the speculative question of whether barbarism could once again destroy the citadel of civilization, as it had done when the Northern tribes conquered Rome. His analysis led him to conclude that the power and resources of the Europe of his day (the late eighteenth century) made the prospect of another successful onslaught of barbarism against Europe highly unlikely. Gibbon then added one further point of assurance: "Should the Barbarians carry slavery and desolation as far as the Atlantic Ocean . . . Europe would revive and flourish in the American world, which is already filled with her colonies and institutions. . . . Whatever may be the changes of their political situation, they [the Americans] must preserve the manners of Europe."[43] Gibbon's argument assumed, at the deepest level, a harmony of the "manners"—we might say values—of the West and of civilization. Defining the West, of course, has never been an easy task. As Gibbon's own work shows, it is based on an uneasy combination of three great components: Jerusalem (meaning the biblical religions), Athens (meaning classical philosophy), and the modern Enlightenment.

The demonization of America by anti-Americanism not only calls into question the community of interests between Europe and America but threatens the idea of the West. It pulls the various pieces of the West apart and sets them at war with one another. Theoretical anti-Americanism is the Trojan horse that has been introduced to destroy Western civilization.

NOTES

1. *What the World Thinks in 2002*, p. 1, A Report of the Pew Research Foundation. Available at the website of the Pew Foundation.
2. Jean François Revel, *La Grande Parade* (Paris: Plon, 2000), p. 308.
3. Ignacio Ramonet, *Guerres du XXIe siècle* (Paris: Galilée, 2002) pp. 88–89.

4. Jean Baudrillard, "L'esprit du terrorisme," *Le Monde*, November 3, 2001, p. 1.

5. George Washington, farewell address at http://earlyamerica.com/earlyamerica/milestones/farewell/text.html.

6. Henry de Montherlant, *Le Chaos et la Nuit* (Paris: Gallimard, 1963), p. 265.

7. Noel Mamčre and Patrick Farbiaz, *Dangereuse Amérique* (Paris: Ramsey, 2002), p. 63.

8. Bernard Lewis, "The Roots of Muslim Rage," *Atlantic*, September 1990, p. 52.

9. Paul Berman, *Terror and Liberalism* (New York: Norton, 2003); Waller Newell, "Postmodern Jihad," *Weekly Standard*, November 26, 2001, p. 26.

10. Richard Rorty, *Achieving Our Country* (Cambridge, Mass.: Harvard University Press, 1998), pp. 98–99.

11. Alexander Hamilton, James Madison, and John Jay, *The Federalist* (New York: New American Library, 1961), p. 33 (Federalist #1).

12. Joseph de Maistre, *Considérations sur la France* (Geneva: Slatkine, 1980, orig. 1797), pp. 133–134.

13. Joseph de Maistre, *Oeuvres complčtes* (Geneva: Slatkine, 1979), 1:87.

14. Nikolaus Lenau, *Samtliche Werke und Briefe*, (Frankfurt: Insel Verrl, 1971), 2:216, 2:213.

15. Heinrich Heine, "Jetzt Wohin?" cited in Ernst Fraenkel, *Amerika: Im Spiegel des Deutschen politischen Denkens* (Cologne: Westdeutscher Verlag, 1959), pp. 106–107.

16. Antoine-Nicolas de Condorcet, *Sketch for a Universal Picture of the Progress of the Human Mind*, trans. June Barraclough (New York: Noonday Press, 1955, orig. 1795), p. 147.

17. Friedrich Nietzsche, *The Gay Science*, trans. Walter Kaufmann (New York: Vintage, 1974), pp. 258–259, 303.

18. Arthur Moeller Van den Bruck, *Die Zeitgenossen* (Minden: Bruns, 1906), p. 13.

19. Cited in Otto Basler, "Americanismus: Geschichte des Schlagwortes," in *Deutsche Rundschau* (August, 1930), p. 144.

20. Theodor Lessing, *Europa und Asien*, fifth edition (Leipzig: Felix Meiner, 1930).

21. *Europa und Asien*, p. 100, 206, 209.

22. Richard Muller Freienfels, *Geheimnisse der Seele* (Munich: Delphin, 1927), translated by Bernard Miall as *Mysteries of the Soul* (New York: Knopf, 1929).

23. *Mysteries of the Soul*, p. 8, 240, 252, 269.

24. Ernst Jünger, "Total Mobilization," translated by Richard Wolin in *The Heidegger Controversy*, ed. Richard Wolin (Boston: MIT Press, 1933), pp. 137–138.

25. Ernst Jünger, "Das Abenteuerliche Herz" in *Samtliche Werke* (Stuttgart: Klett-Cotta, 1979), p. 102.

26. Martin Heidegger, *Holzwege* (Frankfurt: Vittorio Klostermann, 1957), p. 103.

27. Martin Heidegger, "Holderins Hymne" in *Gesamtausgabe* (Frankfurt: Vittorio Klostermann, 1975) vol. 53:179.

28. Martin Heidegger, *An Introduction to Metaphysics*, trans. Ralph Manheim (New Haven: Yale University Press, 1959, orig. 1935), p. 37.

29. *An Introduction to Metaphysics*, pp. 45–46.

30. For his discussion of a "productive dialogue" with Marxism, see Martin Heidegger, "A Letter on Humanism," in *Basic Writings*, ed. David Krell (New York: Harper and Row, 1977), pp. 220–221.

31. Heidegger, "Holderins Hymne," vol. 53:68.

32. Martin Heidegger, "Overcoming Metaphysics" in *The Heidegger Controversy*, p. 84 and "Seminars" in *Questions III and IV* (Paris: Gallimard, 1976), p. 456.

33. Martin Heidegger, *Holzwege*, p. 268.

34. Martin Heidegger, "Andenken, Erlauterungen zu Holderlins Dichtung," in *Gesamtausgabe*, 52:134.

35. Martin Heidegger, "Andenken" in *Gesamtausgabe*, 52:37.

36. Alexandre Kojčve *Introduction a la Lecture de Hegel*, ed. Raymond Queneau (Paris: Gallimard, 1968), p. 436.

37. *Introduction a la Lecture de Hegel*, p. 437.

38. Jean Baudrillard, *Amérique* (Paris: B. Grasset, 1986).

39. *New York Times*, December 12, 1988, A44; *Amérique*, p. 23, 50, 58, 151.

40. Jean Baudrillard, *La Guerre du Golfe n'a pas eu lieu* (Paris: Galilée, 1991), p. 90, 100.

41. Regis Debray, "L'Europe somnambule," *Le Monde*, April 1, 1999, p. 1.

42. Daniel Bensaid, "Leur logique et la notre," *Le Monde*, April 9, 1999, p. 1.

43. Edward Gibbon, *The Decline and Fall of the Roman Empire*, (New York: Modern Library, 1995), p. 1223.

2

ANTHONY DANIELS

Sense of Superiority and Inferiority in French Anti-Americanism

Anyone who reads the French press soon realizes that the word "Anglo-Saxon" is laden with connotation, and not much of it favorable.[1] Britain deservedly having almost sunk below the threshold of French notice, and Australia, New Zealand, and Canada (except for Quebec) never having risen above it, "Anglo-Saxon" now means in effect American. America is the economic, military, technological, and cultural colossus that bestrides, and haunts, the French imagination, at least that of its intelligentsia. Only in contradistinction to America can France retain what it believes to be its rightful place in the world, that is to say the capital of civilization itself. If it is still to be true that every cultured man in the world has two homelands, his own and France, the particularity of French culture must resist the universal solvent of Americanization.

At the center of French fears is language.[2] With a terrible swiftness, English has become the sole world language: even the *Comptes Rendues de L'Institut Pasteur* must be published in English if the scientific world is to take any notice of them, despite the fact that France and its language have one of the greatest traditions of scientific discovery and publication in the world (indeed, there is no field of higher human endeavor to which the French have not contributed disproportionately). Imagine the anxiety of Anglophones if we suddenly realized in fifty years' time that the whole world had decided to speak not English but Mandarin!

If a Frenchman wants to speak to his neighbor the Spaniard or the German, the chances are he will have to do so in English. It takes little knowledge of French national feeling to understand that this is not a source of pride or pleasure to him. It conjures up the fear that French will be relegated to the status of just another European language, a minor one at that, five others being spoken by more native speakers: English, Spanish, Portuguese, Russian, and German. This is a far cry from being the lingua franca of diplomacy and of all civilized men.

Perhaps it is no accident, as the Marxists used to say, that a book by Marc Fumaroli, of the Academie Française, should have appeared recently with the wistful title *Quand L'Europe Parlait Francais* (When Europe Spoke French).[3] French was the court language in Russia; Edward Gibbon, one of the great masters of English prose, published his first book in French, and Frederick the Great, the icon of German nationalism, spoke German only haltingly and never for preference. Not for nothing did he call his palace near Berlin Sans Souci rather than Ohne Sorge.

The Academie Française attempts to preserve the purity of the French language from foreign influence and pollution, particularly Anglo-American, and even makes up words for new technology, as if French were an ancient or dying language undergoing resurrection, like Irish or Hebrew.[4] The French anxiety over the international future of their language is also demonstrated by the Francophone conferences that are held regularly at the highest governmental levels. The countries in which French is—or was—the second language, such as Lebanon, Romania, and Cambodia, are all invited. The desire to preserve the extent of francophonie is widely believed to explain French support for the regime of Juvenal Habyarimana of Rwanda,[5] a support that continued after his death even when it became clear that his successors were intent upon a real, unequivocal genocide (a rare event, mercifully, despite the frequency with which the word is bandied about). The rebels seeking to overthrow Habyarimana were descendants of the Tutsis, who were expelled and fled to Uganda in the wake of the revolutionary upheavals around the time of the country's independence that brought the majority Hutu to power. Having grown up in Uganda, the rebels were Anglophone, and so their victory would, or at least might, result in a passage of Rwanda from the Francophone to the Anglophone camp. A little genocide was the price central Africa would have to pay for the preservation of francophonie and the prevention of the further extension of the hegemony of English.

America represents, and is largely responsible for, the triumph of English over all other languages, French included. Globalization is the other force responsible for the spread of English as the lingua franca of the world: a Chinese trading with an Indian, a Javanese, or a Brazilian has to speak it, or at least something approximating it. But globalization is another word for Americanization, for America is seen not only as the initiator of the process but as its chief, if not only, beneficiary. If Europe benefits at all, it is very much as a junior partner in the enterprise.

This is not the place to discuss whether globalization is a new or unprecedented phenomenon, as if world trade and foreign investment had never occurred before, or whether it is a good or a bad thing. I do have misgivings about it and do not look forward to a world united mainly by its appetites and patterns of consumption; this admittedly is a tourist's viewpoint. I do not wish to travel five thousand miles and discover that everything is the same both at my destination and my point of departure. Whether global uniformity is a realistic possibility is another question; it is nonetheless a widely shared apprehension.

The fear of globalization is sometimes found in strange places, as for example in the thought (or perhaps I should say the feelings) of Bertrand Cantat, the lead singer of the most successful French rock group, Noir Desir, who is now infamous for having killed his actress lover, Marie Trintignant, in a hotel bedroom in Lithuania. Cantat used his fame as a singer to spread his (banal and cliché-ridden) political and social opinions. Among them, almost inevitably, was support for subcomandante Marcos, the scion of the

Mexican bourgeoisie and university teacher turned Indian guerrilla leader, who opposes globalization while using all the techniques of global communication to turn himself into the radical
chic darling of the world's press. Cantat is—or was—a practitioner
of the most globalized, that is to say American, art form (if that is
what it is), namely rock music. A French rock musician is necessarily quasi-Americanized, even if—as Cantat does—he reads
Baudelaire and Rimbaud. Cantat does not appear in a beret and a
striped jersey with an accordion but in jeans and a T-shirt, with an
electric guitar. Physically he is indistinguishable from an American, and he knows it. But though he practiced a quintessentially
American art, he could never, even without the murder, quite
have made it into the very highest league, such as it is, because he
sang in French. He was thus both highly privileged—the Francophone market was still big enough to make him a very rich
man—and at the same time a victim of forces beyond his control.
The beneficiary of a globalized culture, Catat's career was simultaneously limited by it; and for an ego as large as his, such limita-
tion must have seemed intolerable. He therefore turned upon the
hand that fed him, and fed him handsomely too.[6]

When we love, admire, and imitate what we hate, or feel we
ought to hate, our denunciatory tone often becomes shrill, to
drown our doubts about ourselves. This in a nutshell is a characteristic dynamic of anti-Americanism, and not only in France. But
there is more, and worse, to this ambivalence. As everyone knows,
France has one of the greatest culinary traditions in the world,
yet, oddly enough, it is the second-largest market in Europe for
McDonald's restaurants (which are even known familiarly as
McDo). I do not think one has to be anti-American to find this
form of food and the manner of its consumption crude and child-
ish. The very fact that so many Frenchmen have taken to it when
they are heirs to an infinitely superior and more civilized culinary
tradition is alarming, and seems to reflect badly on modern man's
tastes and priorities. At the same time French intellectuals, however privileged their lives, almost always claim to identify, at least
theoretically, with the common man. The latter must therefore always be seen as a victim rather than a perpetrator (in this case, of

bad taste); therefore the common man who enters McDonald's must not do so of his own free will, because he lacks discrimination, but because he is being manipulated by malign forces over which he has no control. These malign forces emanate, of course, from America, whose market economy has given the freest reign to the bad taste of the multitude. The French intellectual is appalled, even more so that his own countrymen should so eagerly follow the Americans. It appears as if the meretricious has universal appeal; but where does that leave Liberté, Egalité, Fraternité? Perhaps Liberté is not such a good idea after all, if it leads to the cultural damnation of McDonald's. When it comes to Egalité, it is clear at the very least that taste divides men fundamentally, between the few who have it and the many who do not. As for Fraternité, how could anyone seriously consider fraternizing with the patrons of that greasy fried muck, gulped in plastic surroundings of violently clashing primary colors, attractive perhaps to a child of four? It is an impossible dilemma. But since our intellectual is also a democrat, of deep sympathy for the masses, he will blame the supply, not the demand. The supply is American, the demand is French. The latter are exploited by the former.

What is true of food is true also of films. The struggle to preserve a quota of French films shown in French cinemas has been widely publicized, mainly because it is a losing one. French audiences—perversely, from the point of view of intellectuals—persist in their preference for the productions of Hollywood. Hollywood, it seems, has found a formula to seduce, captivate, and corrupt French audiences, just as Socrates corrupted youth. The solution to the problem is to make available to them what they do not want, and restrict their access to what they do want—in short, to treat them as minors in need of guidance.

Again, this is not the place to argue whether or not the anxieties of the French intellectuals are justified. Personally I have some sympathy with them. Paris, thanks to the municipal subsidy of small art cinemas, is the best place in the world to see films from the four quarters of the globe, and for my taste, many of the films shown—to audiences of four, three, or even one—are infinitely more interesting than the simultaneously anemic and

}

bloody productions of Hollywood. But once again it is less disturbing to blame the supply than the demand, and to attribute to
it sinister powers. In this way one can avoid thorny questions
about the philosophical basis of liberal democracy. If people
should not be allowed to vote with their francs (or euros), why
should they be allowed to vote with their ballots? The spread of
American tastes and patterns of consumption, especially among
the young, which so appalls intellectuals, soon raises uncomfortable questions that can be avoided only if the people who indulge
in them are not blamed.

The anxious French intellectual assumes that the cultural influence goes like the flight of Time's arrow in one direction only,
itself symbolic of the disparity in the power of the two countries.
In fact, French cultural influence on American life has been considerable, if less immediately obvious (French restaurants do not
ruin a landscape). Deconstruction, an intellectual fad originating
in France, has run through the humanities departments of American universities like a virus through a computer network. It has
destroyed notions of objectivity and scholarship, and has spread
relativism both moral and epistemological. It has turned most intellectual questions into the equivivalent of Lenin's Who Whom?,
that is to say, who does what to whom. Truth is nothing, only
power counts.

Clearly, people imbued with this philosophy are unlikely to
value social harmony or have much of a sense of proportion about
their own dissatisfactions. Whether it will have any long-term practical effect on American life remains to be seen, though in the past
America's vastness and the opportunities it has offered its citizens
have rendered it relatively immune from the destructive ideologies
fomented by intellectuals. Still, the unprecedented does sometimes
happen, and while it may be true that academic disputes are so bitter because there is so little at stake, it would be wrong to suppose
that, in an age of mass education in which feeling so easily trumps
fact, what happens in the humanities departments of universities is
completely insignificant as far as the rest of society is concerned.[7]
The time may yet come when an historian may argue that deconstruction was France's revenge for McDonald's.

Whatever the realities of bilateral cultural influences, the great and growing disparity of power between France and the United States is experienced as a humiliation. This disparity, rather than any particular love of the Germans (who in private are still hated), is what drives the French desire for European unity. Only as a united front, with their differences suppressed, if necessary by decree, can the countries of Europe, France included, compete with the United States on equal terms. This is the meaning of the attempt in Europe to outlaw xenophobia—but only certain forms of it. Xenophobia that hinders the exercise of power will be forbidden while that which favors it will be encouraged.

France's historical experiences as a supposedly great power have not been altogether happy—that is, if the exercise of great power is ever happy, and brings those who wield it anything other than sleepless nights. Napoleon overreached himself, and his supposed glory, or thirst for conquest, resulting in the deaths of hundreds of thousands of his countrymen while his conquests proved ephemeral. His descendant, Napoleon III, brought about the military humiliation of France by Prussia. The wars of colonial conquest were little more than adventurous bullying on a large scale, unequal struggles between those who had the Maxim gun and those who did not. In the case of France, they were undertaken to overcome the humiliation experienced in Europe, with the blessing of Bismarck.[8]

Colonialism in the end inflicted further humiliations on France. The victory in the World War I was at best equivocal, for it was brought about not by France's unaided efforts, despite its great, indeed almost maximal, sacrifices. The extent of the debacle in 1940 hardly needs emphasis. If it had not been so complete and devastating, it would not have given rise to the so-called Vichy syndrome,[9] the collective inability of the country to acknowledge the passivity with which the Occupation was accepted, and the comparatively minor scale, and late development, of the Resistance. It is not, perhaps, for people who have never had so cataclysmic an experience to criticize those who reacted prudently rather than bravely, to save their own skins; after all, most of us know what it is to compromise with evil when it is in our interests to do so, even when less than our lives are at stake. But the liberation of France gave rise to a myth that everyone knew in his heart to be false: that France had continued to fight the Nazis even after the Armistice. That François Mitterand should have had difficulty in acknowledging his past as a high official of the Vichy regime, and to have consistently muddied his biographical waters, is entirely understandable in a man bent on achieving power by presenting himself as a man of the left. What is more curious, and significant, is that there should have been so few critiques of him, even by his political enemies, on this score during his fourteen-year mandate.[10]

The speed with which biographical details were made known after his death suggests that the information had been easily available all along but that no one had chosen to avail himself of it. Mitterand's life mirrored with some precision the history of France as a whole. He changed sides from Pétain to the Resistance when it became clear to him that the war (on Pétain's side) was lost. He re-created himself as a man of leftist principle, a firm resistant. His personal need to obfuscate his past coincided perfectly with his country's need, and that of his opponents, to do the same. And the Vichy syndrome has a lot to do with French anti-Americanism.

The collapse of French power continued after World War II, and 1940 was far from France's last defeat in its attempt to play the great power. First came the loss of Madagascar and Indochina, then Algeria, with Suez in between. True, the collapse of British power was just as complete; but, with one or two exceptions, Suez notable among them, the British accepted it with better grace and fewer defeats than the French. They even managed some victories en route: first in World War II, then in Malaya, where they comprehensively defeated a Communist insurgency, and later in the Falklands. There is nothing quite like a small victory to disguise the bitterness of falling into the ranks of the unimportant, of declining from world power to a province of the English-speaking world.

France was defeated militarily in Indochina, and if not militarily in Algeria, at least politically. A few successful interventions in sub-Saharan African countries, whose collective power is probably less than that of the police department of a medium-sized

American city, could hardly disguise the extent of France's impotence on the world stage, at least militarily.

To be sure, the loss of power matters only if power itself is regarded as very desirable and important. The fact is that the final collapse of French pretensions to global power coincided with a period of unprecedented prosperity, with dramatic improvements in French living standards. From the point of view of the average French citizen, this has been, materially at least, without doubt the best period in the country's history in which to be alive. Furthermore, the glory of France over the past few centuries, which coincided with its military defeats, had nothing to do with its global power. Paris was not the capital of the nineteenth century because France was the most powerful or economically advanced country in Europe; it was the capital because it was culturally and intellectually without rival. Balzac, Baudelaire, Flaubert, Maupassant; Berlioz, Chopin, Debussy; Bichat, Bernard, Charcot, Pasteur; Haussmann, Eiffel; David, Ingres, Delacroix, Daumier, Manet, Degas, Toulouse-Lautrec—these are only a few who brought it fame and influence; such a flowering of human genius rarely seen in history, had nothing to do with the projection of power. Even in the twentieth century, especially the first half, French achievement was considerable. And though everyone agrees that the present is no golden age from the point of view of high culture in France (but then, where is it?), France remains a greatly more cultivated country than, say, Britain.

But prosperity and cultivation are not enough, at least for some people. For them, power is what counts. De Gaulle was of this ilk: although not indifferent to literature, in which he had a conservative, classical taste, he was indifferent to many of the things that—unbeknownst to him, apparently—constituted France's true glory, for example its leadership in the visual arts.[11] He had a certain idea of France, of its *gloire*, that was not principally cultural but largely military-political—hardly surprising, perhaps, for a career military officer. France was not France, he said in the famous opening paragraph of his memoirs, unless it possessed the power to project itself outward.[12] Brute reality in the modern world is against France becoming a preeminent military power.

The Vichy syndrome, as I have indicated, plays its part in the generation of French anti-Americanism. Lack of resistance to a real enemy has been compensated for by symbolic resistance to an imagined one: an enemy, moreover, known to have no intention of retaliating, and one who is actually quite friendly.

In the case of de Gaulle, his opposition to, and dislike of, American power had nothing to do with sympathy for communism or the Soviet Union. (It is sometimes difficult to tell whether the pro-communism of French intellectuals, at least during the cold war, was caused by anti-American feeling, or vice versa.) De Gaulle was not a doctrinal political thinker, at least not in the sense that he derived policy from clearly-stated first principles. Rather, he derived his policy from basic emotions, chief among which was a mystical attachment to an almost platonic notion of France. This was not the France of actual or contemporary Frenchmen, of little civic mindedness but plenty of ordinary human defects and contradictions, not the France so difficult to govern because of its militant interest groups, but an abstract France. De Gaulle's basic emotion, upon which all else was subordinated, gave him both his peculiar intransigence and complete realism; his was realism in the service of transcendence, France being the transcendent reality to be served.

De Gaulle did not open his memoirs with a conventional account of his origins or background but with a confession of faith. He had his famous conception of the French, which was certainly not that of the canny, scheming peasant type whom Maupassant so lovingly depicts, who believes in advantageous marriage, savings in gold stowed under the bed, and legacies obtained by hook or by crook. There is no France for de Gaulle without *gloire*. He would have nothing but contempt for his countrymen who content themselves with being citizens of a reasonably social democratic France, even a France more prosperous materially, than ever before. For de Gaulle, France must be powerful to be prosperous, not the other way round. Every French leader since de Gaulle, whether officially Gaullist or not, has followed him in this belief, for none has been content to be the leader of a prosperous, merely middle-rank democratic power.

De Gaulle was by necessity a realist. He graduated from St. Cyr at the end of the period between the Franco-Prussian War and the outbreak of the World War I. This was a period of intense anxiety for France, or at least for French politicians and the military, because of the size and preponderance of its eastern neighbor, rival, and enemy, Germany. The Wilhelmine Reich had a population double that of France and was in the forefront of the industrial and therefore military technology of the day. This anxiety manifested itself even in French psychiatry, where the dominant idea was that of hereditary degeneration,[13] which was supposed to account for the relative stagnation of French society vis-à-vis the German.

The same anxiety was shown in Britain when during the Boer War it was discovered that more than half the volunteers for the army did not meet the army's not very stringent physical requirements, stimulating arguments for state intervention to raise living standards. World domination or power could not be sustained by a population of runts.

France could not defend itself against, much less confront, Germany with its own unaided strength, and therefore had to rely upon an alliance, including its even more ancient rival and enemy, England. What was true of France's position with regard to Germany is true, a fortiori, of its position with regard to the United States. The war demonstrated to de Gaulle, in the most brutal and irrefutable way, the disparity in the power of France and the United States, a disparity that was not temporary. Initially dependent upon British goodwill, which was humiliating enough, he later had his revenge in 1963 with his famous "Non" to Britain's application for membership in the European Economic Community. Roosevelt treated him with that same disdain that Stalin displayed toward the pope, when he asked how many divisions he had. This was a slight de Gaulle never forgot or forgave, and he communicated it very clearly to his countrymen.

Yet global and military rivalry with the United States was hopeless. The demographic gap, already large, was growing; the difference in national territory was huge, the United States being seventeen times larger than France; in all technological fields the Americans were far in advance of the French and likely to remain so. There was nothing France could do to alter these facts; only a united Europe, under French political leadership, could give the French political (and intellectual) class the world power and influence it missed and believed it merited.

If power is what you seek, there is little satisfaction in being second rank. Envy of the most powerful kind is the natural outcome, especially when you feel yourself superior on historical, cultural, and civilizational grounds to he who wields supreme power.

Reaction to unassailably superior power oscillates between slavish imitation and carping criticism. Admixtures of both in varying proportions are obviously possible. When confronted by a materially more successful and powerful culture, old and proud civilizations often react by consoling themselves with their moral or spiritual superiority. The Slavophile reaction to the challenge of Western Europe took this form.[14] The Slavophiles saw Western Europe as a rich and powerful but crassly materialist and soulless society, governed by an inhumanly impersonal Moloch called Law. In contrast, the muddy mess of Russian society, at least in its village form, was both warmer and more spiritual, and destined in the bargain to redeem the whole of humanity. It did not occur to the Slavophiles that the Rule of Law was, or might have been, itself the product of deep philosophical reflection upon the aims of human life and society, and could therefore loosely be described as a spiritual phenomenon. Nor did they see any connection between the personal freedom that the Rule of Law guaranteed, and the wealth and power that those societies that possessed it generated and exerted.

The Latin American response—or rather, the response of its intellectuals—to such challenges was similar to that of the Slavophiles' bitter contemplation of the power of Western Europe. It was obvious that the Northern colossus had, in a matter of only a century, far outstripped all the Southern republics combined. The U.S. secretary of state, Richard Olney, could write with good reason in 1895 that "Today the United States is practically sovereign on this continent, and its fiat is law upon the subjects to which it confines its interposition."[15] True, the United States was rich and powerful and could send gunboats wherever it wished;

but it was a soulless and materialistic country, uncouth and un-cultured, a physical giant but a cultural and moral pygmy. Its very strength was evidence of its inhuman qualities, for it was con-cerned only with the accumulation of wealth and power. These were themes prevalent in Latin American thought from José Marti and Ruben Dario to Fidel Castro,[16] which doubtless will persist. Dwelling on the defects of others helpfully reduces the need for honest self-examination.

The Japanese response to the challenge of the West, which first became apparent with the arrival of the American Commodore Perry in 1853, was both more mature and more successful.[17] It was immediately apparent to the Japanese that, if they were not to be dominated completely by the foreign barbarians, they would have to learn the techniques that made them powerful. This they did so successfully that within a matter of a few decades they were able, for example, to contribute as much to the new science of bacteri-ology as the British, despite the latter's long history of scientific research and discovery. At the same time, however, the Japanese never lost a sense of their own essential superiority over the for-eigners, a sense that for much of their recent history they were sensible enough to keep to themselves. At times this sense of su-periority found disastrous and brutal political-military expression in the course of the twentieth century, including the treatment of the "inferior" adversaries of Japan, civilian or military. More re-cently it still occasionally emerges in injudicious remarks made by prominent persons. This sense of superiority has both a spiri-tual and a racial component, and it has spread to (if it was ever en-tirely absent from) Southeast Asia, helping explain the region's explosive economic growth.

Buddhist, Confucian, and Asian values, which once explained the region's backwardness to Westerners and consoled its inhabi-tants with a sense of their spiritual superiority in the midst of ma-terial inferiority, have now been invoked to explain its rapid material advance, an explanation highly convenient to leaders who do not wish to extend Western freedoms to their populations.

The hostile Arab response to Western culture is another case in point. Throughout the Arab world, works critical of the West are

widely distributed and translated into English for the benefit of
those they criticize. The point is not that the criticisms are entirely unjustified; they are not, and in many cases correspond almost exactly to the criticisms made by western cultural
conservatives of the deeply unattractive trends within their own
society. (The unflattering portrait of American society painted by
Islamists, not all of which is unjust, is very similar to that put out
by Fidel Castro's propagandists.[18]) Whatever the justification of
these criticisms, however, their function is not to serve knowledge, much less reform; it is to soothe wounded pride. Solace is
sought for the fact that a civilization once in advance of all others
has contributed so little to intellectual or material advance for
hundreds of years, and appears to be in no danger of doing so for
the foreseeable future.

It is hardly surprising, then, and certainly not without historical precedent, that Europeans should react to their displacement
in the vanguard of power (and some aspects of civilization) by the
Americans with resentment and carping criticism. The French,
who regarded themselves, and were regarded by others, as being in
the vanguard of the vanguard, were perhaps the most hurt by these
developments. The undoubted charms of life in the Middle East
have not consoled those inhabitants of the region who concern
themselves with anything more than the day-to-day flux of normal existence, and neither have the charms of la douce France—
greater in many respects (at least in my opinion) than anything to
be found in the United States—consoled French intellectuals.

Just as Arab criticisms of contemporary Western culture are
not necessarily without foundation, so the criticisms by French
intellectuals of the exercise of American power are not necessarily without foundation. It is, after all, much easier to criticize
power than to exercise it wisely. Thus it may not always be easy
to distinguish perfectly reasonable criticisms from those that are
motivated by envy. But it can be done by assessing evenhanded-
ness, that is to say, whether everyone is being judged by the same
standards. For example, in a recent startling memoir of his two periods of captivity in Khmer Rouge hands, entitled *Le Portail* (The
Gate),[19] the French student of Southeast Asian Buddhism François

Bizot makes it clear that he had no anti-American animus before his experiences of the bombing of Cambodia. On the contrary, he claims to have had an affinity for American culture, at least as far as jazz was concerned. But he saw the bombing as crude, vicious, stupid, and hubristic, the ignorant and final destruction of a delicate social fabric for no good military purpose.

Bizot's criticism of the French, who were by then virtually impotent in Cambodia except for some residual cultural influence, was just as strong and pungent. His testimony about the nature of the Khmer Rouge was dismissed haughtily by the French authorities as unthinkingly pro-Communist because it was unthinkingly and frivolously anti-American. He concluded that they were no better than the Americans. If they had had the power, they would have been just as brutally unscrupulous as the American high command; indeed, in their small, Machiavellian way, they were.

Bizot is not motivated in his criticism by a kind of new-age, general anti-Westernism, notwithstanding his great sympathy for the prewar Buddhist rural culture of Cambodia, no doubt somewhat idealized. He does not excuse the conduct of the Khmer Rouge by reference to the colonial past of Cambodia or its war-torn present, thus according them full membership in the human race, with its freedom to do evil. Bizot is a French intellectual who proves that it is possible to criticize American policies without idealizing all things French or some other cultural-political entity.

After the attack on the World Trade Center in September 2001, sentiment among French intellectuals appeared to undergo an abrupt, indeed a sea change. *Le Monde*, hardly noted for its reflexive pro-Americanism, led with the most famous editorial of recent French history, *"Nous sommes tous americains!"* (We Are All Americans).[20] America as victim was a far cry from the usual portrayal of America as the home of savage economic individualism, as if so powerful an economy could have arisen without a framework of rules and standards.

There was, however, a false ring to this newfound solidarity, a straining for feeling rather than feeling itself. And so it was hardly surprising that within a comparatively short time, sentiments had changed once more. The editor of *Le Monde* itself soon published a book entitled *Tous americains?*[21] (The appending of the question mark to the phrase is strongly reminiscent of the removal of the question mark in the title of the second edition of Beatrice and Sidney Webb's vast and silly apologia for Stalin's Russia, *The Soviet Union: A New Civilization?*) Two eminent French intellectuals, who had both exercised a strong, if not beneficent, influence upon the American academy, Jean Baudrillard and Jacques Derrida, both published works holding the United States responsible for terrorism.[22] A journalist published a book claiming that the attack on the Pentagon was carried out by the Americans themselves, for their own political reasons.[23]

Some French anti-American sentiment is more subtle. A recent work by the historical demographer Emmanuel Todd is of this genre, *Apres l'empire: essai sur la decomposition du systeme americain* (After Empire: An Essay on the Decomposition of the American System).[24] Todd is a formidable commentator on world affairs, and one who cannot be accused of sympathy for the far left. In 1976, for example, at the age of twenty-six, he published a brilliant book foretelling the collapse of the Soviet system, entitled, *La Chute finale: essai sur la decomposition de la sphere sovietique* (The Final Collapse: An Essay on the Decomposition of the Soviet Sphere).[25] Using only a few salient economic and demographic trends within the Soviet Union, he correctly predicted the fate of the Soviet system, thus earning the derision of right and left alike. Only Andrei Amalrik's *Will the Soviet Union Last Until 1984?*[26] stands comparison with his book. He is clearly a man worthy of respect.

More recently, using the same method but concentrating on America's trade deficit, Todd implicitly compares the underlying weakness of the United States with that of the former Soviet Union. He also compares America with the Roman Empire in its days of decadence, when it relied on military might and administrative control to act as the world's rentier and consumed beyond its means. The home population is kept quiet by a policy of bread and circuses—plenty of both in America. Persuasive as Todd is in some respects, his analysis is one-sided and suggests a degree of animus toward America. For example, he omits any reference to the tremendous inventiveness of American society. He might reply that a good deal of America's scientific and technological preponderance is now dependent upon people born and initially educated elsewhere, just as many of Rome's most famous figures came to be born in the provinces. But this argument overlooks the fact that these talented people go to America precisely to give scope to their inventiveness, and because America offers them unmatched incentives and opportunities.

The irritation caused in France by the attempt of certain Americans to appropriate the French discovery of the virus that caused AIDS, while justified by the facts, was doubtless exacerbated by an awareness that France was now a much less inventive society than America and therefore needed to defend its discoveries and inventions all the more fiercely.[27]

Todd uses an old technique in anti-American polemics: emphasizing one side of the ledger only. In discussing American financial and manufacturing dependence on the rest of the world, for example, he does not mention the rest of the world's reciprocal dependence on America. Whenever anyone argues that America absorbs a disproportion of the world's resources, he is sure to forget that it also produces a disproportion of the world's wealth, including new ideas.

Whatever Todd's innermost feelings about the United States, his arguments will give much comfort to less sophisticated intellectuals, who will enjoy anticipatory Schadenfreude at the prospect of an American collapse. This, surely, is a human reaction that requires no elaborate explanation, for it is within the experience of us all to have felt pleasure at the humiliation of others more powerful than ourselves. The fact that American power has rarely, if ever, been exercised to the disadvantage of France makes things worse, for it is not against those who have wronged us most that we feel the deepest resentment.[28] Nor is moral outrage always, or usually, proportional to the misdeeds that prompt it. Thus, for example, French complicity in the genocide in Rwanda—which is at least equal to any alleged crime of America—provoked little notice and condemnation.[29]

Thus it is in the venerable commonplaces of human experience and psychology (as well as in historical circumstances) that we find most readily the explanations for French anti-Americanism.

NOTES

1. The French have the lowest readership of newspapers in the Western world. Of the three main journals, *Le Monde, Liberation,* and *Le Figaro,* the first two are more widely read by intellectuals and are more anti-American.

2. See, for example, Jean Dutord, *A la recherche du français perdu,* Paris, 1999, especially the introduction.

3. Marc Fumaroli, *Quand l'Europe parlait français,* Paris, 2002.

4. See, for example, www.academie-francaise.fr.

5. See, for example, Gerard Prunier, *The Rwandan Crisis,* London, 1995. For a fictional treatment, see Gil Coutremanche, *A Sunday by the Pool in Kigali,* Edinburgh, 2003.

6. This is by no means unusual. See Thomas Frank and Matt Weiland, *Commodify Your Dissent,* New York, 1997.

7. In a slightly different context, Keynes famously remarked, "The ideas of economists and political philosophers, both when they are right and when they are wrong, are more powerful than is commonly understood. Indeed the world is ruled by little else." John Maynard Keynes, *The General Theory of Employment,* London, 1936.

8. See, for example, *The Cambridge History of Africa,* Volume 4, Cambridge, 1985.

9. See Henry Rousso, *Le syndrome de Vichy de 1944 a nos jours,* Paris, 1990.

10. See John Laughland, *The Death of Politics,* London, 1994.

11. See, for example, Julian Jackson, *de Gaulle,* London, 2003.

12. Charles de Gaulle, *War Memoirs: Call to Honour,* London, 1955.

13. See, for example, Theodore Zeldin, *France 1848–1945,* Volume 2, Oxford, 1977.

14. See, for example, Andrezej Walicki, *The Slavophile Controversy,* Oxford, 1975.

15. Ernest R. May, *Imperial Democracy,* New York, 1961.

16. On José Marti, see Christopher Abel and Nissa Torrents, *José Marti: Revolutionary Democrat,* London, 1986. For Ruben Dario, see the poem "A Roosevelt," in *Poesia,* Madrid, 1977. The *locus classicus* of this way of thinking is Jose Enrique Rodo, *Ariel,* Boston, 1922.

17. See, for example, Endymion Wilkinson, *Japan Versus Europe,* London, 1983.

18. The burden of both Cuban and Arab criticism is that moral degeneracy and destitution exist in the midst of material superabundance for some.

19. See François Bizot, *Le Portail,* Paris, 2000, translated as *The Gate,* London, 2003.

20. *Le Monde,* September 12, 2001.

21. Jean-Marie Colombani, *Tous Americains?,* Paris, 2002. Interestingly, the author complains that France gives the impression of being "mediocrement represente, en perte de vitesse et d'influence." He also draws attention to the gulf between Europe's wealth, not only in money but in knowledge, and the pettiness of its ambitions.

22. Jean Baudrillard, *L'esprit du terrorisme,* Paris, 2002, and Jacques Derrida, *Voyous,* Paris 2003. Baudrillard writes, "For it is she (the American super-

power), by her insupportable power, who has fomented this violence." Derrida writes, "The most perverse and most violent of the rogue states is therefore the United States."

23. Thierry Meyssan, *L'effroyable imposture*, Paris, 2002.

24. Emmanuel Todd, *Apres l'empire*, Paris, 2003.

25. Emmanuel Todd, *La chute finale*, Paris, 1976.

26. Andre Amalrik, *Will the Soviet Union Survive Until 1984*, New York, 1970.

27. Nationalist rancor over priority in scientific discovery is not unusual. For a dispute over priority in the discovery of insulin, see I. Pavel, *The Priority of N. C. Paulescu in the Discovery of Insulin*, Bucharest, 1976. For the dispute over the discovery of the mosquito transmission of yellow fever, see Sergio Amaro Melendez, *Alas amarillas*, Havana, 1983, and José Lopez Sanchez, *Carlos J. Finlay: His Life and Work*, Havana, 1999. The claims made are not inherently ridiculous, but for our purposes it is their function and the use to which they are put that is interesting.

28. Similar ideas have occurred to different people at different times. There is an old Hindi proverb asking why do you hate me when I have never tried to help you? The seventeenth-century French author of maxims, La Rochefoucauld, remarked that we never forgive those whom we have wronged.

29. For possible French complicity in the Rwandan genocide, see François-Xavier Verschave, *Complicité de Genocide?*, Paris, 1994.

3

MICHAEL MOSBACHER
AND DIGBY ANDERSON

Recent Trends in
British Anti-Americanism

*B*ritain's major military role in the U.S.-led war to disarm Saddam Hussein and remove him from power has brought the issue of British attitudes toward America once more to the fore. Tony Blair's government has allied itself closely to the United States under both the Clinton and Bush administrations. This would appear to be not merely a matter of political expediency. Blair's actions and his pronouncements on Anglo-American relations seem to reflect a widespread British perception, namely that Britain and the United States have a close cultural, historical, and ideological affinity and share many common interests and concerns. There are also, however, strongly critical currents of British public opinion that are deeply skeptical of U.S. intentions, especially under a Republican administration. Blair's decision to support the United States militarily on Iraq, even without a new and specific United Nations resolution, was thus highly controversial in the United Kingdom and carried major political risks for him. These risks were compounded by the fact that many on the left of his own party had already opposed, or at least felt very uneasy about, Blair's earlier decision to participate militarily in the cam-

paign to remove Al Qaeda and the Taliban from Afghanistan. Going to war with Iraq made Blair deeply unpopular with this faction
of the Labour party and among sections of the wider public, especially many of those who might under normal circumstances be
expected to support a government led by a party traditionally of
the left. In the decisive vote in the House of Commons on whether
to support British participation in the war with Iraq, 139 Labour
party members of Parliament, out of a total of 410 Labour MPs,
voted against their own government's decision to send a 45,000-
strong military expedition to Iraq. This was the largest active rebellion in the House of Commons by members of a governing
party in more than a century. The vote does not adequately reflect
the extent of opposition within the parliamentary Labour party to
Blair's policy on Iraq, as many Labour MPs supported their government only under severe pressure from the party leadership.[1]

Even some MPs who supported the war did so in spite of antagonism toward George W. Bush and, in some cases, strong apprehensions about American power in general. The Labour MP
Oona King, a strong supporter of the war and by no means a knee-
jerk anti-American (herself having American roots), remarked
that "the fact that Bush could be in agreement with me on anything is enough to make me reach for a bucket to puke into."[2]
Michael Meacher, who was a minister in the Blair government
during the Iraq War but was dismissed in June 2003, has since
shown a more generalized antipathy toward American power. He
has declared that while he supported the war with Iraq because
"getting rid of a murderous, barbarous, genocidal regime responsible for millions of death overrode everything else," the real reason for the war was that "America wanted to establish a political
and military platform in the Middle East. It saw a need for oil and
of course it wished to support Israel." Meacher argued that an
"aggressive and unilateralist America" was threatening world
peace and the future of the planet, and that the world's great problem was the power of the United States.[3] He has also argued "that
the 'global war on terrorism' has the hallmarks of a political
myth propagated to pave the way for a wholly different agenda—
the U.S. goal of world hegemony."[4]

Meacher's views, with the notable exception of his support for the war with Iraq, are a typical expression of contemporary British political anti-Americanism and its underlying theme: America is too powerful and has imperialistic ambitions.

There was also vociferous opposition to the war with Iraq outside Parliament. A public demonstration against the war on February 15, 2003, organized by the Stop the War Coalition, was the largest ever in the UK. Estimates for the number of demonstrators varied from 500,000 to 2 million.[5] Whatever the exact numbers, the demonstration comfortably exceeded the 400,000 who participated in the previous largest march in the UK that took place in 2002, a mobilization by the Countryside Alliance, against plans to ban fox hunting. Those taking part in the anti-war demonstration included members of far-left groups one would expect to find at any such march. But the numbers indicate that the march drew many who did not fit this stereotype: some were British Muslims, others were what might best be described as "concerned liberals," and many were schoolchildren. Many of the placards were anti–American and specifically anti–George W. Bush.

Much of the opposition to the war with Iraq, as manifested in Parliament and on the streets, was motivated not merely by the debate over the rights and wrongs of disarming and removing Saddam Hussein. More important, it was also motivated by antipathy to what many perceived as excessive U.S. power and by opposition to U.S. foreign policy in general and the policies of George W. Bush in particular. This point has been well made by Michael Ignatieff, an influential liberal commentator and Harvard professor of human rights policy, whose writings have been popular in the UK. Ignatieff wrote: "The cynicism about America on the part of the left and many in Europe depressed me. For them there is nothing to discuss except U.S. intentions. It was never about Iraq. All they want to talk about is the U.S."[6]

Anti-Americanism thrives on the strong opposition to the war with Iraq present in certain quarters in the UK. But British anti-Americanism is not confined to opposition to U.S. foreign policy. The American historian Richard Hofstadter famously stated that "It has been our fate as a nation not to have ideologies, but to be one."[7] He meant that the United States is not just another nation, it is the embodiment of a set of ideas and ideals, some realized, others waiting to be realized and possibly unrealizable. Given its historical origins, there is a tendency to judge the United States in light of its founding ideas and ideals. For such reasons, attitudes toward the United States are likely to have more to do with the worldview of the observer than with any specific U.S. actions. There is also a popular anti-Americanism in the UK unrelated to matters of philosophy or worldview, the kind that is often casually expressed in a pub or on the train. Altogether there are three types of British anti-Americanism—the popular; the kind that is linked to specific U.S. foreign policies; and the ideological. Each in turn must be examined.

But first, how widespread are various anti-American attitudes in the UK? Circumstantial evidence suggests that they have a substantial constituency. Michael Moore, the left-wing American polemicist, author, and filmmaker, whose films and books radiate every variety of embittered anti-Americanism, has enjoyed great success in the UK (as he has had in other countries of Western Europe). His pro–gun control, anti-capitalist film *Bowling for Columbine* was a surprise box-office success, something unheard of for a polemic of its kind. His book excoriating American corporations and George W. Bush, *Stupid White Men*, has sold more than 600,000 copies in the UK, competing with *Dr. Atkins New Diet Revolution* and exceeded only by the popularity of J. K. Rowling's *Harry Potter* books.

For a more thorough and social scientific analysis of British attitudes toward America, the authoritative *Pew Global Attitudes Project* is available. This project, which is chaired by Clinton's secretary of state Madeleine Albright, involves polls in many nations designed to learn about, among other things, the global image of the United States. Its June 2003 survey found that 70 percent of respondents in the UK had a favorable image of the United States, and 80 percent had a favorable image of Americans as people.[8] These figures are considerably higher than those in Germany or France, where in June 2003 only 45 percent and 43 percent respectively held a favorable view of the United States, and 67 percent and 58 percent respectively held a favorable view of Americans. In March 2003, as the conflict with Iraq approached, these figures plummeted in all three countries. Only 48 percent in the UK had a positive image of the United States, though this was still higher than figures in Germany and France—25 percent and 31 percent respectively. It is interesting that in the UK the image of the United States improved rapidly after the Iraq War, almost to the levels before March 2003.

In 1999/2000 83 percent, and in Summer 2002 75 percent of respondents in the UK held a positive view of the United States. These figures show clearly that in the UK, unless there are exceptional circumstances such as the lead-up to the Iraq War, a large majority of the population have friendly attitudes toward the United States. Only a minority, albeit a fairly significant one— somewhere between 20 and 30 percent—hold a steady anti-American outlook. This is a much lower figure than in many other countries, as, for example, France. Even among those in the UK who do hold anti-American beliefs, there is a reluctance to blame America in general. Fifty-nine percent of those who were critical of the United States in 2003 averred that this was due mainly to President George W. Bush; 31 percent said they objected to the United States in general, and 8 percent said it was both. These figures indicate that hard-core anti-Americans in the UK—those who are generally critical of the United States—comprise only about 10 percent of the population, still a significant number of people but a distinct minority. But in Britain, as in many other countries, these anti-American minorities seem concentrated in certain elite groups, for example academic intellectuals, social workers, and those who work for the mass media.

America is not the only country the British have disliked at times. Unlike the United States (with its immigrant heritage and because it was for much of its history more "self-contained" than the UK), the British have a long history of mildly disliking other "foreign" nations. Anti-French and anti-German sentiment in the UK used to be, if anything, much more strident than anti-American sentiment, and has taken not just a popular but also an ideological form. A classic representation of anti-French sentiment is William Hogarth's great print of 1749, *O The Roast Beef of Old England, or the Calais Gate.*[9] It was wildly popular at the time and has endured as a classic icon of English anti-French patriotic xenophobia. The print depicts the Calais Gate, the ancient gateway built by the English in Calais, and shows the French in front of it as impoverished, servile, affected, effete, and oppressed. The French are subsisting on a diet of *soupe maigre* and snails, and suffer the consequences with their puny frames. The only well-fed Frenchman in the print is a gluttonous monk. A sirloin of beef, so large the cook can hardly carry it, arrives from England, to feed English visitors to Calais—with the French reduced to drooling over it. The implied contrast is with the English over the water—large, prosperous, free men who spoke their minds and subsisted on a diet of roast beef. The print illustrates Hogarth's view of the French as marked by "poverty, slavery, and insolence, with an affectation of politeness." Hogarth saw this condition rooted in France's Catholicism and its absolute monarchy.

After the French Revolution, the causes of the Frenchman's poor state changed, but the symptoms as expressed in caricature did not. James Gillray in the 1790s produced a whole series of prints lampooning the promises of the Revolution with the pitiful condition of the French, and contrasting it with the true liberties enjoyed by the English. In Gillray's prints the French remain servile and oppressed but are now gone mad by "reason" rather than papist superstition. The Jacobin had replaced the priest as the source of France's ideological corruption, but the French were still subsisting on a funny diet, more often than not a few bulbs of garlic and the occasional snail or frog. In the following two hundred years many artists and cartoonists produced images lampooning the French, often referring to contemporary events but retaining the old stereotypes.

More recently, in 2003 Jacques Chirac was caricatured on the front page of Britain's best-selling popular newspaper, *The Sun,* as a snail for threatening to veto any new UN resolution authorizing the use of force to disarm Saddam Hussein. The venerable British tradition of lampooning the French in caricature lives on.

The Germans have fared no better in their portrayal by the British. The German as a figure of ridicule has until the 1990s been a mainstay of British television comedy. Understandably enough, popular images of Germany often remain linked to the Nazis and their crimes nearly sixty years after the end of World War II. Nicholas Ridley, who served as Trade and Industry minister under Margaret Thatcher, had to resign from the cabinet in 1990 when he compared German Chancellor Helmut Kohl's supposed economic ambitions and his support for European federalism with the Nazi invasion of most of Europe. Such sentiments can still be detected from time to time in some of Britain's mass-circulation newspapers.

British apprehension of Germany and its ambitions predates the Third Reich. In an aesthetic sense, perhaps the finest statement of British anti-German sentiment comes from the start of World War I in the opening lines of Rudyard Kipling's poem *For All We Have and Are.*

> For all we have and are,
> For all our children's fate,
> Stand up and take the war.
> The Hun is at the gate![10]

Such examples show that the popular expression of anti-Americanism in the UK should not be seen in isolation from other, similar attitudes. At the same time British anti-French and anti-German sentiment may be seen as more rational than anti-Americanism, since both those countries have at various times been a far greater threat to Britain than the United States has ever been. Considered in comparison to British antipathies toward other nations, British anti-Americanism comes across as a milder, less serious phenomenon than it would otherwise appear to be. A society composed of immigrants, such as the United States, cannot afford to disparage other nations if it seeks to retain its internal coherence. Furthermore, due to its size and relative geographic isolation, the United States has for much of its history been much more insulated from foreign nations. Britain, by contrast, has to some extent, defined itself through the semi-jocular disparagement of others, of "foreigners." Nonetheless, Britain has welcomed and successfully integrated successive waves of newcomers into its society. Attitudes towards foreigners have not had much impact on the treatment of individual Americans, French, or Germans in the UK. British popular anti-Americanism is thus best understood as part of a barroom jousting of "foreigners." This makes it probably the most widespread, and also the least important, form of anti-Americanism in Britain today.

Mass Observation, a social research organization founded in 1937 by a group of anthropologists and sociologists, sought to establish the quantitative dimensions of British anti-Americanism alongside other attempts to trace British social-political attitudes through diaries and recorded conversation. Attitudes recorded in the 1940s included opinions of the United States and Americans. British opinion of the United States improved, as would be expected, with increased American support in World War II, first expressed by the Lend-Lease program and later by U.S. participation in the war. Popular anti-Americanism, however, survived even these developments. Americans were seen as "rather vulgar and ostentatious," "truculent and opulent barbarians, glorying in atomic bombs and the almighty dollar," "pushy and arrogant," "immature, too materialistic and immoral," "too self-satisfied, loud spoken, too ignorant," "politically backward, uncultured and half-educated," and "tiresome children with a mental age of 12."[11]

Note how closely these prejudices mirror the British popular anti-Americanism of the present. All of them could easily have been expressed in 2003. The image of Americans as brash, loud, vulgar, uncultured, and unsophisticated has had an enduring appeal in the UK, just as the different prejudiced images of the French and the Germans has had. The portrayal of Americans as unsophisticated is symbolized by the frequent, stereotyped, highly unflattering portrayal of American presidents (Carter, Reagan, George W. Bush) as simpletons. During the 1980s a major theme of *Spitting Image,* a highly successful British satirical TV show using latex puppets, was Ronald Reagan's misplacing his brain and where it might be found. Comments about George W. Bush's supposed lack of intellectual capacity have become a staple that comic writers use to gain a cheap laugh. To give but one typical example, in an article by John O'Farrell, a successful British comic novelist, one finds the throwaway line ". . . unless you yourself happen to be reading this, George W—which let's face it, is unlikely, given the absence of pictures."[12]

Such popular anti-Americanism becomes more significant when its prejudices merge with the attacks on U.S. foreign policy, especially by influential policymakers. Chris Patten, the former British Conservative Cabinet Minister, ex-governor of Hong Kong, and at the time of his comments European Union commissioner in charge of Europe's international relations, in 2002 described U.S. foreign policy in the aftermath of 9/11 as "absolutist and simplistic." He went on to say that the United States was all too ready to see bombs instead of sophisticated policies as the solution to problems: "smart bombs have their place but smart development assistance seems to me even more important."[13] More recently Patten has described U.S. policy toward the Middle East as "too crude."[14] Such descriptions of U.S. foreign policy—as unsophisticated, simplistic, or crude—are drawn straight from the lexicon of popular anti-Americanism.

The apotheosis of popular and visceral anti-Americanism has been reached in a speech by Harold Pinter, not a man occupying a position of political influence but nonetheless a major public figure and arguably Britain's leading playwright. In 2002, on the occasion of receiving an honorary degree in Turin, Italy, Pinter described the aftermath of his cancer surgery that became an occasion for experiencing intense anti-American sentiments:

> I found that to emerge from a personal nightmare was to enter an infinitely more pervasive public nightmare—the nightmare of American hysteria, ignorance, arrogance, stupidity, and belligerence: the most powerful nation the world has ever known effectively waging war against the rest of the world. . . . The U.S. administration is now a bloodthirsty wild animal. Bombs are its only vocabulary.[15]

This was not an exceptional, spur-of-the-moment outpouring; Pinter was so proud of his denunciation that he published it as a pamphlet, alongside anti-American and anti–Tony Blair poems. In speeches such as this, British popular anti-Americanism has taken a much more aggressive, angry, and embittered form. (On the other hand, can this kind of anti-Americanism expressed by an elite intellectual-artist be properly labelled as "popular"?)

The tone and claims of Pinter's speech, and others like it, undermine the assertion that anti-Americanism is simply a rational response to U.S. actions and foreign policy. This claim has been made most frequently and prominently by the American academic Noam Chomsky, whose tone greatly resembles Pinter's. Chomsky's influence on the politics of radical protest in the UK, or for that matter throughout Europe, has been vast. He has argued that the terrorist atrocities of 9/11 and others were motivated not by opposition to globalization or to U.S. cultural dominance, not by opposition to Hollywood or McDonald's, but to what he sees as the iniquities of U.S. foreign policy.[16] Pinter made the same point in his speech, namely, "The atrocity in New York [9/11] was predictable and inevitable. It was an act of retaliation against constant and systematic manifestations of state terrorism on the part of the United States over many years, in all parts of the world."[17]

The comment editor of *The Guardian*, the UK's leading left-liberal newspaper, argued on September 13, 2001, two days after 9/11, in the same fashion: that "for every 'terror network' that is rooted out, another will emerge—until the injustices and inequalities that produce them are addressed." This article was provocatively titled "They Can't See Why They Are Hated—Americans Cannot Ignore What Their Government Does Abroad."[18] Aside from a highly questionable interpretation of American foreign policy, the tone of such statements reveals a deeper and not fully rational antagonism toward the United States. On another occasion, Pinter, addressing his two favorite objects of hate, said, "Blair sees himself as a representative of moral rectitude. He is actually a mass murderer. . . . The U.S. is really beyond reason now. . . . There is only one comparison: Nazi Germany."[19]

What, then, are the supposedly rational bases for Britsh anti-Americanism that is linked to U.S. foreign policy? There appear to be three. The most popular is the objection to the extent of U.S.

power and its uses. This entails apprehension of the United States as the only superpower in a unipolar world, and its perception as a kind of global policeman with nefarious motives . By the same token, some of those in the UK, including Tony Blair, who have been strong supporters of the United States and of an interventionist American foreign policy, have done so partly because they see U.S. power as the most important force in maintaining a semblance of international order and in challenging those states that threaten global security. Second is the objection to U.S. support for Israel, sometimes associated with the traditional pro-Arab policies of Britain. Third is a residual antagonism toward America stemming from cold war politics.

As the United States has become the sole dominant player in the international system of the post–cold war world, it is inevitable that doubts about its role have arisen. This is the fate of any dominant power in a given situation. Fears of U.S. military dominance have often been combined with fears of economic hegemony. Such legitimate concerns, however, are often overblown in the rhetoric of U.S. opponents. Eric Hobsbawm, the renowned British historian and lifelong member the Communist party, has declared, that "A key novelty of the U.S. imperial project is that all other empires knew that they were not the only ones, and none aimed at global domination. . . . The present U.S. policy is more unpopular than the policy of any other U.S. government has ever been, and probably than that of any other great power has ever been."[20]

Calling the United States an empire has become widespread and is used mostly as a term of denigration. But it has also been used by some commentators, most prominently Michael Ignatieff, in support of Americans adopting, whenever possible, an international humanitarian role and in support of its military intervention to remove pariah regimes that threaten the security, indeed the lives, of their own people and those of their neighbors.[21] The Blair government has implicitly supported this reasoning and has also converted sections of liberal and formerly left-wing opinion to become much more supportive of the United States. While part of the British left strongly opposed the Anglo-American-led NATO mission against the former Yugoslavia, others warmly welcomed it as humanitarian intervention. This argument has also been used, admittedly by far fewer, in relation to the Iraq War. For example, Ann Clwyd, a Labour MP on the left of her party who used to be strong supporter of the campaign for Britain to renounce unilaterally its nuclear deterrent, became a strident supporter of the war on Iraq. This was not because of weapons of mass destruction or security issues but as a way of removing an appalling regime that was abusing the human rights of its own people on a massive scale.[22]

For much of the left, however, all Western and especially U.S. interventions remain suspect and perceived as motivated by predominantly nefarious economic gain. There is no analysis of the intervention's individual merits but rather a reflexive rejection of the use of American or Western power. When Noam Chomsky was asked if he could think of any worthy interventions, he said that the British intervention in Sierra Leone might be genuinely humanitarian, "but that's probably because I haven't looked at it properly."[23]

Arguments and suggestions are repeatedly put forth about ways to limit U.S. power. Some of those keenest on European integration (though less so in the UK than in continental Europe) see the European Union (EU) as a bulwark against U.S. dominance. Sometimes the United Nations is portrayed as an institution that might control—or channel in acceptable ways—U.S. power. Much of the more moderate British parliamentary opposition to the Blair strategy on Iraq has argued that acting without a new UN resolution would encourage U.S. unilateralism and thus undermine a major impediment to U.S. power, not just in the current situation but also in the future. Their opposition was thus motivated by an explicit desire to hold U.S. power in check.

For some of the more radical thinkers, neither the EU nor the UN as currently constituted can provide satisfactory constraints on U.S. power. What is needed, they believe, is a whole new global system of governance. An extreme proposal, explicitly developed to shackle the United States economically and politically as well as limit (what he believes to be) the ever-growing power of U.S. multinationals has been put forward by George Monbiot. He is the

UK's leading chronicler and advocate of the anti-corporate protest movement. He suggests that the way to "stop America" is to abolish the UN Security Council, thereby removing the veto powers of the five permanent members, and allow all decisions to be made by the General Assembly, by countries whose votes would be determined proportionally by the size of their population and by how democratic they are. He would also establish a directly elected World Parliament, with each constituency representing ten million voters.[24]

Although this proposal is unlikely to be adopted, its far-reaching nature shows how central to the concerns of today's protest movements objections to U.S. power have become. Many of these protesters began by targeting Nike and McDonald's, but their objections to the United States are much deeper than aversion to fast food or American footwear.

There has also been a connection between British anti-Americanism and events in the Middle East. In recent years Israel has been receiving an increasingly bad press in the UK for its handling of the Palestinian conflict. Too often the reporting does not offer a balanced picture or take account of the complexities of the situation; it simply portrays the Israeli-Palestinian situation as a David and Goliath human rights story. This can partly be explained as a product of a generational shift among those reporting from the Middle East. For many journalists in their thirties and forties now, the Holocaust does not have the emotional immediacy it had for an earlier generation. Its continuing impact and repercussions, along with that of the Arab wars with Israel of the 1950s, '60s, and '70s—the legitimate fears such events have engendered and the need for a secure place for Jews—are too often forgotten. Journalists like to side with those whom they perceive to be the underdog. In the Middle East today, those are the Palestinians—and U.S. support for Israel only compounds this impression. Such support has become a major issue for "concerned" opinion in the UK. Before the Iraq conflict American support of Israel was probably the most widespread source of criticism of U.S. foreign policy. The growth, through immigration, of the Muslim population in the UK has also created another vocal anti-Israeli constituency. Members of the Muslim community have been in the forefront of criticism of U.S. support of Israel.

Such criticism ceases to be rational when such support is attributed to the power of something called the "Jewish lobby." All too often there has been an unhappy conflation of three separate phenomena: U.S. support for Israel, organized pro-Israeli lobby groups, and the American Jewish community. In 2003 Tam Dalyell, a Labour MP who has been a vehement critic of Tony Blair, said in an interview with *Vanity Fair* magazine that, in relation to the war with Iraq, "there is far too much Jewish influence in the United States."[25] Dalyell also suggested that Tony Blair had been too reliant on Jewish advisers, singling out Lord Levy, his special envoy to the Middle East: "I believe his influence has been very important on the Prime Minister and has led to what I see as this awful war and the sack of Baghdad."[26]

Dalyell's remarks caused an uproar in the UK and a debate as to whether they were anti-Semitic or merely the result of infelicitous expression. There has, however, been a wider debate as to whether anti-Semitism is on the rise in the UK and whether it has become linked to anti-American attitudes. Jonathan Sacks, the British chief rabbi, has argued that a new anti-Semitism has emerged: "It is coming simultaneously from three different directions: first, a radicalized Islamist youth inflamed by extremist rhetoric; second, a left-wing anti-American elite with strong representation in the European media; third a resurgent far right, as anti-Muslim as it is anti-Jewish."[27]

Anti-Americanism rooted in the disapproval of U.S. policies during the cold war is often an attribute of a generation whose political outlook was formed in opposition to U.S. involvement in Vietnam. This generation remains sympathetic to Cuba due to its resolute anti-capitalist and anti-American rhetoric. Cuba's long-standing defiance of Washington has endeared it among those who share such hostility in Britain and elsewhere. Thus the positive views of Cuba are an integral part of a more deeply rooted British anti-Americanism.

Before the fall of the Soviet Union liberal, non-Communist observers often noted that various East European regimes had certain redeeming features, such as job security, universal child care, or an effective health system. These dubious assertions are still heard in relation to Cuba. For example, Brian Wilson, a minister in Blair's government until the end of the Iraq conflict, has since said in 2003 that while

> Cuba is not perfect . . . critics should never ignore the fact that Cuba's primary service to the world has been to provide living proof that it is possible to conquer poverty, disease, and illiteracy in a country that was grossly familiar with all three. That is a pretty big service. The fact that it has been delivered in the face of sustained hostility from an obsessive neighbor makes it all the more stunning. . . . For those who go to Cuba only in order to sneer, there are political paradoxes on every street corner. All true, all the inevitable result of 40 years of siege, but also irrelevant to the bigger picture of what Cuba represents as a symbol of human potential.[28]

Brian Wilson goes on to state, perhaps to the surprise of some historians, that Castro was never a true ally of the Soviet Union—Castro's "withering remarks about the Soviet Union confirm just how unloving a marriage of necessity that was."[29]

Brian Wilson's sympathetic remarks in support of Cuba appear mild in comparison to those made by others. Seamas Milne, the comment editor of *The Guardian* previously quoted, has said:

> The historical importance of Cuba's struggle for social justice and sovereignty and its creative social mobilization will continue to echo beyond its time and place: from the self-sacrificing internationalism of Che to the crucial role played by Cuban troops in bringing an end to apartheid through the defeat of South Africa at Cuito Cuanavale in Angola in 1988. . . . Cuba will have to expect yet more destabilization, further complicating the defense of the social and political gains of the revolution in the years to come. The greatest contribution those genuinely concerned about human rights and democracy in Cuba can make is to get the U.S. and its European friends off the Cubans' backs.[30]

Some of the leading British critics of United States romanticize not merely present-day Cuba but even the bygone Eastern Bloc regimes. The Labour MP George Galloway has been probably the most rabid parliamentary opponent of Britain's military alliance with the United States in Iraq and one of Blair's most vituperative opponents within his own party, displaying an abiding loathing for all that Blair represents. In an interview with *The Guardian* in 2002, more than ten years after the collapse of the Soviet Union, Galloway said he had not changed his political position from that of the 1980s and described himself as being "on the anti-imperialist left." When asked if this meant the Stalinist left, Galloway's response was, "I wouldn't define it that way because of the pejoratives loaded around it. . . . If you are asking did I support the Soviet Union, yes I did. Yes, I did support the Soviet Union, and I think the disappearance of the Soviet Union is the biggest catastrophe of my life."[31]

Another prominent opponent of war with Iraq is Andrew Murray, the chairman of the Stop the War Coalition that organized the vast anti-war demonstration discussed earlier. Murray is a leading member of the Communist party of Britain, a Marxist-Leninist organization that was formed in the late 1980s by hard-liners of the old pro-Moscow Communist party of Great Britain who thought that the party had sold out and become "revisionist."[32] The Communist party of Britain has retained control of the main party's low-circulation daily paper, *The Morning Star*, in which Andrew Murray used to write a column. In 1999, ten years after the fall of the Berlin Wall, Murray wrote:

> Next Tuesday is the 120th anniversary of the birth of Josef Stalin. His career is the subject of a vast and ever-expanding literature. Read it all and, at the end, you are still left paying your money and taking your choice. A socialist system embracing a third of the world and the defeat of Nazi Germany on the one hand. On the other, all accompanied by harsh measures imposed by a one-party regime. Nevertheless, if you believe that the worst crimes visited on humanity this century, from colonialism to Hiroshima and from concentration camps to mass poverty and

unemployment have been caused by imperialism, then [Stalin's birthday] might at least be a moment to ponder why the authors of those crimes and their hack propagandists abominate the name of Stalin beyond all others. It was, after all, Stalin's best-known critic, Nikita Khrushchev, who remarked in 1956 that "against imperialists, we are all Stalinists."[33]

The vast majority of those in the UK who oppose war with Iraq or even those who espouse anti-American views are not, and certainly do not remain in hindsight, active supporters of the Soviet Union. Yet the views of George Galloway and Andrew Murray cannot be dismissed as belonging to a tiny irrelevant minority who sully the good name of those who oppose the war or are generally critical of the United States. Both these figures occupied leading, high-profile positions in the campaign against that war, a campaign that became a carrier of anti-American sentiments far more intense than such sentiments have been in the UK for many years. Galloway and Murray remain prominent voices of British anti-Americanism; for whom the battles of the cold war are not over.

These examples demonstrate that many objections and critiques of U.S. foreign policy have deeper and broader ideological roots which are based on an overall rejection of much of what the United States represents. Such ideological anti-Americanism has also been the underpinning of other critiques of the United States. What is at the core of these ideological objections? The prominent American political sociologist Seymour Martin Lipset has argued that "The American creed can be described in five terms: liberty, egalitarianism, individualism, populism, and laissez-faire. Egalitarianism in its American meaning, as Tocqueville emphasized, involves equality of opportunity and respect, not of result or condition."[34] Notions of liberty or egalitarianism may exist in other geographic settings as well. For some in the UK, support for differing aspects of the "American creed," and the desire to see Britain move in that direction and thereby become "more American," has contributed to their pro-Americanism. Tony Blair, for example, as he has pushed the Labour party to abandon its commitment to old-style social democracy, has thought to embrace American notions of egalitarianism—equality of opportunity and its corollary, the legitimacy of wealth creation. He has thus distanced himself from more typical European notions of egalitarianism—of equality of outcome. Blair has specifically defined this debate in terms of learning from U.S. successes and has also used these arguments when attacking the British House of Lords. Jonathan Freedland, a British commentator who has been a leading supporter of Blair in the media and has apparently had a major influence on the thinking of the Blair government, has explicitly put forward the notion that Britain needs to learn from the United States and adopt more of the American creed in order to become a more modern, more progressive society.[35] Other politicians, at other times, most notably Margaret Thatcher, have taken other lessons from the "American creed."

But some in the UK object strongly to aspects of the "American creed," and these objections merge into a generalized anti-Americanism. A conservative critic of these ideas in times past was Edward Wakefield, who in the 1830s was horrified by the absence of European notions of hierarchy and class in America and believed that this made a gentlemanly existence impossible. It turned the United States into an uncivilized, barbaric place:

> A people who, though they continually increase in number, make no progress in the art of living; who, in respect to wealth, knowledge, skill, taste, and whatever belongs to civilization, have degenerated from their ancestors . . . who delight in a forced equality, not equality before the law only, but equality against nature and truth; an equality which, to keep the balance always even, rewards the mean rather than the great, and gives more honor to the vile than the noble. . . . We mean, in two words, a people who become rotten before they are ripe.[36]

Wakefield believed that the only answer to the revolt against nature represented by the United States was, for a cross section of British society, excluding the lowest, to settle and colonize a new/old world—in New Zealand. Here a society could be established that would not represent a "new people" and thus would possess none of the ills of the United States. Rather, it would be an extension of the old, retaining its virtues but eliminating its poverty and overcrowding. Although the importance of his role is still debated, Wakefield's enthusiasm for establishing an un-American colony undoubtedly played a significant part in the decision to annex New Zealand in 1840 and in its subsequent settlement.

Christopher Hitchens, the Anglo-American commentator, has argued that anti-Americanism still has a powerful conservative, right-wing component. "The Cold War succeeded in fixing the idea of anti-Americanism as a syndrome of the left. Forgotten was the long hatred of the old right for the American idea. But now we can see its resurgence in the applause from all of the old and new fascist parties for the attacks of September 11."[37] Notwithstanding this argument, the fact remains that the ideological rejection of the United States today emanates primarily from the left. It is this ideological rejection that is the root of British political anti-Americanism and its various expressions.

Much contemporary anti-Americanism in Britain (and elsewhere) is motivated by opposition to individualism and laissez-faire capitalism and to the great, unjust inequalities believed to be the defining characteristic of American society by those most critical of it. In their eyes, moreover, the United States embodies all that is wrong with Britain. In a world where the existing alternatives to democratic capitalism have failed, raging at the United States has become a popular way of rejecting capitalism without having to provide plausible alternatives. This raises once more the question of why the rejection of capitalism, in Britain and elsewhere, retains such an enduring appeal. A full understanding of anti-Americanism will require a better understanding of the hostility that capitalism continues to stimulate.

NOTES

1. M. White, "Blair Battles on After Record Rebellion," *Guardian*, March 19, 2003.

2. S. Hattenstone, "I'm No Operator: Interview with Oona King," *Guardian*, May 12, 2003.

3. T. Baldwin, "World's Big Problem Is the US, Says Meacher," *London Times*, June 20, 2003.

4. M. Meacher, "This War on Terrorism Is Bogus," *Guardian*, September 6, 2003.

5. J. Vidal, "They Stood Up to Be Counted: And Found Nobody Could Agree on Totals," *Guardian*, February 17, 2003.

6. J. Lloyd, "Between Iraq and a Hard Place: Interview with Michael Ignatieff," *Financial Times Magazine*, August 30, 2003.

7. Quoted in S. M. Lipset, *American Exceptionalism: A Double Edged Sword*, New York, 1997, p. 18.

8. Pew Global Attitudes Project, *Views of a Changing World: June 2003*, Washington, D.C., 2003.

9. R. Paulson, *Hogarth's Graphic Works*, London, 1989.

10. K. Amis, *The Amis Anthology: A Personal Choice of English Verse*, London, 1989, p. 164.

11. R. Taylor, "'Immature, Immoral, Vulgar, Materialistic': Views of America from the *Mass Observation*," *New Statesman*, March 3, 2003.

12. J. O'Farrell, "The Tyranny of George II," *Guardian*, July 4, 2003.

13. J. Freedland, "Patten Lays into Bush's America," *Guardian*, February 9, 2002.

14. P. Stephens, "High Table Talk: Interview with Chris Patten," *Financial Times Magazine*, August 9, 2003.

15. H. Pinter, *War*, London, 2003.

16. N. Chomsky, *9-11*, New York, 2001.

17. Pinter, op. cit.

18. S. Milne, "They Can't See Why They Are Hated: Americans Cannot Ignore What Their Government Does Abroad," *Guardian*, September 13, 2001.

19. A. Chrisafis and I. Tilden, "Pinter Blasts 'Nazi America' and 'Deluded Idiot' Blair'", *Guardian*, June 11, 2003.

20. E. Hobsbawm, "America's Imperial Delusion," *Guardian*, June 14, 2003.

21. M. Ignatieff, *Empire Lite: Nation-Building in Bosnia, Kosovo and Afghanistan*, London, 2003.

22. J. Ashley, "How a Labour Rebel Became Friends with US Hawks," *Guardian*, June 23, 2003.

23. J. Hari, "The Land Where People Want America to Invade," *Independent*, July 2, 2003.

24. G. Monbiot, *The Age of Consent*, London, 2003.

25. M. White, "Dalyell Steps Up Attack on Levy," *Guardian*, May 6, 2003.

26. Ibid.

27. J. Sacks, "A New Antisemitism?" in P. Iganski and B. Kosmin, *A New Antisemitism: Debating Judeophobia in 21st Century Britain*, London, 2003.

28. B. Wilson, "Revolution Revisited," *Guardian*, August 28, 2003.

29. Ibid.

30. S. Milne, "Why the US Fears Cuba," *Guardian*, July 31, 2003.

31. S. Hattenstone, "Saddam and Me: Interview with George Galloway," *Guardian*, September 16, 2002.

32. M. Mosbacher, *The British Communist Movement and Moscow: How the Demise of the Soviet Union affected the Communist Party and its Successor Organisations*, London, 1996.

33. A. Murray, "Eyes Left," *Morning Star*, December 17, 1999.

34. S. M. Lipset, op. cit., p. 19.

35. J. Freedland, *Bring Home the Revolution: The Case for a British Repub-lic*, London, 1998.

36. K. Sinclair, *A History of New Zealand*, London, 1988, p. 59.

37. C. Hitchens, *Regime Change*, London, 2003.

4

MICHAEL FREUND

Affinity and Resentment: A Historical Sketch of German Attitudes

*E*urope would look radically different today if it had not been for America. Direct intervention in both world wars, economic aid, and military, political, and cultural hegemony have made the United States the single most important country to be reckoned with in the Old World. For this reason, negative attitudes toward America reflect not only political and trade differences but a profound unease about social and cultural changes, which can be subsumed under the term "modernity." They have been strongly influenced by the United States, its foreign policies, and its culture.

The relationship between Germany and the United States has been unusual for several reasons. One is the rapid transformation of a Continental power defeated in the two major wars of the twentieth century into an official, "reeducated" ally after the second defeat. Another noteworthy circumstance is that the German view of the New World—from its discovery on—has been especially critical, held by the most "un-Western" of the major European nations. It is a view, as we shall see, composed of resentment mixed with envy and admiration, containing rational and as well as highly irrational elements. It must also be noted that the judgments of philosophers and the gentry differed greatly from those of the "masses" who had less opportunity to articulate their feelings.

Like other strongly held attitudes, "anti-Americanism" entails an overarching and overdetermined way of looking at the world and thus can be grouped with other dogmatic outlooks; it is a far from fully rational disposition. An emphasis on its irrational aspects also dominates Paul Hollander's definition of the concept: *"a predisposition to hostility,* . . . a relentless critical impulse toward American social, economic, and political institutions, traditions and values . . . and a firm belief in the malignity of American influence and presence anywhere in the world."[1] Hollander differentiates between irrational and rational critiques of the United States or American society—that is to say, he recognizes that not all criticisms of the United States are a priori prejudiced, ideological, or otherwise unfounded. I follow this approach.

Anti-Americanism, the Polish-American author Louis Begley recently wrote, "is as old as the Yankee Doodle. It came into being at the same time as the thirteen renegade colonies."[2] "America" as a screen for European projections is even older, dating back to the times when a land beyond the Atlantic was only a mirage, a fantasy held by those looking out for an Eden, a Utopia.[3] As soon as the continent was discovered, it became an "object of European imagination"[4] in a literal and a metaphorical sense. It was populated and shaped by settlers from the Old World, and its promises and fears assumed almost mythical proportions. As Richard Pells has observed,

> The concept of a new world quickly became, for Americans and for Europeans, a means of distinguishing between two entirely different civilizations . . . a disparate set of values and attributes. It emphasized antagonistic ideals and patterns of behavior; it helped the people of each continent define their separate identities by using the other as a foil, a negative image, a lesson in what to avoid.[5]

Or, as Andrei Markovits puts it, "America was . . . a European creation which, however, more than any other form of European extension, consciously defected from its European origins relatively early in the colonial game."[6]

Thus, from the beginning, America was a multi-faceted construction in the eyes of the beholders—the original fatherland. Its reality did not live up to early expectations. Rather than first-hand experience, prejudice or a tendency to prejudgment guided European views of this new experiment. Some of these views were enthusiastic, others skeptical. Many would hold up the "noble savage" against the brutal settlers, and still more embraced the romantic image of a pristine nature to be protected from the onslaught of an inferior civilization. This same primordial nature, however, needed to be "redeemed" by that very same civilization "and by Christianity."[7] As these conflicting attitudes suggest, American realities were bound to fall short of European expectations.

America was soon perceived as vulgar, mediocre, money oriented, a "civilization without culture," especially by those Europeans who thought they owned culture—which they did, in a literal sense: the landowners, the aristocratic gentry, those who frequented the royal court and thus acquired "courtesy." European elites, not given to consensus, nonetheless agreed about the deficiencies of America. Their distaste became even more pronounced when the diffuse alliance of transatlantic settlers coalesced into a distinct political entity, the United States.

After 1776, theories proliferated about the reasons for American inferiority. Various continental and British scientists and *literati* warned of the degenerative effects of the New World on plants, animals, and human beings.[8] These elites had additional reason to be inimical to the "American dream": it promised opportunities for all based on liberty and a mercantile egalitarianism, promises which of course threatened the established order based on entrenched hierarchies and tradition.

The more enlightened French saw this also as "competition" in the field of pioneering democracy. The British held certain sympathies for the transatlantic experiment because of ethnic kinship and because of a similar entrepreneurial spirit. But the German elites felt especially distant from the United States. To them, even France and the United Kingdom represented elements of "the West," which were uncongenial to the highly traditional, rigidly stratified society of the Central European monarchic powers. America was even farther removed from everything the German duchies and later the empire—and, for that matter, the Habsburg monarchy—stood for.

In the early nineteenth century the German Romantic movement inspired the soul-searching, nature-loving, inward-looking attitudes that were alien to the increasingly successful commercial society across the ocean. The poet Nikolaus Lenau is a fine example of these attitudes and of a complete lack of understanding between the two worlds. An early enthusiast who, after spending some time in the United States, returned disappointed, Lenau vividly described his disillusionment. He claimed, among other things, that there were "no nightingales and no singing birds at all" in the New World.[9]

Like Lenau, Heine, Jacob Burckhardt, and Hegel may also be quoted to illustrate the anti-American predisposition of the leading German minds of the nineteenth century. It is only fair, though, to mention a very different and (already in those years) much better-known voice, that of Goethe, whose poem dedicated to the United States starts with the popular lines: "America, you've got it better/Than our old continent. Exult!/You have no decaying castles/And no basalt. . . ."[10] These lines point to a different, more sympathetic interpretation of what "America" might mean and suggest that not all the German elite rejected the United States.

Still, on the whole, German elites retained a far more negative view of the New World than the rest of the population. This became especially clear in 1848, when the vanguard of the more progressive forces, the liberal republicans and democrats, voiced their support for the American model of government during the ill-fated national assembly at the Paulskirche in Frankfurt. It was to no avail. The powers-that-be "restored" the traditional undemocratic order in the German lands and in Vienna.

Nonetheless the transatlantic alternative continued to fascinate, and not only the liberal forces: Karl Marx and Friedrich Engels followed events in the New World with great attention, hoping that European working classes would be encouraged by its example. They would later rejoice in the victory of the Union over the Confederacy, considering it "a major world historical event in which progress clearly prevailed over reaction, which was hardly the case on an autocratic continent dominated by the Habsburgs, Hohenzollerns, and Romanovs.[11] By now America was no longer a purely imagined land but an actual federation of states with numerous attractive features.

After the failed revolutions of 1848, "the country of the future would become the new homeland for many of the Central and East Central European revolutionaries."[12] Not for all, to be sure. Some disappointed 48-ers later joined the ranks of the conservatives, including Richard Wagner and the especially vociferous anti-American critic Ferdinand Kuernberger.[13] By this time it was not only the liberal intellectual vanguard that expressed dissatisfaction with the status quo. The poor also realized that across the ocean was "America the Beguiling."[14] They could not express their feelings as eloquently as the upper echelons of society, but they voted with their feet, with their one-way transatlantic tickets. German immigration after the mid-nineteenth century came to constitute a major ethnic portion of the American population. Even today more Americans claim to be of German than of any other descent: almost 58 million, according to census data of 1990.[15]

Throughout the nineteenth century German sentiments toward America became more complex. The *Bildungsburgertum*, the bourgeois intelligentsia, still—or perhaps more than ever—nourished the cliché of the culturally inferior, primitive West. But entrepreneurs within this same stratum saw the unmistakable success of the American economy and admired it. This was not perceived as a contradiction; on the contrary, it formed a staple of conservative European and perhaps more specifically German anti-Americanism: admiration and envy of the American economy, disdain for the (lack of) culture.

The left concurred with the bourgeoisie and aristocracy in condemning "American materialism" (alleged or real), but for different reasons: not because of egalitarian tendencies which
supposedly led to the dollar as the only standard of value, but because this materialism was seen as an integral part of the capitalist system. Orthodox Marxists, however, welcomed the "more
advanced stage" of societal development in the United States as a
step closer to a socialist revolution; most of the left agreed that the
democratic forms of government were preferable to what Germany or Austria—or most of Europe, for that matter—endured until World War I.

A special instance of a purely projective image of America may
be found in the collected works of Karl May (1842–1912), barely
known in the United States. The Wild West of this immensely popular German author (who did not cross the Atlantic until very late
in life), was populated by noble Indians (*idiots savants* unless corrupted by whites), wheeler-dealing Yankees, and honest and coura-
geous trappers and cowboys hailing mostly from Germany,
preferably from May's home region in Saxony. The impact of his
writings, devoured by several generations of German-speaking children (mostly boys), cannot be overestimated. His writings met two
conflicting needs of his readers: a fascination with the New World
and reassurance about the ultimate moral superiority of the Old.

1900 marked the first time German bonds were floated in the
United States—a borrower was turning into a lender. Less than
two decades later, America presided over the peace negotiation
following World War I. The victor had by now become a real presence in Europe in various capacities: political, military, economic,
and cultural. As C. Vann Woodward wrote,

> The future began to arrive in the present. It arrived at the Euro-
> peans' doorstep, their markets, their press, their schools. It ar-
> rived in the shape of missionaries, evangelists, salesmen,
> advertisements, and movies. . . . The future was an intrusive, un-
> avoidable, living presence. They called it "Americanization"![16]

In defeated Germany and Austria, President Woodrow Wilson
was widely viewed as responsible for all the postwar misery. In

their eyes his Fourteen Points stood for hypocrisy, forced pay-
ments, the humiliation of the proud Reich, and, in Austria especially, a death blow to the nostalgically revered *Vielvoelkerstaat*,
the multi-national, multi-cultural Habsburg Empire. A new wave
of anti-Americanism can be traced to the Versailles and Trianon
treaties and their consequences, imagined or real, but the attitude
soon acquired a life of its own. Distinctions between rational and
irrational critiques, never very distinct, became even more
blurred. *Ressentiments* against the new power united the extreme
left ("Imperialists!") and the radical right ("International finan-
ciers!") against the weak liberal and social democratic political
center in Germany, foreshadowing ill-fated alliances as the
Weimar republic neared an end.

At the same time Germany was probably the most Americanized country in Europe after World War I, and by the late 1920s it
was also regarded as the most modern. The influence of new cultural phenomena such as jazz, cinema, new dances, and other
fashions, as well as realist literature, was powerful, at least in urban settings. And while political extremists decried these developments, many intellectuals were ambivalent about America—or
rather, like Bertolt Brecht, about their image of "America." On the
whole, however, pessimistic, hostile attitudes toward the United
States dominated, especially after the Great Depression of 1929,
which hit Germany and Austria as hard as the earlier economic
crisis (of 1925).

It was a small step from the traditional stereotypes hardened in
the post–World War I period, and from equating America with
"the Jews," to the official propaganda of the Third Reich, which
made anti-Americanism a high priority. The anti-Semitic, anti-
U.S., anti-modern, anti-Roosevelt rhetoric of the Nazis has been
widely documented and need not be reviewed here. As to why millions responded to these repetitive propaganda messages, the answer is inseparable from an understanding of the origins of and
receptivity toward Nazism. Here it is sufficient to point out that
some of the arguments of the Nazis were far from new; they had
formed the staple of anti–New World resentments since the nineteenth century and even earlier.

At the same time a certain "American" lifestyle was alive and well (though of course not viewed favorably by the authorities) even in Hitler's Germany, from swing music to the consumption of Coca-Cola.[17] This grassroots "Americanism" was, according to Dan Diner, counterbalanced and subsequently overwhelmed by an ideologically motivated anti-Americanism.[18]

The end of World War II and of the Nazi regime created a peculiar situation. Germany was once more defeated, but aside from this fact history did *not* repeat itself. Instead of punitive reparations, generous assistance was provided in the form of the Marshall Plan. This time around the Americans came to stay, to rebuild and soon to form an alliance with the defeated enemy against a former ally. As Pells notes,

> For many Germans, the GIs who came to occupy part of the country were the first Americans they had ever seen. They aroused . . . a mixture of feelings, from fascination to exasperation, to envy. As they swaggered down the street, brimming with health and confidence . . . more robust than the local population, the soldiers seemed the embodiments of a vulgar, flamboyant, mythological America. . . . [They seemed] more anti-authoritarian than any occupying force ever seen on the Continent. This was an army imbued with a civilian mentality.[19]

There was political support for the United States and the Western allies in West Germany for obvious reasons: their massive help in the reconstruction effort. They also built the institutions that turned a country in ruins into a functional, prosperous democracy.

Conservative Christian Democrats under Adenauer were more pro-American than the liberal and social democratic forces as they embraced the newly found mission of German politics: to be a good ally in the beginning cold war against Soviet communism. The global ramifications of this new conflict went far beyond the German question. But at a social or mass psychological level, it helped fortify the idea of the *Stunde Null*, the "hour zero"—the belief that with the end of the war, Germany could start from scratch.

It would, however, be unfair to suggest that the Germans were quickly trying to forget their past and rally around a new authority. No survey data from those years are available, but cursory evidence from travelogues and monographs[20] suggests that at least a portion of the population seriously reconsidered the recent past. Many went through a form of U.S.-sponsored "reeducation," which included the establishment of liberal, investigative media.

While a pro-American, anti-Soviet political stance was being established in the postwar years in Germany, in cultural affairs the patterns were far less clear-cut. The old anti-American, culturally superior attitudes survived in German conservative circles, which had little political power. "Basically, the anti-Americanism of the Right in the Bonn republic, in notable contrast to Weimar, was confined to a *cultural* criticism of things American . . . whereas its pre-Bonn *political* component changed to an explicitly pro-American position."[21]

Some of the critics were survivors of the Nazi or pre-Nazi national-conservative elite, like Carl Schmitt. Others joined them as disappointed observers of the "Westernization" of Germany—among them also some emigrants who had returned or who, like Stefan Heym, moved to the Soviet zone (later the German Democratic Republic (GDR).[22]

The latter were the exception rather than the rule. Those among the emigrant intellectuals who returned—and they were not many in Germany and fewer still in Austria—did not usually defend the German way against American "degeneracy." A case in point was the "Frankfurt School" under Theodor W. Adorno and Max Horkheimer. Having emigrated as Marxist, Jewish intellectuals to the United States, these two leading figures of the prewar Institute for Social Research in Frankfurt returned with a modified but still radical view of the pitfalls of progress in a capitalist society, as embodied also, but not exclusively, in America; more often they would speak of "the administered world." Back in Germany they became the targets of critics like the conservative Caspar von Schrenck-Notzing, who accused them of "destroying the German character" in collaboration with the American occupiers.[23]

Anti-American declarations were clearly the rule among the GDR literati, and they could also be found among leftist West Germans in the pre–Vietnam War period.

There was also an equally strong appreciation (in West Germany) of what "America" meant, an appreciation that had both emotional and rational elements. The United States signified cultural liberation and a breath of fresh air in public discussion, the arts, entertainment, and popular culture, especially music.

Much changed on the road to 1968. Most notable was the shift of attitude among many intellectuals toward American foreign policy, from support of the U.S. role in the cold war to a strong critique of it. Two developments are often considered responsible for this change: abroad the Vietnam War, and at home the coming of age of the first post–World War II generation of students and intellectuals, strongly influenced by the Frankfurt School.

The Vietnam War was a watershed in attitudes toward the United States among German leftists and radicals, as well as their counterparts in many other parts of the world, including America itself. German and Austrian students felt they had more in common with their peers at Berkeley and Columbia than with their own governments, and in fact they did. Their tactics in battles against university and state authorities, in protests against the war against what they perceived as social injustices at home, were imported from the United States and called by their English names—"teach-ins," "sit-ins," and "happenings."

Anti-American attitudes among the radicalized young came in various shades. Some of them adhered to traditional Communist party lines or to "Marxist-Leninist" beliefs, some were Maoists, others anarchists. Most of them accused the United States of a wide variety of evils, ranging from the inhumane conduct of the war to imperial attitudes and the airing of mindless sitcoms on television. A distinction was drawn between Washington politics and Americans as a people. Somewhat surprisingly, students who were radicalized under Adorno, Horkheimer, et al. were more action-oriented and radical in their rejection of the United States than their teachers, but at the same time more willing to borrow from American culture and mores. Where the old, ultimately very Germanic professors

saw only shallowness and deceit (even in matters such as synco-
pated jazz music), part of the New Left generation took to these aspects of American life and even drew energy from them. As the
filmmaker Wim Wenders, speaking of the sixties, recently put it: "If
it hadn't been . . . for Bob Dylan, I would never have had the courage
to drop out of college and start on such unsafe territory as my own
creativity."[24] Reference to Dylan has also been made on several occasions by the present German foreign minister Joschka Fischer,
leader of the Green party and former left-radical, to indicate how
pro-Western, and pro-American his cultural socialization had been.[25]

Speaking of the sixties and seventies, Andrei Markovits has
pointed out that leftist criticism was directed at specific events and
policies and "did not, for the most part, extend to a cultural condemnation of the American 'way of life.' Nor did it spare West Germany from accusation of complicity in the capitalist-imperialist
'world order.'" Equating such criticism with an irrational anti-
American prejudice, Markovits continues, would be "both deceptive and dangerous."[26]

Most strata of West German society did not share these forms of
anti-Americanism. Rather more typical were attitudes of "cultural
reservations and political agreement." Pro-American sentiment
was amplified by social forces such as the media conglomerate
Springer. A favorite target of the Springer publications was Hans
Magnus Enzensberger, the writer, poet, and leftist political essayist,
who in 1967 rejected his fellowship as a writer in residence at Wes-
leyan University in protest against what he called "fascist tendencies" in the United States.[27] Instead he went to Cuba to show his
solidarity with the Third World. (Subsequently he also became disillusioned with Castro's Cuba.)

In later reflections, Enzensberger regarded his perception of the
United States as typical of a whole generation of Germans, those
who had experienced the liberation of Germany and imagined
America as a kind of utopia. When reality did not correspond to
such wishful thinking, it led to deep disappointment and to the especially shrill protest of the 1968 generation.

More than ten years later a new wave of protest against the
United States swept over Germany in response to the NATO plan

to install Pershing II and cruise missiles in Western Europe, Germany included. The Green party and the peace movement constituted the main opposition. In contrast to the protests of the late sixties, this time there was a mass base.

Because of romantic tendencies within the Green and leftist movements, an anti-modernist slant became apparent. It opened up the left "to the danger of cooptation from the right by not explicitly distancing itself from the cultural anti-Americanism of the latter."[28] Opposition to modernity was a potential link between the left and right and even to the discredited Nazi past. Both, according to Paul Hollander, "represent . . . a nostalgia for a more authentic and fulfilling past."[29] For the Nazis, the Jews had been the most visible agents of modernity; for the left, the United States played the same role.

Leading figures on the left, such as the novelist Günter Grass, went beyond the fashionable moral equation of the United States and the USSR and maintained even at the time of the Soviet invasion of Afghanistan that "the United States was disqualified from making moral judgments about anything."[30] Yet Grass, like other detractors of the United States, also maintained in 1980 that "I who often visit America and love America and see that they are our ally . . . think that in this situation [the missile deployment], criticism is the best sign of loyalty."[31]

The showdown in Europe between the Reagan administration and the Soviet government under Brezhnev did not, as the pacifists feared, lead to a new war. Instead it contributed to the weakening and dissolution of the Communist bloc. The fall of the Berlin Wall in 1989, the symbolic climax of this development, was credited in good part to the firm policy of the West. The "end of history" was declared by some, and an early form of Pax Americana was widely welcomed. Anti-Americanism in Germany was reduced to small pockets among the cultural right and political left.

This state of affairs was short-lived. The main reasons for the change are well known. The first Gulf War, the war in Afghanistan against the Soviet occupiers, the recent conflict in the Balkans, and above all September 11, 2001, and the consequent wars in Afghanistan and Iraq created a new situation for the United States, by now the only global power. As a result, new forms of anti- as well as pro-American attitudes emerged in many parts of the world including Germany.

As in most Western countries, in Germany too the shock of 9/11 led to an immediate show of solidarity with America; some 200,000 people took to the streets in Berlin, and the sentiments of the headline of *Le Monde* (*"Nous sommes tous Americains"*) were widely echoed in Germany. But soon a more critical stance emerged in Western Europe, and to some extent in Japan, Canada, and other developed nations.

Apprehension about the war in Afghanistan could be found even in the NATO countries, with the notable exception of Great Britain. Debates have raged ever since as to what extent the ensuing estrangement between the United States and Western Europe has been caused by U.S. unilateralism, German neutralist and pacifist tendencies, French oil interests and diplomatic competitiveness, or a combination of all of the above.

As far as U.S.-German relations are concerned, according to some German observers the "fragile sympathy" was destroyed by Bush. By contrast, Markovits sees "a crescendo in condescension, ridicule, irritation, ressentiment, and a new sentiment—Schadenfreude" at work in Europe, including Germany. In his view, the opinion that "Europe's goodwill towards the United States immediately following 9/11 was squandered" was "absolutely untrue as far as the elites were concerned, who had no such good will to squander in the first place."[32] Diner detects similar attitudes in some of the German reactions he analyzed and finds in them echoes of traditional German feelings of superiority, incapable of dealing with a new world.

AN AGORA WITHOUT EQUAL

In an effort to assess whether or not informed or uninformed anti-Americanism dominates public discussion in Germany, I examined a specific reflection of public opinion, namely the Feuilleton, a daily section of up to eight pages in quality newspapers which contains comments, reviews, analyses, and essays on political, so-

cial, cultural, and economic topics. Despite growing financial restrictions and competition from the internet, the daily Feuilletons
still represent the agora, the marketplace of ideas for opinion leaders and better-informed citizenry. The Feuilleton has no direct
equivalent in Anglo-Saxon print media; the op-ed pages of major
American dailies such as the *New York Times* or the *Washington
Post* come closest. The kind of person who in Germany (or Austria or Switzerland) reads such a newspaper and its comment pages
"is constrained in America to read one of the high-quality week-
lies and monthlies. . . . But such journals are read by what is proportionally a much smaller minority even of the elite."[33]

I examined the Feuilletons of the major German dailies: the
Frankfurter Allgemeine Zeitung (FAZ, a slightly conservative
daily and arguably the German paper of record); the *Sueddeutsche
Zeitung* of Munich (SZ, more on the liberal side); and *Die Welt* of
Berlin, the weekly Feuilleton of *Die Zeit* (DZ) and the
newsweekly *Der Spiegel*, both published in Hamburg. In Switzerland the *Neue Zuercher Zeitung* (NZZ) is the paper of record and
carries a widely respected comments section. Finally, I included
the relevant Feuilleton articles of the Vienna-based *Der Standard*
(DS) that appear in the daily cultural pages and in the weekend
supplement for which I am responsible. The period of analysis
ranged from September 2002 to September 2003—that is, the second year after 9/11 and including the Iraq War.

As far as the major contributions were concerned in both FAZ
and SZ, the articles critical of America dominated (forty in all),
whereas roughly one-third (fourteen) took a positive stance toward
aspects of American politics, culture, or "way of life" in general.
Twenty-three contributions were of the "on the one hand and on
the other" variety. I also looked at articles published in some highbrow periodicals. All told I found an impressively broad range of
opinions and perspectives, many critical, but few could be classi-
fied as genuine, irrational anti-Americanism.

In addition to pieces by the staff writers of the papers, there
were critical articles, for example, by the British author Julian
Barnes, on the prospect of a next war against North Korea; by Norman Mailer, on being afraid of Saddam Hussein; by Paul Krugman,

on the entrepreneurial past of George W. Bush; by Paul Kennedy, with suggestions for a new "core" Europe; and by Paul W. Schroeder, the historian emeritus, arguing that 9/11 was no turning point. Richard Rorty wrote twice in SZ (on the permanent militarization of the United States and on the necessity of an assertive Europe); Norman Birnbaum, the sociologist, is a regular contributor to it.

Some of the more recent contributions followed a debate initiated by Juergen Habermas and Jacques Derrida on the "rebirth of Europe" in FAZ of May 31, 2003, and were accompanied by simultaneous articles in five other major European dailies. Hans-Ulrich Gumbrecht, the German-born American comparative literature professor at Stanford, regularly criticizes his former compatriots in the pages of FAZ for their unthinking anti-Americanism; a full-page article in the same paper analyzed the biased anti-U.S. coverage of the Iraq War on German TV channels, comparing them with ABC and BBC.

All these sources pay extraordinary attention to the American media, intellectuals, and opinion-makers (twenty-six articles in FAZ, SZ, and DZ). There are, to name but a few, articles about the *Weekly Standard*, Paul Krugman, and Ann Coulter and Michael Moore (not showing much enthusiasm for either, though Moore is on the best-seller list in Germany and Austria as well as in the United States). There are essays about the *New Yorker* and the *New York Times*, content analyses of the Fox and CNN channels, comments on the writings of Kenneth Pollock and Frederick W. Kagan (and of course on his brother Robert, whose book *Of Paradise and Power* was translated and widely reviewed).

In a series that ran in the weekend supplement of DS from January 11 to July 19, 2003, space was given to a wide range of voices, from the decidedly pro-American German politician Karsten Voigt to the skeptical Austrian EU-parliamentarian Hannes Swoboda, from the "empire" theorist Andrew Bacevich at Boston University and the neo-conservative Max Boot at the Council of Foreign Relations to the liberal editor Alison Smale of the *New York Times*, the critical sociologist Richard Sennett, and the highly critical Indian writer Arundhati Roy.

Such wide coverage does not necessarily immunize German public opinion against irrational attitudes or protect it from slanted reporting. But whatever the ultimate influence, the better media for the most part refrain from taking one-sided, dogmatic positions. If some fraction of the German elite still—or more than ever—subscribes to an irrational anti-Americanism, it is certainly not because of the influence of the reputable publications I briefly surveyed.

As regards other channels of solid and wide-ranging information available for opinion-makers and leaders in Germany, there is also an enormously active book publishing industry which translates a considerable part of Anglo-Saxon and especially American publications, noting topics of transatlantic interest as soon as they appear. The motives may be commercial, but the result is an almost instant access to transatlantic authors encompassing the entire political spectrum. (There is hardly a corresponding interest on the other side of the Atlantic in European authors, publications, and preoccupations, unless linked to some dramatic events.)

In light of these sources of information, it would seem that ignorance is not a major source of, or factor in anti-American sentiments in these parts of Europe.

BEYOND MODERNITY?

An argument frequently put forward throughout the long history of anti-Americanism is that anti-American attitudes are associated with the protest against modernity. Paul Hollander regards this as one of the three types of anti-Americanism, the other two being nationalistic and anti-capitalistic.

Originally used to describe the avant-garde of nineteenth-century culture, modernity came to signify the historic period from the early Enlightenment until today. Sometimes the beginning of this epoch is placed as far back as 1492. Ever since then, America has been its most obvious embodiment. Subsequent critiques of modernity focus on the relentless innovations of the New World, its all-encompassing democratic processes, nontraditional social life, decline of community, competitiveness, and emphasis on the individual pursuit of happiness. These critiques, often closely linked to a romantic view of the world, have been voiced especially strongly in Germany, Austria, and other relatively traditional societies. Whether in an appreciative or derogatory spirit, "America" has been designated as the beacon of modernity.

While the equation of America with modernity has been historically valid, some questions may be raised about its soundness at the present line. Modernity has always been a multi-dimensional concept and not all of its components have been applicable to the United States. Thus, for example, American modernity has proved unexpectedly compatible with the survival of many forms of traditional religious beliefs, attitudes, and institutions. No other modern industrial society harbors so many fundamentalist religious movements and such strong religiously based opposition to abortion. It was also in modern America (after World War I) that the state attempted to outlaw alcohol, also on religious grounds. Another strange phenomenon in contemporary America is the attempt to regulate intimate personal behavior on the campus and in the workplace through "sensitivity training" and various minute, puritanical regulations governing the relationships between men and women. Such attempts to control personal behavior and interaction (and the associated invasion of privacy) are far more characteristic of traditional than modern societies, though of course in the former the mechanisms of control tend to be informal.

Such phenomena may prompt the question whether the United States is still the haven of modernity, the "democratic . . . empire of the future," as some would have it. Much of the criticism I surveyed in the German-language Feuilletons addressed this question.

Guarding civil liberties and some measure of government responsibility for the welfare of the citizenry are also modern ideas, and may no longer be taken for granted in the United States. Moreover, American-style capitalism has in recent years taken a course different from its European counterparts. It remains to be seen which version of capitalism is more compatible with modernity as the concept has been generally understood in the Western world.

NOTES

1. Paul Hollander, *Anti-Americanism: Rational and Irrational* (New Brunswick, N.J., 1995), p. 339.

2. Louis Begley, "Das Washington-Imperium," *Frankfurter Allgemeine, Zeitung*, September 13, 2003, p. 24.

3. Thomas More's *Utopia* was published a mere quarter of a century after the discovery of the new continent—and takes place there.

4. Dan Diner, *Feindbild Amerika. Ueber die Bestaendigkeit eines Ressentiments* (Munich, 2002), p. 14.

5. Richard Pells, *Not Like Us: How Europeans Have Loved, Hated, and Transformed American Culture Since World War II* (New York, 1997), pp. 2f.

6. Andrei S. Markovits, "European Anti-Americanism: Past and Present of a Pedigreed Prejudice." Inaugural lecture of the Karl W. Deutsch Collegiate Professorship, delivered in Ann Arbor, Michigan, September 24, 2003. A version of the lecture is published in the Viennese publication *Juedisches Echo*, December 2003; a book incorporating it is scheduled for publication in 2004.

7. Diner, *Feindbild Amerika*, p. 15.

8. See also, ibid, pp. 42–66; Katja Hirnschrodt, "Zwischen Stereotypisierung und Differenzierung," master's thesis in history, University of Vienna, 2002, pp. 23f; and Markovits, "European Anti-Americanism," for examples of these warnings. See also James Ceaser, *Reconstructing America* (New Haven, Conn., 1997), Chapter 1, "America as Degeneracy."

9. See Andrei S. Markovits, "On Anti-Americanism in West Germany," *New German Critique*, vol. 34 (1985), p. 11; Markovits, "European Anti-Americanism"; and Diner, *Feindbild Amerika*, pp. 44ff. According to Diner, Lenau had traveled to the United States with the mundane plan to invest money in land. When the scheme failed, he went on to decry the very commercialism that had inspired him.

10. Translation by Daniel Platt. See www.schillerinstitute.org/trans/trans_goethe.html.

11. Markovits, "On Anti-Americanism in West Germany," p. 12.

12. Diner, *Feindbild Amerika*, p. 54.

13. Ibid., pp. 54f.

14. This is how Josef Joffe, the journalist and co-publisher of the German weekly *Die Zeit*, defines the attraction that the elites had sensed—and resented—about America, "in contrast to any other country." Quoted in Markovits, "European Anti-Americanism."

15. U.S. Bureau of the Census, 1990 Census of Population, Table No. 56, Population by Selected Ancestry Group and Region. The Irish are second, with 38.7 million, and the English third, with 32.6 million. It could be somewhat flippantly argued that any anti-American attitudes since then diagnosed in the German population are partially biased by the fact that many pro-Americans had left long ago.

16. C. Vann Woodward, *The Old World's New World* (New York, 1991), p. 80, quoted in Hirnschrodt, "Zwischen Stereotypisierung und Differenzierung," p. 31.

17. Goering was actually photographed drinking Coca-Cola. The popular American product was even bottled in Germany until 1942 when the syrup sup-

plies ran dry. See Werner Pieper, ed., *Nazis on Speed. Drogen im 3. Reich,* 2 vols., Edition Rauschkunde (Heidelberg, 2002), pp. 108ff.

18. Diner, *Feindbild Amerika,* p. 97.

19. Pells, *Not Like Us,* p. 40.

20. Cf. Philipp Gassert, "Gegen Ost und West: Antiamerikanismus in der Bundesrepublik,"in Detlef Junker, Philipp Gassert, et al., eds., *Die USA und Deutschland im Zeitalter des kalten Krieges 1945–1990* (Stuttgart, 2001), pp. 944ff.

21. Markovits, "On Anti-Americanism in West Germany," p. 13.

22. For an overview of the array of post–World War II, pre–Vietnam War cultural anti-Americans, see Hirnschrodt, "Zwischen Stereotypisierung und Differenzierung," pp. 58–66, and Diner, *Feindbild Amerika,* pp. 116–136.

23. See Hirnschrodt, "Zwischen Stereotypisierung und Differenzierung," p. 64. In an analogy to the metaphor of brainwashing, Schrenck-Notzing called his pamphlet, published in 1965, *Charakterwaesche* (Character Washing).

24. In *Die Zeit,* October 1, 2003, p. 72.

25. One such occasion was an interview that Fischer gave to Charlie Rose on PBS in mid-November 2002. Obviously Mr. Dylan does not constitute the "official" America that Fischer had come to visit in the fall of 2002; but that does not, in my opinion, mean that by looking at the "other" America, Fischer just looked at his own projection, as Dan Diner argues. Diner sees no validity in a German's reference to "the other America." (Diner, *Feindbild Amerika,* p. 35). In Diner's view, an identification with (sub)cultural American phenomena (whose exponents would often call themselves—or the others—the "other America") is just another form of hostility toward the country. As a fan of Bob Dylan, Robert Crumb, Billie Holiday, Frank Zappa, T. C. Boyle, or Toni Morrison, I beg to differ.

26. Markovits, "On Anti-Americanism in West Germany," p. 14.

27. Diner, *Feindbild Amerika,* p. 141.

28. Andrei S. Markovits and Philip S. Gorski, *The German Left: Red, Green, and Beyond* (New York, 1993), pp. 26f.

29. Hollander, *Anti-Americanism,* p. 380; see also Diner, *Feindbild Amerika,* pp. 143ff.

30. Quoted in Hollander, *Anti-Americanism,* p. 381, from a statement that Grass made in the early 1980s.

31. Quoted in Markovits, "On Anti-Americanism in West Germany," p. 17.

32. Quoted in Markovits, "European Anti-Americanism."

33. Tony Judt, "Hochgezogene Zugbruecken," interview with Michael Freund, *Der Standard,* October 18, 2003, p. A15.

5

PATRICK CLAWSON AND BARRY RUBIN

Anti-Americanism
in the Middle East

The only surprising thing about Middle Eastern anti-Americanism is that anyone should be surprised by it. The history of this antagonism is rooted in the early cold war, well before the United States played any serious role in the region, and its rise is linked to the interests of the regimes, movements, and ideologies propounding the doctrine. Contrary to beliefs and assertions that U.S. policies are responsible for Middle Eastern anti-Americanism, local forces have promoted it in the service of particular political goals. This anti-Americanism has been fanned more by modern ideologies and political interests than by traditional religious values.

CELEBRATING THE ATTACKS OF 9/11

There are many ways to measure Middle Eastern anti-Americanism, but nothing better illustrates the depth and breadth of the phenomenon than the reactions to the September 11, 2001, attacks on the World Trade Center and Pentagon.[1] Whereas in other areas of the world, governments and peoples were repelled by the attacks and demonstrated their solidarity with the people and government of the United States, in the Middle East the attacks drew decidedly mixed reactions from politicians, religious leaders, and elite figures. Some openly supported the attacks. Former Iraqi President Saddam Hussein declared on Iraqi television that the attacks were well-deserved by a nation that "exports evil, in terms of corruption and criminality, not only to any place to which its armies travel, but also to any place where its movies go." Many others doubted that Middle Easterners had anything to do with the attacks. The hard-line Iranian newspaper *Siyasat-e Ruz* expressed the common view that "the operations on [September 11] in America were part of a complicated methodical, technical and intelligence plan and must have been carried out by a group or organization that had precise intelligence, access to America's vital and sensitive center, access to high-quality weapons and explosives, and infiltrators in those organs," suggesting that the attack must have been undertaken by Americans or "Zionists." While the Saudi government made no such assertion, it did deny for many months that its citizens had been involved in the attacks. Indeed, the Saudi government's open acknowledgment to the Saudi public of the role of Saudis in the attacks came only after the May 2003 bombings in Riyadh; it took terror violence at home to shake the Saudi government from its state of denial about the depth of the terror problem.

A larger group condemned the attacks but saw them as understandable if not excusable because of the evil done by the United States. This view was by no means confined to a few extremists. As Saudi cleric Safar bin Abd al-Rahman al-Hawali wrote in his open letter to President Bush in the London newspaper *al-Quds al-Arabi,*

> I will not conceal from you that a tremendous wave of joy accompanied the shock that was felt by Muslims in the street, and whoever tells you otherwise is avoiding the truth. . . . Everyone on earth who claims to love you—and no Muslim is able to make that claim—they only love you like frightened prey loves a brutal predator.

Leading journalists in state-sponsored newspapers in countries friendly to the United States, such as Egypt and Jordan, were more temperate in their wording, but they too argued that the terrorist attacks were only a natural reaction to deeply unjust U.S. policies.

There were also those who condemned the attacks without reservation. That included not only friends of the United States—such as the thousands of ordinary Tehran residents who held a candlelight vigil, to the disgust of the Iranian government—but also many devout Muslims who reject the politicization of their faith by radicals. Salih bin Muhammad al-Luheidan, chairman of the Supreme Judicial Council of Saudi Arabia, wrote bluntly, "Islam rejects such acts, since it forbids killing of civilians even during times of war, especially if they are not part of the fighting. . . . This barbaric act is not justified by any sane mindset or any logic, nor by the religion of Islam."

What are the origins of the fierce anti-Americanism permeating the Middle Eastern reactions to the 9/11 attacks? It has been frequently claimed that its roots lie in U.S. policy and that it flourishes because of traditional religious sentiment. Both claims are basically wrong. To better understand the phenomenon we must examine the two main versions of Middle Eastern anti-Americanism: the radical Arab nationalist and the violent Islamist.

THE GREAT EXCUSE

One of the mainsprings of anti-Americanism is radical Arab nationalism, but that ideology is hardly a reaction to U.S. policy; in fact, it predates active U.S. involvement in the region. Arab radical nationalism began in the years before World War II in opposition to British and French power, as well as its own traditional societies; it rose to power in the decade that followed the war. While fascism had some influence on these groups—notably in Egypt and Iraq—many of their ideas were adapted from Communist ideology and Soviet practice. The incumbent moderate, parliamentary, and pro-Western monarchies were perceived as failures; the revolutionary left was the wave of the future, promising rapid development, national solidarity, geographical unity, and the expulsion of Western influence, to which was added after 1948 the destruction of Israel.

The democratic, free-enterprise, human and civil rights–oriented system of the United States was of little interest for these politicians and politicized military officers. They wanted an authoritarian mobilization society in order to achieve the dramatic changes they sought: the ordering of a new polity from above, the sweeping away of old classes, and the establishment of a militarized state that would achieve order at home and victory abroad. All the basic factors predisposing to anti-Americanism were already in place by 1950, when none of these people or countries could claim to have serious grudges against or conflicts with the United States for its actions in the region.

In fact U.S. policy was friendly to the Egyptian officers who took control of their government in 1952, until they chose to become allies of Moscow and aggressors toward other Arab states. Even after these policies emerged, the United States in the 1956 Suez crisis restrained Great Britain, France, and Israel in their efforts to overthrow Nasser. Rather than showing any appreciation or gratitude for being rescued, Nasser thanked Moscow for its support, setting a pattern for his continued pro-Soviet policy.

The conviction and claim that the United States was an imperialist power opposed to Arab countries and their ambitions grew out of the politics of the 1950s and 1960s, long before the United States developed a special relationship with Israel. It arose from the view that the United States was the ally and successor of Britain and France in international politics as well as from ideas borrowed from the USSR (and to a lesser but significant extent from the Axis fascist powers). Correctly the United States was seen as a status quo power while the USSR was viewed as seeking revolutionary change in the region. The willingness of the United States to help "progressive" nationalist movements—which were neither Communist nor stagnantly traditionalist—was totally misunderstood or ignored.

The most obvious source of anti-Americanism embraced by the radical Arab nationalist forces that seized power in Egypt in 1952, and in Syria during the 1950s, was the disposition of the United States to help defend their adversaries in other Arab countries (notably Jordan, Lebanon, and Saudi Arabia) against aggression by either Nasser or the Ba'th party that ruled Syria after 1963 and Iraq after 1968, or against the aggression of various other radical Arab nationalists.

The notion that the United States was disliked because it supported "unpopular" or "repressive" regimes in the region has
been disseminated by regimes far more repressive and unpopular
than those alleged to be supported by the United States. In fact,
during the second half of the twentieth century, no Arab government owed its existence to U.S. support. On no occasion did Arab
governments receive direct U.S. help against internal threats;
counterinsurgency efforts against radicals were carried out without U.S. pressure or assistance. For example, it was Britain that
helped Oman battle a Marxist insurgency in the 1970s and France
that helped Algeria fight Islamist revolutionaries in the 1990s. If
anything, the U.S. occasionally shielded more moderate Arab
regimes from foreign attack. This tradition found the most dramatic expression in the U.S.-led coalition to free Kuwait from
Iraqi aggression and annexation in 1991.

Earlier American interventions were limited. Thus while U.S.
Marines did land in Lebanon in 1958 to prevent subversion of that
country's independence, they stayed only a few months; Washington advised the Lebanese government to carry out reforms in order to assuage domestic grievances. In any event, with all its
failings, Lebanon was the most democratic and pluralistic of all
the Arab states.

Despite these policies the United States came to be blamed by
radical Arab dictatorships (and other regimes as well) for many of
their failures. It has thus been alleged that the failure of the pan-
Arab nationalists to unite the Arab world was due to U.S. interference, though there is little evidence for that claim. At most,
what might be said is that the United States prevented Egypt, Iraq,
or Syria from conquering their neighbors. Even in that regard
America did little between 1950 and 1990 besides selling arms to
the Saudis or Jordanians that were never used in combat. So reluctant was the United States to become involved in these internal and inter-Arab issues that it told Iraqi President Saddam
Hussein in 1990 that it did not wish to interfere in his quarrel with
Kuwait, thus unintentionally encouraging him to believe that he
could conquer his weaker neighbor.

The inability to develop economically or socially, the failure to raise living standards, or to modernize efficiently were also blamed on the United States. Bernard Lewis has summarized the process of historical decline in the Middle East from what once was an advanced and powerful region (arguably ahead of Europe) to a backward one: "By all the standards that matter in the modern world—economic development and job creation, literacy and educational and scientific achievement, political freedom and respect for human rights—what was once a mighty civilization has indeed fallen low."[2]

While one could at least attempt to argue—albeit on somewhat shaky grounds—that the United States damaged the economic development of Latin American countries, no such claim could be made about the Middle East. The main (almost exclusive) regional product of value has been oil. By the 1970s this resource was controlled by the Arab states and Iran, which were able to set prices virtually at will. American strategy in this regard was much closer to appeasement than intimidation. There were virtually no U.S.-owned factories in the Middle East exploiting cheap labor, or plantations and mines exploiting natural resources at huge profits. Even as a market, the region was hardly a dumping ground for expensive American goods.

Nor was the United States responsible for the incumbent governments in the region that were perfectly capable of keeping themselves in power. U.S. "support" played little role in their domestic politics while, as noted above, American arms were literally never used against insurgents or the local population. By contrast, Soviet-made and -supplied weapons were crucial for the ability of such regimes as those in Syria and Iraq to retain power.

Despite these facts it was widely believed in Arab countries that the United States was so powerful that it controlled even the Arab regimes most hostile to it. Thus it was commonplace to hear even from educated and well-traveled Arabs that Saddam Hussein, Yasir Arafat, Ayatollah Ruhollah Khomeini of Iran, and others were American puppets or agents. One proof given for this claim was that if the United States really opposed them, it would have overthrown them.

By the 1990s it was increasingly claimed that the United States was the force that had blocked democracy in the Arab world by supporting oppressive regimes. At the same time, when the United States pressured existing regimes for change, it was accused of imperialist intervention in the internal affairs of Arab countries.

Of all the anti-American complaints, U.S. support for Israel and objections to its destruction were the most widely held and contributed to conflicts between Arab and American policies. Of course there was no reason why the United States should have acquiesced in Israel's destruction, whether on grounds of international law, humanitarian motives, or national self-interest. The United States sold arms to Israel and provided aid to pay for them, but there was never any direct intervention on Israel's side.

Israel won the 1948 and 1967 wars without American help. It defeated Egypt in 1956 and was then, under U.S. pressure, forced to give up the leverage gained. In 1973 and 1982, and in fighting Palestinian insurgencies thereafter, Israel's victories were diminished by American diplomatic pressure. Thus while the United States certainly helped Israel from the mid-1970s onward, it did not unambiguously assume responsibility for that country's survival. In any event, U.S. assistance to Israel cannot account for the Arab states' failure (despite Soviet support, oil wealth, and superior numbers) to destroy that country.

In short, radical Arab nationalism was unable to attain any of its key objectives; by the standards it had established for itself, it was a failure. But rather than admit its shortcomings, radical Arab nationalists blamed America. This continued the long, lamentable tradition in the Arab world of blaming outsiders for their difficulties rather than looking at the conditions within Arab societies that account for the inability to achieve their objectives. To quote Bernard Lewis again:

"Who did this to us?" is of course a common human response when things are going badly, and there have been indeed many in the Middle East, past and present, who have asked this question. . . . The blame game—the Turks, the Mongols, the imperialists, the Jews, the Americans—continues, and shows little sign of abating.[3]

RADICAL ISLAMISM: A MODERN IDEOLOGY

It is tempting to regard Middle Eastern anti-Americanism as a rejection of modernity and a thus a reflection of traditional religious values. Osama bin Laden, among many others, calls for a return to the values of true Islam and the rejection of Western ways. Many in the Middle East, particularly in Saudi Arabia, cling to traditional beliefs and practices and reject the modern world and outsiders. Indeed, Abdel Aziz bin Baz, the longtime official religious leader of Saudi Arabia, argued until his 1999 death that Muslims have a religious obligation to hate Jews and Christians.[4] Bin Baz rejected American values, but that was part and parcel of his general opposition to modern ideas; he wrote a book on the theme that anyone who believes that the earth revolves around the sun should be killed (this from the man who had to approve all textbooks used in Saudi schools). But "anti-American" may better be reserved for those who dislike America in particular rather than all outsiders, all non-Muslims who have different values and attitudes. Bin Baz was generally opposed to modernity in its broadest sense and was more a narrow-minded traditionalist than anti-American.

It is during the last decade that the traditionalist interpretations of Islam have become strongly influenced by radical Islamist views, which include a highly negative attitude toward the United States.

Those who most vociferously attack America in the name of Islam are the radical Islamists, whose ideology is a modern totalitarian perversion of Islam. Radical Islamist leaders such as Osama bin Laden lack training in Islamic religious thought—no minor problem for a religion based on a rich body of law (the *sharia*) which claims to regulate every aspect of human existence. Bin Laden's pronouncements and actions show ignorance of, or disdain for, traditional learning. He appeals directly to the Quran—reminiscent of early Protestant radicals who appealed directly to the Bible without reference to the teachings of the Catholic church. But unlike those Protestants, he is not seeking the true meaning of the original text. Instead he turns to the holy book to justify the political course he has already charted, namely fierce opposition to the West. Much of his program—and even more of the program of such radical Islamists as the Algerian Armed Islamic Group (GIA) or the Iranian revolutionary hard-liners— is anti-imperialist and anti-capitalist, with strong similarities to the agenda of the radical nationalist Third World socialists of the generation that preceded them.

Islamists have seized on the most intolerant aspects of the old Islamic tradition to justify their radical extremism. The concept of jihad to which they assign such importance is a prime example. From the days of the Prophet Muhammad, Islam has stressed the importance of jihad in the sense of territorial expansion; after all, that is how Muslims came to rule over a vast region within one generation. But jihad is not "holy war" in the sense of a war to forcibly convert those living in the areas conquered. Instead "it means the legal, compulsory, communal effort to expand the territories ruled by Muslims at the expense of territories ruled by non-Muslims"[5]—not only are Muslims enjoined to live under the government of fellow believers, but government by Muslims is supposed to benefit the entire community.

While mystics stress a spiritual meaning of jihad as a struggle for self-improvement—a view that was gaining in influence until very recently—radical Islamists have picked up on and expanded an extremist strand in it that has been around for centuries. For these radicals, moderate Muslims are infidels and therefore legitimate targets of jihad. This concept of jihad best characterizes the modern radical Islamists: when they began to organize, their main targets were their fellow Muslims in Egypt (think of Anwar Sadat), Algeria, Saudi Arabia, and elsewhere. It is a fallacy to believe that the radical Islamists are being bent only on the destruction of Americans. The three thousand dead on September 11, 2001, are only a small portion of their victims, following tens of thousands killed in Algeria and Egypt. Even Saudi Arabia has seen terrorist bombings by Al Qaeda which killed innocent civilians.

Thus it bears repetition that there is no basis for the claim that radical Islamism is a reaction to U.S. policy. In fact the radical Islamists hate America for what it is, not for what it does. They reject core American values such as religious liberty, freedom of the press, and equality before the law as much as they oppose U.S. support for Israel.

Before September 11 there was little if any U.S. opposition to Islamism and its agenda, or to the insurgencies seeking to promote it. As regards the three main such insurgencies in Arab countries—in Lebanon, Algeria, and Egypt—the United States did not provide large-scale aid to the governments under attack, nor did it move against radical Islamist groups. (This situation stands in sharp contrast to the costly, sustained, and comprehensive U.S. efforts against Communist movements and revolutions during the four decades of the cold war.)

On the other hand, the United States provided billions in aid to radical Islamist forces fighting in Afghanistan, whose victory against the Soviet invaders and their local allies would not have been possible without U.S. money and arms.

The radical Islamists came to emphasize anti-Americanism—which was not initially prominent in their agenda—only when they failed to revolutionize their region. These movements blamed the United States for their inability to take over Arab countries, though this was actually due to the skill in repression and cooptation of the existing regimes. Furthermore, conservative regimes themselves encouraged the Islamists to turn to anti-Americanism, using such sentiments as escape valves to deflect anger from themselves. Unhappily, American governments acquiesced in this. In his *mea culpa* after September 11, Martin Indyk (former U.S. ambassader to Israel) described the 1990s policy he supported:

[It was felt that] the United States could not afford the destabilizing impact that pressure for reform would generate in deeply traditional and repressed [Arab] societies. Pushing hard for political change might not only disrupt the effort to promote [Arab-Israeli] peace but could also work against vital U.S. interests: stability in the oil-rich Persian Gulf and in strategically critical Egypt. The United States should therefore . . . leav[e] friendly Arab regimes to deal with their internal problems as they saw fit. . . . The al Qaeda network established by bin Laden (a Saudi) and his associate Ayman al-Zawahiri (an Egyptian) wanted to overthrow the Saudi and Egyptian regimes, but with U.S. support those had become hardened targets. So al Qaeda made a strategic decision to strike at their patron, the more powerful but also more vulnerable United States.[6]

POLITICAL ADVANTAGE, NOT GRIEVANCE

What lies most clearly at the root of Arab anti-Americanism is not so much grievance as the pursuit of political advantage. More radical regimes, such as Syria and Saddam's Iraq, have systematically promoted anti-Americanism among their own people and fellow Arabs as part of their foreign and domestic policies. More moderate regimes too, including Saudi Arabia, have often sponsored anti-Americanism to foster domestic support and deflect the criticism of foreign radicals. And radical Islamists have emphasized anti-Americanism when their efforts to overturn Arab rulers came to naught.

Anti-Americanism did not develop spontaneously but has been consciously and strenuously promoted and propagated by many groups and institutions in Arab societies for a number of reasons:

1) For the regimes in power to prove their militant credentials and provide an excuse for their foreign and domestic policy failures. Opposition to the United States has been one of the few subjects about which free expression is permitted for journalists and demonstrators on the street.

2) The main opposition groups (pan-Arab nationalist, leftist, and Islamist) have used anti-Americanism to discredit incumbent governments as lackeys of the West whose failures are due to their insufficient militancy.

3) Professionals, among them teachers, intellectuals, and journalists, have used anti-Americanism to show that they are politically correct militants who cannot be accused of being American puppets, despite being Westernized themselves to a considerable degree.

4) The mass media (television, radio, the press) have been instruments of states making use of anti-Americanism while also expressing the leftist and nationalist views of the journalists.

5) The educators, servants of the state, have been obliged to promote its goals, which include the dissemination of anti-Americanism; teachers as other professionals have also embraced a personal anti-Americanism for reasons noted in point 3.

6) Religious clerics, as instruments of the state or supporters of Islamist opposition movements, have viewed the United States as a cultural-religious as well as a political threat.

Citizens have thus been surrounded daily by anti-American messages and extreme distortions of U.S. policies, to a degree that has made it difficult to avoid absorbing these views. Anyone who disagrees with this political line is barred from the institutions mentioned above and branded as hostile to the existing regime, Arab nationalism, and Islam as well as an agent of the United States. He faces considerable career and personal risks.

None of this is intended to suggest that there have been no genuine conflicts of interest between the United States and a number of Arab regimes, let alone radical Islamists. The United States did block the ambitions of countries such as Egypt, Syria, Iraq, and Libya as well as Islamist Iran for control of the region. The long-standing alliance of several Arab regimes with the Soviet Union, some of them dating to the 1950s, created an adversarial relationship with the United States during the cold war. Indeed, the radical states in the Middle East were virtually the only non-Communist countries in the world that made common cause with Moscow for an extended period of time.

A striking feature of Middle Eastern attitudes toward the United States has been the systematic refusal to credit America for its positive policies toward the Arab world. These policies have included many years of foreign aid, diplomatic support, the rescuing of Egypt during the 1956 Suez crisis, protection from radical movements, convoying of oil tankers and support for the Arab cause in the Iran-Iraq war, and protection for Muslim minorities in Kosovo and Bosnia. Even American efforts to promote Arab-Israeli peace, culminating in the advocacy of a Palestinian state and coordinating billions of dollars of aid for the Palestinian Authority in the 1990s, has rarely been acknowledged.

For a half-century in the Arab world and a quarter-century in Islamist Iran, there has been an insistence, rarely challenged, that the American record toward the Arab countries has been one of unmitigated hostility. At the same time American grievances over issues such as the cold war policies of various Arab states, the widespread official anti-American rhetoric, and support for terrorism have been ignored.

Arab spokesmen addressing Western audiences, politicians, or media people ascribe anti-Americanism in the Middle East entirely to the Arab-Israeli conflict. To be sure, many in the Arab world passionately reject U.S. policy toward Israel. But this is only part of the picture, and often more a symptom than a cause of anti-Americanism. Moreover, much of the opposition to the U.S.-Israel alliance is based on a highly distorted view of the actual policies and actions of the two countries.

THE IRANIAN EXCEPTION

Judging from the official pronouncements of the Islamic Republic of Iran, it might seem that anti-Americanism has as much resonance in that country as in the Arab world at large—but this is not the case. The millions of Iranians who poured onto the streets during the 1978–1979 revolution to chant "Death to America," and the 1980–1981 hostage-taking at the U.S. embassy in Tehran show that anti-Americanism had broad appeal during the last days of the shah. The new Islamic Republic made anti-Americanism a pillar of its ideology and policies. No government in the Middle East has been more insistent on its opposition to the United States and the rejection of American cultural influences as the Islamic Republic of Iran. For decades Tehran had the only government in the world that refused to talk to Washington on a government-to-government basis, except in such unusual situations as the Iran-Contra affair. Spiritual leader Ayatollah Ruhollah Khomeini declared that discussions between the United States and Iran would be like discussions between the wolf and the lamb. This policy gradually eroded after the 1997 election of the reformist president Mohammed Khatemi, but Iran still refuses to contemplate official diplomatic relations between the two countries. And Iran continues to impose tight controls over any expressions of American culture while state media and clerics pour out invective against what they describe as an American cultural offensive against Iran. While the official Iranian position is one of deep hostility, the United States has now become widely popular among the people of Iran. The principal reason for pro-American sentiments is that the United States is a staunch opponent of the hated clerical regime. President Bush put it exactly right when he said in his 2002 State of the Union message that "an unelected few repress the Iranian people's hopes for freedom." Hopes for reform within the Islamic Republic, which were so high after the unexpected landslide victory of President Mohammed Khatemi in 1997, have died. Khatemi proved unwilling or unable to effect meaningful change, and the clerical hard-liners have reasserted control, shoving aside the president and parliament to run the country through the judiciary and the revolutionary institutions that report directly to Supreme Leader Ali Khamenei (who controls institutions such as the Revolutionary Guard Corps).

The aftermath of U.S. operations in Afghanistan and Iraq provide evidence of how far the pro-American sentiment extends in Iran. On June 22, 2003, the Iranian newspaper *Yas-e Now* published a remarkable poll that had originally appeared on the "Feedback" web page of the Expediency Discernment Council, run by former president Ali Akbar Hashemi Rafsanjani. Those polled were asked the question, "What are the actual demands of the Iranian people?" and were given a choice of four answers. They responded as follows:

• 13 percent chose the answer "solutions to the problems of people's livelihood, and the continuation of the present political policy"—in other words, the current hard-line stance.

• 16 percent chose "political reforms and increases in the powers of the reformists."

• 26 percent chose "fundamental changes in management and in the performance of the system for an efficient growth"—a position often identified with Rafsanjani.

• 45 percent chose "change in the political system, even with foreign intervention."

The endorsement of 45 percent of the respondents of such intervention is all the more surprising considering the continued imprisonment of pollsters who in 2002 found that 75 percent of Iranians wanted to open negotiations with the United States, and in light of the ominous (and unfounded) rumors circulating in Iran that the United States was considering an invasion.

If the poll reflected mass opinion, two interesting letters showed that many in the elite are concerned about the spread of pro-American attitudes. On Mohammed's birthday (May 19), 196 prominent clerics and intellectuals issued an open letter to "express our complete dissatisfaction with the rulers in Iran." The sharp criticism focused on "the unelected institutions" which are "united against the wishes of the people"—phrases that echo those used by President Bush. The letter warned that present policies "might provide an excuse to some groups who desire freedom to sacrifice the independence of the country"—in other words, they might welcome a U.S. invasion. It added, "We must learn a lesson from the fate of the Taliban and Saddam Hussein and understand that despotism and selfishness is destined to take the country down to defeat."

On May 25, 40 percent of the Parliament (Majlis) members signed a letter to Supreme Leader Ali Hossein Khamenei. The letter carefully refrained from any criticism of Khamenei, but its tone was otherwise tough. It warned, "Perhaps there has been no period in the recent history of Iran as sensitive as this one [due to] political and social gaps coupled with a clear plan by the government of the United States of America to change the geopolitical map of the region." Insisting on "fundamental changes in methods, attitudes, and figures," the letter warned, "If this is a cup of hemlock, it should be drunk before our country's independence and territorial integrity are placed in danger" (the hemlock phrase was used by Ayatollah Khomeini to explain his 1988 decision to end the war with Iraq).

Neither of the two letters was mentioned in Iranian media because of a ban imposed by the Supreme National Security Council, chaired by President Muhammad Khatemi. (This ban belies the commonly held notion that Khatemi-era Iran enjoys press freedom.) The council appears to be concerned with the spreading belief that the country is at risk of a U.S. invasion because of provocative actions by the hard-liners. This perceived risk apparently emboldens reformers to step up their criticism of the hardliners, contrary to the assumption widely held in the West that U.S. pressure hurts reformers.

What has occurred in Iran is more than a manifestation of a reflexive "the enemy of my enemy is my friend" attitude. The last few years has seen a far-reaching debate among many groups about the Enlightenment ideas. On issue after issue, intellectuals have come to support the values that America champions, from rule of law to free speech and representative government. Significantly, many Iranians argue that the state should stay out of religious affairs. A leading intellectual has written a book—from prison, no less—arguing that democracy is incompatible with a state religion. Hossein Mostafa Khomeini, the grandson of Ayatollah Ruhollah Khomeini and himself a prominent cleric, speaks eloquently—from the podium of the American Enterprise Institute in Washington—about the importance of individual liberties and a secular state while applauding America as the embodiment of these values.

Certainly there remains much anti-Americanism as well. Cultural conservatives are deeply hostile to what they see as America's crusade to corrupt traditional ways of life. Iranian nationalists are suspicious that the United States wants to block Iran from what they see as its natural place as leader of the region. Leftist Third World socialist ideas have shaped the entire generation that now runs Iran, clerics as well as secular intellectuals (though this ideology has no attraction for the young). Nonetheless it is no exaggeration to suggest that America has won the battle for the hearts and minds of the Iranian people, and the hard-line clerics have lost.

THE BATTLEGROUND OF IDEAS

The Middle East remains an active battleground of ideas. One would think the U.S. government would be vigorously engaged in promoting its vision and values in the region. After all, President Bush has spoken eloquently about how Muslims share the same hopes as Americans. In his 2002 State of the Union message, he said:

> No people on Earth yearn to be oppressed, or aspire to servitude, or eagerly await the midnight knock of the secret police. . . . Let the skeptics look to Islam's own rich history, with its centuries of learning, and tolerance and progress. America will lead by defending liberty and justice because they are right and true and unchanging for all people everywhere. No nation owns these aspirations, and no nation is exempt from them. We have no intention of imposing our culture. But America will always stand firm for the non-negotiable demands of human dignity: the rule of law; limits on the power of the state; respect for women; private property; free speech; equal justice; and religious tolerance. America will take the side of brave men and women who advocate these values around the world, including the Islamic world.

In fact the U.S. government has done little to take the side of those in the Middle East who advocate these values. Sad to say, one reason that anti-Americanism thrives in the Middle East is that the U.S. government does little to counter it.[7] This assertion may seem surprising since after 9/11 much concern was expressed—by administration officials, journalists, and experts—about improving the efforts of the United States to win the hearts and minds of Middle Easterners. Yet the administration has made few efforts to counter anti-Americanism or promote or defend American values or U.S. policies on Middle Eastern issues. Instead its focus has been on celebrating the cultural diversity of America that allows Muslims to lead traditional lives in the United States. More specifically, the Bush administration has placed more emphasis on public diplomacy. Charlotte Beers, a onetime advertising executive, was brought in as undersecretary of state to lead the effort. Beers championed the idea that America could earn sympathy around the world through the sort of image-oriented campaign used by Madison Avenue. The State Department developed a series of expensive initiatives to that end, spending tens of millions of dollars on television commercials. The focus was on everything but U.S. policy. For instance, a glossy publication claimed that America is a diverse society in which Muslims thrive, as if Middle Eastern anti-Americanism stemmed from the belief that Muslims are persecuted in America. (The State Department pictured Muslim women in America wearing head scarves, as if that were the norm for American Muslims.) The results were disastrous. Many television stations in Arab countries refused to air the TV spots, while many damned the ads as puerile propaganda. At home, after complaints about the Madison Avenue approach to diplomacy grew, Beers resigned in March 2003.

Nonetheless the State Department continues to use the approach Beers championed, focusing on common values (such as family, home, religion) and cultural interests (pop music, sports) that Americans share with foreign Muslims. To this end it devotes millions of dollars to a glossy fashion-and-pop-culture magazine targeted at Arab yuppies. It even spends tax money on promoting a Muslim rap group, Native Deen, whose lead singer, Joshua Salaam, once praised the terrorists who blew up the *USS Cole* for having "a lot of guts to attack the United States military."

Broadcasting has been the main instrument in these attempts to counter anti-Americanism. A new Arabic language radio station, Sawa, has started up. Sawa has gained strong congressional support based on a 2002 listener poll showing that it won a large audience in several Arab countries through an innovative mix of pop and Arabic music, interspersed with brief, informative, U.S.-style news reports. Rather than using its acceptance by a large audience as an opportunity to slip in more pro-U.S. content, Sawa staff claimed that its popularity proved its news content was "just right." The result is that Sawa is a music radio station instead of a voice promoting American policies and values. Sawa may have been the first radio network to introduce an enticing music mix to the Middle East, but it will not be the only one for long; already the Moroccan and Jordanian governments have launched stations based on the pop-Arabic music format. Congress, based on the Sawa experience, has appropriated $100 million for a similar style satellite television network.

Concerned about criticism of its public diplomacy, the State Department created an Advisory Group on Public Diplomacy for the Arab and Muslim World, chaired by former assistant secretary

of state Edward Djerijian. In its October 2003 report the group issued the usual appeal for more money but also offered indirect
criticism of the past feel-good approach. In particular it argued,
"Sawa needs a clearer objective than building a large audience,"
and complained that the strong focus on that one objective alone
"may deter Sawa from adding more influential content."

It seems unlikely that the United States will win the battle of
ideas unless it openly and explicitly discusses why the United
States does what it does. It is true that many Arabs disagree with
U.S. policies, but what they know often comes from the highly
distorted, caricatured views of reality propagated by their local
media and by even less professional Arabic-language satellite television stations, competing with one another as to which of can
be more stridently anti-American. These distortions and misrepresentations are rarely challenged by U.S. officials on Arab media.
With rare exceptions, U.S. officials in the Arab world fail to explain to local audiences, plainly and dispassionately, why Americans support Israel, oppose militant Islam, and opposed Saddam
Hussein. Experts whom the U.S. government sends on speaking
tours to Arab countries are overwhelmingly outspoken critics of
U.S. policy toward the region. The U.S. government subsidizes
study visits to the United States by radical Islamist journalists
more often than visits by liberal Arabs interested in promoting
democratic change in their countries.

Anti-Americanism in the Middle East, and the related opposition to the values America champions, will not wither away unas-
sisted. Only a concerted effort can counter the pernicious
misrepresentations that serve the interests of powerful local groups
and fire the imaginations of disaffected radicals. If the U.S. government does not lead the way, Arab liberals on their own are unlikely
to win the battle for the values America represents and supports.

The most extreme voices from the Middle East are the loudest,
and this creates an incorrect impression as to how widely their
views are shared. Thus despite talk about boycotts of American
products, the region's trade with the United States continues to
grow, and American mass culture—from fast food to music and
movies—is popular with the young. More important, American

higher education remains the dream of millions of Arab students and their parents. For all the concern about how America has changed since 9/11, few things are more eagerly sought than a visa to the United States. Even in the world of religion, moderation is more common than extremism. As Daniel Pipes has eloquently described,

> Anti-Islamist Muslims not only exist; in the two years since 9/11, they have increasingly found their voice. They are a varied lot, sharing neither a single approach nor one agenda. Some are pious, some not, and others are freethinkers or atheists. Some are conservative, others liberal. They share only a hostility to the Wahhabi, Khomeini and other forms of militant Islam. They are starting to produce books that challenge the Islamists' totalitarian vision.[8]

The challenge is to find the best way to encourage the voices of moderation and liberalism, which can already be heard in every Middle Eastern country.

NOTES

1. This section draws on the chapter "Middle East Reaction to September 11," pages 279 to 315 in Barry Rubin and Judith Colp Rubin, eds., *Anti-American Terrorism in the Middle East*, Oxford: Oxford University Press, 2002. The quotes in this section by Saddam Hussein, Siyasat-e Ruz, Safar bin Abd, al-Hawali, and Salih bin Muhammad al-Lheiden are from documents printed there.

2. Bernard Lewis, *What Went Wrong? Western Impact and Middle Eastern Response*, Oxford: Oxford University Press, 2002, p. 152.

3. Lewis, *What Went Wrong?* pp. 152, 159.

4. His writings and his influence are analyzed in detail in Antoine Basbous, *L'Arabie Saoudite en Question*, Paris: Perrin, 2002, especially pp. 125–140.

5. Daniel Pipes, "What Is Jihad," *New York Post*, December 31, 2002.

6. Martin Indyk, "Back to the Bazaar," *Foreign Affairs*, January/February 2002, pp. 80–81.

7. This section draws heavily on Robert Satloff, "How to Win Friends and Influence Arabs: Rethinking Public Diplomacy in the Middle East," *Weekly Standard*, August 18, 2003.

8. Daniel Pipes, "Voices of Islam," *New York Post*, September 23, 2003.

6

MICHAEL RADU

A Matter of Identity:
The Anti-Americanism of
Latin American Intellectuals

*T*he idea that Latin Americans are profoundly anti-American may seem implausible to many Americans. After all, they are our neighbors, millions of them have migrated to the United States, and, from Lima to Mexico City, Havana to Buenos Aires, American culture is omnipresent. Miami is close to being Latin America's cultural and financial capital. The approximately thirty million Latin Americans living in the United States, legally or otherwise, give the United States a Latin population larger than that of most countries south of the Rio Grande.

And yet anti-Americanism is deeply imbedded in the culture of Latin America and has been almost from the beginning of the Latin American states' existence as independent countries at the beginning of the nineteenth century. Indeed, although some of the founding fathers of (Spanish-speaking) Latin America, including Simón Bolívar, Francisco de Miranda, and José Martí, briefly lived in the United States and were profoundly influenced by American political ideas, they all shared an ambivalent attitude toward the Northern giant. Their successors have, more often than not, built on only the anti-American elements of their thought.

Moises Naim, formerly Venezuela's minister of trade and industry (educated at MIT) and later the editor and publisher of *Foreign Policy* magazine, correctly made a distinction between "light" anti-Americanism and its "assassin" form.[1] The latter ends up in terrorism, the former pretends to appreciate the American people but rejects its democratically elected leaders: "We love Americans, but hate their elected leaders"—a claim implausibly made by French haters of the United States as well and shared by American "peace" or "anti-war" militants, Arab adversaries of the United States, and others seeking to make their hostility seem more respectable.

THE BURDEN OF HISTORY

Spanish-speaking America's basic attitudes to economics, religion, and personal conduct have always diverged from the Protestant ethic of North America, all the way back to the conflict between the traditional culture of Spain and the (mostly French) ideas of the Enlightenment. The merchant was seen as inferior in colonial Spanish America, and the worker, if Spanish, even more so. Like the United States' Founding Fathers, Spanish America's liberators—Bolívar, José de San Martin, Bernardo O'Higgins, and Francisco de Santander—embraced the ideas of the French Revolution (secular democracy, well spiced with anti–clericalism, equality, individual liberty, and republicanism) and were often Freemasons. But the Spanish Americans never overcame their Spanish contempt for the merchant and producing classes.

The newly established (often on the basis of rather dubious historic or colonial administrative divisions) Latin American countries were culturally vulnerable due to the absence of a true "national" consciousness. Thus Peru was "liberated" by what today we call Venezuelans and Argentines, against the rather stubborn, pro-Spanish resistance of today's "Peruvians"—mostly Indians. As late as the 1980s, Peruvian highlander Indians were referring to the Lima government as *Señor Gobierno* (Mister Government), a personalized and distant boss. Throughout the nineteenth and early twentieth centuries, the result, especially in Central America, was that Latin American political parties, both conservative and liberal, but all *criollos* (Creoles), looked abroad—which, following the Monroe Doctrine, generally meant Washington—for help in defeating their rivals. Naturally enough, the defeated rivals saw Washington as the national enemy and the gringos as the natural adversary, despite the fact that it was their own countrymen who had asked the gringos to help (as the defeated party would too, in its turn).

In South America, where the United States carried out no significant direct military intervention except for the help it gave to Panamanian secessionists, anti-Americanism began as and remains largely a European-derived intellectual trend. Considering the importance Argentina traditionally had in defining the tone of cultural discourse in South America, the fact that the massive immigration to that country was Italian (with significant Irish, Welsh, and English inputs) has also played a role in separating—first economically and then, more permanently, culturally—the educated elites from the United States. And from separation to disdain and dislike there was only a small distance—but Buenos Aires was far from a peculiar exception.

For most of their history, Latin America's elites were culturally and ideologically more European than "American." Bolivar himself was more likely to quote Montesquieu and Diderot than Jefferson or Madison—though he did consider the United States a sister republic. Later on, as Mexico and Argentina provided most of the intellectual fashions throughout the subcontinent, the former's Pavlovian and the latter's fashionable Parisian anti-Americanism spilled over the rest of the region. Even today, when many distinguished Latin intellectuals peddle their anti-Americanism from tenured positions at Harvard, Stanford, or other American elite educational institutions, their attitudes ultimately derive from those institutions' own European ideological biases.

By the 1930s the United States had intervened militarily in a number of Latin American countries—Mexico aside, mostly in Central America and the Caribbean. Interestingly, and with Mexico again the exception, those "victims" of American imperialism are today the least anti-American countries in the hemisphere, at least in the business sector and the lower classes. Salvadoran,

Nicaraguan, and Guatemalan "oligarchs" tend to own Miami apartments and marry American women—or at least have their children born in the United States; El Salvador has branches of Los Angeles–based gangs; Ecuador, Panama, and El Salvador officially use the dollar; English is widely spoken. Once again, it was the intellectual class—with Mexico's and Argentina's as the models—that began and continues to cultivate anti-American trends, partly as a matter of affirming its own identity.

INTELLECTUAL AND IDEOLOGICAL ANTI-AMERICANISM AND ITS CRITICS

An adverse reaction to historic anti–Americanism in Latin America can also be found, but, significantly, it comes from disappointed or "converted" former leftists. One may think it is the nature of the intellectual to rebel against common wisdom, but not in Latin America. There, rebellion in intellectual circles means only one thing—*rebellion in favor* of the old but fashionable and socially friendly ghost of "Yanqui imperialism." Rejection of the established habits of thinking—such as anti-Americanism and its corollary, support for Fidel Castro—is "reactionary" or worse.

Most Latin American critics of anti-Americanism today are former leftists converted to common sense: Plinio Apuleyo Mendoza, Mario Vargas Llosa, Octavio Paz, and others. Their importance at home is well demonstrated by their current position: Paz is dead, Vargas Llosa is widely unpopular in Peru and lives in Spain and the United States, Mendoza is Colombia's ambassador to Portugal. They broke the mold of what an intellectual in Latin America is supposed to be: anti-American, informed by European (read Parisian) cultural fashions, leaning toward Marxist interpretations of life, and well known in Europe. One of the most accurate descriptions of the roots of anti-Americanism among Latin American intellectuals is provided by José Antonio Aguilar Rivera:

> Victimization has always been a part of nationalist sentiment. Anti-Americanism is an emotionally satisfying explanation of our faults. . . . The intellectuals articulated and encouraged this

sentiment for various reasons. Many of them depended on the
state . . . and anti-Americanism was functional for the state's ideology: revolutionary nationalism. This was grasped by a sociology professor in the mid-1980s when trying to explain the sources
of the anti-yanqui sentiment in Mexico. The Mexican intellectuals' dependence on the state contributed to their nationalist attitudes. For different reasons, the left-wing intelligentsia also bore
an acute anti-Americanism. Whether because the United States
was philosophically and materially the enemy of the proletarian
motherland, or because it was the butcher who cut the veins of
Latin America, the leftist intellectuals joined the nationalist supporters of the government in their anti-Americanism. Even some
intellectuals of the Right joined in and bathed in the Hispanist
and conservative nineteenth-century source, which saw the
Protestant modernity of the United States as an enemy of national identity.[2]

Aguilar Rivera is a Mexican, and he is referring to his own country, but his diagnosis applies to the rest of Latin America as well.
And not just because the roots of anti-Americanism in general are
similar from Tierra del Fuego to the Rio Grande, but also because
of the enormous influence Mexican culture and its anti-American
essence have had upon the rest of the Hemisphere.

While a permanent and historic part of Latin American culture,
anti-Americanism never became an autonomous ideology: it always needed new justifying myths. But for some two hundred years
it has been, and still is, the necessary background or supplement to
other, competing ideologies. Those ideologies—nationalism, Marxism, "Third Worldism" and its latest incarnation, anti-globalism—
all needed and used anti-American components. Latin American
nationalism emerged during the nineteenth century in opposition
to the Monroe Doctrine; for twentieth-century Marxists, the trio of
Castro, Allende, and *el Sandinismo*, provided new idols and models. Nowadays, it is the American-controlled International Monetary Fund (IMF) and the World Trade Organization (as well as
NAFTA in Mexico's case) that provides the fuel and slogans of anti-
Americanism.[3]

A good case could be made that the Latin American intellectuals' admiration for Castro and his revolution was as much a product of their love of the word "revolution" and his fundamental anti-Americanism as it was of the Marxism-Leninism some of them believed in and he personified. That combination of attractions may also explain the still powerful popularity of unorthodox (as far as Moscow was concerned at the time) Latin American Marxist Ernesto "Che" Guevara. Guevara—an Argentine active in Guatemala in 1954, when with U.S. help the Communist-controlled Arbenz regime was removed, later a minister in Cuba's government and a *guerrillero* in the Congo, Guinea Bissau, and finally Bolivia—was and remains the quintessential Latin American alumnus of a public (often, Catholic) university. Che-style revolution promises to make Latin America a global vanguard, or at least a symbol of anti-(American) imperialism. It serves the old (and erroneously labeled "Bolivarian") ideal of achieving a united Spanish America via revolution, and it gives a human identity (no matter how romantically touched up by professional ideologues) to all those confused sentiments pretending to be a continental doctrine.

HEROES OF ANTI-AMERICANISM

It has been a widely held myth that Salvador Allende, a "democratically elected" (with 36 percent of the vote) "progressive" leader was overthrown by a cabal of General Pinochet's military gorillas and the CIA on September 11, 1973. The facts that Allende received only slightly more than a third of the popular vote in 1970 (which meant that he was not even constitutionally entitled to be president, as the Chilean Congress was supposed to choose between the two front-runners who were virtually tied at that time), that his democratic credentials were so doubtful that the left-of-center Christian Democrats had to ask him to sign a special declaration that he would respect the Constitution, and that while governing he showed little respect for law and constitutional rule—all this is forgotten. What remains is the notion of a CIA plot to overthrow "democratic Allende"—as if the Chilean military needed CIA assistance to stage a coup d'état. Ultimately the perception of students in Latin America's schools and state universities—shaped by leftist teachers—is that Allende was a democratic hero killed by the monster of the North.

Facts calling into question the Allende myth are beginning to be noted by voices of the left. Some leftist analysts have admitted that his regime made serious mistakes, including the irresponsible and hurried imposition of a revolutionary program upon an unprepared populace, and alienation of the centrist Christian Democrats. As a reformed member of the Chilean Communist party wrote recently:

> It should not be forgotten that on August 22, 1973, in the middle of extreme shortages of basic goods, acute political violence and economic crisis, the Chilean Chamber of Deputies declared [Allende's] Popular Unity government illegal. . . . Castro played a decisive role in wearing Allende down: first, by organizing and financing the Movement of the Revolutionary Left, a guerrilla group that aggressively pursued socialism through a campaign of bombings, assassinations and bank robberies during the Allende years, and, second, through the military training of ultra-Left members of Allende's own Socialist Party and other small leftist parties.[4]

All this was later forgotten in the fog of anti-American ideology, a fog now made thicker by former leftist radicals posing as human rights activists in Argentina, Peru, Chile, and elsewhere. In mostly conservative and highly successful Chile, statues of Allende are erected and his downfall seen as a national failure, rather than as the opening of the path to freedom and economic development it was. Hence Chile had to take a position against the United States on Iraq in the UN Security Council—a bone thrown to domestic public opinion, albeit one that was counterproductive at a time Chile was lobbying Congress for access to NAFTA.

Nicaragua's Sandinistas, like Castroist Cuba before them, were widely seen by most Latin American elites as the Latin David fighting the giant of El Norte. Havana's massive support of the Sandinistas in their overthrow of the Somoza regime only reinforced that image. For Castro, helping Daniel Ortega and his brother, and the sinister secret police of Tomás Borge, were part and parcel of fighting American imperialism. Nicaraguan "socialism" might have meant sacrificing Nicaragua's Miskito Indians, who opposed the Sandinistas, but humiliating Washington was more important. The result was that, like Allende's Chile, Nicaragua became a magnet for all the failed totalitarian guerrillas of the Southern Cone—people like the recently pardoned continental assassin Enrique Gorriarán Merlo of Argentina, who murdered the most competent anti-Sandinista commander and assassinated Somoza himself in Paraguay at the Sandinistas' command. That he also ordered and planned an assault on an Argentine military barracks in 1986, under a left-of-center, democratically elected government was apparently less important in Latin American intellectual circles than his career of revolutionary murder. Hence, not surprisingly, in 2003 his pardon became the last decision of the outgoing Argentine president.

The Sandinistas, for reasons including their imitation of and control from Havana, became heroes of the anti-American left, who mistook the Nicaraguan guerrilla leader Augusto Sandino's combination of anti-communism, nationalism, and physiocracy for an actual philosophy.[5] Like Allende, Sandino became what his ideological manipulators wanted him to become: an anti-American saint.

Fidel Castro, above all others, remains the preeminent hero of Latin Americanism because he endured—and thus personified anti-Americanism as a lasting and feasible belief. The thinning ranks of Castro's supporters among Latin American intellectuals were, however, somewhat shaken in the spring of 2003 when Havana executed three hijackers and imprisoned seventy-five peaceful dissidents. José Saramago, the Portuguese Communist party member and Nobel laureate for literature, touched off a debate when he withdrew his support of Castro, saying the regime had "lost my confidence, damaged my hopes, cheated my dreams."[6] In a letter to the *Reforma*, Mexican novelist Carlos Fuentes congratulated Saramago for drawing a line, but managed to expand the discussion to include Bush and the war on Iraq, adding, "I am against Bush and against Castro"—as if the two were morally or politically equivalent. Uruguayan Eduardo Galeano, author of Latin America's most popular, and most primitive book, *The Open Veins of Latin America* (1971),[7] joined the debate. In "Cuba Hurts" (*Progressive*, June 2003), he wrote of being saddened by the executions and arrests, but nonetheless found a way to lay blame at America's door:

> The recent wave of executions and arrests in Cuba is good news for the universal superpower . . . that indefatigable mill of world dictators . . . which remains obsessed with removing this persistent thorn from its paw. . . . They make martyrs for freedom of expression certain groups that operated openly from the house of James Cason, representative of Bush interests in Havana. . . . Do true revolutions . . . like Cuba's, need to learn bad habits from the enemies they are fighting? The death penalty has no justification. The revolution, which was capable of surviving the fury of ten American Presidents and twenty CIA directors, needs the energy that comes from participation and diversity to face the dark times that surely lie ahead.

Galeano's book was a rehash of theories of world development and dependency—including, naturally, Frantz Fanon's *The Wretched of the Earth* (1961; introduced, not surprisingly, by Jean-Paul Sartre). Simplifying nineteenth-century anti-Americanism in fashionable post-1968 terms, Galeano attributed all of Latin America's ills to the evils of American imperialism and capitalism. As postulated by dependency theory, wealthy countries are rich because poor countries are poor, world trade is a zero-sum game, and "the International Monetary Fund and World Bank emerged to deny underdeveloped countries the right of protecting their national industries and to discourage state action in those countries."[8]

Only the tightest ideological blinders could lead to the conclusion that Latin America's economic underdevelopment is due to international institutions created for the benefit American interests. Sweeping claims of Latin American underdevelopment themselves are far from well established. During the 1930s, Argentina had a higher per capita income than Canada or Australia; Chile today is, by all standards, a developed country, even if its neighbors are not. No matter—Galeano and his book are still the Bible of the anti-American left.

Here we come to a major misconception shared by Latin America's left and right alike: the belief that they are incapable of doing anything of importance independent of Washington's manipulation or control. Thus generals or colonels cannot stage coups without the CIA telling them when and how, and guerrillas cannot become a threat without leftists in Washington encouraging them and weakening their patriotic opponents. In this paternalistic view Latin Americans are children in Washington's care, a belief shared by elitist Marxists and conservative nationalist officers alike.

Aguilar Rivera observes the often unnoticed fact that anti-Americanism has multiple and ideologically incompatible sources. While the left is still the most vocal, effective, and persistent standard-bearer of hatred for the United States, the farther one moves to the right, the more common anti-Americanism becomes. The same meeting of the extremes is apparent in Europe as well.

During two decades of travels to countries such as Guatemala, El Salvador, and Peru, researching revolutionary movements, I have been confronted many times by military officers and their allies in the business community who accused the United States of supporting terrorism, of being controlled by Jewish leftists, and of using human rights as a pretext for destroying tradition, Catholic values, and ultimately the sovereignty of their countries. Such sentiments peaked during the Carter administration, which was widely perceived by Latin conservatives and rightists as supporting Marxist subversion.

It is a common error on the part of both American and Latin American analysts to single out Marxism as the prime source of the Latin American intellectuals' hostility to the United States. A better case could be made by proposing that Marxism was, and remains, a convenient device for expressing, justifying, and articulating a preexisting, underlying sentiment; that is to say, many Latin intellectuals became attracted to Marxism because it provided them with a framework for articulating and validating an anti-Americanism already strongly felt. The influence of European (usually French) intellectuals, from Sartre to Frantz Fanon, and often years of living in Paris, added to the appeal of these ideas.

THE ROLE OF THE LEFT, MARXISM AS FASHION

By the 1920s, under the influence of Marxism-Leninism, Latin Americans who had previously expressed a combination of envy of and frustration with America increasingly articulated their feelings in new, convenient terminology borrowed from Europe. Correspondingly the tone and structure of the new anti-American discourse were largely European imports. The most influential Latin American writers were educated in Europe, often Paris. The great Nicaraguan poet Rubén Darío lived in Paris, and Nobel laureate Miguel Angel Asturias (a Communist sympathizer at home) was Guatemala's ambassador there. Chilean Pablo Neruda, another Nobel laureate, was a prominent activist and Stalinist and a leader of his country's Communist party, while Peru's best-known and beloved poet, César Vallejo, was a Paris-based Marxist. At the same time his fellow Peruvian (and a still influential philosopher among the country's Maoist terrorists), José Carlos Mariátegui, founded the country's Communist party after spending time in Paris.

Not all Latin American intellectuals hated the United States with the same intensity, or acted upon that sentiment. Miguel Angel Asturias blamed American companies in his country, Guatemala, for all its problems, but that did not interfere with his becoming Guatemala's ambassador to Paris and a supporter of his country's elected pro-American and non-Marxist government. Neruda, on the other hand, went much further: as Chilean consul in Paris (to the Spanish Republican government in exile) he virtually sentenced to death Spanish Republicans who were not Communist party members by denying them the chance to obtain an emigration visa—phony as that might have been. By doing so he contributed to the liquidation of democratic and anarchist refugees from the Spanish Civil War of whom the Soviet Union did not approve; he also wrote hymns to Stalin. By contrast, although a Communist, César Vallejo mostly confined himself to writing poetry; and Argentine Julio Cortázar moved from supporting Franco to "progressive" causes.

In the post–cold war world, anti-globalism and human rights have replaced communism as causes associated with opposition to everything American. This opposition—again from the left and often disguised as a concern for human rights—became especially virulent after September 11 as the Bush administration embarked on its war on terror. Argentine Adolfo Perez Esquivel, a devoted anti-American who, evidently for some politically correct reason won the 1980 Nobel Peace Prize, characterizes the 2003 war on Iraq as a "crime against humanity":

> The novelist Gore Vidal has made the point clear: the true motive behind the war against Iraq is oil and empire. Apparently, the cost of human lives and resources does not concern Bush and company as long as they reach their economic and political objectives. . . . A related situation . . . is militarization on our continent by US forces—including the Plan Colombia and, in Central America, the Puebla Panama Plan. Bush is . . . threatening to free all the evils of the apocalyptic beast, seeking destruction and death.[9]

Perez Esquivel's rather unoriginal if fierce anti-Americanism is nurtured and shared by Americans in the United States or elsewhere (Gore Vidal lives in Italy). He would be another obscure Argentine leftist without the Nobel Committee's providing him with the legitimacy conferred by the 1980 Peace Prize.

The likes of Perez Esquivel are relative moderates compared to the remnants of the defeated totalitarian revolutionaries of the Southern Cone (Chile, Argentina, Uruguay), best represented by the Argentine Mothers of the Plaza de Mayo, led by Hebe de Bonafini, whose hatred for the United States puts her to the left of Havana. In a post-9/11 interview, Bonafini declared that "In the Twin Towers died the powerful. And the powerful are my enemy; because it is the same that killed my children [i.e., her terrorist Montoneros "children" killed during Argentina's civil war of the mid-1970s]." Asked about the fact that office workers of African, Argentine, and Muslim origin were also killed, she answered, "What does that have to do with anything? . . . It is true: I am happy and celebrate the fact that this savage capitalism which destroys us has for once been hit. I do not feel sorry over them." While admitting that there are a few "good Americans," such as Noam Chomsky and SUNY Binghamton's James Petras, she made it clear that she hates the American people as such. She concluded, "Now things are clear. Revolution is the only way people could succeed . . . you are either imperialist or Marxist."[10]

The Reverend Miguel D'Escoto, a U.S.-educated Maryknoll priest and former Sandinista foreign minister, said shortly after 9/11 (and just before the Nicaraguan presidential elections, in which former president Daniel Ortega once more lost his bid for election):

> We must congratulate Washington because their intimidation tactics worked. . . . They are now into electoral terrorism [in Nicaragua, that is] among a people here where the wounds are still open. We did not lose 5,000 people like in New York, we lost 50,000 in a war that was invented, organized, armed and financed by the United States.[11]

The problem is not just that D'Escoto used to be a supporter of the Somozas before 1979. His explanation of why the Sandinistas seemed poised to again lose an election, as they had in 1990 and 1996, is another example of the belief of the Latin left that nothing they are opposed to can occur without American ill will and interference.

Faced with the increased popularity of the dollar and masses of their compatriots trying to get into the belly of the beast (that is, illegally migrate to the United States), Latin American elites had to find new flags to march under against the imperialists of El Norte. The new face of the American monster is *neoliberalismo*. The term itself demonstrates how far behind global developments Latin America's intelligentsia and a growing number of politicians remain. What they mean by neoliberalism is free-market, free-enterprise economies and free international trade with low or nonexistent barriers—that is to say, what is normally considered modern capitalism or liberalism in its original nineteenth-century and contemporary European meaning. But, on a continent where capitalism of this type has never existed, only its savage, corrupt, protectionist, and unregulated version—modern capitalism is indeed new. Hence *neoliberalismo.*

INTELLECTUALS AND THEIR COUNTRIES

In her foreword to the twenty-fifth-anniversary edition of Galeano's book mentioned earlier, Isabel Allende writes, "I could not miss the opportunity to write this introduction and thank Eduardo Galeano publicly for his stupendous love for freedom, and for his contribution to my awareness as a writer and as a citizen of Latin America."[12] That says it all: her political ideas came from Galeano (or similar sources), and she sees herself as a "citizen of Latin America" rather than a Chilean. Such a sought-after Latin American identity is one of the hallmarks of the intellectuals' deep anti-Americanism. They live in a closed circle of often exiled and always denationalized, rootless individuals, known, published, and applauded abroad more than in their own countries. The members of this narrow international fraternity bear closer resemblance to their European, American Ivy League, and New York colleagues than to the hundreds of millions of ordinary citizens of Latin America, few of whom could read or afford to buy their books.

Being socially unrepresentative does not make such intellectuals less influential where it counts, either at home or abroad. University education has been much more accessible in Latin America, especially in public institutions such as Mexico's National Autonomous University (UNAM, the world's largest university, which introduced its first non-Marxist course on economics less than a decade ago) as well as in older and until recently respected universities such as San Carlos in Guatemala and San Marcos in Peru. While a dubious investment of scarce public funds in countries with high levels of illiteracy, these universities have greatly expanded the influence of radical, or simply fashionable, intellectuals and strengthened the traditional social respect they have always enjoyed within Latin America.

The Nobel Peace Prize Selection Committee was of late also drawn to anti-Americanism. Esquivel in Argentina and Rigoberta Menchú in Guatemala have been exceedingly critical of, even hostile to, the United States. Esquivel is a man of the left and demonstrates it with every statement he makes. In turn, Menchú is a committed Marxist revolutionary and the poster woman of international political correctness. In awarding her the 1992 prize, the Nobel Committee was able to honor a woman, a leftist, and an Indian all at once—important in a year that celebrated the quincentenary of the discovery of the Americas by Christopher Columbus and the beginning of what Galeano calls "five centuries of the pillage of a continent." The prize also gave Menchú an international forum for denouncing the war in Iraq as "the threshold of an announced genocide" and an opportunity to call on the people of the world to "oppose the New Imperial Disorder."[13]

EUROPEAN VERSUS INDIAN

It would be futile to try to find a statue of Hernán Cortés in Mexico, a country he founded; likewise in Peru, statues of Francisco Pizarro, essentially the country's founder, are rare. The ethnic European origins of Latin America are increasingly played down everywhere, it seems. Correspondingly the United States has come to symbolize the ills of this European heritage in Latin America. Nonetheless it was the European intellectual influence that created what Carlos Rangel called the process of change from "the good savage to the good revolutionary," and from the noble savage to the noble revolutionary, from Cuauhtémoc or Atahualpa to Che or Fidel.

Since the Spanish Conquest was made possible by Spain's numerous Indian allies against the romanticized Aztec mass murderers and Inca would-be totalitarians,[14] it takes a priori anti-Westernism á la Galeano to explain the post-Cortés history of Latin America as a story of European exploitation: first Spanish, then British, and for the past century or so, American. The idealized and victimized image of "the Indian" has become the latest stimulant of anti-Americanism among Spanish-writing Latin American intellectuals, including such self-appointed advocates of the Indians as Rafael Guillén, a.k.a. Sub-comandante Marcos, the blue-eyed, middle-class ex-professor at a public university and self-appointed representative of the Indians of Mexico's Chiapas region. Equally fair-skinned Uruguayans of European origin, such as the Tupamaros leader Raúl Sendic (of Croatian background) or his Argentine counterpart, also of Croatian background, Mario Firmenich of the "Montoneros," have offered themselves as guardians of an imaginary non-European "America," all of them holding forth on behalf of the Indians in Spanish, needless to say.

All of them undertook to wage revolutionary war against European exploitation in the name of "authentic" Indian symbols—such as Gabriel Condor, a.k.a Tupac Amaru II, another ambiguous case of an eighteenth-century mixed-blood Indian claimant to purity. And so it went, from the similarly implausible Victor Polay, a Sorbonne-educated leader of the Peruvian Revolutionary Movement Tupac Amaru (MRTA), to the so-called Movimiento Estudiantil Chicano de Aztlán (MECHA) of the U.S. Southwest, seeking separation from the United States of an imaginary region, Aztlán, defined in pre-Colombian terms.

Once again, it all comes down to an imitation of the European and European-influenced North American admiration for the noble savage. It goes all the way back to the French Enlightenment, to Voltaire, Diderot, and, especially, Rousseau. Simply put, "stone-age culture is good, modern culture—especially European—bad." The outlook is widely embraced by the elites.

ANTI-AMERICANISM AND THE CATHOLIC CHURCH

Arguably the Catholic church, or at least those parts of it never rebuffed by the Vatican until the papacy of John Paul II, had greater responsibility for anti-Americanism in Latin America than any other force, save possibly the Marxist left. Samuel Ruiz García, a now (forcibly) retired Chiapas Catholic bishop, was the actual founder of the popular Frente Zapatista de Liberación Nacional

(FZLN) and responsible for hiring "Sub-comandante Marcos" as its spokesman. In Guatemala, Maryknollers worked closely with the Castroite guerrillas, recruiting and indoctrinating on their behalf. Jesuits, wherever they could, radicalized the young at Catholic universities or locally disseminated anti-capitalist, anti-U.S. "liberation theology." Catholic radicals legitimized violence against governments, elected or not; against the "structural violence" alleged to be inherent to capitalism and against U.S. influence. It may well be that it was precisely the Guatemalan church's close association with Marxism and the Castroist guerrillas that explains why Guatemala today is Latin America's only country where the majority of the population is no longer Catholic.

Most of the Catholic clergy involved in these activities were either European or American, like the American-born James Carney, a.k.a. Padre Guadalupe, who was killed in 1983 in Honduras while a member, if not a leader, of a pro-Sandinista guerrilla unit. Again, it is notable that while anti-Americanism has deep historic roots in Latin America, its recent articulation and organization has required European and even North American assistance and influence.

POLITICS AND ANTI-AMERICANISM

In November 2002, Evo Morales, Bolivian presidential runner-up and leader of that country's second-largest party, the Movement to Socialism (MAS), urged Brazil's President Inacio Lula da Silva, Venezuelan President Hugo Chávez, and Ecuador's President Lucio Gutiérrez to join together to oppose the Free Trade Area of the Americas (ALCA) proposed by President Bush earlier that year. By rejecting the proposal, he said, "for the first time in Latin America the Empire could be defeated. . . . ALCA is a neocolonization project. . . . It should be called [the] area of free gain of the Americas. If it is approved it would be a policy of economic genocide."[15] What makes Morales's statements important, besides being made in Havana, is that except for Lula, the other two presidents—or "comrades," as he called them—although democratically elected, were both former military officers involved in failed coups d'état against democratic governments in Caracas and Quito, respectively. Anti-

Americanism, anti-capitalism, and contempt (or, at the very least, a highly ambiguous attitude) toward democracy are the hallmarks of Latin anti-Americanism, whether of the left or the right.

Whether or not a coalition of the newly elected or otherwise powerful leftists of Latin America will join together in a coherent anti-U.S. strategy remains to be seen. Gutiérrez and Lula must deal with the reality of dependence upon IMF loans, sniping from the left, and opposition from conservatives, while Chávez faces strong internal opposition, including that of the trade unions. Nevertheless, rhetorically at least, the anti-American left is again on the march south of the Rio Grande. Argentine students celebrated the 9/11 terrorist attacks; Mexico and Chile joined French hostility to Washington in the UN Security Council during the run-up to Iraq; Rigoberta Menchú still insists that imperialism and capitalism (read the United States) are the root of the problems of indigenous people everywhere and Castro's image, albeit somewhat tarnished, remains largely positive in elite intellectual circles in most Latin American countries.

At the same time a creeping cultural revolution has also been occurring in Latin America since the 1970s. It started where it should have: in the universities. It used to be that Latin Americans with ambitions for higher education had only two options: if wealthy or lucky enough to obtain scholarships, they could study abroad; if not, they would have to study at state universities, which had been dominated by the Marxist left since the 1950s and where the study of revolution rather than economics or engineering was the fashion. Attempts to find an alternative have been made since the 1960s, such as the locally and privately funded University of Central America José Simeón Cañas in El Salvador, founded in 1965; however the former Marxist Catholics (mostly Jesuits) who took control of it not only copied but added legitimacy to the radical curriculum of the public institutions. Genuine change began with the appearance of such small and plucky institutions like the Francisco Marroquin University in Ciudad de Guatemala, where politics are banned and the library is named after free-market economist Friedrich Hayek. Such trends have snowballed since, with private, nonpolitical institutions, such as the Universidad del Pacifico in Lima, becoming dominant in many countries. Private universities have given middle-class youth a chance to study something other than guerrilla warfare, the romantic exploits of Che, or the virtues of Marx's social and economic analysis. Today in cultural bellweather Mexico, the Instituto Tecnologico de Monterey, established on the MIT model eight decades ago, is more respected and sought over than UNAM. It has real or virtual campuses in most Mexican states and is seen by ambitious young people as the best path to a career in business.

CONCLUSIONS

Latin American anti-Americanism is not a superficial, imported cultural-political phenomenon, much as it may be influenced by certain trends abroad. It is a deeply rooted disposition, also shared by the many illegal or legal immigrants to the United States who seek prosperity but not citizenship; by intellectuals who accept well-paying sinecures at prestigious Ivy League institutions, only to use those platforms to attack the country making them welcome; and by politicians who hide from their constituencies their actual support of U.S. policies. This being the case, it would be hard to dispel these attitudes with a propaganda offensive by the U.S. government. Culturally there is not much that Washington can do about anti-Americanism south of the Rio Grande. As long as the rejection of and hostility toward the United States and American culture continue to dominate the elite U.S. universities in which many Latinos get educated, these sentiments will persist both south and north of the border. Making the United States look good in Buenos Aires, La Paz, or even Santiago is not only an expensive but ultimately hopeless task.

Change, however, is coming from within Latin America itself. Private, nonpoliticized universities provide the best hope in the long run to make a dent in the stale attitudes of anti-Americanism and anti-capitalism and increase the appeal of political democracy and free-market economics among young Peruvians, Colombians, Mexicans, and others.

In the final analysis, the root of Latin American anti-Americanism lies in the insecurity of its intellectual class, torn as it is between admiration for Europe and the distance separating their countries from it, between their own beliefs and those of the masses and between the reality of American proximity and power, and, after almost two centuries of independence, the often vague and undefined sense of nationhood of their compatriots. Add to this the financial crisis that Latin American intellectuals are experiencing as government cuts in spending and competition from private educational institutions reduce the availability of sinecure positions. Consequently many intellectuals, feeling marginalized and frustrated, seek refuge in the mushrooming nongovernmental organizations (NGOs), especially those specializing in human rights. These positions depend heavily upon outside (American and European) financing, and that financing is accompanied by a congenial dose of anti-Americanism, anti-globalism/*altermundism*, and, naturally enough, anti-capitalism. Being part of what Naim calls "a global anti-American chorus"[16] gives these intellectuals a sense of importance and belonging to a larger cause—just as the myth of the "noble savage," reinvigorated under the guise of "indigenous rights" and the persistent admiration for the failed Che, did before.

There is also an element of escapism in present day anti-Americanism in Latin America and elsewhere. Jacques Julliard, an editor of *Le Nouvel Observateur*, has aptly described anti-Americanism as the "socialism of imbeciles."[17] The nostalgic purveyors of "socialism" continue to project their old dreams (which vanished when socialism ended in Prague and Bucharest in 1989) onto figures such as Chávez and Lula and the old Fidel. Consequently the United States is hated more as a symbol of the values it stands for (including opposition to socialism) than for anything it has done or does. Anti-Americanism today, associated as it is with nostalgia for failed and discredited socialist regimes, experiments, and ideas, is profoundly reactionary, whether it comes from the "progressive" left, as it does more often than not, or from the unreconstructed right.

NOTES

1. Moises Naim, "Los peligros del antiamericanismo 'light,'" *El Pais*, Feb. 22, 2002.

2. José Antonio Aguilar Rivera, "El mito del antiamericanismo," at www.nexos.com.mx/aguilar.html. Author's translation.

3. Roberto Ampuero, "The Left Killed Allende, Too," *Washington Post*, Sept. 8, 2003.

4. Ibid.

5. According to Plinio Apuleyo Mendoza, Carlos Alberto Montaner, Alvaro Vargas Llosa, *Manual del perfecto Idiota latino americano*, Plaza & Janes, Barcelona, 1996.

6. *Pubicado en el Pais Madrid*, at http//www.arnoldbaguilla.com/saramgo.html

7. Eduardo Galeano, *Open Veins of Latin America: Five Centuries of the Pillage of a Continent*. With a new Foreword by Isabel Allende, twenty-fifth anniversary edition, Monthly Review Press, New York, 1997, p. 204.

8. Ibid.

9. Adolfo Perez Esquivel, "In the Event of War, Bush Should Be Declared 'Criminal Against Humanity,'" *Global Viewpoint*, Mar. 6, 2003, at www .digitalnpq.org/global_services/global%20viewpoint/03-06-03.html.

10. For complete text in Spanish, see www.eurosur.org/rebelion/internacional/hebeo31101.htm.

11. David Gonzalez, "Nicaragua Voters Reject Ortega's Bid for the Presidency," *New York Times*, Nov. 6, 2001.

12. Galeano, op. cit., p. xiii.

13. "Rigoberta Menchu calls to stop the war," *América Latina en Movimiento*, Mar. 20, 2003, www.alainet.org.

14. The literature on the Aztecs' downfall is too abundant to be quoted; for the Incas, see Waldemar Espinoza Soriano, *La destrucción del imperio de los Incas*, *Amaru Editores*, Lima, 1996. On the other hand, denials of the mass murder dependency of the Aztec state are often explained away as politically incorrect.

15. Gerardo Arreola, "Fidel Castro encabezó el encuentro hemisférico de lucha contra el irea comercial. Llama Evo Morales a Lula, Chivez y Lucio Gutiérrez a rechazar el ALCA," *La Jornada*, Nov. 28, 2002.

16. As in the Latin quip it is only a slight exaggeration that an Argentine is a Spanish-speaking Italian who pretends to be British—an example of ambiguous identity.

17. Jacques Julliard, "Miseria del antiamericanismo," *El Mundo* (Madrid), Nov. 16, 2001.

7

DAVID BROOKS

Nicaraguan Anti-Americanism

If he [George W. Bush] is really to capture Bin Laden, then all the President has to do is to look in the mirror. That way he [Bush] can—with our help if he so desires—hang himself, shoot himself, cut his own throat, cut out his own guts or do whatever he thinks will make his enemy suffer more, an enemy that is, in the end, [Bush] himself.—Fredy Quezada, "George Bush Is Bin Laden," *El Nuevo Diario*, October 11, 2001.

In these crucial moments for humanity's future, please accept in your own name and in the name of your people the strongest possible signs of solidarity from the Sandinista National Liberation Front (FSLN) and from the people of Nicaragua, defenders and lovers of peace.—Letter from FSLN General Secretary Daniel Ortega to President Saddam Hussein of Iraq, made public in Havana, Cuba, March 18, 2003.[1]

If judged by size, population, and proximity to the United States, Nicaragua would hardly seem a likely setting for significant anti-Americanism. The country is small, containing a population of just over five million. Nicaragua has historically depended on the United States for investment and aid. Many Nicaraguans, particularly those in the upper classes, have had strong cultural and family ties to the United States. Baseball, a game learned from the U.S. Marines, is the country's most popular sport. Nonetheless Nicaragua has developed a persistent strain of anti-U.S. feeling that has dramatically and, I believe, destructively influenced the country's history.

Several important features distinguish the Nicaraguan case from others among its hemispheric neighbors. Nicaragua is the only country in Latin America, aside from Cuba, to undergo a successful Marxist-Leninist revolution during the cold war. It is also the only country in the world—other than the United States—that has ever had a president who was an American national. And Nicaragua is one of the few places in the Western Hemisphere where the United States has suffered significant military setbacks. From 1927 to 1933, Nicaraguan General Augusto Cesar Sandino fought the U.S. Marines in a bitter guerrilla war. His resistance made him a folk hero for some Nicaraguans and for many across Latin America.

These characteristics have not so much set Nicaragua apart from the rest of Latin America as they have placed the country in the forefront of anti-Americanism. Nicaragua has been from time to time a symbol, a vehicle, and even a battleground for both Latin American and extra-hemispheric opponents of the United States. In the 1980s, for example, Nicaragua became the destination for many leftist "political pilgrims" from around the world (myself included).[2] Its confrontations with the United States have, at key moments, lent Nicaragua and some of the country's leaders a hemispheric and even global prominence they would otherwise never have achieved. At the same time, the transformation of Nicaragua from a country into a cause has carried a high price for the majority of Nicaraguans.[3]

This essay is divided into three parts. The first traces the historical roots of Nicaragua's complex and conflicted relationship with the United States. The second discusses the Sandinista period during which (from 1979 to 1990) the Marxist-Leninist Sandinista National Liberation Front (FSLN) ruled Nicaragua. The FSLN attempted to transform Nicaragua into a socialist state aligned with Cuba and the USSR. As part of this program the party tried to create and promote an official or state sponsored anti-Americanism resembling Cuba's. The Sandinistas' anti-Americanism had an important international dimension that gave them a global following even as it weakened them internally

The final part of this essay deals with anti-Americanism since 1990, a period during which Nicaragua ceased to be a cause célèbre of the global left and the country's political actors were compelled to adjust to competitive democratic politics. This section focuses on the decade's end, a time when the terrorist attacks in New York, the U.S. war against the Taliban in Afghanistan, and the U.S.-led overthrow of Saddam Hussein raised the profile of anti-Americanism worldwide. Some Nicaraguans interpreted those events through the prism of classic anti-American themes and tropes. This last section suggests that while Nicaraguan anti-Americanism is not a mass phenomenon, it is likely to be an enduring one.

YANQUIS AND ANTI-YANQUIS IN NICARAGUAN HISTORY

Many Nicaraguans and outside observers have lamented Nicaragua's misfortunes. In just the last three decades, the country has suffered a devastating earthquake, a revolution, civil war, and two hurricanes. Throughout its history, regimes of both the left and the right have engaged in systematic corruption that has created much misery for the country's people. Nicaragua enters the twenty-first century as the second poorest country in the Western Hemisphere after Haiti and the poorest in Central America.[4]

The proximity of Nicaragua to the United States, the contrast between Nicaraguan poverty and U.S. prosperity, and, most important, the long history of U.S.-Nicaraguan conflicts and frequent U.S. interventions have caused some Nicaraguans to conclude that their country's greatest problem is the United States. For members of this group, resistance to Washington is the defining character of their national identity. Nicaraguan author and former FSLN vice president Sergio Ramírez describes this tradition in his recent memoir *Adios Muchachos* when he writes,

> For more than a century, no other Latin American country has been more subject to the abuse and victimization of the United

States than Nicaragua, from the moment that William Walker, an adventurer from Tennessee, proclaimed himself president of the country in 1855. . . .[5]

As a result, Ramirez continues, when the Sandinistas took over Nicaragua in 1979, their conflict with the United States was predestined:

> The [FSLN's] discourse had no fissures. They [the United States] were the cause of all the bad things in our history; they had sustained the [Somoza] dictatorship by an obscene patrimony and had nurtured country-selling politicians; they had sacked our natural resources, the mines, the forests; the declaration of our sovereignty could only be realized against the United States.[6]

Miguel D'Escoto Brockmann, FSLN foreign minister in the 1980s and still a leading adviser to Sandinista leader Daniel Ortega, expressed this globalized version of Nicaraguan anti-Americanism recently when he attacked the U.S. intervention in Iraq. D'Escoto suggested that U.S. intervention in any part of the world is nothing more than

> . . . the logical development of the pernicious ideology of Manifest Destiny that, while only so named in 1845, was present [in U.S. history] from 1776 with the genocide of the American Indians, with the Monroe Doctrine in 1823, with William Walker, with the Roosevelt Corollary in 1904, with the atomic bomb, with the uninterrupted aggression against Cuba for more than forty years, with Vietnam, with the war against Nicaragua in the 1980s and with hundreds of criminal interventions against countries all over the world.[7]

The historical record shows that both individual Americans and the U.S. government have frequently had a strong and, to say the least, controversial impact on Nicaraguan affairs. From 1855 to 1857 an American soldier of fortune, William Walker, took over Nicaragua and tried to transform it into an English-speaking, slaveholding state. In 1909 President William Howard Taft's administration insisted on the resignation of Nicaraguan President José Santos Zelaya after Zelaya had executed two Americans who had fought with his political rivals. Three years later Taft sent the Marines into Nicaragua, and they stayed for more than twenty years. They returned in 1926 and became embroiled in the guerrilla conflict with Nicaraguan Liberal General Augusto Sandino. During the 1980s the United States aided and the CIA trained an army of anti-Communist Nicaraguan guerrillas, the Nicaraguan Resistance (RN), which forced the Sandinista regime to agree to internationally supervised elections in 1990.

From slaveholding soldiers of fortune to U.S. Marines to CIA-supported rebels, Nicaraguan history provides ample ammunition for those inclined to blame the United States for the misfortunes of the country. The problem with the story of U.S.-Nicaraguan relations as described by Ramirez D'Escoto and others similarly disposed is not what it tells, but what it leaves out.

REVISITING NICARAGUAN HISTORY

Nicaragua has been more than passive clay molded by the United States. From its origins, the country has been afflicted by poverty, natural disaster, and political division. Since independence there have been only two periods of extended stability, institutional development, and economic growth: the so-called Thirty Years of the Conservative Republic in the late nineteenth century, and the Somoza period in the twentieth century. Other than those years and the last decade, Nicaragua has been ruled by autocrats, suffered internal political divisions, been involved in confrontations with the United States, and experienced economic difficulties.

The Spanish Conquest left Nicaragua with a doleful legacy of caste and class divisions that continues to this day. A privileged elite of mainly European origins rules a large, indigenous, and impoverished underclass. The Nicaraguan elite, however, has suffered more internal divisions than those in other Latin American countries. Soon after gaining independence, Nicaragua's leaders, like those in other Latin American countries, divided into rival groups, Conservatives and Liberals. In practice these divisions were far more fluid than the dichotomy suggests. Both sides produced strong-man leaders, *caudillos*, adept at using oratory and personal courage to raise large armies of impoverished followers who fought both out of personal loyalty and for personal gain.[8]

The importance of *caudillo* leadership, or *caudillismo*, cannot be underestimated in Nicaraguan politics. Nicaragua, in the words of E. Bradford Burns, was a society of lighter-skinned patriarchs and more ethnically Indian folk. The patriarchs engaged in near-constant warfare with one another, warfare carried out according to male codes of personal and familial rivalry that gave Nicaraguan conflict a feudal flavor.

These deep personal rivalries between Liberal and Conservative leaders were intensified by a seemingly contradictory phenomenon, and one that persists to this day in Nicaragua: the intimate ties that bind political rivals and their families. Despite mutual antagonisms, Liberal and Conservative elites were members of the same high society (*"la sociedad"*) and were frequently connected by marriage.

During the 1980s Nicaragua's most famous clan, the Chamorros, became similarly divided. The children of former Nicaraguan President Violeta Chamorro were split between the Sandinistas, the anti-Communist Nicaraguan Resistance, and the internal civic opposition to the FSLN. This has led more than one observer of Nicaraguan politics to describe the country's politics as a "family affair."[9]

The deadly jousting among Nicaraguan elites continued into the twentieth century, giving rise to the oft-repeated Central American lament, "In Nicaragua, there are no Nicaraguans, only Liberals and Conservatives."[10] Nicaraguan politics revolved around intense struggles between patriarchal male leaders of the country's most important families. In what might seem almost a caricature of Max Weber's model of charismatic authority, these figures were frequently lionized by their lower-class followers and invested with allegedly preternatural powers. Conservative *caudillo* Emiliano Chamorro was known as *"El Cadejo,"* a mythical wolflike creature that could disappear at will. Augusto Sandino was thought to possess special abilities to elude his enemies.

In Nicaragua the culture of charismatic attachment also included foreigners. U.S. Marine Lt. Lewis B. Puller led an elite unit of pro-U.S. Nicaraguans against Sandinista guerrillas during the war with Sandino, from 1927 to 1933. Reportedly, the Nicaraguans called Puller "the Tiger of the Mountains." Decades later, Nicaraguans would fall for John Kennedy, "the most popular American in the history of Nicaragua," in a way that confirms the importance of charisma in Nicaragua's political culture of *caudillismo*.[11] As Arturo Cruz, Jr., concluded, "What tied a Nicaraguan leader to his followers was finally something personal—a form of loyalty appropriate to a world of atavisms."[12]

This kind of political culture made compromise difficult. Coming to an agreement with a hated rival would fatally undermine one's personal dignity. In Nicaraguan history when such pacts take place they usually result in tactical cease-fires rather than true bi-partisanship. They also usually result in the political self-destruction of at least one of the parties who makes the agreement.

INTERVENTION BY INVITATION

If the domestic social and cultural tradition fed conflict in Nicaragua, the country's relations with its neighbors also sharpened the country's civil wars. Because the Central American states originally had formed part of a single federation, throughout the nineteenth century Nicaraguan Liberals and Conservatives had little compunction about calling in aid from their counterparts in neighboring countries. The introduction of these outsiders added to the savagery of Nicaragua's internal conflicts.

Nicaragua's struggles became so severe that in 1855 the country's Liberals contracted an American, William Walker, to fight for them. Walker's easy takeover of Nicaragua frightened not only the local elites but the country's neighbors, who in 1857 banded together defeat the American.

Although Walker had nearly conquered and kept Nicaragua, the Nicaraguans' tradition of looking for outside allies persisted. Because foreign intervention could mean the difference between defeat and victory against hated rivals, Nicaraguans became adept at manipulating outsiders. No foreign intervention in Nicaragua—whether U.S. or Cuban or Soviet—has ever taken place except at the behest of a substantial domestic faction. In 1912 it was the Conservatives' turn to ask the United States to send in the Marines. When the Taft administration responded, the conservative "ladies of Granada" sent a message to the commanding U.S. admiral, praising the intervention and expressing the wish that "our elder sister, the great Republic of the United States, so wise, so powerful, will bring us permanently the benefits which all her sons enjoy throughout her vast and peaceful domain."[13]

While Conservatives heaped praise on the U.S. navy, a Liberal poet of León wrote of "the blond pigs of Pennsylvania [home of the U.S. Marine commander, Smedley Butler] advancing on our garden of beauty."[14] Thus did the United States descend into the whirlpool of Nicaragua's deep and deadly internal divisions and become a factor in them.

The 1912 Marine intervention initiated a long period of American attempts to modernize Nicaragua through legal and financial reform. The United States sought to create a fiscally solvent state that could conduct clean elections, several of which the U.S. supervised. This experiment was judged a success in 1924 when the Nicaraguans elected a promising Conservative-Liberal coalition candidate for president. The Marines left soon after.

STIMSON, SANDINO AND SOMOZA

In response to renewed violence in Nicaragua, in 1927 President Coolidge sent Henry Stimson to the country as his personal envoy. Stimson was determined to solve the country's endemic internal chaos. He proposed that the Liberals and the Conservatives move their competition from the battlefield to the ballot box, and that both agree to the formation of a bipartisan national army to guarantee peace. Stimson's plan was an enlightened one. It would founder, however, on the rocks of Nicaragua's internal divisions. Nicaraguan Liberal General Augusto C. Sandino rejected Stimson's intervention and took his men into the northern hills, declaring war on the Americans and on any Nicaraguans who would cooperate with them.

Sandino's resistance inspired great admiration, particularly among intellectual and cultural elites both in Nicaragua and across Latin America. Most admirers of the Nicaraguan guerrilla have described him as a simple nationalist, a patriot who resisted foreign intervention. While certainly a nationalist, this characterization overlooks the political and psychological complexity of Sandino's revolt, which tapped deep feelings that went far beyond politics.

Born on May 18, 1895, Augusto Sandino was the illegitimate son of a middling coffee planter and a woman who had been his servant. Though Don Gregorio Sandino would not be seen as wealthy today, he was undoubtedly considered so within the tiny community where he lived. His son lived in extreme poverty, until at around age ten he was taken in by his natural father. He spent time in Mexico as a young man, returning to Nicaragua to join the Liberals in 1926 as civil war broke out.

Sandino showed talent as a military and political leader but found his pathway blocked by Liberal leader José Maria Moncada. Sandino hated Moncada for this, and when Henry Stimson chose to negotiate with Moncada, the de facto leader of the Liberals, Sandino rejected Stimson's formula for pacification and began his war against the United States and against the majority of Nicaragua's political leaders.

The United States made several overtures to Sandino, hoping he would accept electoral supervision, a scheme that, at an earlier juncture, he had appeared to favor. The local Marine commander, Captain Hatfield, wrote Sandino, urging him to cooperate with the U.S. plan, one already agreed to by all other Nicaraguan political leaders. Sandino's reply to Hatfield is instructive for what it reveals about the military-feudal values, the ethic of dueling, and the absence of compromise that dominated Nicaragua's political culture.

No, degenerate pirate, *you do not even know your father* in your real language. I do not fear you. If you would like to avoid your countrymen's loss of blood, they having no interest in our political affairs, make up your mind like a man. *Come to me personally,*

*choose the terrain you prefer outside your control, and I will do
the same,* so that we may measure the power of our weapons in
the following way. Either you will fill yourself with glory killing a
patriot, or I will make you eat the dust in the manner demonstrated by the official seal of my army [which depicted a Sandinista beheading a Marine with his machete.][15] (emphasis added)

Sandino's romantic intransigence was not entirely impractical.
His tactics flowed from his rhetoric. An underappreciated aspect
of Sandino's revolt was the Nicaraguan guerrilla's use of extreme
brutality, not so much against Americans but against other
Nicaraguans. For Sandino, those who cooperated with the United
States had sacrificed all dignity and honor, and ceased to be
Nicaraguan. In effect, Sandino "excommunicated" these individuals from their Nicaraguan identity. Thus they were, in his words,
"dogs, traitors, cowards"; "traitors, impostors, toadies, mercenar-
ies, and acolytes"; "chicken Liberals, eunuchs, sellouts"; "worm-
eaten and degenerate"; mere "eunuchs and swamp geese."[16] Such
individuals deserved a slow death. Sandino's writings celebrated a
macabre series of carving and dismemberment techniques that his
men used against these ex-Nicaraguans, as he defined them.

Sandino outlasted Washington's will to defeat him, and the
United States withdrew its Marines on January 1, 1933. Unfortunately for Sandino, with the American departure the Nicaraguan
guerrillas lost perhaps the only power that might have guaranteed
a fair settlement of the war. Within two years Sandino was dead,
assassinated at the orders of Anastasio Somoza, leader of the U.S.
Marine-trained National Guard. Much has been made of Somoza's
pro-American leanings, his fluent English, and his reputed flair on
the dance floor with Mrs. Hannah, the U.S. ambassador's wife. In
fact, in his betrayal of Sandino and transformation of the Guard
into his personal force, Somoza was following not the path suggested by Stimson in his pacification plan, but the pattern of many
Nicaraguan military leaders who had preceded him. The United
States had created the National Guard in the hopes of depoliticiz-
ing the military. In the end, Somoza came to dominate and shape
the Guard in the Nicaraguan tradition.

THE SOMOZAS IN POWER

The five-decade rule of the Somozas was itself a complex phenomenon. The first Somoza, though an autocrat, wielded power in shrewd fashion, showing his flair as a populist in key political crises and building up the Liberal party as his political vehicle. Assassinated in 1956, he was succeeded by his two sons. Nicaragua was not a democracy, but neither was it a totalitarian dictatorship. A vigorous opposition press was tolerated, and during the 1960s the opposition Conservative party ran a strong candidate. Economically the Somozas reaped significant benefits from their rule, but Nicaragua as a whole also grew rapidly. The country became known as the breadbasket of Central America, and Nicaraguans took pride in the seemingly perpetual one-for-one convertibility between Nicaraguan currency, the Cordoba, and the U.S. dollar. While not the most attractive regime from a U.S. point of view, the Somoza administration was far from the totalitarian dungeon later described by its left-wing critics. And in the meantime, economic growth brought increasing contacts with the United States.

These contacts affected Nicaragua profoundly. As Arturo Cruz, Jr., has observed, in the postwar era Nicaraguans "went crazy for America: the best tractors (Caterpillars), the best cigarettes (Camels), the best razor blades (Gillette)."[17] Images of American consumer goods flooded the country's airwaves, attracting the buying power of Nicaragua's rapidly expanding middle class. Admiration for the United States went beyond mere consumerism. Many Nicaraguans identified the United States with progress and as the model for the development in Nicaragua. As Cruz puts it, to Nicaraguans,

> Americans made money, sense and power. Americans built the Panama Canal. Americans forged the highest buildings in the world, they built the cars, they built the highways for the cars, in America and in Nicaragua. Since the 1860s, Nicaragua had felt that the railroad, along with the telegraph, was the symbol of the future. The Americans came and explained that railroads were old, that automobiles were progress. American roads and cars followed.[18]

The Somozas skillfully manipulated both the image and the reality of U.S. influence in Nicaragua. They cultivated contacts with Washington and aggressively sold the idea to the Nicaraguan people that they enjoyed unstinting U.S. support. Many Nicaraguans have criticized the United States for its apparent acquiescence in the Somozas' rule.

In the 1970s a variety of factors converged against Anastasio Somoza Debayle, the last of the dynasty to rule. Economic growth created new middle-class rivals for the Somozas' power. And, with the 1972 earthquake and the 1973 Arab oil embargo, Nicaragua suddenly began to falter economically, threatening that new middle class. Finally, and perhaps most important, new winds were blowing in Washington with regard to human rights.

During the late 1970s the Carter administration sought to distance itself from dictators who had no respect for American democratic principles. In the wake of the Cuban Revolution, fresh currents made themselves felt in Latin America. Jesuit faculty in Nicaraguan universities began teaching liberation theology to the disaffected children of the Nicaraguan elite, many of whom came from Conservative families that were the historic enemies of the Somozas. As opposition to the dictatorship rose, the last Somoza came to depend increasingly on the National Guard to retain power. After Somoza's rival Pedro Joaquin Chamorro was assassinated in 1978, urban areas of the country rose in rebellion. The Somoza dynasty collapsed when Washington distanced itself from the dictator by imposing an arms embargo. Jubilation followed his fall and the rise to power of the Sandinista National Liberation Front.

ENTER THE FSLN

The Somoza regime inspired a wide variety of opponents, both civic and military, left-wing Marxist and anti-Communist. A number of these groups claimed allegiance to Augusto Sandino, who, after his assassination, became a martyr for opponents of the regime.

Ultimately the most successful of the anti-Somoza resistance organizations was one that would have been considered least likely to prosper, the Sandinista National Liberation Front, a group founded in 1961 in Cuba by Nicaraguan Marxist intellectual Carlos Fonseca. A Marxist, Fonseca nonetheless believed that Marxism, to succeed in Nicaragua, would have to be wrapped in a tradition with which Nicaraguans could identify. Consequently he blended Marxism-Leninism with the traditions of Augusto Sandino to create a Nicaraguan variant of Marxism-Leninism that he called *Sandinismo*. Fonseca made a breakthrough introducing leftist doctrine to Nicaragua. Nonetheless Sandinismo was not a unitary movement. Throughout most of the 1960s and 1970s the Sandinistas were split into three factions and failed to attract mass support. Of the three FSLN factions, two espoused Marxist doctrines based on peasant and proletarian revolution. The third, known as the Terceristas (or the Third Way advocates) and led by the brothers Camilo, Daniel, and Humberto Ortega, thought the time frame for revolution could be radically compressed. Using spectacular military actions to humble the last Somoza and destroy his aura of invincibility, the Terceristas touched off an insurrection by the urban poor that defeated the dictatorship. Acting as the vanguard for the anti-Somoza forces, they then sought to steer the country in a Marxist-Leninist direction.[19]

Events began to break the Terceristas' way in the late 1970s. When the United States failed to take decisive action against Somoza in 1978, the situation in Nicaragua spun out of control. As the dictator depended more and more on his military to repress an increasingly restive population, the number of people who identified with the FSLN mushroomed (though the party's elite membership, its *militancia*, always remained limited). In the insurrection that followed, the FSLN took the military lead of a broad coalition of Nicaraguans who had become sick of Somoza. Within months after taking power, however, moderates like Violeta Chamorro and Alfonso Robelo deserted the ruling junta. The Sandinistas then began to mix state and party, creating Sandinista organizations for all levels and areas of society—unions, students, the media, the church, the peasants.

From the beginning, the Sandinistas saw the United States as an inevitable enemy and Cuba and the Soviet Union as essential friends. The Sandinistas soon monopolized the country's military and police forces, incorporating them into their party. They dramatically expanded the military, renaming it the Sandinista Army. They invited representatives of various radical groups from around the world to set up shop in Nicaragua, including the Palestinian Liberation Organization and the Argentine Montaneros.[20] They sent aid to the guerrillas in El Salvador, hoping to tip the regional balance of power even further in their favor.[21]

For FSLN activists as well as many pro-FSLN intellectuals, anti-U.S. feeling was visceral and an essential part of the mobilization plans described above. The Sandinistas wrote a new national anthem that included the proposition, "The Yankee is the enemy of humanity." They created a huge state apparatus for both didactic and political mobilization. Managua abounded in books and pamphlets that lionized Sandino, demonized the Somozas, and attacked the United States. The walls of Nicaraguan cities fairly dripped with pro-Sandinista and often anti-U.S. graffiti.[22]

Yet the Sandinistas encountered two major challenges. First, they needed international support, including the left in the United States. Second, they ran up against the basically pro-American feelings of many Nicaraguans. The FSLN attempted to square this circle by promoting a dichotomous view of the United States—they did not oppose the American people, they stated, only the policies of their government, particularly those of the Reagan administration.

While sympathetic Americans who visited Nicaragua eagerly swallowed this line, it foundered against realities: President Reagan and his tough policies were popular with the American people, and the majority of Nicaraguans, while overall anti-Somoza and at times critical of the United States, were not committed Marxist-Leninists but pragmatic neighbors of the United States. In contrast, the Sandinistas were revolutionary internationalists with a set of convictions that earned them alliances with faraway socialist states and the sympathy of many on the global left, but these convictions were of little help to the majority of Nicaraguans.

THE 1980S: ONE DECADE, TWO NICARAGUAS

By the mid-1980s Sandinista beliefs and policies had created two Nicaraguas. One was a country of symbols, the country as a cause, and a place inhabited by the internationally celebrated Sandinistas and their supporters. In this Nicaragua the FSLN's anti-U.S. line dominated the state-controlled airwaves, echoed at mass rallies, and was splashed on walls in every major town and city, presenting the image of a population united by Third World nationalism and in its resistance to the United States. Visitors from abroad—left-leaning European and U.S. academics and activists—embraced this image as the definitive Nicaraguan reality, since it flawlessly conformed to with dominant currents in the post-Vietnam academy and, more broadly, with what has been called the adversary culture.

By contrast, the other Nicaragua was nearly invisible in the official mass media. In this Nicaragua, Sandinista rule had led to economic disaster, impoverishment, and confrontation with the United States. Far from being revolutionary internationalists, the majority of this Nicaragua felt like dupes, people who had been sacrificed on an ideological altar at which others worshiped.[23]

In 1987 I visited Nicaragua with a group of academics from the Latin American Studies Association (LASA) and experienced Nicaragua's "double reality," as Paul Berman would later call it. For several weeks our little collection of professors and graduate students encountered overwhelmingly pro-Sandinista Nicaraguans. When the rest of the group left the country, I remained and immediately ran into a firestorm of criticism of the FSLN, an experience incarnated in the encounter I recorded later in an article for the *Atlanta Constitution*. It described a scene I had experienced in Matagalpa, a provincial capital. While at the time the town was filled with Sandinista soldiers, in the privacy of homes, people expressed sentiments like these:

"When the Americans come," he said, his eyes alight . . . "the Sandinistas will turn and run! And then . . ." As he finished, the Nicaraguan rose from his couch and, striking a sudden Rambo pose, he fired a long burst from an imaginary machine gun into his living room wall. But Ronaldo (not his real name) is . . . a

man in his 50s with a slight paunch and graying goatee beard.
. . . The Sandinistas would call him a Somocista, someone who
would sell out his country for the privileges he possessed in the
past. Yet Ronaldo is more than that. . . . Under pressure, many
in [Nicaragua] have become not Sandinistas but Reaganistas.
These Nicaraguans vented their anger on their . . . government
by admiring its enemy, the American president.[24]

Ronaldo's admiration for the United States was based on more
than his sufferings under FSLN rule. Although anti-American feeling has strong roots in Nicaragua, pro-American feelings are
equally deeply rooted. They grew even more intense as the Sandinistas led the country down a path that lent the FSLN interna-
tionalist glory and meant ruination for the rest of the country.

In a spectacular event that calls to mind other recent predictive
failures of left-wing critics of the United States, Nicaragua's "double reality" was exploded by the election of 1990.[25] Compelled by
the Contra War to hold free elections, the Sandinistas ran their
leader, Daniel Ortega, against an opposition coalition led by the
widow of former Somoza rival Pedro Joaquin Chamorro. For many
outsiders—American and European academics, left-leaning political activitists from the churches, NGOs and international solidarity organizations, and even some in the press corps—the
Ortega-Chamorro contest was a critical battle in the global struggle between President Reagan and the Sandinistas, the U.S. and
Latin America, capitalism and socialism, imperialism and revolutionary nationalism, et al. Most such observers, steeped in post-
1960s theories of dependency, Marxism, and Third World
nationalism at American and European universities, predicted a
big Ortega win.[26]

In February 1990 Mrs. Chamorro won a landslide victory, defeating her FSLN opponent by almost twenty percentage points. In
so doing she destroyed the myth of vast, mass-based Sandinista
popularity rooted in historical resistance to the United States. At
the time, many who were sympathetic to the Sandinistas argued
that the vote against the party was merely a product of the pressures created by the policies of the Reagan administration. Events

since 1990 have shown this to be untrue. FSLN candidate Daniel Ortega has run in every election since and has never come close to winning. In fact, Ortega has not improved his share of the vote (40 percent) since losing in 1990.

FROM THE SANDINISTAS' DEFEAT TO SEPTEMBER 11

The Sandinistas' electoral defeat in 1990, along with the general retreat of socialism worldwide, dealt a major blow to anti-Americanism in Nicaragua. As they left power, the Sandinistas engaged in a wholesale seizure of state resources reminiscent of Somoza's last days, the so-called *piñata*, an act that further deligitimized them. The subsequent shrinkage of the state and its ideological apparatus under the Chamorro administration stranded many left intellectuals without jobs. Some moved into the university system, others shifted to the burgeoning NGO sector. On the whole, however, anti-American voices became muted, as the illusion of a Nicaragua united in opposition to the United States ran up against new political, economic, and geopolitical realities.

Anti-American feeling was further diminished following massive U.S. assistance after the devastation wrought by Hurricane Mitch in 1998, including a $100 million emergency aid program from Washington. U.S. military forces worked side by side in relief efforts with their former Sandinista counterparts in the Nicaraguan military.

In recent years tough U.S. stands against corruption have also proved popular with many Nicaraguans, who increasingly see their problems not as created by the colossus of the north but rooted in their own political practices and habits. Finally, Nicaraguans have grown closer to the United States because of immigration. By March 2003, Vice Minister of Foreign Affairs Salvador Stadthagen estimated that there were 800,000 Nicaraguans living abroad, most of them in the United States, and that they contributed $500 million annually in remittances to Nicaragua, a staggering sum for a country with a GDP of around $2.5 billion per year.[27]

After 9/11 Nicaraguans from across the entire political spectrum expressed solidarity with the United States, including the

FSLN candidate for president, Daniel Ortega. The U.S. embassy was inundated with flowers and condolences. Some Nicaraguans offered to give blood for victims of the attacks. Masses and marches were held in Managua to commemorate the casualties in New York City, Washington, D.C., and Pennsylvania.

The landslide election of Liberal presidential candidate Don Enrique Bolanos over Daniel Ortega less than three months later confirmed that Nicaraguans en masse felt little if any hostility to the United States. Throughout the campaign, both candidates had competed as to who could better handle relations with Washington, a contest that Bolanos won easily.

ANTI-AMERICANISM AFTER SEPTEMBER 11

Yet anti-Americanism is by no means dead in Nicaragua. Maintained by a small group of writers, cultural figures, and left-leaning academics, Nicaragua's anti-American critics kept up a steady drumbeat of anti-American criticism during the 1990s, most of which was featured in small publications, some associated with the FSLN, or in the editorial pages of *El Nuevo Diario*, the country's most important left-wing newspaper after the official FSLN newspaper, *Barricada* (The Barricade), folded in 1998.

The smoke had barely cleared from the Twin Towers' collapse when these groups mobilized and updated their message for the post–September 11 world. Nicaraguan anti-Americans employed certain tropes which as arguments often do not stand up to close scrutiny but are useful as polemics in a country where literacy has been the tool of a privileged few and poverty constitutes a daily reality for the majority.

The following are now the major elements or themes of Nicaraguan anti-Americanism (also found in other countries):

MORAL EQUIVALENCE

The fantasy that leads off this chapter—"George Bush is Bin Laden"—written by Nicaraguan polemicist Fredy Quezada, is a classic example of this approach. Although as a purveyor of lurid images and rhetoric he represents the more extreme responses to the U.S. war on terror, Quezada's contention that President Bush is the moral equivalent of bin Laden is an oft-repeated theme in left-wing criticisms of the United States. Polemicists in Nicaragua also repeatedly ask the question, "Is Bush a fundamentalist?"[28]

THE FRANKENSTEIN IMAGE

In a variant of the moral equivalence theme, Nicaraguan critics complain that the United States, in fighting bin Laden (and later Saddam Hussein), is in conflict with a Frankenstein of its own creation. During the 1980s the United States supported the Afghan mujahedeen, the partisans who fought Soviet domination of their country, a group with which Al Qaeda leader Osama bin Laden was also allied. Ergo, Osama was a creation of the United States. As one author put it, "Just as with Manuel Noriega in Panama or Saddam Hussein in Baghdad, the United States created a monster 'Made in the USA.'"[29]

GENOCIDE

In the fall of 2001, Nicaraguan critics charged that the United States was carrying out "genocide" in its attacks against Taliban forces in Afghanistan.[30] The example of the U.S. atomic bombing of Hiroshima was frequently cited as historical antecedent of the allegedly "genocidal" policies of the United States in Afghanistan and later Iraq. News reporting of the war also emphasized the allegedly indiscriminate way in which the United States used its military power. An *El Nuevo Diario* story from April 2, 2003, for example, described a "massacre" carried out by U.S. aircraft.[31] Another longer article, a retrospective on Hiroshima curiously timed to coincide with the Iraq War, alleged that the U.S. bombing of that city had killed 260,000 people. (More reliable estimates place this total at 66,000.[32])

THE MILITARY-INDUSTRIAL COMPLEX

Critics of the United States commonly assert that the United States goes to war, particularly in Iraq, to solve its economic problems. It is taken for granted by such authors that Washington wants to control the world's oil supply. More specifically, they allege that elements of the military-industrial complex demanded the war in part because the U.S. economy was near collapse; war provided a desperate solution to its problems. As one Nicaraguan author described it,

> Apart from petroleum, the war sector . . . is the only dynamic sector [of the U.S. economy]. This country has entered into a terrible recession. It cannot compete with Japan, China and Europe. [So] it wants to take over the political economy. It can't do it. So, war becomes a big business. . . . Without this military conflict the North American economic recession could become a collapse.[33]

THE AMERICAN NIGHTMARE

An inconvenient fact for anti-Americans in Nicaragua is the great number of Nicaraguans who have family in the United States or would like to move there—a trend accelerated by the economic catastrophe of the 1980s. During the run-up to the Iraq War, *El Nuevo Diario* found a way to turn this reality on its head. The paper ran a number of stories on the fears of Nicaraguan parents who had children in the U.S. military. One such parent was Carlos Mejia Godoy, a famous Nicaraguan musician who was the author of the Sandinista hymn that describes "the Yankee" as "the enemy of humanity." Such articles strongly suggested that Nicaraguans in the U.S. military were forced to serve for economic reasons. In a similar piece, *El Nuevo Diario* claimed that the U.S. army unfairly denied a Nicaraguan recruit the opportunity to become an astronaut. It alleged that the young Nicaraguan "had wanted to study in NASA, but they [the Americans] closed the portals of space to him because of his nationality."[34]

One former FSLN official from the 1980s summed up the U.S. war on terror as follows:

. . . The descendants of those who literally burned alive the majority of inhabitants of Hiroshima and Nagasaki, those who painted red the countryside of Vietnam and Korea, those violators of young women, those who propagate AIDS across the whole world, the most important conventional and non-conventional weapons makers on the planet, [they] have now decided to avenge themselves by blood and blows against terrorists, former friends of theirs, [the terrorists] who have dealt them a blow, not so much in their hearts, but in their pride.[35]

This appeared on September 22, 2001, well before U.S. military action against either Afghanistan or Iraq, scarcely a week and a half after the fall of the Twin Towers.

Hostility toward the United States can also be conveyed by a show of solidarity with its arch-enemies. Thus on March 18, 2003, FSLN General Secretary Daniel Ortega sent a personal letter to then-Iraqi President Saddam Hussein. Ortega was in Cuba at the time. In the letter Ortega described how the politics of the Bush administration represented nothing more than "a continuation of the politics of death" that "different U.S. administrations have carried out in the most diverse regions of the world. . . ."[36]

THE ARGUMENTS OF THE ANTI-AMERICANS

After all is said and done, Anti-Americanism in Nicaragua is more a matter of style and emotion than empirical substance. Little care is taken to make well-argued assertions, and supporting statistics are either wildly skewed (as in the case of causalities from Hiroshima) or altogether absent. The assertion that the military-industrial complex drives U.S. foreign policy and sustains the U.S. economy is not based on any evidence. (Until 2002 the United States spent just over 3 percent of its GDP on weapons.) Terms like "genocide" are thrown around without reference to historical context. (The United States, for example, was at war with Japan when it used the atomic bomb.) Many claims are made with the help of dubious internet sources or by relying on individuals with obvious bias such as Noam Chomsky.[37]

Despite their harsh words about the United States, Nicaragua's anti-Americans—like Augusto Sandino—have reserved their bitterest attacks for their internal enemies, their fellow citizens who either worked with Washington, agreed with the United States or enjoyed better relations with the Americans than they did.

For the anti-Americans, the distinction between themselves and their pro-U.S. Nicaraguan counterparts is not a matter of a difference of opinion but a fundamental moral divide. In words rich in irony and sarcasm, Miguel D'Escoto denounced "*Los* 'nice,'" ("the nice ones"), the "pragmatic" Nicaraguans who agree with the United States, those who, in D'Escoto's words, "are never absent from U.S. Embassy receptions." He described such Nicaraguans as "concubines of the beast."[38] For another anti-U.S. critic, identification with the United States amounts to a loss of national identity, akin to the excommunications Sandino levied against his opponents. As he lamented, ". . . In this little and beautiful country, there are many people who feel more North American than Nicaraguan. . . ."[39]

From the beginning of Nicaragua's history, the existence of two power centers in a country permeated by a feudal political ethos created deep divisions among the Nicaraguan elite. This history of division and civil war preceded U.S. intervention. After Americans first appeared on the Nicaraguan scene (in the odious form of William Walker), Nicaraguans continued their tradition of division. For most of them, identification with the United States became a source of pride, for others the hallmark of betrayal. But even this difference is more apparent than real. As journalists and other keen observers of the Nicaraguan scene have noted, anti- and pro-Yankee feelings can be collapsed into a single entity: nimble Nicaraguan politicians praise U.S. actions that favor their interests but decry U.S. interventionism that works against them.

Nicaraguan anti-Americanism is at least as much, and possibly more, a product of the country's history of internal division than the result of U.S. policies. In this sense, despite generously borrowing from abroad, Nicaraguan anti-Americanism has at least one important homegrown attribute: it is used as a weapon in the impassioned internal struggles Nicaraguans have waged against one another since independence from Spain. Anti-Americanism will moderate only when the anti-Americans cease to demonize not just the United States but, more important, their fellow citizens, these pro-U.S. Nicaraguans with whom they so passionately disagree.

NOTES

1. *El Nuevo Diario*, Managua, March 22, 2003.
2. See Mark Falcoff, "Revolutionary Tourism," *Public Opinion*, Summer 1986. On the roots of this phenomenon, see Paul Hollander, *Political Pilgrims*, Oxford University Press, New York, 1981. George Orwell, *Homage to Catalonia*, Harvest Books, 1969, is also useful.
3. The formulation of cause and country was recently coined by Mexican intellectual Jorge Casteneda.
4. Nationmaster.com puts Nicaragua's per capita GNP as USD 384 per year. See: www.nationmaster.com/country/nu/Economy. The same figure for neighboring Honduras is more than twice that.
5. Sergio Ramirez, *Adios Muchachos*, Aguilar, Mexico, D.F., 1999, p. 137.
6. Ibid., p. 138.
7. Miguel D'Escoto Brockmann, "Desnudando el Enemigo de la Humanidad," *El Nuevo Diario*, April 11, 2003.
8. Much of the subsequent analysis of Nicaraguan political history is drawn from E. Bradford Burns, *Patriarch and Folk: the Emergence of Nicaragua, 1798–1858*, Harvard University Press, Cambridge, 1991.
9. Shirley Christian, *Revolution in the Family*, Random House, New York, 1985. For the best account of the ties that bound divided Nicaraguans in the 1980s, see Arturo Cruz, Jr., *Memoirs of a Counter-Revolutionary*, Doubleday, New York, 1989.
10. Cited in Glenn L. Busey, "Foundations of Political Contrast: Costa Rica and Nicaragua," *Western Political Quarterly*, September 1958, p. 631.
11. Cruz, cited, p. 46.
12. Arturo Cruz, Jr., "One Hundred Years of Turpitude," *New Republic*, November 16, 1987, p. 33.

13. Lester D. Langley, *The Banana Wars: An Inner History of the American Empire*, University of Kentucky Press, Lexington, 1983, p. 75.

14. Ibid., p. 75.

15. Robert E. Conrad, *Sandino: The Testimony of a Nicaraguan Patriot, 1921–1934*, Princeton University Press, Princeton, 1990, p. 81.

16. Ibid., pp. 41, 58, 74, 90, 91, 118.

17. Cruz, *Memoirs*, cited, p. 40.

18. Ibid., p. 39.

19. See Humberto Ortega, "The Strategy of the Victory," in *The Sandinistas Speak*, Pathfinder, New York, 1984, p. 65. See also David Nolan, *The Ideology of the Sandinistas and the Nicaraguan Revolution*, Institute for Interamerican Studies, Coral Gables, 1984, especially Chapter 5.

20. Christian, cited, pp. 169–170.

21. Sergio Ramirez, *Adios Muchachos*, Aguilar, Mexico, D.F., 1999, pp. 144–146.

22. For an account of the use of Sandino as a symbol for political mobilization, see David E. Whisnant: *Rascally Signs in Sacred Places: The Politics of Culture in Nicaragua*, University of North Carolina Press, Chapel Hill and London, 1995. For an account of the Sandinistas' embrace of anti-Americanism, see Christian, Chapter 9. As Christian puts it, after their takeover, "the Sandinista *comandantes* and their propaganda organs were suddenly making the United States the main culprit for everything they found wrong with the world. This outbreak of gringo-baiting after the insurrection surprised U.S. officials because they had previously judged leaders of the Sandinista Front not be inherently anti-Yankee." *Revolution in the Family*, pp. 164–165.

23. Robert Leiken was among the earliest and most prominent observers to sense that the idealization of Sandinista Nicaragua was groundless. See his article "The Sins of the Sandinistas," *New Republic*, October 8, 1984. Paul Berman would eventually coin the term "double reality" to describe the two Nicaraguas. See Paul Berman, "Double Reality: The People's Revolution Versus the Sandinista Revolution," *Village Voice*, December 5, 1989.

24. David C. Brooks, "Misled 'Reaganistas' in Nicaragua Are Overlooking Best Chance for Peace," *Atlanta Constitution*, December 17, 1987.

25. The Nicaraguan elections of 1990, the predictions that preceded them, and the results that followed were but one in a series of monumental misjudgments by academic and activist observers hostile to U.S. policies. There were similar predictions of the U.S. failure in Gulf Wars I, the invasion of Panama, and the war in Afghanistan. Discussions of how the ideological baggage of American professors, activists, and journalists caused them to misread major events in Nicaragua (and, by implication, in other areas) can be found in Robert L. Leiken, *Why Nicaragua Vanished: A Story of Reporters and Revolutionaries*, Rowman and Littlefield, Lanham, Md., 2003; Arturo J. Cruz, Jr., and Mark Falcoff, "Who Won Nicaragua?" *Commentary*, May 1990; and Paul Berman, "Why the Sandinistas Lost," *Dissent*, Summer 1990. A provocative reflection on the meaning of the end of the cold war for the left can be found in José Arico, "Rethink Everything (Maybe It's Always Been This Way)," *NACLA: Report on the Americas*, May 1992.

26. See also Leiken.

27. Octavio Enriquez, Interview with Vice Minister Stadthagen, "The Silent Majority," *El Nuevo Diario*, March 31, 2003. U.S. Embassy sources estimate that 500,000 Nicaraguans live in the U.S. and 300,000 in Costa Rica. Together they send back $600 million per year, the bulk of that coming from the U.S. The sum constitutes about 25 percent of Nicaragua's GDP.

28. Gustavo Adolfo Vargas, "Is Bush a Fundamentalist?" *El Nuevo Diario*, October 12, 2001.

29. Carlos Escrocia Polanco, "The '380' of Afghanistan," *El Nuevo Diario*, October 13, 2001.

30. Miguel D'Escoto Brockmann, "The New Era Backs Genocide," *El Nuevo Diario*, February, 28, 2003.

31. French Press Agency, "Another Massacre!" cover story, *El Nuevo Diario*, April 2, 2003. The story led with a picture of an Arab man in tears as he leaned over the casket of a member of his family.

32. See The Avalon Project at Yale Law School: www.yale.edu/lawweb/avalon/abomb/mp10.htm.

33. Interview by Valeria Imhof with Orlando Nunez Soto, sociologist, "What Orlando Nunez Soto Sees Behind the War: A Financial Business," *El Nuevo Diario*, March 20, 2003.

34. Edwin Sanchez, "Cries of Pain from the North: Another Parent Weeps," *El Nuevo Diario*, March 21, 2003.

35. Oscar Merlo, "With Whom Shall We Settle Up?" *El Nuevo Diario*, September 22, 2001.

36. Managua, March 22, 2003.

37. Columns and references to Noam Chomsky abound in *El Nuevo Diario*, Miguel D'Escoto quoted Chomsky admiringly in his article, "Denuding the Enemy of Humanity," *El Nuevo Diario*, April 11, 2003. Canards about the Bush family's supposed Nazi connections were repeated from *George H. W. Bush [Sr.]: the Unauthorized Biography*, in an article by Juan Gelman entitled "Lineages," *El Nuevo Diario*, December 6, 2001. Howard Zinn as well as left-wing sociologist James Petras are also favorites of left-oriented Nicaraguan academics. Petras has a Spanish-language website. For the Zinn reference, see Miguel D'Escoto, "The Mother of All Bombs," *El Nuevo Diario*, March 19, 2003.

38. Miguel D'Escoto, "Denuding the Enemy of Humanity, *El Nuevo Diario*, April 11, 2003, and "Concubines of the Beast," *El Nuevo Diario*, March 27, 2003.

39. Oscar Merlo, "With Whom Shall We Settle Up?" *El Nuevo Diario*, September 22, 2001.

8

MARK FALCOFF

Cuban Anti-Americanism: Historical, Popular, and Official

Cuba today is probably the most anti-American political system in Latin America, perhaps as anti-American as any in the world. This is most obviously and massively reflected in the Cuban official media as well as in the pronouncements of Fidel Castro, the supreme leader. Through its numerous propaganda outlets, the Cuban government paints a consistently bleak picture of the United States as a country of homelessness, poverty, inadequate medical attention, racism, and violence. For example, the official daily newspaper recently reported that "twelve million families [in the United States] do not have sufficient purchasing power for food and 32 percent of them are actually suffering hunger at one time or another."[1] Another article begins, "While thousands of children die every day, either of hunger or incurable diseases, the United States of America is investing more and more money in the development of its nuclear arsenal."[2] Every incident, real or imagined, that implies the persistence of racism in the United States is given wide publicity.

In many ways all this is paradoxical, because Cuba has been, and remains, one of the nations most heavily influenced by, and oriented toward, the United States. One might almost argue that Cuban anti-Americanism is the dark side of an obsession with its powerful neighbor, the product of a necessarily unequal relationship.

Of all Communist systems, extinct or surviving, only in Cuba has anti-Americanism had deep historical roots which have made the population more receptive to the anti-American propaganda of the authorities. Both popular and official anti-Americanism have been nurtured by these historical roots.

Although Castro's revolution began in the early 1960s to reshape the island along Marxist-Leninist lines, it has never subscribed to a version of "socialism in one country." Rather, it has always proceeded with a glance over its shoulder to the United States, explicitly aspiring (or claiming) to replicate (or even surpass) its achievements and to challenge its role in world affairs. The Cuban Revolution has been driven in large measure by a desire to provide an alternative to the American way of life, not just for the rest of Latin America or the Third World but (and perhaps even principally) for itself.

This obsession has been arguably counterproductive as regards Cuba's practical needs as an impoverished Caribbean nation. It is not, and can never be, a serious rival to the United States. Outside its borders, however, its rhetoric and its self-image find remarkable resonance among many countries around the world who have failed to achieve satisfactory levels of development in the postcolonial era. This phenomenon is particularly evident at the United Nations, where Cuba is extraordinarily active, and where the basic currency of its anti-Americanism is negotiable over a wide range of cultures, religions, and national boundaries. Indeed, anti-Americanism plays so vital and so central a role in Cuban official discourse and even in the country's sense of self that it is difficult to imagine how the island would function if and when the Castro regime achieves its principal stated foreign policy objective—recognition by, and normal relations with, the United States.

MAJOR HISTORICAL THEMES

The reasons for this obsession with the United States are, evidently, historical. Cuba achieved its independence three-quarters of a century after the rest of Latin America, and then only under truncated circumstances. It fought two wars of independence, one in 1868–1878, which ended in clear-cut defeat, and another, in 1895–1898, which led to the collapse of Spanish rule, but only after the United States intervened in the last weeks of what had been a long Cuban-Spanish struggle. The American expeditionary force defeated its Spanish counterpart—or, more accurately, destroyed its will to continue the war—and the American navy effectively destroyed its Spanish counterpart. But entering the conflict in its final phase, the United States proceeded as if the patriot armies were of no military or political consequence, and in the peace conference that settled the island's future shortly after the Spanish surrender, not a single Cuban diplomat, soldier, or politician was present.

Well before its involvement in the Spanish-American (technically the Spanish-Cuban-American) War, the United States had shown a keen interest in Cuba. As Secretary of State John Quincy Adams wrote in 1823, "Cuba, almost within sight of our shores, from a multitude of considerations has become an object of transcendent importance to the political and commercial relations of our Union. . . . Looking forward to the probable course of events . . . it is scarcely possible to resist the conviction that the annexation of Cuba to our federal republic will be indispensable to the continuance and integrity of the United States itself."[3] In the same year Thomas Jefferson "candidly confess[ed]" to President James Monroe that "I have ever looked on Cuba as the most interesting addition which could ever be made to our system of States. The control which . . . this island would give us over the Gulf of Mexico, and the countries and isthmus bordering on it . . . would fill up the measure of our political well-being"—though Jefferson added that he was unwilling to acquire it at the cost of war.[4]

The Louisiana Purchase and the subsequent continental expansion of the United States to its south and west eventually sated the territorial appetites of most Northern politicians. Southerners, however, continued to look favorably upon the acquisition of Cuba, then a slave society, as a way of tilting the balance within the American Union. During the run-up to the Civil War, politi-

cians and business interests in Mobile, New Orleans, and elsewhere along the Gulf of Mexico launched various abortive
schemes aimed at annexing Cuba—typically in collusion with
anti-Spanish Cuban activists.[5]

For various reasons, none of these projects came to fruition; the
abolition of slavery in the United States eliminated the single
most important incentive to annexation, and the gradual entry of
U.S. capital into the Cuban sugar industry, in which it became
dominant by 1895, made formal incorporation unnecessary and
perhaps even undesirable. Spain respected American commercial
interests on the island, which grew by leaps and bounds in the last
quarter of the nineteenth century, and the United States evinced
no great interest in incorporating into its political union a population that by century's end was largely of African origin. This probably explains why, in the very act that authorized American
intervention in the Cuban-Spanish war, a congressional resolution
committed the United States to withdraw once Cuban independence was secured.

This is precisely what happened, but not until after three years
of military occupation, during which the United States attempted
to reshape Cuba in its own image. A military occupation authority under General Leonard Wood moved firmly and vigorously to
rehabilitate a society shattered by war. Needed repairs were carried out; yellow fever was checked, roads were constructed,
schools and hospitals were built, modern streets were laid out.
Cuba's first public school system was established, with a view to
replacing rote learning with a more dynamic system of student-
teacher interchange. Some reforms were of short duration since
they ran against the grain of local culture—for example, the introduction of a jury system, the creation of local self-government, the
abolition of lotteries.

Together with the Philippines, which the United States acquired as a result of the same conflict, Cuba was the United States'
first experience at "nation-building." For all its good intentions, it
was not particularly successful. Moreover, once Washington found
itself saddled with the administration of the island, contact between Americans and Cubans on one side, and Americans and

Spaniards on the other, produced an abrupt change in attitude. Before U.S. entry into the war, the American media and political classes typically attributed to the Cuban patriots a scarcely credible level of courage, idealism, and nobility while depicting the Spanish authorities as cruel, vindictive, and obscurantist. Once on the island, however, U.S. authorities began to view the Spaniards as gentlemen with whom one could do business. If they were, as they seemed to be, anxious to cooperate in every way, it was perhaps because they much preferred to be ruled by U.S. occupation forces than by Cubans. As for the quondam Cuban freedom fighters, at close range they now appeared to the Americans as intractable, irresponsible, and untrustworthy, when not hopelessly corrupt.

This change of attitude provoked a slight but crucial shift in U.S. intentions for the island. The constituent assembly that met to draw up the country's constitution was forced by the occupation authorities to insert a proviso that granted to the United States the right to intervene in the nation's affairs whenever it judged "life, liberty, or property" to be in peril—a word-for-word Spanish translation of a rider to a U.S. army appropriations bill known as the Platt Amendment. This qualification constituted, as one writer has put it, "both the birth certificate and the gravestone of Cuban independence."[6]

It is impossible to exaggerate the centrality of the Platt Amendment to Cuban nationalist beliefs and traditions. While the new republic would probably have performed just as miserably without it, its very existence provided a ready-made excuse for failure. True, the U.S. protectorate (for that is what the proviso effectively created) settled relatively lightly over the political geography of Cuba, particularly compared to similar arrangements elsewhere in Africa and Asia imposed at the time by European colonial powers. Nonetheless, to this very day it remains the centerpiece of Cuban nationalist discourse, cited on all occasions as the *fons et origo* of the republic's ills, and not merely by Cuban supporters of the Castro regime.

Ironically the Platt Amendment had precisely the opposite effect intended by its authors: far from assuring Cuban stability, it encouraged those forces defeated in (frequently fraudulent) elections to create the very disorder that would force the United States to intervene and depose the offending authorities—an eventuality that occurred in 1906–1909, and in a different way in 1932–1933. On neither occasion did U.S. involvement improve the local situation; in the second instance it probably worsened matters for the duration.[7] Small wonder that President Franklin D. Roosevelt succeeded in persuading Congress to revoke the Platt Amendment unilaterally in 1934—a gesture which, however, drew only scant appreciation from Cuban patriots. In spite of the fact that it was consigned to the dustbin of history more than three-quarters of a century ago, it continues to be invoked by the Castro regime as the first cause of all the country's misfortunes.

At just about the same time, a U.S.-Cuban Reciprocity Treaty established a special place for the island in the American domestic sugar market. This was particularly significant on two counts. World sugar prices in the late 1920s were deeply depressed, and many countries in Europe and elsewhere were moving to close their markets to Cuban produce. At the same time the establishment of a permanent, fixed Cuban place in the U.S. market (the so-called "sugar quota") assured a minimal price floor for the Cuban harvest; sugar from the island was to be sold in the United States at the same (subsidized) price as the American product. Although this was done largely as a favor to American corporations which at the time controlled most of Cuba's production, the effect was extremely salutary for Cuban society as a whole, producing a significant and continuing flow of hard currency. In the 1940s and 1950s, moreover, the industry was increasingly "Cubanized" or, perhaps more accurately, "re-Cubanized," so that the full benefits of the quota were "grandfathered" into the local economy. Even so, Cuban critics complained that by rescuing their country from the most serious effects of the Great Depression, the United States had saddled it with a monoculture and in so doing rendered it excessively vulnerable to the price of sugar futures.

The political history of the Cuban republic, even after 1934, is one of frustration and failure. Its economic history is quite another matter. By 1958 Cuba had the third-highest standard of living in Latin America, higher in many aspects than some

European countries like Spain, Italy, and Greece.[8] It was not, however, to Latin America or even to Europe that Cuba compared itself, but to the United States. On this score it would always be found wanting—a comparison providing a wound to national self-esteem that could never be healed.[9]

The comparison with the United States was inevitable given not only geographical proximity or economic dependence but a familiarity (unusual for the period) with American lifestyles, products, and personalities. Before Castro's revolution, Cuba was far more Americanized than, say, Mexico, the Dominican Republic, or other countries of the Caribbean. Cuban business and technical elites were typically trained in the United States; wealthy Cubans owned homes in Florida or New York; American popular culture—especially baseball and motion pictures—had an enormous impact on the Cuban imagination. Although the Spanish demographic presence on the island grew exponentially after 1898 (ironically, more Spaniards emigrated to Cuba between 1898 and 1920 than during the entire four hundred years it had been a colony), at an official level there was a deliberate rejection of Spain and all things Spanish; many educated Cubans actively sought an alternative to replace it. As a character in Robert Redford's film *Havana* (1990) puts it, "We Cubans want to be just like you Americans."

To be sure, this fascination with the United States did not run very deep, and anti-Americanism was a persistent theme in Cuban intellectual and political circles. If Cuba had been anywhere near as pro-American as some members of the exile community profess to recollect, it would have been far more difficult for Fidel Castro to capture and retain so much popular support with his anti-American discourse over such a long period of time.[10]

Another way of looking at Cuban attitudes toward the United States is to characterize them as a variant of the classic "love-hate" relationship that most Latin American countries have long sustained with their powerful neighbor to the north—but in the Cuban case, far more intense and enduring. Whereas for Mexico or Panama the objection to American policy or American presence (or the loss of territory to the United States) was rooted in specific grievances which at least theoretically could be alleviated, for anti-

American Cubans the *very existence* of the United States was a permanent reproach, continually reminding them of their failure to achieve the greatness and global significance which was theirs by right.

It was precisely this sentiment that recommended the Soviet Union to Fidel Castro as an ally and trading partner. The Soviets appeared not merely as an alternative source of military and economic support—and therefore, on pragmatic grounds, a highly recommended ally—but as a system diametrically and ideologically opposed to everything the United States represented. Cuba's strategic partnership with Moscow provided guns, oil, machinery, and access to a global network of political support, but also an entire worldview which already dominated a third of humanity and seemed likely to win yet another third in the foreseeable future. Perhaps nowhere else did Third World nationalism so readily blend with Soviet Communist ideology.

The disappearance of the Eastern bloc has been a particularly bitter pill for Fidel Castro, but since the bedrock of his ideology has been anti-Americanism rather than communism (the latter merely being an instrument to realize the former), the implosion of the Soviet Union has had a far less devastating psychological impact upon him or his regime than might otherwise have been expected.

CUBAN NATIONALISM AND ANTI-AMERICANISM

This succinct history should make it obvious that the Cuban nationalist brief against the United States has been long, relentless, and unforgiving. Many decades before Fidel Castro came upon the scene, Cuban historians were complaining about U.S. aspirations to annex the island, the Platt Amendment, the "imposition" of monoculture, and the suppression of the country's cultural identity and legitimate aspirations. The guns of 1898 had hardly fallen silent before Cubans began to transfer their hatred and resentment of Spain to the United States.

The Cuban nationalist narrative has shown remarkable continuity. As Carlos Alberto Montaner writes, Cuban history has

always been rendered as "an epic tale in which the Cubans, always good and always selfless, suffered the attack and the cruelties of the enemies of their freedom and independence."[11] Thus
the United States came to be depicted as *always* having plotted
to seize the island from Spain, and when this proved impossible
(thanks to the supposed intransigence of Cuban patriots), it intervened at the last minute to snatch the fruits of victory from
the patriot forces. Some Cuban commentators have even suggested that the destruction of the battleship *USS Maine*—in
which dozens of American sailors died—was intentionally
arranged by Washington to invent an excuse to enter the conflict
when it appeared that the Cubans were on the verge of defeating
the Spanish enemy. In more moderate versions, Cubans claim
that the battle plans at the decisive engagement of San Juan Hill
were purloined from Cuban military strategists, or (somewhat
more credibly) that the problematic landing of the U.S. expeditionary force at Daquirí was made possible only by the diversion-
ary activities of the insurgent forces.[12]

The brief against the United States continued well into the period of national independence. The role of Cuban political forces
in deliberately provoking the American occupation of the island
between 1906 and 1909 was air-brushed out of the history books;
instead that event was attributed to mercenary motives or imperialist arrogance. The gradual descent of the government of Gerardo Machado (1925–1933) into dictatorship and violence was
blamed on Washington, since it was obvious to most politically
active Cubans (if not to most Americans) that if the United States
had *really wanted to*, it could easily have forced the strongman to
respect the rules of the game.

Yielding to moral blackmail and the growing prospect of disorder, shortly after taking office in March 1933 President Roosevelt
dispatched Ambassador Sumner Welles to the island to play the
role that Cubans of all political tendencies expected of him:
Machado was forced to resign and go into exile.

Had Roosevelt's envoy stopped there, the damage would have
been limited. Instead he took it upon himself to decide what kind
of government should replace the dictatorship. The problem was

that in the agitation that preceded the fall of Machado, new political forces were emerging in Cuba—revolutionary in style if not in substance—of which the Welles mission took little notice. They included the infant labor movement, middle-class professionals, radical students at the University of Havana, and, remarkably, noncommissioned officers in the Cuban army. Under Sergeant-Stenographer Fulgencio Batista the NCOs had seized control of the barracks in the first and only social revolution ever carried out within the ranks of a Latin American army.

While Welles selected Carlos Manuel de Céspedes, scion of a distinguished Cuban family, as Machado's successor, the revolutionaries put forth Ramón Grau San Martín, a professor of physiology at the University of Havana medical school. Although Céspedes' government fell apart even before it was formed, Welles steadfastly refused to recognize Grau's new government and even implored Washington to send in the Marines. When President Roosevelt refused the latter course, Welles connived to separate Sergeant (soon to be Colonel) Batista from the revolutionary coalition; without military support, Grau's government collapsed, and the former noncommissioned officer became the most important political personality in Cuba.

It is obvious, and not just in hindsight, that the U.S. envoy had greatly overstepped the bounds of his mandate. Grau should have been allowed a chance to govern. But it is unlikely, as many Cubans have later claimed, that by recruiting Batista as its "man in Havana" the United States had derailed a wholesome and needed social revolution which would otherwise have made Fidel Castro's career impossible. This much is obvious from the fact that Grau (and his associate, Carlos Prío, leader of the students at the University of Havana) were both eventually elected to the presidency in their own right in the late 1940s; their administrations were notable for cynicism and corruption, discrediting much of the country's traditional political class.

As the man behind the throne in the period 1934–1940, and then as president in his own right (1940–1944), Fulgencio Batista showed himself to be an exceedingly nimble and imaginative politician, even in ways, a revolutionary. Among other things, he

sponsored Cuba's 1940 constitution, the most advanced such char-
ter in Latin America; invited three Communist ministers into his
cabinet (the first to serve anywhere in Latin America); and devised
social reforms that in many respects went considerably further
than the New Deal in the United States. Futhermore, at the end
of his term in 1944 he bolstered his image as a reborn democrat by
presiding over honest elections so that Grau San Martin (now
older but also more cynical and corrupt) could have a turn at ruling the island. Grau was followed four years later by Carlos Prío,
who in 1933 had been a student leader at the University of Havana
during the tumultuous events of 1933.

The point is worth emphasizing here because the bad reputation of Batista dates from 1952, when he seized power by force to
forestall elections in which success appeared to lie beyond his
reach. The failure of the United States to deny recognition of this
de facto regime has been brandished to "prove" that it either favored Batista's forcible return or at any rate was indifferent to the
fate of Cuban democracy. (In fact Washington was practicing a version of nonintervention that it adopted—at the specific urging of
the Latin American states themselves—just about the time the
Platt Amendment was revoked.[13]) What is true is that Washington
was slow to realize that the Batista of the 1950s was not the same
man he had been two decades before, and that although U.S. interest in Cuba, both economic and political, had declined somewhat in the intervening years, Cubans continued to regard the
U.S. embassy in Havana as the real center of power in their country.[14] If this had been the case, as many Cubans imagined, there
could be no other explanation for the persistence of Batista's dictatorship than the malign purposes of the United States, which he
presumably served.

By the time Washington woke up to the unpleasant facts on
the ground and began working to replace Batista with a legitimately elected successor, it was too late. In spite of the attributions of the opposition, the dictator had no interest in serving any
purposes but his own, and therefore refused to step down. Batista's
refusal to cooperate with Washington, more than anything else,
discredited the traditional political opposition and paved the way

for Fidel Castro. There is good reason to think that Batista's purpose was precisely to narrow the choices between himself and the one alternative, which he knew Washington found distasteful and even unacceptable. Nonetheless, in the narrative of both the Castro regime and its exile opponents, Washington is responsible for the communization of Cuba by persisting in its support of Batista when his mandate was no longer politically viable.[15]

CUBA AND THE COLD WAR

Although official Washington had serious doubts about Fidel Castro and many of his associates from the very beginning, there is no truth to the legend that because of its lack of understanding and sympathy for its social reforms, it forced the new government into an alliance with the Soviet Union. The persistence of the myth is strange not only because it flies in the face of much historical evidence but because Fidel Castro himself has persistently denied it—as well he might, since it reduces him to the role of a subject of history rather than a protagonist in his own right.

In spite of its own misgivings, the United States promptly recognized the new Cuban government and prepared to do business with it. Ambassador Earl E. T. Smith, a political appointee, was replaced by Philip Bonsal, a career diplomat of long and distinguished experience in Latin America. Even before his departure for Havana, however, as Bonsal writes in his memoirs, "I became aware of developments and trends which clouded the relatively hopeful prospect." From the very beginning of his rule, "Castro and his sycophants bitterly and sweepingly attacked the relations of the United States government with Batista and his regime."[16] Although the United States had embargoed arms sales to the fallen Batista regime in 1957—late in the day perhaps, but nonetheless psychologically and politically devastating—it was claimed that partiality for Batista persisted to the very day of the dicator's flight. Bonsal wrote:

> Much poisonous nonsense was poured forth to the effect that the United States was officially harboring and protecting the "war criminals" of the fallen regime. It was even alleged that they

were being helped in their conspiracies against their successful opponents. No evidence was adduced to support these charges. Indeed, if the United States had wished at that time to overthrow Castro, the least efficient tools it could have selected would have been the representatives of the hated regime just expelled to the applause of an overwhelming majority of the Cuban people.[17]

More significantly, he goes on to say:

This fraudulent hate propaganda went far beyond the relations of the United States and the Batista dictatorship. It embraced the common history of the two countries in all its aspects since the Spanish war. It attempted to rewrite that history so as to achieve a maximum of odium for a crudely imperialist United States and its Cuban "lackeys" and of indignant sympathy for a noble, virtuous, and constantly oppressed Cuban people.

With the advent of Castro, the history of Cuban-American relations was subjected to a revision of an intensity and cynicism which left earlier efforts in the shade. . . .

Castro's concept of himself as the spokesman of the righteous infallibility of the Cuban people . . . led him to demand from the United States government, the mass media, and other organs of American public opinion respectful applause for his every action and pronouncement. When this expectation was disappointed, as it was in the case of the executions of those allegedly guilty of committing war crimes under Batista, his reaction was severe and hostile.[18]

Even before it became evident that Castro intended to align his country with the Soviet Union—a process which we now know from declassified Soviet archives actually began slightly before his accession to power on New Year's Day, 1959[19]—the new Cuban government was behaving provocatively by sponsoring expeditions or subversive movements in Panama, the Dominican Republic, and Nicaragua. Once it became a formal ally of the Soviet Union—and as such, a piece on the chessboard of the cold war—it prompted a more stringent and activist policy in Washington. From March 1960 the United States sought by various means to undermine the Cuban economy with a view to provoking popular dissatisfaction with the new government, and when this proved unproductive, to arm and equip an expeditionary force. The failure of the Bay of Pigs exile invasion in the early days of the Kennedy administration (1961) inspired other forms of covert action—including, most famously, a plot to cause Fidel Castro's beard to fall out[20]—none of which came to fruition. Meanwhile, Castro's growing support of guerrilla movements in Latin America, and later military interventions in Africa, caused his anti-imperialist imprecations to become a self-fulfilling prophecy. Cuba became a major strategic enemy of the United States and was regarded and treated as such.

By the late 1960s Cuba had cast itself in a new and more grandiose role: rather than just a small Latin American country fighting to liberate itself from U.S. influence, it now saw itself as part of a vanguard of history, globally aligned with progressive countries and forces, and destined to reshape the world. As Ernesto Ché Guevara, onetime minister of industries and Castro's envoy extraordinary to the Third World, told the Havana Tricontinental Conference in 1968, "Our hopes for victory [are] the total destruction of imperialism by eliminating its firmest bulwark: the oppression exercised by the United States of America. This means a long war. And once more we repeat it, a cruel war. . . . It is almost our sole hope for victory." In this context Che singled out the conflict then under way in Southeast Asia and urged "two, three, or many Vietnams" (a slogan adopted by violent American radicals in the 1960s). He concluded that "our every action is a battle cry against imperialism, and a battle hymn for the people's unity against the great enemy of mankind, the United States of America."[21] The impact of such rhetoric on official Washington was to regard the Cuban threat seriously and to take appropriate measures to neutralize it wherever possible. This included military and intelligence assistance to countries threatened by Cuban-sponsored insurgencies, many of whom would otherwise not have qualified for Washington's aid and support.

One of the earliest tools of U.S. cold war policy against Cuba was a trade embargo which not only denied entry to Cuban exports

and forbade the sale of essential goods but established strict controls over travel to the island. Curiously enough, for the thirty
years during which the island was a formal ally of the Soviet
Union, official Cuba rarely complained about this measure. Indeed, Havana generally emphasized its futility, since the embargo
did not prevent it from trading with most other countries, including many Western nations, and since much of its machinery was
retooled early on so that spare parts from the United States were
no longer needed. Only since the collapse of the Soviet Union and
the disappearance of the socialist bloc has the embargo become the
sole and unique explanation of the island's parlous economic state.

If there are no pencils or textbooks in schools, no medicine in
clinics, no rice or beans in the state bodegas—in short, if there is
anything wrong with Cuba today, Cuban officials tell foreigners,
particularly American visitors, it is all due to the U.S. embargo. As
they see it (or pretend to see it), Cuba's difficulties have nothing
to do with the end of the annual $6 billion subsidy from the Soviet
Union, with the structural inefficiencies of a socialist economic
system or the chronic meddling of Castro in the economy.

By suddenly discovering the centrality of the embargo to his
country's ills, Castro has chosen well, since it is the one U.S. policy unlikely to change during his lifetime, especially since the passage of the Helms-Burton Act (1996) which raises the obstacles to
its repeal to almost impossible levels. The fact that the embargo
has endured more than ten years after the end of the cold war has
permitted the Cuban government to garner considerable international support, since the island today can hardly be said to represent the kind of threat to the United States that is was during the
years of its alliance with the Soviet Union, when it had on its soil
Soviet military bases and listening posts. Blaming the embargo
also allows the Cuban regime to luxuriate in victimhood and self-
pity, comfortable and time-tested consolations.

Just how successful Castro has been in selling his people the
notion that their present troubles are entirely due to the U.S. embargo is difficult to measure. Independent and open opinion polls
of the Cuban population on its political or foreign policy are impossible to conduct. Visitors to the island report a variety of views

on the subject of the embargo and relations with the United States; they are generally related to whether or not the Cuban in question supports the continuation of the Castro regime or is critical of it. On the other hand, many leading dissidents, notably Elizardo Sánchez Santacruz and Osvaldo Payá, favor lifting the embargo, not because they accept the regime's line that it is the cause of the island's economic difficulties but because the continued hostility between the United States and the Cuban government puts them in a precarious position, accused as they often are of being the agents of American "imperialism."[22]

THE CENTRALITY OF FIDEL CASTRO

To propose that Cuban anti-Americanism long precedes Fidel Castro does not mean that the dictator-president has not played a central role in its furtherance and diffusion. Had he chosen a different, more cooperative and pragmatic kind of relationship with the United States, he could easily have convinced other anti-American Cubans to follow him, since in the months and even years after his accession to power he enjoyed unprecedented influence and credibility with his people. On the other hand, such a posture would have diminished his regional and international importance. It would also have inhibited him from leveraging economic, strategic, and political support from the only power willing to finance his confrontation with Washington, the Soviet Union, and quite possibly also inhibited his conquest of all the spaces of power in Cuban society, depriving him of the ideological weapons needed to discredit and eliminate many early supporters and even cabinet members who were drawn from the sectors of Cuban society most closely identified with the United States.

Certain details of Castro's biography may also provide a clue to the origins of his intense, lifelong anti-Americanism. His father was a Spaniard who had originally come to Cuba as a conscript to fight the patriot forces and later the Americans. He soon settled in the province of Santiago, where through determination, guile, and brutality he became a landowner of some importance. The peninsular ancestors were constantly thrown in young Fidel's face in school, possibly encouraging him to exaggerate his *cubanidad*. At the exclusive Catholic boy's high school where he was sent, many of the teachers were Spanish Jesuit priests who subscribed to the fascist doctrines espoused by dictator Francisco Franco. Some of his surviving schoolmates—both in Santiago and later at the University of Havana—recall the young Castro expressing admiration for Mussolini and Hitler.[23] In 1948 he went to Bogotá with two other Cuban students to take part in a Latin American "anti-imperialist" and "anti-U.S." student Congress financed by Argentina's president Juan Perón, staged to coincide with (and protest) the founding meeting of the Organization of American States.

For all his Yankeephobia, Castro has had relatively little first-hand experience of the United States. He spent his honeymoon in New York; he may have visited once or twice to raise money for his revolutionary struggle against Batista. He made one (unofficial) visit in March 1959, shortly after coming to power, when he was generally well received by the public and the media, and three more since aligning with the Soviet Union, to attend the United Nations General Assembly in New York. Unlike many Cubans of his class and generation, he has never lived in the United States and his English has never been more than provisional. In meetings with Americans he appears to understand much of what is said by his guests but still relies on an expert interpreter for both ends of the dialogue.

None of this has stopped Castro from discoursing at great length on the deficiencies of American society. To be sure, much of what he has to say merely replicates the clichés that have long been popular in Spain, France, and much of Latin America. For example, he told an American visitor in the late 1960s that "the percentage of mentally disturbed people in the United States is very high. . . . From the time the individual gets up in the morning, he feels as if they were trying to influence his will in some way: he is a person with a thousand pressures." With no irony whatsoever he suggested that in Cuba, by way of contrast, "you can light a cigarette . . . and not see any advertising, or drink a soft drink, read a newspaper, go out in the street, turn on the radio. You can live somewhat more calmly. No one is trying to influence your will so incessantly, in every way." People in the United States, he concluded, "live under a great strain . . . and have great feelings of frustration."[24]

The same visitor—an American by no means unsympathetic to Castro and his regime—nonetheless could not help pointing out that the Cuban media and educational system constantly provided a one-sided (not to say distorted) view of the United States. He saw this as a possible problem for the day when the two countries would eventually have normal relations. What did Castro think of this? The dictator's response is enormously revealing:

That is not an easy question to reply to. Besides, nobody has ever before posed this question. Actually it is the first time that I have heard it posed by a North American. Nor have we posed it to ourselves; it can be said that we have never been consciously concerned about that problem.

To which he added somewhat condescendingly, "Perhaps that is due to our great pessimism about whether the American people really have much opportunity to express their own opinions, or to change a situation."[25]

Quite apart from the historic influences to which he, like all Cubans of his generation, have been exposed, Castro's views of the United States have probably also been shaped to some degree by the Americans he tends to meet. While he has had the opportunity over the years to meet a wide range of U.S. citizens—including politicians, diplomats, businessmen, journalists, academics, and members of the clergy—the people who speak his language, figuratively if not literally, tend to come from adversarial elements of the American elite. American radicals without such elite credentials were also welcome, including black radicals like Eldridge Cleaver and Stokely Carmichael.[26] At one time Cuba even supported radical groups in the United States, like the Puerto Rican *macheteros*, and provided safe haven for fugitive criminals and individuals wanted in the murder of policemen. For a time it financed an English-language station known as Radio Free Dixie beamed at the black population of the American South.

In recent years Castro has spent extensive periods of time with more sophisticated (and more mainstream) critics of the United

States—maverick former officials of the American diplomatic service as well as members of the congressional Black Caucus and prominent American writers and media figures (William Styron, Arthur Miller, Ted Turner). He has also entertained celebrities of the American entertainment world, particularly the movie industry, whose politics tend to the extreme left of the U.S. mainstream. Some of these people share Castro's views of the United States, or at least of its world role, and doubtless provide him with additional anecdotal material to buttress his prejudices.[27]

It may also be noted here that, as Irving Horowitz pointed out, "there is scarcely a dictatorship in the world—from Kim Il Sung's in North Korea to Muammar Qadaffi's in Libya—that has not enjoyed the benefit of Castro's warm embrace," including of course the Sandinistas in Nicaragua and most recently Chavez of Venezuela.[28] These connections too help to validate Castro's anti-Americanism.

Much ink has been spilled over the question of whether Castro was a Marxist-Leninist before taking power. One might rather ask whether he has ever really been one, as opposed to a political opportunist and adventurer who simply grasped at the one ideology capable of attracting the kind of foreign allies that would help him to implement the Cuban nationalist agenda in its most extreme form.[29] True, since the disappearance of the Soviet bloc there has been much rhetorical claim that he and his country are a kind of saving remnant of Marxism, and that at some nebulous future date his regime will be vindicated by history. On the other hand, the compromises he has been willing to make to survive in power—including the legalization of the U.S. dollar, which has introduced new and drastic inequalities in Cuban society—suggest that his commitment to communism is shallow, useful mainly to intimidate American innocents and attract European sympathizers.

After 9/11, while on the one hand Castro condemned terrorism he also seized the opportunity to reiterate his old anti-American sentiments: "After the uproar and sincere regret of all the peoples of the earth . . . the most belligerent hawks . . . have taken control of the most powerful country of the planet. . . . Its capacity to destroy and kill is enormous." He also claimed that Cuba is "subject today of an unprecedented campaign [by U.S. authorities] to sow hatred and vengeance."[30]

ANTI-AMERICANISM AND THE CUBAN EXILE COMMUNITY

All great revolutions of modern history have produced emigra-
tions, but few exile communities have turned out to be so
geographically concentrated, politically well organized, and proximate to their country of origin as the Cuban diaspora in southern
Florida. Moreover, because their numbers include many businessmen and professionals, Cuban-Americans have come to be the
most successful and prosperous Hispanic community in the
United States. They have made Miami a second and far more im-
pressive Cuban capital, and by their very existence act as a goad
and reproach to the revolution and the country they left behind.
The fact that so many Cubans have succeeded in the United States
(or rebuilt careers that were ruined by the revolution) only pours
salt into the open wounds of Cuban national self-esteem.

Because so many ordinary Cubans have relatives in the United
States with whom they communicate by telephone or in person
(in the annual visits that Cuban-Americans are permitted to make
under existing U.S. Treasury regulations), there is widespread
awareness on the island of the gap of well-being that separates the
two communities.

Unquestionably Cubans harbor ambivalent feelings about the
U.S. diaspora. Some are openly envious of its material success;
others fear that in the event of Castro's disappearance the island
will suddenly become vulnerable to an invasion of Miami Cubans
determined to recover their properties—particularly their houses,
into which citizens loyal to the revolution have since moved—or
to settle scores with those who have deprived them of pride and
place, or even of their children or grandchildren. On the other
hand, the constant outflow of people, now drawn from the less-
exalted ranks of society, and the visits back and forth have confused the whole notion of national boundaries. As one émigré
remarked to me, "For many Cubans, the United States isn't a foreign country at all; rather, it is a place where all the dreams of the
revolution have been realized."

The regime has attempted to neutralize the effect of a
"counter-Cuba" in four different but related ways. First, the government insists that those who have left for American exile have

somehow ceased to be real Cubans, as if becoming American citizens suddenly demoted them to a lower class of person; it constantly refers to the émigré community as the "Miami mafia." Second (with far more justification), the Miami community is accused of being the power behind Washington's "anti-Cuban" policies, particularly the embargo. Third, to the extent that the exile community has lately come to support the dissident movement in Cuba, it and its allies on the island are accused of planning to effect the annexation of Cuba to the United States. Fourth and finally, relentless official propaganda paints a bleak picture of life in the United States. The very fact, however, that so many Cubans (including, increasingly, people of recognizable African descent) line up for one of the twenty thousand entry permits that (under the 1994 migration accords) are granted each year—let alone the thousands who have perished on the high seas attempting to make the trip on makeshift rafts—suggests that the official characterization of exile life in the United States has not been entirely convincing to the population.

It should be added that Cuban official perceptions of the exile community have a somewhat dated quality. For one thing, the most extreme elements—those, for example, who favor a U.S. invasion to topple Castro—are passing from the scene while younger Cuban-Americans are more moderate in their politics and more firmly grounded in the United States. The United States today is not the country it was when Castro seized power in 1959; it is far more plural, both linguistically and culturally, a place where Spanish-speaking people can feel more at home. While the boundaries between Spanish and Anglo-Saxon America have been slowly dissolving in the decades since Castro's seizure of power, the pathologies of Cuban nationalism require that they be artificially preserved in myth and vituperation.

THE CUBAN CONTRADICTION

To return to a point made at the very beginning of this essay: the principal stated objective of Cuban foreign policy today is to normalize relations with the United States. Such a normalization would undoubtedly bestow many significant benefits on the regime. Diplomatic recognition would put an end once and for all to the question of whether Fidel Castro is or is not the legitimate leader of the country, humiliating his enemies and critics abroad and possibly many of his opponents at home. Such recognition would raise his already high prestige in the international community and allow him to crow that he had finally "defeated" his adversary, the world's only surviving superpower. It would also provide new sources of income to the regime through tourism and presumably some trade in tobacco, biomedical products, nickel, and other exports, on the other hand such recognition would deprive him of the excuse for an authoritarian political system, a security policy based on the fantasy of an imminent U.S. invasion, and an explanation and excuse for the deficiencies of its economic system. The disappearance of the "Yankee peril" would greatly weaken the overall legitimacy of the Castro government. Anti-Americanism is the glue that holds together an otherwise fraying revolutionary heritage, and it must persist for that reason if for no other.

Rather than resembling a former Communist Eastern European country, Castro's Cuba today is more like a typical patrimonial Latin American dictatorship with some unusual ideological trimmings, though admittedly it continues to utilize some of the organizational features associated with Soviet-type regimes. Even so, at this point the Cuban military is arguably a far more important institution than the official (Communist) party—a feature that Castro's regime shares with Trujillo's Dominican Republic or Somoza's Nicaragua.

If the Castro regime lasts another seven years—a by no means impossible prospect—it will comprise more than half the country's entire independent history. However one might wish, this regime can hardly be relegated to an unfortunate parentheses in a long and glorious history. Rather, it *is* Cuban history, or at least a very large part of it. Many expect that with the physical disappearance of Fidel Castro the country will be able to start anew, but it is not easy to anticipate in what directions the country would move. Building on Cuba's historic frustrations and grievances, Castro has given his people a largely negative collective self-definition, one which may well survive the dissolution of his system.

He has also institutionalized a "xenophobic nationalism" in combination with economic backwardness shaped by doctrinaire
Marxist policies. It will be the task of the next generation of
Cubans to replace such a self-definition with one less dependent
on the relationship with the United States and on the remnants of
an excessively nationalistic sense of identity.

NOTES

1. "Crece cifra de families en EE.UU. que pasan hambre," *Granma digital*
(Havanna), November 3, 2003.
2. Norges Martínez Montero, "Sam el gran policía?" *Juventud Rebelde*,
October 23, 2003.
3. Quoted in Robert Freeman Smith, ed., *What Happened in Cuba? A Documentary History* (New York: Twayne Publishers, 1963), pp. 27–28.
4. Ibid, p. 30.
5. See Robert E. May, *The Southern Dream of a Caribbean Empire* (Baton
Rouge: Louisiana State University Press, 1973) and Albert Z. Carr, *The World
and William Walker* (New York: Harper and Row, 1963).
6. Boris Goldenberg, *The Cuban Revolution and Latin America* (New
York: Frederick A. Praeger, 1965), p. 102.
7. See Luis Aguilar, *Cuba, 1933* (Ithaca, N.Y.: Cornell University Press,
1972); also Justo Carillo, *Cuba 1933: Students, Yankees and Soldiers* (New
Brunswick, N.J.: Transaction Publishers, 1996).
8. See the data in Mark Falcoff, *Cuba the Morning After: Confronting Castro's Legacy* (Washington, D.C.: AEI Press, 2003), pp. 30–31, 33–37.
9. C. A. M. Hennessy, "The Roots of Cuban Nationalism," *International
Affairs*, XXXIX (July 1963).
10. As one perceptive Cuban essayist has written, "The Cuban elites constantly underestimated the depth and breadth of [anti-Americanism] in the national outlook." Julién B. Sorel (pseud.), *Nacionalismo y revolución en Cuba,
1823–1998* (Madrid: Fundación Liberal José Martí, 1998), p. 95.
11. Quoted in Sorel, *Nacionalismo y revolución . . .*, p. 11.
12. For a useful survey, see Duvon C. Corbitt, "Cuban Revisionist Interpretations of Cuba's Struggle for Independence," *Hispanic American Historical Review*, XLIII (August 1963).
13. See L. Thomas Galloway, *Recognizing Foreign Governments: The Practice of the United States* (Washington, D.C.: American Enterprise Institute,
1978) and Bryce Wood, *The Making of the Good Neighbor Policy* (New York:
Columbia University Press, 1961).
14. Unfortunately, so did some American ambassadors. Earl E. T. Smith,
who served there as U.S. representative from 1957 to 1959, is famous for having
told a congressional committee after Castro's seizure of power that "the Amer-

ican ambassador in Cuba was as important as the president of the republic, and at times even more important."

15. See Mark Falcoff, ed., *The Cuban Revolution and the United States, 1958–1960: A History in Documents* (Washington, D.C.: U.S.-Cuba Press, 2002).

16. *Cuba, Castro and the United States* (Pittsburgh: University of Pittsburgh Press, 1971), p. 31.

17. Ibid, p. 32.

18. Ibid, pp. 33, 36.

19. Aleksandr Fursenko and Timothy Naftali, *"One Hell of a Gamble": Khrushchev, Castro and Kennedy, 1958–1964* (New York: W. W. Norton, 1997), pp. 12–19.

20. Select Committee to Study Governmental Operations with Respect to Intelligence Operations, *Alleged Assassination Plots Involving Foreign Leaders,* U.S. Senate, 94th Congress, First Sess. (Washington, D.C.: Government Printing Office, 1975), pp. 32–191.

21. John Gerassi, ed., *Venceremos: The Speeches and Writings of Ernesto Che Guevara* (London: Weidenfeld and Nicholson, 1969), pp. 423–424.

22. This was my impression after a long conversation with Sánchez at the U.S. Interests Section in Havana in February 2001.

23. Georgie Anne Geyer, *Guerrilla Prince: The Untold Story of Fidel Castro* (Boston: Little Brown and Co., 1991), pp. 24–25, 41–43, 51, and Robert E. Quirk, *Fidel Castro* (New York: W. W. Norton and Co., 1993), pp. 21–22.

24. Lee Lockwood, *Castro's Cuba, Cuba's Fidel* (New York: Vintage Books, 1969), p. 191.

25. Ibid, p. 117.

26. Van Gosse, *Where the Boys Are: Cuba, Cold War America and the Making of the New Left* (New York: Verso Books, 1993).

27. One of the most fatuous of these is Robert Redford. For a devastating critique of his views on Cuba, see Merle Linda Wolin, "Hollywood Goes Havana: Fidel, Gabriel and the Sundance Kid," *New Republic,* April 16, 1990.

28. Irving Louis Horowitz, "One Hundred Years of Ambiguity: U.S. Cuba Relations in the 20th Century," *National Interest,* Spring 2002, p. 64.

29. Horowitz wrote: ". . . Castro came into power—not as a living vindication of Marxism-Leninism, but as part of an effort to move Cuba beyond ambiguity and to a nationalist closure, and, in consequence beyond the suffocating sphere of American influence. . . . Castro's strength is less a function of the authority of Marxism-Leninism as an ideology than of . . . nationalism as a mobilization tool." [Horowitz cited p. 60, 64].

30. *Granma* (the official Communist daily), September 23, 2001.

9

WALTER D. CONNOR

Anti-Americanism in Post-Communist Russia

" **O** fficial" anti-Americanism is very much a part of Russian history, especially of the history of the Soviet Union of which Russia was the core. It persisted from 1917 to the Gorbachev period beginning in 1985, when all manner of things began to change in ways inconceivable to Russians and to outside observers. Unofficial or grassroots anti-Americanism emerged after the 1991 dissolution of the Soviet Union.

At the outset, two points are to be made. First, Russian anti-Americanism is not of the sort that is common and well established among the left intelligentsia in Paris or Berlin (or Cambridge or Berkeley). Russian social and economic life is still too unsettled to afford a stable base in academia, the media, or the arts for an "adversary culture" that is routinely and predictably critical of the United States and whatever it does. Second, the anti-Americanism to be found among Russians is also different from the high-pitched, near impenetrable kind found in the Muslim lands of the Middle East and elsewhere that is associated with a fierce rejection of secular modernity. To be sure, *one* of the sources of Russian anti-Americanism is religious and cultural, but it is not of the same intensity as other varieties found elsewhere.

What follows is an attempt to specify and describe, first, four distinct (if sometimes overlapping) "sources" from which Russian anti-Americanism derives, and, second, to provide survey data about its dimensions among Russians who hold these sentiments—a large number indeed, though not always a majority of Russia's 144 million souls.

ANTI-AMERICANISM AS SOVIET RESIDUE

Russians who were formed as Soviet citizens in the pre-Gorbachev era were force-fed a steady—if stale and boring—diet of official anti-Americanism through education, the mass media, and day-to-day explicit political propaganda. From the outset the USSR sought to foster suspicion and distrust of all things foreign, "Western" and capitalist in particular. The spread of literacy, mass education, and the media assured that the message reached the population. Tight restrictions on foreign travel, preemptive censorship, and the "jamming" of foreign radio broadcasts limited the discrepant messages that Soviet citizens could receive.

Fed tendentious versions of reality, domestic and foreign, the Soviet audience may have suspected these were not quite on the level. But they could not compare them against the external world nor freely share discrepant perceptions of their domestic reality. Before World War II, Great Britain was presented as the core state of capitalism, to be replaced after the war by the United States. In the cradle-to-grave political socialization of Soviet citizens, anti-Americanism was a major theme. Its key symbol was the poster-art Uncle Sam, fat-bellied and well fed, scheming against proletarian revolution and global progress, ever the enemy of emerging nations taking "the noncapitalist road" after the wave of decolonization in the early 1960s.

This brand of anti-Americanism is still found among older people, the less educated, the smaller-town rural population—people who largely accepted the Soviet "official" version of reality and were habituated to the "normal totalitarian society" of the pre-1985 USSR. After 1985 a Soviet leader himself offered a new version of reality, leaving such people more disoriented, confused, and angry than grateful or hopeful. They learned that their "Soviet way of life" was not the envy of the world; that some 50 to 60 of the world's 180-odd nations enjoyed higher living standards; that in their daily life they were as much objects of Western pity and contempt as of fear. For them the end of the cold war was not a triumph of bilateral negotiation, of realistic Gorbachevian diplomacy, but a surrender to the U.S.-led West, a capitulation to "the enemy" by the very leader who had already disturbed their life with new and subversive ideas and information.

As these people see it, they have gained little since 1991. They do not appreciate their new freedom to complain and are nostalgic for numerous aspects of the old order. Their habits are maladaptive in the new market economy. They are losers. They have seen capitalism come to Russia—and it *is* the capitalism they read about yesteryear in their schoolbooks and in the media—rough, unequal, competitive, and juxtaposing a few very rich winners to a mass of poor losers.

Such people vote Communist in large numbers. The Russian Federation Communist Party—the KPRF—is not explicitly "restorationist," but it is close enough to old ideas (and views of the United States) to generate significant protest votes. The KPRF won 22.3 percent and 24.95 percent of the parliamentary vote in 1995 and 1999, respectively. Its non-charismatic leader, Gennadi Zyuganov, received 40 percent of the presidential vote in 1996 versus Yeltsin's 53.8 percent, and 29 percent versus the quasi-incumbent Putin's 52.9 percent in March 2000. Besides the KPRF, there are explicit Soviet restorationist groups such as "Communists—Working Russia—For the Soviet Union," a coalition with more than a hint of street thuggery about it, which won only 4.53 percent and 2.22 percent of the vote in the 1995 and 1999 parliamentary elections, but with these numbers outscored many other small parties.

The anti-Americans who thus manifest their feelings at the ballot box certainly view the past through their own biased perspective, but that past, and what they value about it, is *not* entirely imaginary. A fast-moving, unforgiving, "freer" society and economy that rewards and sanctions unequally and *publicly* is far removed from the old, grey, low-level, secure egalitarianism that formed these people. Americans may be used to such conditions; they live with them. Russians—*these* Russians—are not, and cannot imagine how other Russians can. They are bound to be anti-American. The United States is both symbol and agent of all that has befallen them, the embodiment of forces of history that, as it turned out, were *not* on their side. The Soviet system failed—but these are still Soviet men.

AN "ORTHODOX CHRISTIAN NATION"

Russia—as a society, state, civilization—is the largest national component of the non-Western part of Europe. Its heritage is in Byzantium, not Rome; its alphabet is the modified Greek that is Cyrillic, rather than the Latin of the West; its religion is "Orthodox" rather than the Catholic/Protestant mix of the West. The "markers" of textbook Western Civilization—feudalism, Renaissance, Reformation/Counter-Reformation, the Enlightenment—are not part of Russian history. Nor are they of the other Christian Orthodox lands of Eastern Europe—Serbia, Montenegro, Macedonia, Bulgaria, Romania—with which Russia has at times claimed special affinity.

Not all Russians, by any means, are aware of these differences—or, more to the point, see them as important. But the differences endure. Even in the nineteenth century, reformist intellectuals split into Westerners and Slavophiles, the latter rejecting Western political and economic models in favor of the ideal of a Russia transformed according to its own (deeper, more "authentic," religious) roots and resources. For Slavophiles, the West was a shallow, rootless, secular civilization that Russia would try to emulate only at its peril. Better to be faithful to itself, "better to be poor and backward but close to nature than to be rich and civilized like the French and English, whose advanced development proved only that they were on the brink of decadence."[1]

The Soviet order effectively suppressed *this* debate, imposing another ideology. After its demise, both Slavophiles and Westerners reemerged, the latter especially in the writings of the authors of a hopeful "Atlanticist" foreign policy and approach to America. The Slavophile strain, the emphasis on Russia's Eastern Orthodox identity, draws a line between Russia and the West, with specific implications for attitudes toward the United States as well. Russians of this persuasion are sensitive to any indication, past and present, of Western contempt, patronization, or disrespect for their Orthodox world. Tsarist Russia positioned itself as "big brother" to the Orthodox people of the Balkans, long under the Ottoman Turks. "Western" Christians seemed to care little about the Serbs, Bulgars, and similar peoples. And, though all sorts of realpolitik were entangled in August 1914, it was Serbia's difficulties with the Austro-Hungarian Empire that "drew" Russia toward war.

The journalist Aleksei Pushkov, in late 1993, characterized this mind-set:

> Its [Russia's] leaders have inherited the old communist "hate" of the United States, but they bring to it much more passion and paranoia, along with strong anti-Semitic overtones. They depict the United States as *the center of a Western anti-Russian, anti-Slavonic, and anti-Orthodox conspiracy that aims to destroy Russia as a state and reduce it to a Western colony* [emphasis added].[2]

The U.S.-NATO intervention in Bosnia in 1995 provided grist for these mills. It was seen as intervention against brotherly (Orthodox, Eastern) Serbs on behalf of (Catholic, Western) Croats and, worse, Slav Muslims. This was evidence of "Western animosity toward Russia," "an important element of the West's master plan to destroy" Russia.[3] Four years later the Western intervention in Kosovo—again, against Serbs, in defense of (non-Slav) Albanian Muslims, once more produced strong feelings among the partisans of this line.

This anti-Western anti-Americanism is *not* ubiquitous, and it has many critics in Russia itself.[4] But to those who contemplate the nature of *Muslim* anti-Americanism, the resemblances are striking. This type of anti-Americanism is strident and obsessive: the writer Vasil Belov in 1997 condemned "people like Brzezinski and Kissinger who hate the Orthodox conscience of the Russian people and their religious and monarchic aspirations."[5]

Similar attitudes emerged in connection with the NATO action in Kosovo against the Serbs, as one *member* country, Greece, sharing such sentiments was quite reluctant to participate. In both mass and elite opinion, Greece was on the wrong side. This had less to do with inconvenient location than with civilizational and religious ties to the Orthodox Serbs.

In this perspective much of Russian foreign policy from 1991 to the present appears excessively pro-Western—a policy misguided, doomed to failure, and, perhaps most important, undignified and unworthy of historic "Great Russia." For these critics, despite manifest differences, there is little essential difference between the United States and Western Europe, except for America's size and power. While protectiveness toward "Christian Orthodox civilization" is not the major force behind Russian anti-Americanism today, it is likely to be among the most *durable* kind being as much about what the United States *is* as what it does.

FRUSTRATION: SUPERPOWER NO MORE

Not surprisingly, anti-Americanism is also fed by a powerful combination of frustration and envy: frustration that Russia is not the superpower the USSR used to be, and envy of the United States as sole superpower since the Soviet collapse.

David Remnick wrote after a recent visit to Russia that "obsession with American power is universal. The Russians are obsessed with American power in their own way. Theirs is a reaction of the humbled rival learning to deal with an unaccustomed sense of weakness. This may be the most important emotion in all Russian politics."[6] This emotion is not necessarily tied to any particular political ideology. Even those with pro-West tendencies can feel it.

Superpower status guarantees respect. For many people, even being a small cog in the state machine of a superpower was a source of psychological gratification. In the past many Russians, as Soviet citizens, understood that only they and the Americans "counted" in this global sense. By contrast, the USSR's Warsaw

Pact "allies"—Poles, Czechs, Hungarians, and the rest—counted
hardly at all. Neither did the U.S.'s NATO allies (with the special
exception of West Germany for older Russians).

For some this type of "civic" gratification was compensated for
the material deprivations experienced in their daily lives. (Although it is well to remember that even in the Brezhnev era the
average Soviet citizen had little real awareness of how his living
standard compared to that of Western or even Eastern Europe's average citizen.) Thus onetime *Financial Times* correspondent
David Satter reported that when people in a Moscow foodstore
queue in 1981 complained, an old woman silenced them with the
reminder that "the whole world is afraid of us."[7]

With the Soviet collapse, the gratification of being feared vanished. Life for many of the educated, metropolitan, and better-
situated improved markedly in the material sphere, but the old
sense of partaking of the superpower "clout" was gone. Many not
given to any love of the old regime found they missed this.
Vladimir Shlapentokh makes the point comprehensively:

> Paradoxically, the "new" attitude toward the West . . . does not
> incorporate an individual inferiority complex. . . . However,
> while Russian politicians, business people and journalists re-
> joice in their newfound wealth, what they have lost is the self-
> esteem and pride of representing a superpower, a great country
> . . . which could compete on almost any level. . . . Today, the
> Russian elites feel not dignity, but national humiliation. With
> their material needs fully satisfied . . . [they] are particularly sen-
> sitive to the view that their country lost, probably forever, its
> special standing in the world.[8]

Many who welcomed the approaching end of the cold war as
Gorbachev dealt with Reagan and Bush as a seeming equal inclined to see the future as one of partnership and cooperation between two great powers of undiminished stature. This was an
unrealistic expectation given the impact of the USSR's economic
decline on its political and military capacity. Others anticipated
that the Soviet Union would transform itself into a somewhat
downsized Union of Sovereign States, with Russia dominating any

formal "union." And some anticipated a complete dissolution and an independent Russia. In any case it was hoped that a measure of Western—and especially American—sympathy and aid (along with continuing nuclear status) would allow Russians to maintain the dignity of superpower status in the post–cold war era.

It did not work out that way, and it was an unrealistic expectation from the beginning. Hence there was a sense of wounded dignity, the feeling that Russia was being treated in a way appropriate for a small, run-of-the-mill country, but not for—a Russia. Some observers see this view as a deep, continuous thread in the mass consciousness; others regard it as ephemeral.[9] Many Russians see the United States, leader of the West, as a selfish state rich in economic resources, capable of giving Russia a much softer economic landing, that has withheld help and turned to "exploiting" Russian riches where it can, while carping about Russia's assumption of liability for the USSR's debts.

People of this persuasion have great difficulty accepting the notion that "Russia" is not an equal of the United States. For them the Western moves that *have* given Russia special status (arguably, some would say, *beyond* its entitlements)—such as expanding the G-7 into the G-8, or signing the NATO-Russia "Founding Act"—are cold comfort.

"America," its actions and failures to act, have defined more than any other country or countries Russia's reduced status. For those with the ex-superpower blues, it is hard not to be anti-American.

THE SPURNED SUITOR

The early foreign policy line of Yeltsin's Russia—from August 1991 to early and mid-1993—was pro-Western and pro-American to a fault. This Atlanticist policy was articulated by the foreign minister Andrei Kozyrev, a polished product of the international organizations section of the old Soviet foreign ministry, who had joined Yeltsin's Russian government in 1990. In the Kozyrev policy, Russia offered partnership to the United States, and to all indications would have been satisfied with a junior partnership. Russia sought entrance to many Western "clubs," but, as Kozyrev made its case, it was not making claims to special treatment because of its history. There was an element of "eager learner" in all this, a foreign policy line that complemented, and aimed to serve, the domestic objectives of Yeltsin's economic team led by Yegor Gaidar. The aims were price liberalization, economic stabilization, privatization of the state-built monopoly economy, and the development of institutions alien to the Soviet economy but normal and necessary in the "civilized economic world" Russia sought to join. Both in foreign and domestic policy, Russia was trying to show the Western world that it was determined on this new course and sincere in its pursuit. As Aleksei Pushkov summarized it:

> . . . The radical democratic wing in Russian politics . . . professes the idea of strategic alliance with America and major concessions to Western countries in return for financial assistance and a gradual integration of Russia into international economic and political institutions.[10]

This policy had to be sold, however, to many outside the radical democratic wing. Yeltsin and Kozyrev had to justify it to the fractious, disorderly congress of People's Deputies, the legislature elected in mid-1990. Kozyrev and Co. overestimated the benefits to be reaped from pursuing a course many of his critics judged to be overly "eager" and concessionary, and one that disregarded the new Russia's legitimate interests.

Kozyrev thus found himself pressured to deliver goods he promised but could not produce because the United States, and the rest of the West, were not delivering them to *him*. Economic recession, the mistaken anticipation of "peace dividends," and the rising expense of the thickly woven social safety nets characteristic of the European NATO/EU states made the West less generous than it could have been in its treatment of Russia in the critical years 1992–1993. Much-ballyhooed aid packages in the mid-$20 billion range turned out to include large amounts of noncash benefits (like the reduction or rescheduling of debt that Russia could not pay in any case).

The Russian political audience could not take these disappointments in stride. To much of the public, Russia seemed to be reaping little reward for the pains and dislocations it was experiencing, and the West was insufficiently supportive and set unrealistic standards for the niceties of market transition. By late 1992, Kozyrev and those aligned with him were increasingly on the defensive, and frustrated. The criticisms came by no means only from the political fringe but from respectable players in the new Russian politics who were not in the thrall of pro-Soviet nostalgia.

The critics had a point. The Yeltsin-Kozyrev "oversell" had been an extension of the euphoria from the recent past, when Gorbachev and Shevardnadze had done so much to "settle" the cold war. It had further inflated an unrealistic but appealing image of the Soviet Union, later Russia, entering the family of free nations, supported by its big American friend politically as well as financially.[11]

Euphorias do not endure, and Russia's post-Communist landing was not nearly as soft as the Atlanticists had promised nor as the majority of Russian citizens would have liked. The Atlanticists' failure underlined the differences, as Vladimir Shlapentokh put it, between the "old liberals" (effectively the Kozyrevs and Gaidars) and the "new liberals."[12]

When in 1993–1995 the Russians discovered that Western financial aid would be limited and that Western private firms were more interested in profit margins than in pulling Russia out of its economic morass, they were extremely disappointed. The "new liberals" began using the West, particularly the United States, as a scapegoat for the Russian economic predicament. There was considerable resentment against the United States, which despite its sympathetic declarations refused to grant Russia the status of a favored nation.[13]

QUANTITATIVE DIMENSIONS: THE U.S. IN RUSSIAN MINDS

Despite the multiple roots of Russian anti-Americanism, poll data show Russians often well inclined toward the United States. National sample polls (the number of respondents usually around 1,600) by the All-Russian Institute for the Study of Public Opinion

(VTsIOM) have since 1992 asked Russians about their "attitude as a whole" toward the United States, with the following results.[14]

Date	Positive %	Negative %
11/1991	70	8
8/1992	70	8
4/1993	69	7
3/1995	65	13
3/1997	71	19
12/1998	67	23
3/1999	38	49
4/1999	33	53
5/1999	32	54
12/1999	55	31
2/2000	66	22
7/2000	69	23
2/2001	59	27
9/2001	72	19
10/2001	61	28
1/2002	68	22
3/2002	50	41
8/2002	67	22

Majorities or pluralities held positive attitudes during the period up to 2002, save for the exceptional soundings of 1999. Russians who have a pronounced positive attitude toward the United States rarely fall below 80 percent—only around one in five Russians "doesn't know" or "doesn't care" about the United States.

To a significant degree, the variations in attitudes over time are driven by events (and the media spin on them). In March through May of 1999, positives plummeted, negatives exceeding 50 percent. At the time, Russians were responding to the U.S.-led NATO moves against Milosevic's Yugoslav regime, in defense of the Albanians in Kosovo. And even though this was an instance when the Russian government too was critical of U.S. policy toward the "Orthodox little brother" Serbs, public ire was rather short-lived. By December the positive-negative balance had reversed itself.

The notable positive "spike" in September 2001 is of course the effect of 9/11. Sympathy came quickly and readily, it seems, prompted by scenes of graphic destruction from a people also concerned about terrorism with Islamic fundamentalist roots. Putin, a popular and decisive president whom many Russians regarded as the "tough" leader the times required, led and augmented popular sentiments with his declaration that Russia stood in solidarity with the stricken Americans.

Negative attitudes have a dynamic of their own. Three polls over 1991–1993 reflect a honeymoon of sorts, a hopefulness in the Atlanticist foreign policy of the time. Russians knew little, and had little experience of, the United States from the pre-Gorbachev past. Very moderate negative attitudes are registered in this hopeful period. They grow as time wears on and no "quick fix" comes from the West for the grinding economic and social problems that preoccupy Russians in the mid-1990s. The "spurned suitor" has soured on the object of earlier aspirations.

Over the long haul, though, post-Kosovo and 9/11 positive responses have dominated. America and Americans became more familiar as Russians gathered more information and developed more "nuanced" views. U.S. and Western policies and actions— NATO expansion, Kosovo, etc.—came to be seen as reflecting indifference to, even hostility toward, Russia's legitimate interests. While Russians who are still psychologically "Soviet" remain impervious to variations in Western behavior, figures show that there is a Russian population with varying attitudes over time, capable of positive turns (after 9/11) but also reverting rapidly to the more typical reservations once the "event effect" lessens, as the October 2001 figures show.

AMERICA THE EXPLOITER?

Marxism-Leninism taught Soviet citizens that large capitalist economies exploited weaker, smaller ones, often ex-colonies of major Western capitalist powers. Inequalities and exploitation within capitalist economies were reproduced in the massive inequalities among states.

Soviet citizens were told in Brezhnev's time—and in a certain sense accurately—that their economic order protected them from the rapacity of global capitalism. But since 1992, according to one oppositional refrain, Russia lies prostrate, still rich in human talent and natural resources, but now the target of unscrupulous foreigners and Russians who will deal with them for their own profit.

There are reasons for Russians to feel vulnerable, though engagement with foreigners is not a major one. The arms trade aside, the USSR, and now Russia, exported mainly raw materials—oil, natural gas, timber, minerals—not unlike a Third World country. It has been dependent—for some, overdependent—on commodities whose prices fluctuate markedly. Growth since 1998 has been based significantly on high oil and gas prices. These will, at some point, fall, as they did in the early to mid-1980s, darkening the Soviet economic outlook in the years before Gorbachev's 1985 accession.

Many in 1992–1993 feared what they called "Kuwaitization." International oil interests would somehow "grab" Russia's energy sector, assisted by a small stratum of Russians ready to act as a *comprador* class. These groups would enjoy Western-style wealth while the vast Russian majority stagnated in poverty and marginalization. While fears of this type were not unrealistic given precedents in many of the world's oil economies, things worked out somewhat differently. Many of the early "oligarch" fortunes were based on buying oil at the absurdly low domestic Soviet/Russian price, bribing or otherwise acquiring export licenses, and selling the oil abroad at the world price. Russians were exploiting the Soviet legacy of nonmarket pricing and exploiting their fellow Russians as well.

Attitudes toward foreign economic involvement, especially American, are likely to carry a lot of "freight," given the recent and more distant history, and the failure of the world economy in the earlier 1990s to provide enough economic benefits from the rich West to suffering Russia. There *had* been optimism—polled in December 1991, a majority felt "foreign companies should be allowed to establish their own businesses in Russia." By January 1993, a plurality was against this; in January 1996 a 56 percent majority favored discouraging foreign investment. Poll results into 2000 saw virtually the same anti-investment majority.[15]

Through much of the post-Communist period, direct foreign investment in Russia, on a per capita basis, was very small compared to that in Poland, Hungary, and other transition economies. Thus American "penetration" of the Russian economy was far from massive. But attitudes are not the result of measured reality. Major branded consumer items (Marlboro cigarettes, Snickers bars) carry an American identity, feeding the notion of an American "hyper-presence," of the rich surviving superpower making money off the Russian consumer.

Poll data support these observations. A recurrent Russian-administered poll, commissioned by the USIA/Department of State, asks for responses to the statement, "The U.S. is utilizing Russia's current weakness to reduce it to a second-rate power and producer of raw material." Over the course of 1995–2000, respondents answered thus:[16]

Date	% Agree	% Disagree
Aug. 1995	59	27
Apr. 1996	71	18
Apr. 1997	71	18
Jan. 1999	76	13
Feb. 2000	81	12

A spring 1996 four-city study (St. Petersburg and Moscow, Ekaterinburg in the industrial Urals, and Vladivostok on the Pacific) posed essentially the same question, with results not quite as negative as later. Asked whether the United States wanted "to help Russia revive, as it helped Germany and Japan revive after 1945," or whether its aim was "to reduce Russia . . ." as above, they replied:[17]

	St. Petersburg	Moscow	Ekaterinburg	Vladivostok
Help revive	31%	29%	34%	30%
Reduce	48	54	49	56
Uncertain	22	18	17	14

1996 was a presidential election year: Yeltsin was up for a second and last term, his major opponent the Communist Gennadi Zyuganov. The same poll examined subsamples in Moscow and Vladivostok sorted by intent to vote for either of these, or other contenders.

Zyuganov backers were much more likely to feel that the United States aimed at "reduction" than Yeltsin supporters (78 percent versus 43 percent in Moscow, 70 to 46 percent in Vladivostok). Yeltsin supporters saw the United States aiming to "revive" the economy much more than Zyuganov's people (Moscow: 39 to 13 percent, and 46 to 18 percent in Vladivostok.) Notable, still, is the lukewarm assessment of American intentions even by Yeltsin's backers.[18]

History and attitudes formed in an earlier era, persistent economic problems, the unfamiliarity of full engagement in the world economy, and the "looming" American presence will probably conserve these attitudes in the foreseeable future.

WHAT KIND OF A FOREIGN POLICY?

As far as foreign policy preferences are concerned, there is no sign that the public is being manipulated by elites into extreme anti-Western positions. Absent as well is any massive groundswell of popular emotion that would constrain foreign policy makers. Russians, like most other people, seem for the most part "deferential" to elites in matters foreign—they have had enough domestic issues to fill their plates in the decade-plus since 1991.

But there have been events which call for a reaction. NATO's first post-Soviet expansion, encompassing Poland, Hungary, and the Czech Republic, initiated in the mid-1990s, met with strong objections from Moscow at the time and was grudgingly tolerated when it was consummated in 1999. On Putin's watch, the second expansion (involving Slovakia, Slovenia, Romania, and Bulgaria, as well as Estonia, Latvia, and Lithuania, the latter three former republics of the USSR) effectively took place in 2002–2003. "Old" NATO typically assured Russia that expansions were not aimed at it, minimizing or denying what drove the new Central and East European members to seek inclusion. Russia tolerates the new NATO, its interests acknowledged in the NATO–Russia Founding Act giving it "a voice, but not a veto."

There is little indication in poll data that Russians feel particularly threatened by these developments, however unwelcome they have been. An early 1997 VTsIOM poll found that negative reactions to the *idea* of NATO expansion to include former (Soviet-era) "allies" had risen from 34 percent a year earlier to 41 percent at that point. At the same time reactions to the prospect of former Soviet republics joining went to 50 percent negative from 41 percent in 1996. These are *moderate* reactions, given the gravity of the symbolism of these events; if most Russians did not welcome these developments, few were deeply disturbed.

The same (1997) respondents, asked about an appropriate alliance policy for the Russian Federation, responded thus to the alternatives presented:[19]

Avoid all blocs	26%
Cooperate with NATO	22
Link with former WTO states, ex-Soviet republics	17
Join NATO	8
Hard to say	27

These views largely held over the next few years. Later studies showed significant numbers advocating cooperating with or joining NATO (37 percent in January 2000, 36 percent (August) and 43 percent (November), and back down to 32 percent in February 2001.[20]

The stimulus of 9/11 evoked sentiments of "outrage" from 52 percent in a poll a few days later, and 38 percent expressed sympathy with the United States. But 33 percent said the U.S. "got what it deserved"—and by the end of the same month 50 percent held this view.[21] In February 2002, several months after the U.S. reaction, another VTsIOM poll sought to measure Russian sentiment. Asked about bilateral relations, only 16 percent of the respondents thought that the United States and Russia had grown closer; 28 percent saw more drifting apart; and 46 percent little change. Only 7 percent were willing to support sanctions on suspect states (Libya, Iraq, Syria) while 20 percent opposed moves against these "historic allies" of the former USSR.[22]

A Pew Foundation multi-national poll in June 2003 asked whether respondents were happy or unhappy with the lack of Iraqi military resistance to U.S./UK military forces. The unhappy Russians, 45 percent, outnumbered the 24 percent who were happy.[23] Independent of events in Iraq, a June 2003 VTsIOM poll found 61 percent agreeing that the United States tried to "dominate" and "impose its values" on the world[24]—but as far back as April 1995, precisely the same portion had responded that way to the question. In early 2000, shortly after Kosovo and well before 9/11, 85 percent had expressed the same view of the United States.[25]

It is hard to know how deep and stable are such opinions since polls capture the attitudes of the moment. Tangential factors and events can produce changing judgments. Tracking the run-up to Bush's 2002 visit with Putin, a February poll found 44 percent regarding the United States as "unfriendly" to Russia, a figure that spiked in March to 71 percent, and declined to 58 percent in May on the eve of the visit. The spike, as the pollsters interpreted it, was due to (1) controversies over the figure-skating judgment at the Salt Lake City Winter Olympics, and (2) a heavily-publicized bilateral scrap over "Bush legs"—the massive export of U.S. frozen chicken to a hungry but sensitive Russian market.[26]

Such fluctuations in Russian views of the United States have also been reported recently by David Remnick, relying on "two of Russia's leading pollsters" who told him that "anti-Americanism . . . comes and goes. . . . Generally Russians have a positive attitude toward the United States, but there is a complex of defeat and humiliation and even neurotic sensitivity that flares up."[27]

On the whole, the Russian public's assessments of the United States do not come across as alarmist. Repeated polls indicate that however negatively Russians "feel" about NATO expansion, they do not express any deep conviction that NATO actually threatens them. Many accepted, however grudgingly, that Russia's unenthusiastic cooperation with the West via the IFOR force in Kosovo in 1999 made sense, even though the West was seen by many as illegitimately taking the (Muslim) Albanian side versus the (Christian Orthodox) Serbs. Similarly, asked about what most needed attending to in pursuit of Russia's long-term national security interests, many suggested less emphasis on NATO issues and more on improving the performance of Russia's domestic economy.

EUROPE AND AMERICA? EUROPE VERSUS AMERICA?

Strains in the Western alliance were dramatized in 2003 by the run-up to "Operation Iraqi Freedom." In the UN Security Council the UK aligned with the United States. Permanent Security Council—and NATO—member France opposed Washington and was joined by NATO and (temporary) Council member Germany. They both thus joined permanent Council member Russia. What this disjunction among NATO members implies in an age when it has been asserted that "Americans are from Mars, Europeans from Venus"[28] need not detain us here. But it introduces the question of how Russians distinguish the United States from the "rest of the West," if they do.

A March 2001 poll showed a tendency to draw such distinctions when asked. Twenty percent were "equally favorable" to the United States and "Europe," 5 percent disliked both. Of the remaining 75 percent, five times as many (51 percent) favored Europe, only 11 percent the United States. The better educated tended more than others to see distinctions, and tended to favor Europeans. Asked whether Russia should develop partnership with the United States or the European Union, 46 percent chose the EU, only 10 percent the U.S., and 28 percent not unreasonably said "both." However far-fetched it was in 2001—and has been since—59 percent thought Russia should seek membership in the EU, a sentiment especially common among the younger, better educated, and affluent.[29]

Studies over 1995–2002[30] showed clear trends in Russian evaluations of specific countries.

	Positive		Negative	
	1995	*2002*	*1995*	*2002*
United States	77.6%	38.7%	9.0%	45.5%
UK	76.6	64.1	4.2	14.5
France	78.9	78.0	3.0	7.1
Germany	69.0	68.1	11.5	14.9

Evaluations of the United States substantially declined; European countries retained their positive ratings. In 2002 those polled responded to broader regional/cultural concepts, thus suggesting stronger reservations about the United States per se and as a component of the West.

	Positive	Negative
America	43.3%	49.6%
Europe	79.0	13.6
The West	51.6	39.1

Apart from judgments about the actions and intentions of other countries, there is the question of whether Russians see "models" to emulate—in pursuit of material and political benefits—either in America or Europe or both. Expressions such as "a market economy, but not a market society" (used by 15 percent) suggest an acceptance of greater state involvement in the production of "social goods" than is the case in the United States.

Recent poll data provides little help in assessing the balance of pro-European versus pro-American attitudes. A May 2000 VTsIOM poll,[31] just before a Clinton visit to Putin, asked Russians whether "the West European and American type of social system" was appropriate for them—conflating the two. The respondents did not seize on either as models. Only 4 percent said "entirely," 15 percent that it could be "adapted" to suit. A full 37 percent at the other end said "totally unsuited" and "contrary to Russian ways of life," with 31 percent more moderately judging it "not entirely suited" or "unlikely to take root." These results are in line with the earlier-mentioned 1996 survey of four cities where respondents were asked about whether "Russia should try to emulate the American economic system." We have averaged the four cities' results, as there was little variation. The tilt was negative: 8.75 percent fully agreed, but 21 percent fully disagreed. One-quarter partly agreed, but 34.3 percent partly disagreed—well over half, then, were inclined against the American model.[32]

Focus-group research, more than polling, encourages the exploration of questions like what "U.S. vs. Western Europe as potential model" means. In July 1999, eight groups assembled by a Russian firm with USIA funding explored questions about America.[33] Perhaps it was to be expected that while some were attracted to the

United States as model, more respondents were drawn to the "safety nets" that Western European societies provide. "We need a democratic but probably less liberal system than in the States. It would rather be some socialist model, of the Scandinavian type," said a twenty-five-year-old St. Petersburg man, backed by another in Samara who thought that "Germany . . . Scandinavian countries, are closer to us." Some saw *scale* as critical and therefore Europe less attractive as a model ("The American model . . . is the only one that can be applied. All other countries considered are very small. . . . Here everything is similar, the same geographical scale"). But others saw a poor fit with America because of what might be called a moral gap: "Extreme freedom will be harmful to us, because such honesty as in America is impossible here."

The 1999 sentiments in favor of the European welfare state replicated those expressed in a focus-group study of youth much earlier (in 1994). There is something poignant and wistful, given the weakness of the Russian economy, in the words of a St. Petersburg student quoted in one such study:

> There's a very good system in Germany. . . . Even those who don't work are completely protected socially, with the kind of stipend a person can live on easily. . . . Those who work pay very high taxes. . . . A person who's not working can have an apartment and a car and feed himself. By working, he can afford to travel.[34]

In conclusion it may be observed that phenomena like "anti-Americanism" are always volatile and variant, driven by a wide range of factors. The political/social/economic dynamic of Russia today, hopeful in many ways, remains distinct from that of the states of Western Europe and Third World countries, which have maintained or generated high levels of anti-American sentiments in recent times. Russian anti-Americanism is a unique blend of European-style cultural superiority, Third World–style envy and ambivalence, and historically conditioned nationalistic resentment.

Russian Anti-Americanism seems more than marginal but less than epidemic, broad but not necessarily deep. It is less confined to a self-reproducing intelligentsia, unlike in Western Europe, but often displayed by substantial portions of the so-called masses.

Certain aspects of Russian anti-americanism have more to do with Russia than with the United States (as is true in many other countries); some of its components are obviously related to what the United States *does*, others to what it is or stands for. Since some U.S. policies will always be irritants in some part of the world, Russia included, and since the basic characteristics of American society are unlikely to change in the foreseeable future, Russian anti-americanism will persist, albeit in a fluctuating manner—especially since there is so much in America that appeals to the Russian desire for modernity, affluence, political stability, and a rooted democracy.

NOTES

1. William Pfaff, "Russia's Foolish Gesture," *Boston Globe*, June 21, 1999, p. A23.

2. Alexei K. Pushkov, "Letter from Eurasia: Russia and America: The Honeymoon's Over," *Foreign Policy*, Winter 1993–1994, p. 81.

3. Vladimir Shlapentokh, "'Old,' 'New,' and 'Post' Liberal Attitudes Toward the West: From Love to Hate," *Communist and Post-Communist Studies*, no. 3, 1998, p. 212.

4. See, e.g., the commentator Otto Latsis in *Novye Izvestiia*, March 26, 1999, pp. 1–2 trans. in *Current Digest of the Post-Soviet Press (CDSP)*, April 21, 1999, pp. 11–12.

5. Vasili Belov, *Sovetskaia Rossiia*, Feb. 13, 1997, cited in Shlapentokh, op. cit., p. 212.

6. David Remnick: "Post-Imperial Blues," *New Yorker*, October 13, 2003, p. 88.

7. David Satter, *Age of Delirium: The Decline and Fall of the Soviet Union* (New York, 1996), p. 46.

8. Shlapentokh, op. cit., p. 206.

9. See e.g., Mikhail Kochkin, "Russia and the United States Post September 11: What Do the Russians Think?" The Jamestown Foundation *Russia and Eurasia Review*, no. 11, 2002 (online).

10. Pushkov, op. cit., p. 77.

11. Ibid., p. 83.

12. Shlapentokh, op. cit., p. 205

13. Lev Gudkov, "Otnoshenie k SshA v Rossii i problema anti-amerikanizma," *Monitoring obshchestvennogo mneniia*, no. 2, 2002, p. 35.

14. Department of State, Office of Research, Opinion Analysis, "Russians Queasy Over Chechens, Taliban, NATO," August 23, 2000, p. 6

15. Department of State, Office of Research, Opinion Analysis, "Russians' Mistrust of the U.S. at New High," March 14, 2000, p. 2.

16. USIA, Office of Research and Media Reaction, Research Report, "Four Russian Regions View the United States," May 1996, p. 25

17. Ibid.

18. *Trud*, Jan. 21, 1997, p. 1, trans. in Feb. 19, 1997, p. 24.

19. *Vremya Novostei*, March 12, 2002, p. 6, trans. in *CDSP*, April 10, 2002, p. 24.

20. *Izvestiia*, Sept. 28, 2001, p. 4, trans. in *CDSP*, Oct. 24, 2001, p. 5.

21. *Vremya Novostei*, op. cit., above.

22. Pew Research Center for the People and the Press, "Views of a Changing World 2003: War With Iraq Further Divides Global Publics," June 3, 2002, p. 3 (online).

23. Interfax Moscow, May 15, 2003, online via Johnson's Russia List, no. 7182, May 15, 2003.

24. "Russians' Mistrust," op. cit., p. 1.

25. *Izvestiia*, May 21, 2002, p. 4, trans. in *CDSP*, June 12, 2002, p. 8.

26. "Four Russian Regions," op. cit., p. 22.

27. Remnick, cited, p. 88.

28. See Robert Kagan, *Of Paradise and Power: America and Europe in the New World Order* (New York, 2003).

29. *Noviye izvestiia*, March 24, 2001, p. 1; trans. in *CDSP*, April 25, 2001, p. 7.

30. *Izvestiia*, Oct. 8, 2002, p. 7; trans. in *CDSP*, Nov. 13, 2002, pp. 1–4.

31. *Trud*, June 3, 2000, p. 4; trans. in *CDSP* , July 5, 2000, pp. 6–7.

32. "Four Russian Regions," op. cit., p. 20.

33. USIA, Office of Research and Media Reaction, Anatole Shub, "Russian Attitudes Toward America After the Kosovo Conflict," Sept. 1999 (the quotes are drawn from pp. 11–12).

34. USIA, Office of Research and Media Reaction, Richard B. Dobson and Anatole Shub, "Russia's Future: Perspectives of Young Russians, 1994–1995," March 1995, p. 20.

PART II

Domestic Denunciations

10

ROGER KIMBALL

Anti-Americanism Then and Now

"Beware! America is a mad dog!"—Jean-Paul Sartre, 1953

"America has become a criminal, sinister country—swollen with priggishness, numbed by affluence, bemused by the monstrous conceit that it has the mandate to dispose of the destiny of the world." —Susan Sontag, 1967

"The real matter is the extinction of America, and God willing, it will fall to the ground."—Mullah Mohammed Omar, Taliban leader, 2001

Anti-Americanism is hard to argue with. I don't mean that there is an abundance of good arguments in favor of the phenomenon. Quite the contrary: in so far as arguments enter the arena at all, they usually lean heavily on assertion backed up by belligerence and cliché. But it is seldom that argument *does* enter. Anti-Americanism has always been more a matter of attitude than argument. It depends on, it draws its strength from, the wells of passion, not reason. The composition of that passion is complex and shifting. Envy generally enters into it, as do a congeries of political attitudes that the literary critic Frederick Crews aptly dubbed "Left Eclecticism": a bit of cut-rate Marxism to start with, leavened with a dollop of some trendy academic theory, a dash of

239

utopian fantasy and snobbery, seasoned to taste with resentment and paranoia. Paul Hollander's classic *Anti-Americanism: Irrational and Rational* (1995) provides a connoisseur's overview of the favored configurations.[1]

Reading through Hollander's inventory, one is again and again struck by the combination of virulence and absolutism that fuels expressions of anti-Americanism. Hollander quotes the Russian writer Vassily Aksyonov, who emigrated from the Soviet Union to the United States in the late 1970s: "Even now, after living in America for more than five years, I keep wondering what provokes so many people in Latin America, Russia, and Europe to anti-American sentiments of such intensity that it can only be called hatred. There is something oddly hysterical about it all."[2]

Indeed. What Aksyonov omits is the prevalence of such hatred and hysteria in both European and even homegrown American expressions of anti-Americanism. There may be—in fact there assuredly are—many things to criticize about the United States. But anti-Americanism has almost nothing to do with *criticism*. It is more a pathology than a position, operating not by evidence but emotion.

Apparently it was always thus. What we might call contemporary anti-Americanism—as distinct from the simple *haut-en-bas* snobbery and prejudice that preceded it—was born in the aftermath of the Second World War. In part, I suppose, it was an illustration of the old adage that "no good deed goes unpunished." As the French novelist and essayist Pascal Bruckner observed in *The Tears of the White Man* (1986), his brilliant anatomy of "third-worldism" and "compassion as contempt": "Western Europe knew that, without the help of the Marines, they would purely and simply have been wiped off the map. But some forms of generosity are insulting."[3]

The insult festered in the years following 1945, a period when Sartre's explosive anti-Americanism set the tone of elite opinion in Europe and, increasingly, in the United States. Vietnam fanned the smoldering resentment into a raging conflagration. "It must be understood," Bruckner observed,

> how in this emotionally overheated context, America could be the focus of so much hostility in the post–World War II period,

and particularly during the 12 years of the Vietnam conflict. She
provided the ideal guilty party. She was guilty on many counts,
particularly because of the help she had given us. Neither
France, nor Italy, nor Germany could forgive America for having
liberated them from the Nazi and fascist yokes. . . .

The hatred was essentially aimed at the fact that America
was what she was. America's actions were seen as following
from her perverted nature, and came to be simply consequences
or illustrations of it. The polemical escalation went on and the
controversy degenerated into a kind of metaphysical confrontation: America did not commit misdeeds, she herself resulted
from a fundamental injustice. She was execrated not for this or
that, but purely and simply for existing. Everywhere, at all
times, it was necessary to denounce "the planetary empire of
North American hegemonic capital," the underlying pathology
of barbarism.[4]

The image of America as essentially evil and corrupt was
widely taken up and parroted by American intellectuals in the
1950s and 1960s. More and more, anti-Americanism became a necessary badge of authenticity for writers and intellectuals. One
thinks of Norman Mailer and his excoriation of "the totalitarian
tissues of American society" in "The White Negro,"[5] or Susan
Sontag's unending denunciations of American society as "inor-
ganic, dead, coercive, authoritarian," etc., etc. "America," she
wrote in 1969, "is a cancerous society with a runaway rate of productivity that inundates the country with increasingly unnecessary commodities, services, gadgets, images, information."[6]

It is often said that the Vietnam War was the great catalyst for
the sudden upsurge of anti-American sentiment in the United
States. Almost overnight, it seemed, the entire climate of elite
opinion in the country underwent a startling metamorphosis.
Opinions, like those of Norman Mailer, which had hitherto occupied the fringe suddenly went mainstream. The ostensible issue was U.S. military involvement in Vietnam. But it soon
became clear that Vietnam was merely the occasion for disparagement and demands that went far beyond any specific government policy. Vietnam became the banner under which the entire

range of radical sentiment congregated. Michael Lind was right when he observed in *Vietnam: The Necessary War*[7] that the conflict in Vietnam "uncovered, but did not create, deep divisions in the American body politic." Vietnam provided a rallying point, a crusade large enough to submerge all manner of ideological differences. Susan Sontag spoke for many left-wing intellectuals when she noted that "Vietnam offered the key to a systematic criticism of America." As Paul Hollander wrote, Vietnam was "more a catalyst than a root cause of the rejection of American society in the 1960s."[8]

The Yippie leader Jerry Rubin put it even more bluntly: "If there had been no Vietnam war, we would have invented one. If the Vietnam war ends, we'll find another war."[9]

As the sixties evolved, it became increasingly clear that what was at stake was not only the war. The real issue was our way of life: what used to be called without apology "the American way of life," with its social and political institutions, its moral assumptions, its unspoken beliefs about what mattered. One measure of the change wrought by this cultural offensive is the fact that even now, thirty or more years on, it is nearly impossible for anyone with a college education to speak of "the American way of life" without irony or condescension. To a large extent, that is the case because it is now practically taken for granted that going to college involves not so much the "questioning" as the repudiation of traditional moral and political values. (Or to put it another way: the academic "questioning" or "interrogation" of traditional values has only one outcome: rejection or ridicule.) The greater the exposure to higher education, the more thorough the repudiation is likely to be.[10]

Not that such exhibitions of adversarial animus are confined to the academy. Far from it. They are part of the air we breathe: implicit as much in our degraded pop culture as they are in our assumptions about our responsibilities as citizens and moral agents. To put it somewhat paradoxically: one of the most profound effects of the cultural revolution of the 1960s was to institutionalize the assumption of institutional illegitimacy. Accordingly, anti-Americanism became less a response to events than a simple reflex—less a matter of cynicism than a rejection of established authority, as if the very fact of being established undermined the legitimacy of an idea or institution.[11]

One of the most conspicuous and influential bastions of reflexive anti-Americanism in the 1960s (and since) has been the *New York Review of Books*, the highbrow near-weekly review that was started in 1963.[12] The *Review* began to fill a void in American letters for the serious review and discussion of ideas. This it did with extraordinary energy and success. But what began as a distinct liberal bias lurched sharply to the left in the aftermath of the assassination of John F. Kennedy and the escalation of the Vietnam War. The *Review* reflected and abetted the growing anti-Americanism of America's cultural elite. It was in the middle 1960s, for example, that Noam Chomsky began contributing his lugubrious diatribes against American foreign policy, replete with such delicacies as his description of the Pentagon (in a piece called "On Resistance") as "the most hideous institution on earth." It was then, too, that Mary McCarthy filed her three-part report on the socialist paradise being prepared in North Vietnam and that I. F. Stone began bludgeoning readers with his interminable essays on the American military establishment (sample title: "The War Machine Under Nixon").

In the mid-sixties, upper-class English dons and trendy American writers were joined by a more demotic element. Suddenly, political firebrands like Jerry Rubin, Stokely Carmichael, and Tom Hayden began appearing in the paper along with radical fellow-traveler Andrew Kopkind, a refugee from *Newsweek*. Of the ten pieces that Kopkind wrote for the *Review*, the most notorious came in the issue of August 24, 1967. Headlined "Violence and the Negro," the cover announced in outsize type Kopkind's piece on Martin Luther King and Black Power and Hayden's report on the riots—what he called "The Occupation"—of Newark. Underneath was a large diagram instructing readers on the exact composition of a Molotov cocktail. According to former SDS leader Todd Gitlin, a Berkeley commune that habitually trashed neighborhood stores believed that "massive retaliation might be imminent, . . . and for that contingency they kept a

Molotov cocktail in the basement, designed to the specifications of the *New York Review of Books* cover of 1967."[13]

It was about this time that even some of the *New York Review*'s ideological allies began having doubts about the direction the journal was taking. Irving Howe, himself a socialist and founding editor of *Dissent*, noted scathingly in 1968 that the *Review* had managed to achieve "a link between campus 'leftism' and East Side stylishness, the worlds of Tom Hayden and George Plimpton." Howe continued:

> Opposition to communist politics and ideology is frequently presented in the pages of the *New York Review* as if it were an obsolete, indeed a pathetic, hangover from a discredited past or worse yet, a dark sign of the CIA. A snappish and crude anti-Americanism has swept over much of its political writing. . . . And in the hands of writers like Andrew Kopkind . . . liberal values and norms are treated with something very close to contempt.[14]

Howe was not the only former contributor to express alarm. The liberal sociologist Dennis Wrong, who had appeared in the *New York Review*'s inaugural issue, wrote a lengthy and thoughtful piece on the journal for the November 1970 issue of *Commentary*. Noting, with basic approval, the *New York Review*'s early campaign against the Vietnam War, Wrong pointed out that

> by 1966 and 1967 a new tone of extravagant, querulous, self-righteous anti-Americanism began to creep into the NYR's reports on Vietnam, especially those of Noam Chomsky, Mary McCarthy, and I. F. Stone. The war seemed increasingly to provide the occasion for an extreme and bitter repudiation, marked by an unmistakable touch of *Schadenfreude*, of a great deal more in American life than the Johnson administration's foreign policy, the Pentagon, the military-industrial complex, and the wretched clichés of cold-war propaganda.[15]

The May 1971 *Esquire* went even further, predicting in a press note that "from among [the *New York Review*'s] authors the next Stalin, and his speech writers, will emerge."[16]

As Dennis Wrong suggested, although the Vietnam War occasioned much of the *New York Review*'s radicalism, the real target was not U.S. policy about Vietnam but America itself. Indeed, anti-Americanism—a prominent feature in almost all countercultural rhetoric—became a major leitmotif, almost a unifying theme, in the *New York Review* within a few years of its birth. For example, when Mary McCarthy traveled to Vietnam early in 1967 for the *New York Review*, she began the first installment of her report—the cover story for April 20—with this admission: "I confess that when I went to Vietnam early in February I was looking for material damaging to the American interest and that I found it, though often by accident or in the process of being briefed by an official." In the course of her reports, McCarthy naturally places the phrase "Free World" in scare quotes and consistently portrays Americans as venal monstrosities. (When she converses with a CIA agent, his "lips flexed as he spoke like rubber bands.") Glorifying the industry and pluck of the North Vietnamese, she tells her readers that the "sense of fair play . . . has atrophied in the Americans here from lack of exercise." At the beginning of her second installment, McCarthy famously declared that "the worst thing that could happen to our country would be to win this war."

Years later, in 1979, after the horrific spectacle of the Vietnamese boat people and similar phenomena consequent on America's withdrawal and defeat in that war, she was asked if she had changed her views on Vietnam. Noting that her ideal was still "socialism with a human face" (one might as well wish for wooden iron), she nevertheless acknowledged that

> as for my current views on Vietnam, it's all rather daunting. I've several times contemplated writing a letter to [the Vietnamese premier] Pham Van Dong (I get a Christmas card from him every year) asking him can't you stop this, how is it possible for men like you to permit what's going on? . . . I've never written that letter, though.[17]

The combination of arrogance and naiveté implicit in Mary McCarthy's retrospective musings about Vietnam was a staple of the *New York Review*'s anti-Americanism. Jason Epstein provided a

truly vertiginous example in an essay called "The CIA and the Intellectuals" (April 20, 1967). Following up on the revelation that the
CIA had covertly funded some student and cultural organizations
(including, most famously, *Encounter* magazine in England), Epstein's piece was a meditation on how "organized anti-Communism
had become as much an industry within New York's intellectual
life as Communism itself had been a decade or so earlier." Among
other things, "The CIA and the Intellectuals" was an early master-
piece of what came to be called "moral equivalence." In one remarkable passage, Epstein writes that Stalin

> not only purged and tortured his former comrades, killed millions
> of Russians, signed the pact with Hitler, and suppressed the writ-
> ers and artists. He had also done something which directly affected
> their own lives, much as the CIA and the State Department have
> not only burned the crops and villages and peoples of Vietnam, but
> have also brought so much anguish into the lives of so many young
> people today. What Stalin did to the generation of intellectuals
> who came of age between the Thirties and Fifties was to betray the
> idealism and innocence of their youth. By perverting revolutionary
> Marxism, he cheated them, as it were, in their very souls.

Epstein concludes sadly that certain radical intellectuals,
robbed of their Communist ideals by nasty Joe Stalin, devoted
"the rest of their energies to retribution." Hence, you see, the
birth of neoconservatism. It's not simply that Epstein transforms
a principled rejection of communism into a psychological tic; he
also insinuates an equivalence between the murderous behavior of
Stalin and the activities of the CIA. What Epstein does not see is
that his friends who turned against communism did so not because Stalin *perverted* "revolutionary Marxism" but because they
finally understood that Stalinism was the natural *fulfillment, the
outcome* of revolutionary Marxism.

Epstein's essay is notable for its exhibition of the way liberal
disillusionment can be elevated into a kind of metaphysics of anti-
Americanism:

> The facts are clearer now than they were ten years ago. Then it
> surprised us to find that the country seemed to have fallen into

a frenzy of self-destruction, tearing its cities apart, fouling its landscapes, poisoning the streams and skies, trivializing the education of its children, and not for any substantial human happiness, . . . but for higher profits and rapidly increased economic growth. . . . What we were experiencing was the familiar philistine expansionism (of which the Vietnamese are only the latest victims), this time attached to a formidable technology whose alarming possibilities were as yet unclear, but which was even then depressingly out of human scale and growing larger and more autonomous every day.

Now at last, Epstein concludes, it is clear that "pursuit of money and power became openly America's main, if not its only, business."

By psychologizing politics and attempting to replace basic political commitments with a melodrama of virtue, Epstein is really engaged in a species of moral blackmail. As Diana Trilling observed in a withering response to "The CIA and the Intellectuals,"

Epstein would have us believe that "depending on how we respond to the poisoning of our streams and skies we will take either a Left- or a Right-Wing position on—say—the Vietnam War. Whoever abhors polluted air and desecrated landscapes will have adequate grounds on which to judge American foreign policy. He will recognize it in all its 'philistine expansionism.' What further guide to decision in foreign affairs does anyone need?[18]

In the end, the *New York Review*'s anti-Americanism has to be seen as part of a larger project of political, intellectual, and moral delegitimation. For example, over the years the *Review* has run some distinguished pieces on science. But it has also been prey to a kind of countercultural technophobia that borders on irrationalism. Consider, for example, John McDermott's "Technology: The Opiate of the Intellectuals," that appeared in July 1969. The amazing conclusion of this long and tedious piece is that the spirit of scientific curiosity and the promotion of technology

should be frankly recognized as a conservative or right-wing ideology. . . . It succeeds in identifying and rationalizing the interests of the most authoritarian elites within this country, and the expansionism of their policies overseas. Truly it is no accident that the leading figures of *laissez innover* . . . are among the most unreconstructed cold warriors in American intellectual life.[19]

It is no accident, either, that this sort of politicized attack on science and technology became a prominent item on the menu of academic radicalism in the decades to come.[20]

Although the Yippie leader Jerry Rubin made only one appearance in the *New York Review*, his "Emergency Letter to My Brothers and Sisters in the Movement" (February 1969), written while he was in custody, is nonetheless significant as a reminder of the kinds of views the editor Robert Silvers and his colleagues were willing to countenance in its pages. Rubin begins by boasting that, although the forces of repression are on the rise, "We are stealing the youth of America right out of the kindergartens and elementary schools." After some remarks about how "America's courts are colonial courts," her jails "black concentration camps," he goes on to declare that

> . . . smoking pot is a political act, and every smoker is an outlaw. The drug culture is a revolutionary threat to plasticwasp9–5america [sic].
>
> Who the hell wants to "make it" in America anymore? The hippie-yippie-SDS movement is a "white nigger" movement. The American economy no longer needs young whites and blacks. We are waste material. We fulfill our destiny in life by rejecting a system which rejects us.[21]

Accordingly, Rubin calls for widespread demonstrations near jails and courthouses to "demand immediate freedom for Huey P. Newton, Eldridge Cleaver, Rap Brown, all black prisoners, Timothy Leary, the Oakland Seven, all drug prisoners, all draft resisters, Benjamin Spock, . . . me," etc. To be sure, Rubin was always something of a buffoon. And his later conversion from Yippie freak to Wall Street investment counselor makes his adolescent antics seem even more puerile than they perhaps were. Today it is tempting to look back on erstwhile countercultural heroes like Jerry

Rubin as comic figures, more preposterous than menacing. But it is a great mistake to believe that the preposterous is the enemy of the malign. On the contrary, such qualities often feed upon and abet each other.

The malevolence of the preposterous has been reinforced by the upsurge of anti-Americanism in the wake of the terrorist attacks of September 11. Thus when the playwright Harold Pinter was granted an honorary degree in Turin in 2002, he explained that the attack of 9/11 was "a predictable and inevitable" "act of retaliation against the constant and systematic manifestation of state terrorism on the part of the United States over many years, in all parts of the world."[22]

Pinterism (if I may thus eponymize this brand of intellectualizing self-hatred) is not a new phenomenon. George Orwell noted something similar in his anatomy of the pacifism that was rampant in English intellectual circles before and during World War II. The "unadmitted motive" of pacifism, Orwell wrote, was "hatred of Western democracy and admiration of totalitarianism."[23] Harold Pinter is no John Walker Lind. You won't find him joining up with the Taliban. But you will find him in sympathy with his spiritual colleague-in-rhetoric, Susan Sontag, who explained that the assault of September 11 was "not a 'cowardly' attack on 'civilization' or 'liberty' or 'humanity' or 'the free world' but an attack on the world's self-proclaimed superpower, undertaken as a consequence of specific American alliances and actions. . . . Whatever may be said of the perpetrators of [September 11's] slaughter, they were not cowards."[24]

Does she say, then, that they were murderous fanatics? Hardly. Sontag (like Pinter) is at once too ambivalent and too admiring for that: too ambivalent about the "world's self-proclaimed superpower" (or "rogue state," as Pinter put it) and too admiring of the insurrectionists, perhaps on account of the authenticity of their committment. In this context, it is worth remembering Orwell's observation about the "processes by which pacifists who have started out with an alleged horror of violence end up with a marked tendency to be fascinated by the successes and power of Nazism."

Orwell noted that pacifism was "objectively pro-Nazi" because it inculcated an attitude that aided England's enemies. Just so, anti-Americanism is objectively pro-terrorist. It was not surprising that the Nazis did all they could to encourage pacifism among the English (just as the Soviets actively aided the anti-war movement in America in the 1960s and 1970s). Similarly, anti-Americanism helps to create a climate where terrorism is excused, rationalized, explained, and explained away. We deserved it; we had it coming; arrogance; poverty; the environment; root causes . . .

Pacifism was built around phrases that sounded pleasant (peace, love, understanding, nonviolence) but that were essentially deceptive because they were unrealistic—that is, untrue to the nature of reality, to the way the world actually works (as distinct from the way we might wish that it did). "To abjure violence," Orwell noted, "it is necessary to have no experience of it." Looking back on the Spanish Civil War in 1942, he criticized "the sentimental belief that it all comes right in the end and the thing you most fear never really happens." He also wrote:

> Nourished for hundreds of years on a literature in which Right invariably triumphs in the last chapter, we believe half-instinctively that evil always defeats itself in the long run. Pacifism . . . is founded largely on this belief. Don't resist evil, and it will somehow destroy itself. But why should it? What evidence is there that it does?[25]

While pondering that question, let us also step back and ask what America's role in the world has been over the course of the last century. The British journalist Brian Appleyard, writing in the London *Times* on September 23, 2001, registered his amazement at the orgy of anti-Americanism that greeted the terrorist attacks of September 11. In one sense, he noted, there was nothing new about anti-Americanism.

> I, certainly, have always lived in a world suffused with savage anti-Americanism. In my childhood the grown-ups were all convinced that the apparently inevitable nuclear holocaust would be the fault of the Americans. In my student years I saw the Vietnam war used as an excuse for violence and intimidation that

would have made Mao Tse-tung proud—indeed, my contemporaries were waving his Little Red Book, his guide to mass murder, as they attempted to storm the American embassy. . . .

But the access of anti-Americanism that followed al Qaeda's attacks proceeded in a shriller, more virulent register than most earlier examples. It also seemed less rational.

Appleyard duly noted that America was far from a perfect society. But what role had Americans actually played in "that most awful of all centuries," the twentieth?

They saved Europe from barbarism in two world wars. After the second world war they rebuilt the continent from the ashes. They confronted and peacefully defeated Soviet communism, the most murderous system ever devised by man, and thereby enforced the slow dismantling—we hope—of Chinese communism, the second most murderous. America, primarily, ejected Iraq from Kuwait and helped us to eject Argentina from the Falklands. America stopped the slaughter in the Balkans while the Europeans dithered.

There is a sense in which anti-Americanism—certain aspects of it, anyway—is the predictable function of envy, a phenomenon pointed to by the English authors of *1066 and All That*[26] when they noted that since the time of World War I America has been the world's Top Nation. As political thinkers since Pericles have noticed, distinction breeds envy, envy breeds resentment, and, unchecked, resentment breeds hatred. But that sort of animus—lavished on Athens in her day, on Rome in hers, and on Great Britain in hers—is not by itself the sort of "anti" sentiment with which we need to concern ourselves.

Walter Bagehot came closer when he noted, in *Physics and Politics* (1872), that the enormous benefits the English had conferred upon India—education, hygiene, the rule of law—were received with distinct ambivalence by the native population. The benefits were real, but, Bagehot apostrophized,

What puzzles them is your constant disposition to change, or as you call it, improvement. Their own life in every detail being

regulated by ancient usage, they cannot comprehend a policy
which is always bringing something new; they do not a bit believe that the desire to make them comfortable and happy is the
root of it; they believe, on the contrary, that you are aiming at
something which they do not understand—that you mean to
"take away their religion"; in a word, that the end and object of
all these continual changes is to make Indians not what they are
and what they like to be, but something new and different from
what they are, and what they would not like to be.[27]

The journalist Henry Fairlie made a cognate point in 1975 in
his essay "Anti-Americanism at Home and Abroad." "The energy
of the American presence in the world," Fairlie wrote,

is both welcomed and feared, both a cause of hope and a source
of anxiety, because with its idea it keeps unsettling the established forms of the past. Not merely old but ancient customs are
surrendering to a presence that is not imposed and yet seems ir-
resistible, to an idea that appears to be more powerful than the
slogans of any revolution.[28]

The unsettling of what Bagehot called "fixity" is a great source
of cultural anxiety. It is, I suspect, a much larger ingredient in foreign complaints about the baneful influence of "vulgar" American
culture than is usually acknowledged. (Not, I hasten to add, that
those complaints are without merit: it is a curious irony, though,
that the most effective criticisms of American culture have
tended to come from conservative pro-American sources rather
than from the anti-American left.) But explanations, however accurate, however deep, can take us only so far. They always bring
with them a tendency to dismiss the thing being explained—"*tout
comprendre, c'est tout pardonner*." It is wise to take account of illuminating explanations. But it is a mistake—a mistake to which
well-meaning liberals are especially prone—to believe that by understanding why a vicious character came to be the way he is, we
thereby purchase immunity from the effects of his viciousness.

It has been suggested that the current outbreak of anti-
Americanism, although broad, is not necessarily deep. There may

be some truth in that, at least in so far as it applies to European and American anti-Americanism. (The Arab version is a more resilient strain.) Certainly anti-Americanism comes in several versions and in differing levels of toxicity. But there is not a lot of comfort to be gleaned from that fact. For anti-Americanism is like certain infections: it can begin as a minor nuisance and, if untreated, blossom into a life-threatening condition.

Nor is there much comfort to be had from the contention that anti-Americanism in its homegrown versions is synonymous with political dissent, that it is merely a vigorous form of self-criticism. In the first place, it isn't true. Dissent is one thing; anti-Americanism is closer to its opposite. Indeed, anti-Americanism, because of its adversarial moralism, tends to short-circuit self-criticism. This was a point that Henry Fairlie underscored when he observed that the expression of anti-Americanism is "not criticism of one's own society; in fact it prohibits just and effective criticism" by substituting utopian fantasies for political realities.

One of those realities is the responsibility that accrues to states that wield great power. It is a lesson that liberal regimes are continuously tempted to forget, to their own peril and the peril of the societies they influence. The dissolution of the British Empire—one of the most benevolent and enlightened political forces in history—took place for many reasons, including, sad to say, pressure from the United States. But part of the reason for its dissolution was inner uncertainty, weariness, a failure of nerve. By the middle of the last century Britain no longer wished to rule: it wanted to be liked. The promiscuous desire to be liked, for states as much as for individuals, is a profound character flaw. It signals a faltering of courage, what Pericles castigated as *malakia*, "effeminacy," and a dangerous loss of self-confidence. At the height of the cold war, the political commentator James Burnham observed that "Americans have not yet learned the tragic lesson that the most powerful cannot be loved—hated, envied, feared, obeyed, respected, even honored perhaps, but not loved."[29]

In the immediate aftermath of the terrorist attacks on New York and Washington, we saw plenty of repellent, deplorable outbursts of anti-Americanism: the dancing "Death to America" multitudes in the Middle East as well as the predictable responses of the Chomsky-Sontag-Pinter brigade. But we also witnessed a vast outpouring of sympathy. Some of the sympathy no doubt was genuine; much of it was oleaginous and depended on the novel spectacle of America appearing as victim. The trouble was that America was not content to remain a victim. And when a victim fights back, he may earn respect but he forfeits sympathy and kindred sentimentalizing emotions.

When Susan Sontag said that the terrorist assaults on the United States were "undertaken as a consequence of specific American alliances and actions,"[30] she offered that observation as a partial justification or extenuation of the attacks, which it most certainly was not. But there is, I believe, another sense in which growing anti-Americanism, together with a growing climate of terrorism, can be seen as a predictable result of American actions or, more to the point, of American inaction. I am not offering a candidate for the "cause"—much less the "root cause"—of terrorism. Determining the cause of terrorism is not a difficult hermeneutical problem. Jonathan Rauch had it essentially right when he argued that the cause of terrorism is terrorists. Nevertheless, when we ask what nurtures terrorists, what allows them to flourish and multiply, one important answer is the failure of authority, which is the failure to live up to the responsibilities of power.

In the course of his reflections on anti-Americanism, Henry Fairlie observed that "Anti-Americanism abroad tends to be strongest when America itself seems to have lost confidence in its own idea." Some such loss of confidence has repeatedly afflicted the American spirit, at least since the end of the Vietnam conflict. It is by now a familiar litany but is nonetheless worth reviewing. From the mid-1970s the United States has vacillated in discharging its responsibilities to power. Whatever the wisdom of our involvement in Vietnam, our way of extricating ourselves was ignominious and an incitement to further violence. The image of that U.S. helicopter evacuating people from our embassy in Saigon is a badge of failure, not so much of military strategy as of nerve.

Even worse was our response to the hostage crisis in Iran in 1979 and 1980. Our hesitation to act decisively was duly noted and found contemptible by our enemies. The fiasco of President Carter's botched rescue attempt, when a transport vehicle and one of our helicopters collided on the sands of the Iranian desert, was a national humiliation. President Reagan did effectively face down the Soviet Union, but his halfhearted response to the terrorist bombing of a U.S. Marine barracks in Lebanon in 1983 contributed to the tattered reputation of America as (in Mao's phrase) "a paper tiger."

The Clinton administration sharply exacerbated the problem. From 1993 through 2000 the United States again and again demonstrated its lack of resolve even as it let its military infrastructure decay. In Somalia at the end of 1992, two U.S. helicopters were shot down, several Americans were killed, the body of one was dragged naked through the streets of Mogadishu. We did nothing; such inaction prompted Osama bin Laden to reflect that his followers were "surprised at the low morale of the American soldiers and realized more than before that the American soldier was a paper tiger and after a few blows ran in defeat."[31]

It was the same in 1993, when terrorists bombed the World Trade Center, killing six people and wounding scores. More inaction followed in June 1996, when a truck bomb exploded outside a U.S. military barracks in Saudi Arabia, killing nineteen Americans. There were some anguished words but no response. It was the same in 1998 when our embassies were bombed in Kenya and Tanzania, killing hundreds. The response was to rearrange some rocks in the Afghan desert with a few symbolic cruise missiles.

It was more of the same in October 2000, when suicide terrorists blew a gigantic hole in the *USS Cole*, killing seventeen sailors and almost sinking one of the navy's most advanced ships. Like Hamlet, we responded with "words, words, words" and only token military gestures. The harvest was an increase in contempt and a corresponding increase in terrorist outrage, culminating in the events of September 11.

In my judgment the current orgy of anti-Americanism, fanned by the war with Iraq, will dissipate in proportion to the resoluteness demonstrated by the United States. If America continues to act decisively in Iraq and elsewhere in the war on terrorism, there will eventually be a corresponding diminution in the fury of anti-American sentiment. I do not expect it will end the drivel of fantasists like Harold Pinter or connoisseurs of contempt like Susan Sontag. Nothing could do that. But I am confident that it will help move anti-Americanism off the agenda.

Time and again history has shown that strength legitimately exercised has a pacifying effect. It instills a sense of security, backed up by an attitude of respect. And in that atmosphere anti-Americanism ceases being a threat to world stability and recedes to its proper role as the pastime of cranks and impotent malcontents.

NOTES

1. Oxford University Press, 1992; updated paperback edition published in 1995 by Transaction Publishers.

2. Quoted in Hollander, *Anti-Americanism*, p. 336.

3. Free Press, 1986, p. 15 (originally published as *Le sanglot de l'homme blanc*, Editions du Seuil, 1983).

4. *The Tears of the White Man*, p. 16.

5. "The White Negro: Superficial Reflections on the Hipster," was first published in *Dissent* and later reprinted in Mailer's collection *Advertisements for Myself* (Harvard University Press, 1992, orig. pub. 1959), pp. 337–358.

6. "Some Thoughts on the Right Way (for us) to Love the Cuban Revolution," *Ramparts*, April 1969, pp. 6–19.

7. *Vietnam: The Necessary War. A Reinterpretation of America's Most Disastrous Military Conflict* (Free Press, 1999), p. 215.

8. *Political Pilgrims: Western Intellectuals in Search of the Good Society* (fourth edition, Transaction Publishers, 1998), p. 198.

9. Rubin, cited in *Political Pilgrims*, p. 198.

10. How durable such repudiation remains through adult life is another question. Evidence is by no means clear-cut. On college campuses today there is often a gulf to be found between the "tenured radicals," die-hard ideological veterans of the sixties, and large numbers of apolitical or outright patriotic undergraduates not predisposed to find corruption in every corner of American society and even sympathetic to its military forces, especially when engaged abroad.

11. This is an idea that one can trace back at least to John Stuart Mill's attack on "the despotism of custom" and the "tyranny of [established] opinion" in *On Liberty*. For a criticism of Mill's position, see my essay "James Fitzjames

Stephen v. John Stuart Mill," in *Experiments Against Reality: The Fate of Culture in the Postmodern Age* (Ivan R. Dee, 2000), pp. 159–188.

12. For a more detailed discussion of the *New York Review of Books*, its anti-Americanism, and its place in the radicalism of the 1960s, see "A Nostalgia for Molotovs" in my book *The Long March: How the Cultural Revolution of the 1960s Changed America* (Encounter Books, 2000), pp. 225–246.

13. Todd Gitlin, *The Sixties: Years of Hope, Days of Rage* (Bantam, 1987), p. 401.

14. Quoted in Philip Nobile, *Intellectual Skywriting: Literary Politics and "The New York Review of Books"* (Charterhouse, 1974), p. 4.

15. "The Case of 'The New York Review,'" *Commentary*, November 1970, p. 49.

16. Quoted in Nobile, *Intellectual Skywriting*, p. 5

17. Quoted in *Political Pilgrims*, p. xcv.

18. Quoted in Nobile, *Intellectual Skywriting*, p. 45

19. *New York Review of Books*, July, 31, 1969, p. 35.

20. For a thorough and illuminating examination of these trends, see Paul R. Gross and Norman Levitt, *Higher Superstition: The Academic Left and Its Quarrels with Science*, Baltimore, 1994.

21. Jerry Rubin: "Emergency Letter to My Brothers and Sisters in the Movement," *New York Review of Books*, February 13, 1969, p. 27.

22. Address delivered by Harold Pinter on November 27, 2002, at Turin University. The text is available at: www.haroldpinter.org/home/turinunispeech.html.

23. Quotations from Orwell are from "No, Not One," "Pacifism and the War," and "Looking Back on the Spanish Civil War" in *The Collected Essays, Journalism and Letters of George Orwell*, Vol. II (Harcourt, 1968), pp. 165–171, 220–223, and 249–267.

24. Susan Sontag, *New Yorker*, September 24, 2001, p. 32.

25. "Looking Back on the Spanish Civil War," in *Orwell Collected Essays*, New York, 1968, Vol. II, p. 259.

26. Walter Carruthers and Robert Julian Yeatman, *1066 and All That: A Memorable History of England*, New York, 1931, p. 115.

27. *Physics and Politics: Thoughts on the Application of the Principles of "Natural Selection" and "Inheritance" to Political Society*, edited by Roger Kimball (Ivan R. Dee, 1998), pp. 139–140.

28. *Commentary*, December 1975, pp. 29–32.

29. *Containment or Liberation? An Inquiry into the Aims of United States Foreign Policy* (J. Day, 1953), p. 191.

30. *New Yorker*, September 24, 2001, p. 32.

31. Interview with John Miller in 1998, available at http://abcnews.go.com/sections/world/DailyNews/miller_binladen_980609.html.

11

HARVEY KLEHR AND JOHN EARL HAYNES

The Rejection of American Society by the Communist Left

No political movement in American history has been more clearly identified with the sweeping rejection of American society than the Communist Party of the U.S.A. (CPUSA) and the organizations it controlled. From its militant origins in 1919 to its resolutely moderate tone in the late 1930s; from 1940 when it opposed American participation in World War II to late 1941 when it fervently advocated such involvement; to the late 1940s and early 1950s when its officers were prosecuted for conspiring to teach and advocate the overthrow of the government by force and violence, and members were hauled before congressional committees investigating un-American activities, the American Communist party has been the emblem of opposition to the American political and social order.

At the same time no political movement in American history has figured in more court cases dealing with fundamental issues of American civil liberties. Members and sympathizers of American communism have challenged a host of federal state and local laws and ordinances designed to impede, rein in, or outlaw activities and practices seen as threatening to the social order. Numerous Supreme Court cases from the 1920s through the 1960s established fundamental principles of the civil rights of all American citizens, including the right to hold a passport, freedom of speech and association, the limits on the investigatory powers of legislative bodies, and others as a result of the use of the court system by Communists. Many of the legal battles in which Communists participated grew out of political struggles and activities that few people would characterize as inherently anti-American. Individual Communists and the CPUSA itself were active at various times in the struggles to build industrial labor unions, fight fascism, and end racial segregation. To many Americans these commitments and activities were far from un-American or anti-American but rather represented an effort to fulfill the American creed and extend and protect democratic values.

The relationship between the CPUSA and anti-Americanism is complicated. Through much of its history the CPUSA was passionately and unequivocally opposed to basic American values, beliefs, institutions, and prevailing political-economic practices— though sometimes not because of a special animus toward the United States but due to its deep, doctrinal antagonism toward capitalism and all bourgeois societies. At times it was enthusiastically and even mawkishly pro-American, boasting of its patriotic fervor and denouncing its enemies as traitors to the American dream. Sometimes CPUSA members presented themselves as squarely in the tradition of American democratic reformers; at other times they regarded those reformers as frauds and sellouts.

By the same token, the nature of the party's membership changed over the years, as did the motives of those joining it. The committed revolutionaries who were early party members and looked forward to the overthrow of capitalism had a very different relationship to both communism and Americanism than the labor organizers or opponents of fascism who joined in the late 1930s when the CPUSA was active in those causes. The majority of American Communists remained in the party for only a few years; their motives and attitudes were probably different from those of the devoted, long-term members who remained committed despite frequent changes of party line and emphasis. In turn, rank-and-file members, who may or may not have intellectually absorbed the party's ideology, differed from cadres, who were trained at party schools, worked in party organizations and often lived in a party cocoon where non-Communist views were totally alien and proscribed. But in the final analysis it was the cadre who guided the party, no matter what the views and motives of the rank-and-file and the short-term members who had little impact on party policy.

There was, however, one constant theme throughout the many incarnations of American communism. Whether in its early years or during its decline, the party's gaze was always firmly fixed on Moscow. As one American Communist poet of the 1930s, H. H. Lewis, put it:

I'm always thinking of Russia
I can't get her out of my head.
I don't give a damn for Uncle Sham
I'm a left-wing radical red![1]

The CPUSA came into existence because of events in Russia, endured a decade of struggles and internal conflict in response to and often due to the heavy-handed interference of the Soviet Union acting through the Communist International (or Comintern), and, even during its period of greatest independence, continued to follow, respond, and report to authorities in the Soviet Union and often depended on its secret financial subsidies. Even after the dissolution of the Comintern in 1943, the CPUSA formulated its policies in accord with what it thought the USSR wanted, so much so that an effort to establish an independent American organization in the mid-1950s provoked such an extreme crisis that it destroyed the party. What was left was a tiny rump, still beholden to Moscow's vision of the world, while the vast majority of its members realized that it could not be reformed or weaned from its pro-Soviet orientation. John Gates, a leader of the defeated reform Communists of 1956–1957, bitterly commented on the discussion inside the CPUSA at the time, which was focused on the need to "Americanize" the party: "For us now, after 38 years of existence as an American Party, made up of Americans most of whom were born here and have no problems of language or customs, to have to admit that we must still Americanize ourselves, reveals our situation better than anything I could possibly say."[2]

As the nature of the relationship between the Soviet Union and the United States changed, so too did the attitude of the CPUSA toward the country in which it existed. When the USSR was the center of world revolution and the United States was but one of the many capitalist states that stood in the way of realizing that goal, American Communists were anti-American because they despised capitalism, not because they particularly despised America. When the Soviet Union and the United States were allied in the struggle against fascism, American Communists enthusiastically promoted American values and traditions, in part because some believed in them, but mostly because such a stance helped create alliances with liberals and progressives that in turn strengthened the American-Soviet alliance. When the United States became the Soviet Union's greatest enemy during the cold war, American Communists demonized it as the fount of evil in the world.

The founders of the CPUSA declared their revolutionary intent without equivocation. Radicals on the verge of breaking with the nonrevolutionary Socialist party, they pledged themselves in 1919 "to work unceasingly for . . . the establishment of a Socialist Federated Soviet Republic in America." Militant "Wobblies," proclaiming that "the bloody seizure of power by the working classes is the only possible way," abandoned the Industrial Workers of the World for the new Bolshevik movement. The American Communist party's founding manifesto denounced reformism, saying, "Communism does not propose to 'capture' the bourgeoisie parliamentary state, but to conquer and destroy it," and "it is necessary that the proletariat organize its own state *for the coercion and suppression of the bourgeoisie* [emphasis in the original]."[3]

There was nothing specifically anti-American about the declarations of the newborn American Communists. They saw themselves as internationalists equally hostile to all capitalist states. Many of the founding members of the American Communist party were also more concerned with events in Europe than in America. The great majority were first-generation immigrants who did not speak English and were more attuned to the politics of their native lands than to conditions in the United States. To the frustration of American party leaders, thousands of members of the new party, particularly those from the old tsarist empire, returned to join the revolutionary upheavals there, some voluntarily, others deported by the American government as alien revolutionaries.

Even with these losses, the majority of the American Communist party remained foreign-born, and the organizational weight of the party rested with its many foreign-language federations. Each of these was organized around a different ethnic/immigrant group rather than in the party's central apparatus. The party's isolation from American life was exacerbated by the decision to go underground in 1919. Partly occasioned by government persecution and partly by the romance of the Russian model of revolution, the underground years, (ending in 1922) solidified the pubic impression, even among its sympathizers, that the Communist movement was fundamentally out of touch with American reality. With its cadres hiding their identity, using assumed names, and skulking about the country holding secret meetings, American Communists resembled more a revolutionary European sect operating in a dictatorship than anything remotely American.

As was so often the case in the history of the CPUSA, Moscow intervened to force American Communists to face reality. Comintern emissaries ordered dissolution of the underground. The Comintern itself demanded that the different factions and splinter parties unite into one organization. In 1925 the Organizational Bureau of the Comintern ordered a drastic restructuring of the party based on a set of model statutes reflecting the organizational arrangements of the Communist party of the Soviet Union. "Bolshevization" aimed at rooting the party in industry by changing the basic party unit from ethnic language branches to clubs based on the place of work. Even so, the immigrant character of the party changed only slowly. In 1929 two-thirds of the party's members were still recorded as non-English speakers, leading the Comintern to rebuke it for being "for many years . . . an organization of foreign workers not much connected with the political life of the country."[4]

At the same time the immigrant composition of the CPUSA served as a useful means of Americanization for many of its foreign-born members. When Whittaker Chambers attended his first meeting of a party branch in 1925, he wrote, "There were several nationalities, but broken English, Greek and Yiddish seemed to be the prevailing languages. . . . It was called English-speaking . . . to indicate that the business of the meeting would be conducted in English, however broken."[5] Broken English was, however, a step toward assimilation compared to the insular and linguistically isolated Communist language-federation club meetings of the previous era. In one sense, then, the Comintern promoted the Americanization of the CPUSA by ending its organizational emphasis on foreign-language federations and orienting the party toward domestic concerns and the use of English. At the same time, however, the process underscored Moscow's domination and the supremacy of the Soviet model for CPUSA behavior.

The Comintern's most dramatic interference in the affairs of the CPUSA took place in 1929 when it removed Jay Lovestone as party leader and ordered the expulsion of dozens of his supporters, many in the party leadership, just months after the Lovestone faction had won the support of 90 percent of the party membership in an inner-party conflict. Lovestone was guilty of several sins, most prominently having supported Nikolai Bukharin instead of Joseph Stalin in the struggle within the Soviet Communist party, but his chief ideological error was advocacy of the theory of American exceptionalism. At Stalin's urging, in 1928 the Comintern had proclaimed the onset of an era of capitalist decay and renewed revolutionary upsurge. Lovestone had argued that the American economy was still advancing, constituting an exception to the general trend. The special commission appointed by the Comintern to consider Lovestone's case, chaired by Joseph Stalin, brushed aside Lovestone's theory:

It would be wrong to ignore the specific peculiarities of American capitalism. . . . But it would be still more wrong to base the activities of the Communist Party on these specific features, since the foundation of the activities of every Communist Party, including the American Communist Party, on which it must base itself, must be the general features of capitalism, which are the same for all countries, and not its specific features in any given country.[6]

Convinced that world capitalism was on its last legs, American Communists returned to the ultrarevolutionary rhetoric that had marked their founding days. In America the most bizarre manifestation of this spirit was William Z. Foster's *Toward Soviet America*, written in 1932 when he was running for President of the United States on the Communist ticket. Hailed by the party press and lauded by party organs as the definitive statement of the Communist position, *Toward Soviet America* frankly stated that the overthrow of capitalism in America would require a civil war to transform the United States into a Soviet government organized along the lines of the Soviet Union.[7] The capital would be transferred from Washington to an industrial center like Chicago or Detroit; all industry would be nationalized and agriculture collectivized; a Red Army would be built to crush counterrevolutionaries; government would take control of all means of communication; education would be reoriented to reflect dialectical materialism; churches would be curbed and religious training for minors prohibited; fraternal groups would be abolished and political parties liquidated with "the Communist Party functioning alone as the Party of the toiling masses."[8]

Foster did not derive his disdain for America's democratic values and institutions from a particular hatred of America; they were products of his fierce loyalty to the revolutionary vision enunciated by Moscow. Testifying before a congressional committee investigating communism in 1930, Foster had proclaimed that "workers are understanding that the Soviet Union is really their only fatherland" and that "the workers of this country and the workers of every country have only one flag and that is the red flag"[9]

The 1930s were both the height of the American Communist party's influence and the era of its greatest emphasis on its "Americaness." In large part this was driven by the Comintern's abandonment of its earlier policy, the so-called Third Period line. Although party membership had grown and the party had become more active in the early 1930s, not until after the Seventh Comintern Congress (held in the late summer of 1935) had officially inaugurated a new era of the Popular Front Against Fascism, did the CPUSA begin to make major strides. By the second half of the 1930s a majority of the party's membership was native-born and spoke English as their first language. In part this was a matter of demography: large-scale immigration had ended by 1922, and immigrants were a declining source of recruitment. The CPUSA also began to take in new members from among those radicalized by the Great Depression who were convinced that capitalism had failed and that only the Communist party offered a viable alternative to the rapid expansion of fascism. For the first time the party gained a substantial membership from among those in the professions and employed in cultural pursuits. Some were from "old stock" American groups with little or no previous involvement with radicalism, but many were the children of first-generation immigrants who had been in or near the Communist movement. For many of these "second-generation" American Communists, the trajectory of the CPUSA in the 1930s was another step on the path to assimilation. As the party began to operate more successfully with American workers in the 1930s, young Communists anxious to connect with the working class anglicized their names as they left their ethnic enclaves. Stjepan Mesaros, a young Croatian-born worker, became a prominent party figure from the 1930s to the 1950s as Steve Nelson. John Gates, a leading figure in the party's top leadership in the 1940s and early 1950s, changed his name from Sol Regenstreif when he dropped out of City College of New York to organize for the Young Communist League in Warren, Ohio, and Arvo Halberg, a young Finnish Communist from Minnesota, adopted the name Gus Hall in the mid 1930s after being assigned to organize in Youngstown, Ohio. Hall later became the leader of the CPUSA from 1959 to 2000.

Leading the party into the Popular Front era was Earl Browder, who spoke with a Kansas twang and came from old-stock American ancestry, in contrast to earlier party leaders with foreign ties and New York City accents. Browder dressed like the small-business accountant he once had been; during the Popular Front, Communist activists were encouraged to abandon the bohemian or Russian-style clothing many had affected. Communist "cultural workers" who had attempted, with little success, to create working-class music using cutting-edge modernist styles and dissonant tonality, discovered Appalachian and Southern folk music, which they infused with politically correct didactic lyrics. Ponderous proletarian literature with cartoonish working-class heroes and one-dimensional portraits of American life gave way to more realistic novels. Party organs encouraged members to participate fully in all walks of American life; the *Daily Worker* inaugurated a sports page and gave extensive coverage to such mainstream activities as baseball and boxing.

During the Popular Front era, party conferences still displayed red banners, but they were mixed with American flags, and portraits of Washington, Jefferson, and Lincoln hung beside those of Marx, Lenin, and Stalin. Browder announced that the American Declaration of Independence should be understood as a foreshadowing of Marx's Communist Manifesto, and he arranged for "Yankee Doodle" to be played at party conventions. "Communism is Twentieth-Century Americanism" became the quintessential party slogan of the Popular Front. Attractive to potential recruits and garnering considerable and often approving attention from the mainstream media, the slogan encapsulated the party's public embrace of American values and the political mainstream. Its history, however, also demonstrates the limits and shallowness of the CPUSA's commitment to those values. Moscow thought American flags at a party convention and pro-union lyrics set to banjo music were useful ways to promote the Popular Front. "Communism is Twentieth Century Americanism," however, went too far implying as it did that Marxism-Leninism-Stalinism should be understood as an expression of American political traditions. In early 1938 the Comintern secretly ordered the CPUSA to drop the slogan, and it did so at once.[10]

However enthusiastic party members were about their newfound discovery of American history and culture, this policy was always subordinated to the party's loyalty to the USSR. A Comintern order could alter a slogan about Americanism. A change in line could alter a pledge. Just before the inauguration of the Popular Front, new members of the CPUSA recited a pledge to "defend the Soviet Union, the land of victorious Socialism" and to bring about "the triumph of Soviet Power in the United States."[11] The party's 1935 manual of organization stated that the CPUSA's goal was "the revolutionary overthrow of capitalism . . . the establishment of a Socialist Soviet Republic in the United States" and declared "the Soviet Union is the only fatherland of workers all over the world" and "therefore, the workers all over the world must help the Soviet Union in building socialism and must defend it with all their power"[12] In 1940 young organizers marked for future party leadership heard senior leaders lecture:

> The single country where the dictatorship of the proletariat has triumphed represents a wedge driven into world capitalism by the world proletariat. The USSR is the stronghold of the world proletariat; it cannot be looked on as merely a nation or a country; it is the most advanced position of the world proletariat in the struggle for a socialist world. When the Red Army marches, it is the international proletariat marching to extend its sphere of operations in the struggle against world imperialism. In the period of capitalist superiority in strength, the Party splits world imperialism by taking advantage of its inherent contradictions; it also builds up the strength of the USSR to provide the world working class with greater might. Stalin, the great genius of socialism, stands like a colossus of steel as the leader of the world proletariat.[13]

The intense loyalty to the Soviet Union of so many American Communists contributed to the willingness of hundreds of them to spy for the USSR during World War II. Small groups of party members employed by the federal government had formed secret cells in Washington during the 1930s. In addition to collecting party dues, circulating literature, and discussing Marxism, these units also collected information and passed it along to both the party leadership in New York and Soviet agents. Whittaker Chambers served as a courier to one such cell—the Ware group, which included Alger Hiss, John Abt, and Nathan Witt. When Germany attacked the Soviet Union, a number of devoted party members, anxious to do everything in their power to assist the beleaguered regime, volunteered to transmit military, diplomatic, and technical information to the socialist fatherland. Many felt even less compunction about their actions when the United States and the Soviet Union became allies in the fight against fascism in December 1941. Several scientists employed by the Manhattan Project were driven by their Communist sympathies to seek out Soviet agents and transmitted vital secrets about the atom bomb. Economists and engineers passed along important defense data on weapons production, technological developments, and military procurement. Diplomats and lawyers informed their Soviet masters about key diplomatic issues and plans. More than three hundred Americans worked on behalf of Soviet intelligence agencies during the war.

Serving as sources of information for Soviet intelligence while their country was allied with the USSR enabled these men and women to rationalize their activities as ultimately or indirectly in America's interests, or at least not harmful to them. With the end of the war and the increasingly tense relationship between the two former allies, such justifications became untenable. The first sign that American Communists would have to choose between loyalty to the United States and the Soviet Union came in June 1945 when a French Communist journal published an article by Jacques Duclos signaling Moscow's conviction that the postwar world would see conflict, not cooperation, among the allies. The article, obviously written in Moscow, denounced the CPUSA's decision in 1944 to transform itself into a political association working within the American two-party system. American Communists were put on notice that the era of alliances and mutual interest with progressives and liberals, dating back to the mid-1930s and interrupted only by the Nazi-Soviet Pact, was coming to an end. They would be called upon to challenge American policies and institutions obstructing Soviet interests. When Earl Browder balked at repudiating his plan to "normalize" the CPUSA by bringing it into the political mainstream, he was replaced as party leader and expelled from the party.

The CPUSA was organizationally and ideologically bound to Moscow, and anyone who remained in the party for more than a brief period knew that Soviet interests would override the desires or preferences of American Communists. But until the post–World War II period, loyalty to the USSR and to the Communist movement did not necessarily entail a special aversion to the United States. This, however, changed with the coming of the cold war.

World War II ended with communism once again on the march. The Soviet Union was now one of the two great world powers. Communist governments modeled on Stalin's regime took power, usually with Red Army sponsorship or direct help, in Poland, Hungary, Czechoslovakia, Bulgaria, Romania, Albania, Yugoslavia, and eastern Germany. The USSR's prewar annexations of Latvia, Lithuania, and Estonia went unchallenged. Meanwhile communism was on the offensive in Western Europe. Germany and Italy were defeated nations in political chaos and economic ruin. France and other continental nations were also in economic crisis and politically demoralized by the legacy of occupation and war. The Communist parties of Italy and France became mass movements with realistic prospects of obtaining national power through elections. Victory had left Great Britain in dire economic straits and beginning a long retreat from empire. In Asia a Communist enclave protected by the USSR was created in northern Korea. Communist armies under Mao Zedong defeated the Nationalist government of China in 1949 and won control of the world's most populous nation.

Communists had experienced the intoxication of expansion in the earlier revolutionary era of 1917–1920. Charles Ruthenberg, then the chief figure in the American Communist movement, had proclaimed in 1919 that "new Soviet governments will arise as the months go by and it will not be long until the . . . boundary of Soviet Europe is the Rhine. . . . The Soviet movement will sweep forward and onward until the Soviet Republic of the World comes into being."[14] The Red Army was repulsed on the outskirts of Warsaw in 1920, however, and Soviet power was contained for more than two decades. But in 1945 the radiant dream of world socialism once again seemed to dawn. With the capitalist West in disarray and Soviet power triumphant in Eurasia, many Communists exuberantly expected that the imminent worldwide triumph of Marxism-Leninism.

Only American power stood in the way. The American economy, untouched by war damage, was the largest and most productive in the world. American military power was both formidable and could be projected around the globe. The CPUSA remained hopeful that the United States would not challenge Communist expansion but accept it. Some liberals, most notably former Vice President Henry Wallace, had articulated a belief in a hazy worldwide Popular Front that would concede Soviet hegemony in Europe. But in 1947 President Truman moved boldly to set the contours of what became America's cold war commitment for the next forty-five years. Great Britain notified the United States that its financial crisis had reached the point that required it to withdraw support for the Greek government fighting a civil war against Communist insurgents. At the same time the USSR made demands on the Turkish republic. Truman responded with the "Truman Doctrine" of military and economic assistance for any nation resisting a Communist takeover, and Congress approved aid for the Greek and Turkish governments. Then in June 1947 Secretary of State George Marshall announced a plan to deal with Europe's deepening economic crisis, a crisis that had brought recovery from the war to a halt and threatened to bring Communist parties to power in France and Italy. The Marshall Plan provided massive American aid for a coordinated European recovery program that soon put Western Europe on the road to prosperity and frustrated Communist electoral hopes. President Truman had dissolved America's World War II foreign intelligence agency, the OSS, in 1945 as no longer needed, but in 1947 he created the Central Intelligence Agency with a mandate not only for espionage but for worldwide covert political and ideological warfare against communism.

Driven by opposition to Truman's policies, Wallace ran for president on the Progressive party ticket in 1948 with Communist support. Controlling the party's convention, the Communists and their allies adopted numerous platform planks vigorously condemning American foreign policies that stood in the way of Soviet goals. The Vermont delegation sought to dilute the platform's one-sided criticism of American policies by proposing a sentence: "Although we are critical of the present foreign policy of the United States, it is not our intention to give blanket endorsement to the foreign policy of any other nation." Progressive party leaders denounced the amendment as a betrayal of the party's reason for existence, and it went down to overwhelming defeat, leaving the clear impression that the Communists and their allies did give blanket endorsement to Soviet foreign policy.

While challenging Soviet foreign policy, the Truman administration also mounted a vigorous attack on domestic communism as a threat to internal security and American values. The president issued an executive order in 1947 establishing a comprehensive loyalty/security program to remove Communists from federal employment. The administration indicted and convicted the top leadership of the CPUSA under the Smith Act in 1948 and prosecuted spies such as Alger Hiss and Julius Rosenberg. The FBI began a sustained campaign to infiltrate the CPUSA and disrupt its activities. Anti-Communist liberals organized in Americans for Democratic Action (ADA) denounced Communists as inappropriate participants in the Democratic party and fought them and their Popular Front allies.

When the votes were counted in 1948, Truman retained the presidency and the Democrats regained control of the Congress. As for Wallace, he polled only 2.3 percent of the vote, coming in fourth behind Dixiecrat Strom Thurmond. All across the country candidates aligned with Wallace went down in overwhelming defeat, and Communists and their Popular Front allies lost their position in mainstream politics. Next their institutional base collapsed. Trade union leaders, furious with Communist attempts to turn unions against Truman that threatened hopes of Democratic control of Congress, initiated a purge of Communist-dominated unions. One-time Communists abandoned the party to retain their union offices, and party-controlled unions were expelled from the CIO by 1950. Under sustained attack, by the mid-1950s the CPUSA had been driven to the margins of American society.

America's decision to fight the cold war and the crumbling domestic prospects of the CPUSA led many Communists to denounce the United States in hyperbolic vitriol. In 1949 William Z. Foster, then chairman of the CPUSA , declared, "American imperialism . . . is the organization of the most ruthless gang of fascist-minded capitalists on earth." He further described "American imperialism" as "a monstrous, all-consuming spider" and insisted that "Goebbels . . . was a novice compared with the war propagandists of the United States."[15] In 1951 Howard Fast, writing on behalf of the CPUSA-aligned Civil Rights Congress, described the United States as a "police state" and "a land of loyalty oaths, witch hunts, and terror for all who might hate war and love peace and democracy."[16] And in 1953 Herbert Aptheker, a leading Communist ideologue, described the American ruling class as having "the morals of goats, the learning of gorillas and the ethics of— well, of what they are: racist, war-inciting, enemies of humanity, rotten to the core, parasitic, merciless."[17] These were memorable examples of sure anti-American sentiments.

Although Aptheker and other party ideologues still sought to distinguish between the American ruling class and the American public, they found it harder and harder to do so as the cold war lengthened, and they tried less and less. Benjamin Davis had been one of the CPUSA's high-profile leaders during the World War II years of the Popular Front, winning election to the New York City Council in 1943. But as the cold war got under way, so embittered had he become that at a 1949 public rally in New York he announced that he "would rather be a lamppost in Moscow than president of the United States."[18] And in late 1950 Gus Hall, then party secretary, stated in the leadership's official report to the CPUSA's national convention that America had embarked on a "drive to enslave the world."[19] The United States was no longer just a single, albeit powerful, capitalist state but the largest and most formidable obstacle to Communist power and ideology in the world.

While the CPUSA nearly vanished in the late 1950s, reduced to a few thousand true believers, the extreme anti-Americanism of its last years lived on and was transmitted into mainstream discourse by its heirs: former Communists who remained radicalized although outside the party; the sons and daughters of Communists ("red-diaper babies") who avoided the party but carried its habits of thought into the New Left movement of the late 1960s and 1970s; and newly minted radicals who idolized newer, less stodgy, more strident Communist heroes like Fidel Castro, Ho Chi Minh, and Mao Zedong. When the radical student movement fell apart, and with it the millenarian hope of the New Left, many of its acolytes carried their beliefs and hopes into the academic world, where alienation and hostility to American values remain endemic. Marxism may be invisible in the larger American society, but it remains entrenched and taken seriously in the academy.

As the decades passed, radical frustration grew as one after another socialist cause failed. Variants of Soviet communism (Castroist, Maoist, Titoist, and Eurocommunist) either collapsed or proved unworkable. Various Third World socialisms (Nasserite and Baathist Arab socialism, Nkrumah and Nyerere's African socialism) ended in dictatorship or economic ruin, and usually both. Even the democratic socialists of British Labour and European Social Democracy abandoned Marxist formulas and made their peace with the free market. In all its variations, the socialist dream failed.[20] Yet it still has many fervent adherents who continue to seek a scapegoat for socialism's failure.

To the further indignation of leftists, American culture has become an even more powerful magnet than American capitalism. An early Communist saw it coming. Tom Mann, a radical trade unionist and a founder of both the British and Australian Communist parties, in 1922 wrote the preface to a book aptly named *Americanism: a World Menace*, wherein he warned his fellow radicals, "If we refuse to travel towards Communism, the only alternative is to become Americanised."[21] For many radicals there is no fate worse. Joel Kovel, the Alger Hiss Professor of Social Studies at Bard College, dedicated one of his books, *Red Hunting in the Promised Land,* not merely to one Soviet spy, Hiss, but also to a second, Harry Magdoff. Kovel described America as the "enemy of humanity" and explained that the colonial Americans made Indians the "object of the first 'red scare'" due to Indians being "the first communists in America." From the colonial era to the 1980s, American anti-communism fed on hatred of the ideal of the "classless society" and was "an exploitation of the deep structures of racism for the purpose of managing threats to capitalist rule," as well as "a pathology which had become the civil religion of the U.S." It had plunged the entire world into a nightmare: "millions of innocents lie dead, whole societies have been laid to waste, a vigorous domestic labor movement has been castrated, and the political culture of the United States has been frozen in a retrograde position." So satanic was American opposition to communism that it "destroys time itself"[22]—whatever that means.

Communism was ideologically incompatible with basic American values, although Kovel's diatribe misconstrues the nature of Americanism. Unlike other nations, the United States had been founded on allegiance to certain ideas and values, not ancestry or blood. Democracy, property rights, individualism, and the rule of law were the bedrock values of Americanism, not disposable ideas that could be abandoned once a Communist society was established. People who rejected these values or glorified political systems that scorned them were regarded as un-American and anti-American. Marxism-Leninism insisted on seeing not individuals with rights but classes with preordained virtues and vices. It regarded bourgeois democracy as a sham, property rights as the codification of exploitation, and law as the instrument of repression of the ruling class. Communism's incompatibility with American values became especially intense and apparent once the cold war began after World War II. The cold war was not only a military confrontation and a geopolitical contest but also a global ideological war. American Communists unreservedly allied themselves with America's arch rival in that war, an allegiance that contributed to, as well as reflected, their homegrown anti-American disposition.

The fragility of the ties that connected many of the members of the CPUSA to mainstream American society further contributed to the American Communist movement's alienation from American life and values. Until the mid-1930s a majority of CPUSA members were foreign-born, did not speak English as their first language, and were more attuned to politics in their native lands than in the United States. Most of the native-born Communists who came to dominate the party in the late 1930s were children of immigrant Communists only partly assimilated to American culture. While they did speak English, their ideological alienation from America and loyalty to the Soviet Union were profound and complementary. In some cases their attraction to the Soviet system was reinforced by a residual Russian patriotism. A number of the American Communists who spied for the Soviet Union were immigrants from Russia or the children of immigrants. The parents of Saville Sax, a young American Communist who assisted Soviet espionage against the United States, were radical Russian Jewish immigrants who lived in an apartment building with similar families. Saville Sax's family, his son recalled, had "barricaded themselves" in this "very closed community" that "identified American society with the people who were responsible for persecuting the Jews in czarist Russia."[23] Meanwhile they believed that back in Russia the Bolshevik regime had ended anti-Semitism and repaired all injustice. The twin pull of Communist and Russian loyalties produced in these immigrants and their children a form of Soviet patriotism that overwhelmed their weak ties to American national traditions and values.

Another Communist son of Russian immigrants, Theodore Hall, went to Harvard where his brilliance in physics earned him recruitment into the Manhattan Project. He repaid his country by seeking out Soviet intelligence officers and offering to hand over the secrets of the atomic bomb to the USSR. When a KGB agent interviewed Hall in 1944 to assess his fitness to be a spy, he inquired why Hall was offering to reveal America's atomic secrets. Hall explained, "There is no country except for the Soviet Union which could be entrusted with such a terrible thing."[24] In 1997, after his treachery had been revealed, Hall wrote a statement justifying his actions. He allowed that he had been "mistaken" about the nature of the Soviet state, but he did not regret his espionage. His statement bristled with hatred of the United States and fantasies; he insisted that American democracy was but a façade for an "alliance between the weapons industry and the military" that was "prepared to blow up the world in their Messianic zeal."[25] Hall's illusions about Soviet communism were emblematic but they withered over the years, just like those of much of the revolutionary left. What remained and what he and others on the far left continued to cling to was the loathing for America.

There are, of course, numerous reasonable grounds for criticizing various aspects of American society and America's role in the world. But the irrepressible hostility of American Communists and their latter-day sympathizers is not such criticism; rather it is a cry of pain and frustration at the defeat of the Marxist-Leninist project and rhetorical revenge against the agent thought responsible for the vanishing of the utopian dream.

NOTES

1. H. H. Lewis, *Thinking of Russia*, pamphlet (B. Z. Hagglund, Holt, Minn., 1932), 1 (located in H. H. Lewis Papers, series 4, box 1044, Special Collections and Archives, Kent Library, Southeast Missouri State University). Known as the Plowboy Poet of the Gumbo and the Mayakovsky of Missouri (after the famed Bolshevik poet Vladimir Mayakovsky), Lewis's work won approval from CPUSA aesthetic commissar Mike Gold as well as praise from more prominent and mainstream poets such as William Carlos Williams.

2. John Gates, *The Story of an American Communist* (New York: Nelson, 1958), 173.

3. Letter of the Socialist Party of the Eighth Assembly District, N.Y., April 21, 1919, to L.C.A.K. Martens (representative of Russian Socialist Federated Soviet Republic), editorial of the Finnish-language Wobbly journal *Luokkataistelu*, May 1919, "The Communist Party Manifesto," all quoted in New York (State) Joint Legislative Committee Investigating Seditious Activities, *Revolutionary Radicalism: Its History, Purpose and Tactics with an Exposition and Discussion of the Steps Being Taken and Required to Curb It* (Albany: J. B. Lyon Co., 1920), 639, 776–798, 1191.

4. Nathan Glazer, "The Social Basis of American Communism," Ph.D. Dissertation (Columbia University, 1962), 59.

5. Whittaker Chambers, *Witness* (New York: Random House, 1952), 203–204.

6. Joseph Stalin, *Stalin's Speeches on the American Communist Party, Delivered in the American Commission of the Presidium of the Executive Committee of the Communist International, May 6, 1929, and in the Presidium of the Executive Committee of the Communist International on the American Question, May 14th, 1929,* pamphlet (New York: Central Committee, Communist Party, U.S.A., 1931), 11.

7. In response to prosecution assertions in the late 1940s that the CPUSA was a conspiracy to overthrow the government, assertions made in *Dennis vs. U.S.*, the Smith Act trial of CPUSA leaders, Foster submitted a deposition claiming that after the Seventh World Congress of the Communist International in 1935 the CPUSA abandoned violent revolution and sought only a peaceful road to socialism. In June 1950, after the trial's end, Foster repudiated his disavowal in an article in the party's theoretical journal *Political Affairs,* stating that it was "naive" to believe that capitalists would allow a peaceful transition. Joseph R. Starobin, *American Communism in Crisis, 1943–1957* (Cambridge: Harvard University Press, 1972), 207.

8. William Z. Foster, *Toward Soviet America* (New York: Coward-McCann, Inc., 1932), 275.

9. U.S. House Special Committee to Investigate Communist activities in the United States, *Investigation of Communist Propaganda* (Washington, D.C.: U.S. Govt. Print. Off., 1930), part 1, vol. 4, 358–359, 380, 384.

10. Harvey Klehr, John Earl Haynes, and Kyrill M. Anderson, *The Soviet World of American Communism* (New Haven: Yale University Press, 1998), 36–40.

11. J. Peters, *The Communist Party: A Manual on Organization* (New York: Workers Library Publishers, 1935), 104–105.

12. Ibid., 8, 16.

13. Julius Irving Scales, *Cause at Heart: A Former Communist Remembers,* assisted by Richard Nickson (Athens: University of Georgia Press, 1987), 93–94.

14. Ruthenberg statement, *Ohio Socialist,* April 23, 1919.

15. William Z. Foster, *The Twilight of World Capitalism* (New York: International Publishers, 1949), 37, 39–41.

16. Howard Fast, *Peekskill: USA a Personal Experience* (New York: Civil Rights Congress, 1951), 105.

17. Published in 1953 as part of a book review under the title "The Filthy Rich" and reprinted in Herbert Aptheker, *History and Reality* (New York: Cameron Associates, 1955), 112.

18. Gates, *The Story of an American Communist,* 165.

19. Gus Hall, "Report to the 15th National Convention of the Communist Party, USA," in *Highlights of a Fighting History: 60 Years of the Communist Party, USA,* ed. by Philip Abraham Bart, Theodore Bassett, William W. Weinstone, and Arthur Zipser (New York: International Publishers, 1979), 269.

20. Joshua Muravchik, *Heaven on Earth: The Rise and Fall of Socialism* (San Francisco: Encounter Books, 2002).

21. W. T. Colyer, *Americanism: A World Menace* (London: Labour Pub. Co., 1922), vi.

22. Joel Kovel, *Red Hunting in the Promised Land: Anticommunism and the Making of America* (New York: Basic Books, 1994), dedication page, x–xii, 74, 95, 233; Joel Kovel, "The Victims of Anticommunism," *Zeta Magazine*, January 1988; David Evanier and Harvey Klehr, "Anticommunism and Mental Health," *American Spectator*, 22, no. 2 (February 1989), 28, 30.

23. Michael Dobbs, "Unlocking the Crypts: Most Spies Code Revealed Escaped Prosecution," *Washington Post*, December 25, 1995.

24. Allen Weinstein and Alexander Vassiliev, *The Haunted Wood: Soviet Espionage in America: the Stalin Era* (New York: Random House, 1999), 196.

25. Joseph Albright and Marcia Kunstel, *Bombshell: The Secret Story of America's Unknown Atomic Spy Conspiracy* (New York: Times Books, 1997), 288–289.

12

CATHY YOUNG

The Feminist Hostility Toward American Society

L ess than a month after the September 11, 2001 attacks on the World Trade Center and the Pentagon, a speaker at the Women's Resistance Conference in Ottawa, Canada, denounced "the most dangerous and the most powerful global force unleashing prolific levels of violence all over the world"—one that, she said, was particularly dangerous to women. She did not have in mind Al Qaeda, the international terrorist network responsible for the bombings, or the Taliban, Afghanistan's fundamentalist Islamic ruling clique which has harbored terrorists and subjected women to the most misogynistic regime in modern history; the characterization was aimed at the United States.

The speaker, Tanzanian-born Sunera Thobani, was not a lone eccentric. A professor at the University of British Columbia, she had previously served as the head of Canada's National Action Committee on the Status of Women. Nor was she speaking at a gathering of some lunatic fringe group. The Women's Resistance Conference was funded by the Canadian government to the tune of over $100,000 and was considered mainstream enough to be attended by Canada's secretary of state for the status of women, Hedy Fry.

In her widely reported incendiary speech, Thobani declared:

U.S. foreign policy is soaked in blood. And other countries of the West, including shamefully Canada, cannot line up fast enough behind it. All want to sign up now as Americans, and I think it is the responsibility of the women's movement in this country to stop that, to fight against it.

These policies are hell-bent on the West maintaining its control over the world's resources. At whatever cost to the people. . . .

. . . The people, the American nation . . . is a people which is bloodthirsty, vengeful, and calling for blood. They don't care whose blood it is, they want blood. And that has to be confronted. We cannot keep calling this an understandable response. . . . We have to stop condoning it and creating a climate of acceptability for this kind of response. We have to call it for what it is: bloodthirsty vengeance.

. . . This kind of jingoistic militarism . . . the most heinous form of patriarchal, racist violence that we're seeing on the globe today. The women's movement, we have to stand up to this.

Thobani dismissed "all this talk about saving Afghani women" ("Those of us who have been colonized know what this saving means"). She averred that "There will be no emancipation for women anywhere on this planet until the Western domination of this planet is ended."[1]

Thobani's speech sparked outrage in Canada. Her virulent anti-Americanism was assailed in numerous editorials, and some criticism was even leveled at Fry for not walking out during her rant. Some commentators such as Sun Media columnist Licia Corbella called Thobani's comments a disgrace to feminism, pointing out that Western countries were the source of women's emancipation. "Let me get this straight: the western world—where women enjoy more freedom and power than anywhere else—must disappear before women can be free?" women's studies student Rachel Sa wrote in the *Toronto Sun*. "If Thobani wishes to attack a country that truly oppresses its women, then she should look to Afghanistan where women are denied such basic rights as education and access to health care and can be murdered if they are accused of impropriety."[2]

Thobani also had many supporters. During her speech she received several standing ovations from the five hundred women in attendance. Some feminists spoke out not only in support of Thobani's right to voice her opinion but also in support of her views. In the *Calgary Sun*, guest columnist Brenda Wadey charged that the widespread condemnation of Thobani was "racist [and] sexist."[3] Across the border, writer Sharon Lerner echoed this theme in the *Village Voice*, describing the backlash against Thobani's comments as evidence that "these days, it's hard for anyone to stray from the political mainstream, and harder still for women."[4] The *Vancouver Sun* reported that female students interviewed in the women's lounge at the University of British Columbia were also overwhelmingly supportive of Thobani: "The same thing is being said on campuses and in coffee houses everywhere," a third-year social work student was quoted as saying. According to the report,

A few conceded women have little freedom in Muslim countries like Afghanistan. . . . Yet the women at UBC appeared more critical of the U.S. than of Muslim regimes and in a rousing, spontaneous discussion, none volunteered a word of criticism of the terrorist attacks on New York, Washington and Pennsylvania.[5]

It is also worth noting that at the Ottawa conference, Thobani's views were echoed by an American speaker, Julie Sudbury from Mills College in Oakland, California: "September 11 has created a blank slate for global domination of the Bush agenda of militarism and global capitalism," Sudbury said. "He's no longer the Texas hangman. He appears to have become the global hangman."[6]

Additional evidence that these statements are not an aberration among academic feminists comes from Daphne Patai's and Noretta Koertge's book *Professing Feminism: Education and Indoctrination in Women's Studies*. After the events of September 11, writes Patai, a discussion on the Women's Studies list on the Internet addressed the question of how to deal with these events in the classroom. A typical message asked "whether it is OK to speak with our students right now, in the aftermath of this tragedy, about its roots in US imperialism and terror."[7]

How and why did feminists take such a position in a conflict between a country where women arguably have more freedom and equality than anywhere else in the world, and a violent global movement that seeks to impose a misogynist theocracy? This is all the more puzzling since the liberation of women seems to be one of the attributes of America and the West the radical Islamists particularly detest.

Women's groups in North America and Europe had done some admirable work publicizing the oppression of women under the Taliban; a few leading feminists such as Eleanor Smeal, former president of the National Organization for Women and later of the Feminist Majority Fund, expressed satisfaction over the downfall of the brutal Taliban regime and the role of women in the American war effort.[8]

Yet the majority of feminists seemed at best ambivalent about America's war on terrorism, even when this war was still limited to the strike against Afghanistan and widely supported by the international community. They resisted admitting that the West holds the moral high ground on issues of personal and group freedoms, including those of women. Author Barbara Ehrenreich told the *Village Voice*, "What is so heartbreaking to me as a feminist is that the strongest response to corporate globalization and U.S. military domination is based on such a violent and misogynist ideology."[9] Another leading feminist writer, Katha Politt, in a column for the *Nation*, explained her opposition to her daughter's desire to fly an American flag from their window after September 11 due to the "the flag stand[ing] for jingoism and vengeance and war."[10]

In June 2002 prominent feminists, including activist and journalist Gloria Steinem, novelist Alice Walker, poet Adrienne Rich, and playwright Eve Ensler (author of *The Vagina Monologues*), were among the signatories of a petition titled "Not in Our Name," which barely said a word about the threat of terrorism and militant fundamentalism but urged Americans to "resist the war and repression that has been loosed on the world by the Bush administration." Steinem, Walker, and Ensler had earlier opposed the U.S. war in Afghanistan on the ground that it would do nothing to liberate that country's women from oppression by the Taliban. The sight of Afghan women and girls celebrating their liberation and attending school for the first time in years had not changed their minds.[11]

FEMINIST HISTORY:
TURNING AWAY FROM THE LIBERAL IDEAL

The intersection of feminism and anti-Americanism is particularly paradoxical since feminism has deep roots in American history. American political philosophy and American culture, with its emphasis on individual rights and its rejection of social status as something ascribed rather than achieved, led to the questioning of traditional notions of "woman's place." Indeed, the 1848 Seneca Falls "Declaration of Sentiments" that launched the organized feminist movement in the United States was self-consciously modeled on the Declaration of Independence:

> We hold these truths to be self-evident: that all men and women are created equal; that they are endowed by their Creator with certain inalienable rights; that among these are life, liberty, and the pursuit of happiness; that to secure these rights governments are instituted, deriving their just powers from the consent of the governed.[12]

Elizabeth Cady Stanton, who wrote the 1848 Declaration, continued to emphasize in her later work that the movement for women's rights was seeking to apply fundamental American ideals to women. In an 1892 address before the U.S. Senate Committee on Woman Suffrage, "Solitude of Self," Stanton said:

> The point I wish plainly to bring before you on this occasion is the individuality of each human soul—our Protestant idea; the right of individual conscience and judgement—our republican idea. . . . In discussing the rights of woman, we are to consider,

first, what belongs to her as an individual. . . . Her rights under such circumstances are to use all her faculties for her own safety and happiness.

Secondly, if we consider her as a citizen, as a member of a great nation, she must have the same rights as all other members, according to the fundamental principles of our Government.[13]

In the nineteenth and early twentieth centuries, the women's suffrage movement continued to embrace this patriotic model. Indeed, during World War I, suffragist leader Carrie Chapman Catt successfully urged feminists, and women in general, to support the war effort in order to prove themselves worthy of full citizenship.[14]

After the passage of the Nineteenth Amendment giving women the franchise in 1920, the women's movement ran out of steam and virtually disappeared from the American scene for nearly half a century. In the 1960s, "Second Wave" feminism started out as a liberal movement, seeking, as formulated in the 1966 statement of purpose of the National Organization for Women, "to bring women into full participation in the mainstream of American society now, exercising all the privileges and responsibilities thereof in truly equal partnership with men."[15]

Recently some critics of feminism have made much of the revelation that Betty Friedan, one of the founders of NOW and the author of the 1963 best-seller *The Feminine Mystique*—often credited with almost single-handedly reviving feminism in America—had a history of far-left political activism. In the 1940s and early '50s she was a labor journalist for UE, the United Electrical, Radio, and Machine Workers of America, which has been described as the most radical of American labor unions at the time and "the largest communist-led institution of any kind in the United States." Historian Daniel Horowitz, who first publicized Friedan's leftist background, stresses that it was not unique: others who "helped shape post-1963 feminism" and who had been previously active in the radical labor movement included historian Gerda Lerner and feminist politician Bella Abzug. Horowitz, himself a leftist, concludes that the 1960s revival of American feminism owes a much greater debt than was previously believed to the old left of the 1940s. If so, Second Wave feminism was influenced by a movement that was not only socialist but Stalinist in its allegiances.[16]

Still, it is worth noting that while some of Friedan's critique of American society in *The Feminine Mystique* had radical-extremist overtones—in particular her description of the American suburban home as a "comfortable concentration camp" that stripped the housewife of her individual identity—her vision was rooted in humanistic psychology rather than Marxism.[17] She urged women to reject full-time domesticity and take an equal role in the workplace and in politics, rather than repudiate all American institutions. As Horowitz points out, in the 1970s she was harshly critical of the ascendancy of a feminist model based on "a false analogy with obsolete or irrelevant ideologies of class warfare or race separatism."[18]

Whatever some feminists' roots in the old left may have been, the New Left proved to be a far greater influence on the women's movement. Many feminists had started out as activists in anti-war and other radical groups that saw themselves as a revolutionary anti-capitalist vanguard. These feminists, while becoming bitterly disillusioned with the prevalence of misogynist attitudes in these groups, wholeheartedly embraced their view of American institutions as intrinsically oppressive, corrupt, and malevolent, intended to perpetuate the unjust power of the ruling class and stifle liberation movements worldwide. As Christina Hoff Sommers wrote, "The idea that women are in a gender war originated in the mid-sixties, when the anti-war and anti-government mood revivified and redirected the women's movement away from its Enlightenment liberal philosophy to a more radical, anti-establishment philosophy."[19]

These more radical beliefs came to dominate academic feminism, which emerged in the 1970s and found expression in the birth and proliferation of women's studies programs across America as well as in feminist political activism off the campuses. Academic feminist philosophers such as Alison Jaggar explicitly rejected liberal Enlightenment values and liberal democracy as not only insufficient for achieving gender equality but antithetical to what they saw as real equality: the basic concept of individual rights was reinterpreted as "masculinist," rooted in the supposedly masculine values of cognitive rationality and personal autonomy.[20] On a more popular level too, the feminist philosophical critique of Enlightenment values often merges into a suspicious and dismissive view of liberal democracy. In her *Calgary Sun* column defending Sunera Thobani's anti-U.S. diatribe, Brenda Wadey writes,

> I have been hearing that liberal democracy created feminism and we need to thank that system for our rights and privilege. Wrong! Feminism happened in spite of liberal democracy, not because of it. . . . It has been liberal democratic systems that feminist movements—suffragette movements before them—fought against to gain the rights women have.[21]

These claims overlook the fact that it was only under liberal democracies that feminist movements had a chance to succeed, thanks precisely to values such as individual rights and freedom of speech and association.

WOMEN'S LIVES IN AMERICA: "ONE IS LOOKING AT ATROCITY"

According to Andrea Dworkin, the radical feminist author and activist,

> When one thinks about women's ordinary lives and the lives of children, especially female children, it is very hard not to think that one is looking at atrocity. We have to accept that we are looking at ordinary life; the hurt is not exceptional; rather, it is systematic and it is real. Our culture accepts it, defends it, punishes us for resisting it.[22]

Dworkin is widely known for her maverick views, including the belief that sexual intercourse is by its very nature oppressive to women. But the view of American women as a gender under siege is not limited to a lunatic fringe. Susan Faludi's book *Backlash: The Undeclared War Against American Women*, which purported to chronicle a society-wide effort to roll back women's rights with the collusion of government, business, advertising, and the media, was a best-seller in 1991. A 1995 review in an academic journal of a book dealing with the persecution of women accused of witchcraft in medieval Europe noted the role of the witch-hunts in silencing and repressing women and cited *Backlash* as evidence of "how women are confronting this today."[23]

A 1993 collection of essays by feminist writers and activists, *Transforming a Rape Culture*, characterizes America as a "rape culture"—one that "encourages male sexual aggression and violence against women" and "condones physical and emotional terrorism against women as the norm."[24] According to the activist website[25] "Breaking the Silence," "Many feminists, scholars, and activists argue that the United States of America is the paradigmatic Rape Culture."[26]

Few would deny that violent crime against women is a serious issue and that sex discrimination persists in many spheres. Many feminists' claims, however, go far beyond such a sober assessment. Their often exaggerated assertions about the pervasive victimization of women in America have been refuted by several authors, including Sommers. For instance, Americans have been told that:

Battering by men is the leading cause of injury or of emergency room visits by American women;

Domestic violence is the leading cause of birth defects in America;

One out of three American women is raped at least once in their lifetime;

One out of three girls is sexually abused before reaching adulthood;

American schools systematically discriminate against girls;

Every year, 150,000 girls and young women in America die from anorexia, literally starving themselves to death because of societal pressures to be thin.[27]

Investigations by Sommers and others have shown these "facts" to be largely fictitious. Far more women are injured in car crashes and accidental falls than in incidents of domestic violence; the alarming statistics are taken from studies that focus on emergency rooms in high-crime urban neighborhoods (and that typically look at *all* violence, domestic or not).[28] The claim about battering as a leading cause of birth defects apparently originated in a feminist activist's misunderstanding of a comment by a maternal nurse who had said that according to research by the March of Dimes, pregnant women are screened for domestic abuse far less often than they are for potential birth defects.[29] While accurate statistics on the frequency of rape and sexual abuse are difficult to obtain, even studies that use a fairly broad definition of these crimes put a woman's lifetime risk of victimization at close to one in eight.[30] The figure of 150,000 anorexia deaths comes from a confusion of total anorexia *cases* with fatalities; actual fatalities may number as low as 100 a year or fewer.[31] At the time feminist organizations were claiming that bias against girls was rife in schools, young women in the United States were attending college at a higher rate than men.[32]

False or exaggerated claims about women's victimization have been circulated—often even after they have been convincingly debunked—by reputable organizations such the National Organization for Women and various anti-domestic violence groups (often funded with government grants). Often these claims are accompanied by melodramatic rhetoric: in her 1992 best-seller *The Beauty Myth*, Naomi Wolf compares the alleged death toll of anorexia to that of the Holocaust ("a vast number of emaciated bodies starved not by nature but by men").[33]

The message that women are generally mistreated in Ameican society finds expression in the mass media as well. *Washington Post* columnist Judy Mann has described women as "a class of people . . . beaten up at home and raped almost routinely on college campuses," while *New York Times* columnist Anna Quindlen has written that "the greatest public health threat for many American women is the men they live with." The 1998 tragedy in Jonesboro, Arkansas, in which two boys opened fire on their classmates, killing four girls and a female teacher, elicited commentary in the *Philadelphia Inquirer* about boys "being trained by their parents, other adults, and our culture and media to harass, assault, rape, and murder girls." After a New York man was acquitted in the assault of a former girlfriend, *New York Daily News* columnist Linda Stasi wrote, "Welcome to the U.S. of A., where life is cheap and women's lives are always at a discount."[34] While feminists are doubtless sincere in their beliefs in the bleak life that women lead in America, some acknowledge that painting a negative picture is essential for keeping the women's movement alive. In her 1997 book, Stanford Law School professor Deborah Rhode grudgingly acknowledges that American women have made some progress in the past decades. "Yet ironically enough," she writes, "this progress has created its own obstacles to further change. Women's growing opportunities are taken as evidence that the 'woman problem' has been solved." On the contrary, she asserts, "No just society could tolerate the inequalities that women now experience in status, income, power, and physical security."[35] Judy Mann puts it even more starkly: "I am now convinced that one of patriarchy's most effective lies is to entice us into believing that women and men are treated equally in this culture."[36]

Feminist critiques of American society are intertwined with the belief often voiced by feminists that virtually all of human civilization is a more or less unbroken chain of male abuse of women. In the 1992 book *The War Against Women*, for instance, Marilyn French asserts that "the vast majority of men in the world are guilty of various abuses and atrocities against women (ranging from rape and battering to "treat[ing] women disrespectfully at work or at home").[37] If so, can the feminist critique be seen as anti-American, or is it "simply" anti-male and directed at "patriarchal" civilization in general?

To settle this question it will be instructive to compare many feminists' approach to American culture and society with that to other societies, particularly in the Third World, which are self-evidently far more patriarchal and unkind to women.

WOMEN ACROSS CULTURES

In June 1992 I attended a conference of the National Council for Research on Women, called "The Eye of the Storm: Feminist

Research and Action in the 1990s," held at Radcliffe College in Cambridge, Massachusetts, and attended by several leading figures of academic feminism (such as Catharine Stimpson, dean of the Graduate School of Rutgers University, and Nan Keohane, president of Wellesley College). In one of the more memorable moments of this conference, Deborah Rhode (quoted above) declared, "Only 8 percent of the world's population are white men. That's a very encouraging fact"—an observation met with laughter and obvious delight from the audience. No one, apparently, questioned the implication that white men were uniquely inimical to women's interests.[38]

Three years later, women's status in different cultures came into focus when the United Nations was criticized for holding a women's conference in Beijing despite reports of rampant abuse of women's rights in China. Feminist author Barbara Ehrenreich, then a *Time* magazine columnist, commented on the controversy in a column tellingly titled "For Women, China Is All Too Typical." Arguing that the criticism of China was misguided because there was no truly female-friendly place in the world, Ehrenreich listed abuses of women's rights in countries such as Saudi Arabia, Iran, Poland, and Brazil. She added, "There's always the U.S., of course, the very birthplace of organized feminism," wrote Ehrenreich. "But . . . wouldn't it be depressing to meet in a land where abortion rights are under violent assault, where affirmative action looks to be doomed, and where the percentage of congressional seats held by women is sinking back toward the single-digit level?" Ehrenreich also suggested that Hillary Clinton should have "follow[ed] up her criticisms of China with some heartfelt reflections on the situation of women in America, herself included. She might have admitted she comes from the only industrialized nation that has refused to ratify the 16-year-old U.N. treaty on women's rights, a country where an outspoken woman in public life risks constant revilement."[39]

This bleak assessment, essentially equating the United States with countries that are among the most repressive of women (such as Saudi Arabia and Iran) and the worst violators of human rights in general, has been all too typical of the rhetoric of the feminist left.

In the comparisons of the status of women in various countries, many feminists give the United States low ratings because the less-regulated American marketplace has less room for the social programs they regard as essential for women's equality outside the home. Scandinavian countries—particularly Sweden, where women's workforce participation is high, and social programs including day care and maternity leave are extensive—are often cited as feminist models, though women in these countries lag considerably behind American women in workplace status.[40]

It is also of interest that even today some feminists give the benefit of doubt to Communist regimes because of their allegedly enlightened policies regarding women and their leftist sympathies, old or new. For instance, reviewing the 1997 book *Sex and Revolution: Women in Socialist Cuba* in the *National Association of Women's Studies Journal*, Ann Ferguson, a professor of philosophy at the University of Massachusetts–Amherst and at one point director of the women's studies program at that university, acknowledged that the Cuban Communist regime had failed to give full equality to women. Nonetheless she faulted the authors of the book, Lois Smith and Alfred Padula, for failing to "consider, let alone adequately weigh, the impact of imperialism on the policy choices open to the Cuban government":

> While Smith and Padula rightly critique Castro for being autocratic, militaristic, and paternalistic, and fault the Cuban Communist Party for not allowing the Cuban Federation of Women a stronger voice, they ignore the fact that since 1961 when an American embargo was established, Cuba has been in a difficult economic and political and military situation. . . . [A] nationalist defense of the Castro government has been the response of the majority of Cubans, hindering the possibility of successful democratic social movements, like women's, environmental, or lesbian and gay movements in Cuba.[41]

It is also noteworthy that left-wing feminists such as Barbara Ehrenreich have been less than enthusiastic about the fall of Communist regimes. She wrote that in "most of the post-communist world . . . the advent of market economies has been a decidedly mixed blessing for women. Female unemployment is up, female-supportive services like public child care are getting as scarce as public portraits of Stalin." She also noted that "the percentage of women elected to national legislatures has dropped worldwide almost 25% in the past seven years" (that is, in the late 1980s and early 1990s), overlooking the fact that most of this decline had taken place in formerly Communist countries where the "national legislatures" had been meaningless, rubber-stamping bodies with quotas of women to fill the seats.[42]

These misplaced feminist sympathies may partly be explained by the fact that Communist regimes, for all their general brutality and abuse of human rights, have proclaimed a commitment to the equality of the sexes and have provided women with educational opportunities and access to occupations they were excluded from or underrepresented in earlier times (including street cleaning and heavy manual labor).

Many feminists also continue to find it difficult to acknowledge American and Western superiority in the treatment of women over those countries that still deny women the most basic rights in the name of cultural and religious tradition. Thus, for example, in 2001 a writer in *Labyrinth*, a journal of philosophy and feminist theory, criticized Susan Moeller Okin, a liberal feminist critic of women's oppression worldwide, for portraying Third World cultures in a negative light and thus running the risk of "ethnocentricism" [sic]. Mary-Kate Smith wrote:

> I am not arguing that women are not often abused in the countries that are named as "Third World," nor am I arguing that the abuse does not occur at a greater extent than in the "First World." . . . Okin assumes that generally "Third World" men systematically abuse "Third World" women and this adds support to the stereotype that "brown" men abuse "brown" women more than white men. She makes this generalization, which is most likely an exaggeration, across numerous regions of the world without any real justification. . . . She also does not take into consideration the possible effects of her position which can be understood as equal to a colonizing gaze which treats "Third World" people as more barbaric than their Western

"counterparts" because the people of the "Third World" are less developed and uncivilized.[43]

Smith's argument is shared by prominent feminist scholars such as Hamilton College women's studies professor Chandra Mohanty, co-editor of the 1991 anthology *Third World Women and the Politics of Feminism* and the second-most-popular author in a 1997 survey on the Women's Studies List.[44] It has also been forcefully articulated by prominent feminists, such as Germaine Greer in her 1999 book *The Whole Woman*, which was a best-seller in England. Greer depicts men in the United States and Western Europe as engaged in, as one reviewer put it, "an unprecedented assault on womanhood."[45] At the same time she romanticizes and rationalizes such Third World customs as sexual segregation ("I gazed at women in segregated societies and found them in many ways stronger than women who would not go into a theatre or a restaurant without a man") as a form of female empowerment and even manages to see female genital mutilation as an acceptable assertion of cultural identity, writing that the drive to criminalize this practice "can be seen to be what African nationalists since Jomo Kenyatta have been calling it, an attack on cultural identity."[46]

Anti-colonialist feminists do raise some valid questions, pointing out, for instance, that Western liberal feminists often fail to respect the desires, choices, and preferences of actual Third World women who may not appreciate Western feminist ideals and do not wish to be "liberated" from their traditional roles. Yet left-wing feminists seem incapable of applying the same argument to Western women who have similar (though far less restrictive) traditional preferences, particularly those in conservative religious communities such as fundamentalist Christians.

When feminists are less hesitant to criticize the oppression of women in non-Western cultures, they often fall back on the kind of moral equivalence (exemplified by Ehrenreich's column), that lumps together female genital mutilation in Africa and attempted rollbacks of affirmative action in the United States. This approach makes it possible to take a critical position toward their own society even when they note with seeming detachment horrendous practices (such as genital mutilation) widespread in others.

Consider a feminist response to the deadly riots in Nigeria in November 2002, when Muslim extremists rampaged in protest against the Miss World beauty pageant being hosted in that African country's capital. The same groups that rioted against the pageant, forcing its relocation to London, had also imposed in parts of Nigeria strict Islamic codes that were especially oppressive to women—resulting, for instance, in female rape victims being sentenced to death by stoning for adultery. Commenting on these events on the msnbc.com website, journalist Jill Nelson wrote, "As far as I'm concerned, it's equally disrespectful and abusive to have women prancing around a stage in bathing suits for cash or walking the streets shrouded in burkas in order to survive." (She failed to note that women have not been forced to participate in beauty pageants in the West, but are forced to wear burkas in Muslim societies.)[47]

In the November 2001 *Village Voice* article on feminist reactions to the war in Afghanistan, Sharon Lerner acknowledges the urgency of freeing women from the Taliban's rule. Yet she cannot help sneering that "no doubt, many Americans are feeling somewhat smug about our heroic, enlightened men just now," despite the fact that "the power structure remains overwhelmingly male."[48] Meanwhile, at California State University at Hayward, a course on "The Sexuality of Terrorism" treats both terrorists and soldiers who participate in anti-terrorist missions as examples of male violence. According to Professor Roxanne Dunbar-Ortiz, "Terrorism is on a continuum that starts with violence within the family, battery against women, violence against women in the society, all the way up to organized militaries that are supported by taxpayer money."[49] As author Kay Hymowitz put it, "Gender feminists are little interested in fine distinctions between radical Muslim men who slam commercial airliners into office buildings and soldiers who want to stop radical Muslim men from slamming commercial airliners into office buildings."[50]

Another startling example of such moral equivalence is reflected in a play, *American Burka*, by Southern Methodist University professor Rhonda Blair, which was staged in Dallas in 2002.

According to a review, "A burka is a body-length veil that the Taliban decreed mandatory for Afghan women—to make them invisible in public. *American Burka* asks whether American women have analogous inhibitions imposed on them to prevent them from being seen as they are." Ironically, the only time the play deals with an actual Afghan burka, it is in a fairly positive manner: "Sara Weeks talks about a genuine Afghan burka and admits that wearing it gives her a sense of solitude and peace." Meanwhile the performers discuss such metaphorical "burkas" as "other people's expectations" and "the constraints of brassieres."[51]

Such a play produced by a small Texas theater company may be regarded as a marginal phenomenon. But seemingly mainstream feminist leaders too sometimes come very close to equating the status of women in America and in some of the world's most oppressive dictatorships. The motto for the 2002 International Women's Day, marked by feminist groups worldwide and officially recognized by the United Nations, was "For women, Afghanistan is everywhere."

On that day, National Organization for Women president Kim Gandy affirmed at an anti-war rally her patriotism as well as her opposition to the war. Here again it was not hard to detect moral equivalence:

> Yes, Saddam Hussein is a maniacal tyrant, cruel and vicious. But where are these brave opponents of tyranny when the threat is here at home? Women and children—in the U.S. and around the world—know what it is like to live under Code Red—the highest alert and the greatest risk to our safety. Our tyrants, complete with weapons of mass destruction, are hunger and homelessness, violence and poverty. We face that tyranny in our homes, our workplaces, and our schools.[52]

It is safe to say that the female Iraqi exiles familiar with the cruelties of Hussein's secret police (whose methods included raping women in front of their families) are unlikely to agree with the suggestion that women in the United States face similar tyranny.

WHITHER FEMINISM?

In the wake of September 11, the climate of opinion in the United States has changed. Radical feminism appears to be less influential. This may be the case partly because the unprecedented attacks have promoted greater social-national solidarity: all groups of Americans, women and men, find themselves in the same boat as a people under attack. Radical feminism may also have been weakened by new attention to the status of women in fundamentalist Muslim societies, making people realize what *real* patriarchy looks like. No wonder Sunera Thobani's assertion that Western hegemony is the worst threat to women's emancipation was widely questioned.

For the most part, however, feminism has not caught up with this shift in attitudes, as indicated by recent feminist publications.

In the *Women's Review of Books* in July 2002, English professor Harriet Malinowitz reviews a collection of essays by writer Barbara Kingsolver, *Small Wonder*. Kingsolver is a left-of-center author who opposed the war in Iraq, asking, "How does the rest of the world keep a straight face when we go riding into it on our latest white horse of Operation-this-or-that-kind-of-Justice, and everyone can see perfectly well how we behave at home?" Yet for the *Women's Review*, she was apparently too pro-American. Malinowitz writes sarcastically about Kingsolver's insistence that right-wing "bully-patriots" and "hoodlum-Americans" should not be allowed to "steal" the American flag from progressives:

> The flag, she later amplified on a public radio show while promoting the book, "stands for courage, justice, and kindness." The problem is, their flag and our flag happen to look exactly alike, and the casual onlooker usually can't tell which intended message is fluttering from any particular mast. And Kingsolver, insisting that, as a "good American," she will "defend the American ideals of "freedom and human kindness," imagines she can, with a stroke of the pen, nullify the "Americanness" of the ideals and people that horrify her. But that's called denial. White supremacy, xenophobia and other forms of bigotry are, along

with some nobler principles, an inescapable part of our collective national history.

For Malinowitz as for Katha Pollitt, the flag is a symbol of "jingoism and vengeance and war."[53]

There is little doubt that radical feminism, in academia and in the wider culture, has succeeded in promoting among a substantial if undetermined number of women a pervasive sense of victimization and alienation from their own society. But, it has also alienated many more young women from feminism itself. Only a quarter of women now describe themselves as feminists, and the lack of interest in feminism on the part of most female college students is widely lamented by academic feminists.

In *Reason* magazine, Catherine Seipp wrote:

One of the minor casualties of 9/11 was patience for listening to privileged Americans complain . . . about their privileged American lives. If feminism doesn't want to completely wear out women's patience—and men's, too—it had better find a new agenda. Perhaps one that is, to start with, less blatantly foolish, and more engaged with the issues that women regularly tell pollsters they care most about: crime, the economy, child care, balancing work and motherhood, their children's schools. It might help if organized feminism recognized that, among other things, legal equality already exists. If feminism wants to become vital again, it must first acknowledge the successes that it helped to achieve.[54]

If feminism is to regain its relevance, it must also acknowledge the role Western and specifically American democracy has played in its successes. However much we would like to regard women's liberation as a natural right, it has been the product and achievement of a complex, advanced civilization. Recent events remind us that this civilization is fragile and that its enemies are hostile to freedom for anyone—especially women. Feminists, perhaps more than anyone else, should realize that Western values and institutions are worth defending.

NOTES

1. "It's bloodthirsty vengeance": Transcript of UBC professor Sunera Thobani's speech at the Women's Resistance Conference, *Vancouver Sun*, October 3, 2001, p. A6. See also Licia Corbella, "A Black, Black Day for Feminism," *Edmonton Sun* (Alberta, Canada), October 3, 2001, p. 11.

2. Rachel Sa, "Thobani's an Insult to Western Feminists," *Toronto Sun*, October 6, 2001, p. 16.

3. Brenda Wadey, "Thobani Correct: Liberal Democratic System Encroaches on Women's Rights," *Calgary Sun*, October 21, 2001.

4. Sharon Lerner, "What Women Want," *Village Voice*, November 6, 2001, p. 53.

5. Yvonne Zacharias, "Students Support Thobani's Comments," *Vancouver Sun* (British Columbia, Canada), October 3, 2001, p. A7.

6. Corbella, "A Black, Black Day for Feminism."

7. Daphne Patai and Noretta Koertge, *Professing Feminism: Education and Indoctrination in Women's Studies* (Lanham, Md.: Lexington Books, 2003), pp. 303–304.

8. Lerner, "What Women Want."

9. "The Empire Strikes Back," *Village Voice*, October 9, 2001, p. 53.

10. Katha Pollitt, "Put Out No Flags," *Nation*, October 8, 2001, p. 9.

11. Lerner, "What Women Want." See also Sarah Wildman, "Arms Length: Why Don't Feminists Support the War?" *New Republic*, November 5, 2001, p. 23.

12. "Seneca Falls Convention," in Alice S. Rossi (ed.), *The Feminist Papers: From Adams to de Beauvoir* (New York: Bantam, 1973).

13. "The Solitude of Self": Stanton Appeals for Women's Rights. Available online at http://historymatters.gmu.edu/d/5315/.

14. Sara M. Evans, *Born for Liberty: A History of Women in America* (New York: Free Press, 1989), p. 171.

15. The National Organization for Women's 1966 Statement of Purpose, www.now.org/history/purpos66.html.

16. See Daniel Horowitz, "Rethinking Betty Friedan and *The Feminine Mystique:* Labor Union Radicalism and Feminism in Cold War America," *American Quarterly*, v. 48, No. 1, 1996, pp. 1–42.

17. Betty Friedan, *The Feminine Mystique* (New York: Dell, 1963).

18. Horowitz, op. cit.

19. Christina Hoff Sommers, *Who Stole Feminism?: How Women Have Betrayed Women* (New York: Simon & Schuster, 1994), p. 23.

20. Alison M. Jaggar, *Feminist Politics and Human Nature* (Totowa, N.J.: Rowman and Littlefield, 1988); for other examples of this attitude see, e.g., Iris Marion Young, *"Throwing Like a Girl" and Other Essays in Feminist Philosophy and Social Theory* (Bloomington: Indiana University Press, 1990).

21. Wadey, op. cit.

22. Andrea Dworkin, *Life and Death: Unapologetic Writings on the Continuing War Against Women* (New York: Free Press, 1997), p. 132.

23. Susan Faludi, *Backlash: The Undeclared War Against America Women* (New York: Crown, 1991); Tanice Foltz, book reviews, *Gender and Society* 9, 1995, pp. 514–515.

24. Emilie Buchwald, Pamela R. Fletcher, and Martha Roth (eds.), *Transforming a Rape Culture* (Minneapolis, Minn.: Milkweed Editions, 1993).

25. Wadey, op. cit.

26. The Rape Culture: An American Epidemic, www.rohan.sdsu.edu/~gwick/rapeculture.html.

27. See Sommers, *Who Stole Feminism?*; also, Cathy Young, *Ceasefire!: Why Women and Men Must Join Forces to Achieve True Equality* (New York: Free Press, 1999).

28. Young, *Ceasefire*, p. 105; Sommers, *Who Stole Feminism*, pp. 188–208.

29. Sommers, pp. 12–13.

30. Sommers, pp. 209–226.

31. Sommers, pp. 11–12.

32. Young, *Ceasefire*, pp. 71–72.

33. Naomi Wolf, *The Beauty Myth: How Images of Beauty Are Used Against Women* (New York: Doubleday, 1992), p. 207.

34. Judy Mann, "Our Culture as a Cause of Depression," *Washington Post*, December 7, 1990, p. B3; Anna Quindlen, "Time to Tackle This," *New York Times*, January 17, 1993, p. E17; Jenny Stromer-Galley and Kate Kenski, "Gender May Hold Some Answers in Tragic Wave of School Killings," *Philadelphia Inquirer*, April 28, 1998; Linda Stasi, New York *Daily News*, May 15, 1995, p. 4.

35. Deborah L. Rhode, *Speaking of Sex: The Denial of Gender Inequality*, pp. 1, 20.

36. Judy Mann, *The Difference: Growing Up Female in America* (New York: Warner Books, 1994), p. 276.

37. Marilyn French, *The War Against Women* (New York: Simon & Schuster, 1992), p. 182.

38. See Cathy Young, "How They Spent Their Summer Vacation," *Heterodoxy*, September 1992.

39. Barbara Ehrenreich, "For Women, China is All Too Typical," *Time*, September 18, 1995, p. 130.

40. See, e.g., Ann Crittenden, *The Price of Motherhood: Why the Most Important Job in the World Is Still the Least Valued* (New York: Metropolitan Books, 2001), pp. 239–249.

41. Ann Ferguson, Book Review: "Sex and Revolution: Women in Socialist Cuba," *NWSA Journal*, Summer 1997, pp. 193–194.

42. Mary-Kate G. Smith, "Is Western Liberal Feminism Bad for Women?" *Labyrinth*, v. 3, Winter 2001.

43. See Ehrenreich cited p. 130.

44. Chandra Talpade Mohanty, "Under Western Eyes: Feminist Scholarship and Colonial Discourses," in Chandra Mohanty, Ann Russo, and Lourdes Torres (eds.), *Third World Women and the Politics of Feminism*, (Bloomington, Ind.: Indiana University Press, 1991), pp. 51–80. Popularity on Women's Studies List: Feminist Theory: Suggested Readings, Women's Studies List archives, http://research.umbc.edu/~korenman/wmst/fem_theory1.html.

45. Margaret Talbot, "The Female Misogynist," *New Republic*, May 31, 1999, p. 34.

46. Germaine Greer, *The Whole Woman* (New York: Knopf), pp. 3, 102.

47. Jill Nelson, "The Ugliness of a Beauty Pageant," msnbc.com, November 25, 2002.

48. Lerner, "What Women Want."

49. Kay S. Hymowitz, "Why Feminism Is AWOL on Islam," *City Journal*, Winter 2003, pp. 36–51.

50. Ibid.

51. Lawson Taitte, "Lifting Personal Veils; Four Women Examine Social Limitations in 'American Burka,'" *Dallas Morning News*, April 23, 2002, p. 27A; Mark Lowry, "'American Burka' Unveils Frustration," *Fort Worth Star-Telegram* (Texas), April 21, 2002, p. 6.

52. "NOW Celebrates International Women's Day with a Rally for Peace," March 8, 2003, statement of NOW President Kim Gandy, www.now.org/press/03-03/03-08.html.

53. Harriet Malinowitz, "Down-home Dissident," *Women's Review of Books*, July 2002, p. 36.

54. Catherine Seipp, "You've Lost Your Way, Baby: How Organized Feminism Has Made Itself Irrelevant," *Reason*, October 1, 2002, p. 38.

13

ADAM GARFINKLE

Peace Movements
and the Adversary Culture

Every time the United States uses force in the course of its statecraft, some stand in opposition to it. This has been the case since the founding of the Republic and looks to be the case for the foreseeable future. Those who oppose and protest American military operations have done so for a multitude of reasons, and they themselves have been, and remain, a diverse group. Some oppose only certain wars on prudential grounds, or for morally based reasons, or because they think a particular policy harms the national interest. Others oppose all American wars as a matter of principle. Among the latter, some are pacifists opposed categorically to all violence while others are revolutionaries fundamentally opposed to the character of American polity and society.

Only this last group of self-styled revolutionaries can reasonably be described as anti-American. America is a nation born not of a common bloodline but of a common idea about the public weal. Hence to be unalterably opposed to that common idea is to be anti-American by philosophy.

This typology of opposition and protest applies most directly to Americans, but to a lesser degree also to foreigners. Many people in the NATO countries of Western Europe during the Vietnam

War opposed that war because they thought it weakened and di-
verted the attention of their superpower protector. Others were
pacifists, but more were leftists who hoped that an American defeat in Vietnam would diminish, if not destroy, American influence in the world.

Since such heterogeneity of protest, at home and abroad, has
been in evidence in the past, it is not surprising that opposition to
Operation Iraq Freedom (OIF), as the Pentagon calls it, was similarly heterogeneous. Protest against the Iraq War abroad was espe-
cially robust. Even in countries whose governments supported
American policy, opinion polls showed more or less solid majorities opposed to the war—Spain being a particular case in point,
Italy only a bit less so.[1] Even more striking, the citizenry in what
Secretary of Defense Donald Rumsfeld called the "new Europe"
was at best ambivalent about U.S. policy, as polling data from
Poland and the Czech Republic indicated. Aside from the United
Kingdom, Israel, and maybe Singapore, it is difficult to name a sin-
gle foreign country whose majority body politic sincerely supported U.S. policy. Not even Kuwait.

Public support for the war in the United States, on the other
hand, was consistently high. The president enjoyed a solid majority throughout the lead-up to war and during its roughly three-
week period of greatest intensity. He won an early congressional
resolution of support, and by the onset of hostilities, even the
Washington Post editorial page supported the essential war policy.[2] (The New York Times under Howell Raines did not, but the
Times featured a compelling pro-war argument by Bill Keller, who
replaced Raines not long afterward as executive editor.[3])

Yet even in the United States, anti-war sentiment was loud
enough—in the universities and among many free-floating intellectuals of note, ethnic lobbies, and, of course, the several venerable organizations of the sectarian and pacifist left.[4] Anti-war
sentiment had its moments too, inside the Democratic party. This
welling up of radical anti-war protest surprised some observers,
who thought the paltry anti-war movement of the first Gulf War,
in 1991, was the last gasp of protest sentiment whose motives ex-
pired with the losing side of the cold war. But the adversary cul-

ture, as Lionel Trilling dubbed it many years ago, had never really gone out of business. The Iraq War provided it with another opportunity to take advantage of considerable, if still minoritarian, unease over a war and to connect it to other issues and discontents.

The question arises: what was new, at home and abroad, about the anti-war movement in regard to the Iraq War, and what was not? In answering this question we need to recall long-standing patterns in the conflicts between the adversary culture and the "establishment." The first part of this essay will lay out these patterns and offer examples for them. The examples come mainly from the Vietnam anti-war movement, which for most readers of this essay was their defining experience of the subject. The second part examines the American experience during the Iraq War, with an emphasis on how it differed from the Vietnam War. The third part looks at a foreign example of anti-war sentiment during the Iraq War: Germany.

I have chosen Germany for several reasons. One is that I spent the war there, from the "shock and awe" bombing campaign to the fall of Baghdad and beyond. Another is that Germany is the largest, wealthiest, and most profoundly confused country in the European Union. As such, its future political vicissitudes will invariably have a major impact on U.S. foreign policy, not to speak of those of other EU member states. More generally, it is worth paying closer attention to opinion about the United States in the world at large. To the extent that the world has become unipolar after the cold war, the United States has become the major actor and concern for members of educated and not-so-educated publics nearly everywhere. Much as it may be admired by many—and visa and green card applications to the United States tell that tale best of all—its extraordinary power is also feared in many quarters and some of its major attributes held in contempt. This matters, for a liberal great power such as the United States depends to a considerable degree on the goodwill and benign expectations of others. We are wise to act and speak in ways that produce common security for the maximum number of countries, and persuade them that their own interests are best served when they run parallel to ours. When we fail to do so, the impact can be significant. The Iraq War is a case in point.

PATTERNS OF PROTEST

Historically, the core of the American adversary culture has been constituted by those who are categorically opposed to all uses of violence, or to the nature of the American political system itself. The pacifist element of the adversary culture that is the oldest. It nearly brought about the secession of New England during the Mexican War. It was joined toward the end of the nineteenth century by sectarian socialist, anarchist, and eventually Communist organizations. Despite differences of aims and spirit between pacifists and leftist revolutionaries, in times of war and crisis the two streams of the core adversarial culture managed to cooperate at least to some extent. This is why during the Vietnam anti-war protests, organizations as different as the War Resisters' League, the American Friends Service Committee, the Women's International League for Peace and Freedom, the Communist Party USA, the (Trotskyite) Socialist Workers party, the (Maoist) Progressive Labor party, the Black Panther party, Students for a Democratic Society, and others managed to get along well enough for most purposes.

The periphery of such movements usually consists of those who are one layer removed from professional activism: those connected to Christian churches of politically liberal and pacifist persuasions, and those of the liberal left, including their respective organizations. During the Vietnam period, such groups included SANE, Americans for Democratic Action, the Council for a Livable World, Clergy and Laity Concerned, and many others. Protest occasions have a tendency to push core and periphery groups toward cooperation, though such cooperation is never easy and often does not endure. The longer the occasion lasts—and the Vietnam War lasted a long time—the more such tendencies of coming together, recombining, and splitting apart have time to develop. As they do, and as they did in the mid-1960s and early 1970s, their influence is transmitted toward the center, into the mainstream of American politics. The first consequential impact is usually felt in the Democratic party.

Invariably those closer to the mainstream are skeptical of the motives of adversary culture groups and try to marginalize them on all occasions of protest and opposition. They suspect, rightly, that association with such groups will harm efforts to persuade the great middle of American public opinion, where ultimate electoral leverage lies. Those in the adversary culture pull the other way, trying to insinuate themselves into the protest coalition of decision-making and, ultimately, to attract those farther to the right to their positions.

As a rule, in cases where the events vindicate, or seem to vindicate, the views of the adversary culture, more centrist groups—and even the Democratic party—*are* pulled to the left. Organizations like SANE and WILPF were transformed by the Vietnam era, and, judging by its 1972 national convention, so was the Democratic party.

The end of the cold war hurt the organizations of the adversary culture, and the uses of American force during the first post–cold war decade, (mainly) of the Clinton administrations, provided few occasions for effective protest. This, and generational change in adversary culture organizations, seemed to diminish the energies and power of the adversary culture.

Nonetheless the consequences of the Vietnam era accelerated and deepened countercultural trends, pushing much of the country to the left. Even self-described conservative Republican administrations have not been "conservative" as the term was used before the mid-1960s. Thus the allegedly "far right" current Bush administration has merely slowed the growth of government rather than reversed it. It wrangles over the size of new middle-class entitlements, not whether there should *be* such new entitlements. It nods to the Supreme Court and accedes to the principle of affirmative action and thus to the priority of group over individual rights.

To the extent that the supporters of the adversary culture manage to influence protest tactics and messages, the effect tends to be counterproductive. If long-haired and irreverent protesters wave Viet Cong flags for the television cameras, throw rocks and bottles at police, burn their draft cards, incite violence, and otherwise break the law of the land, they tend to drive those uncertain about foreign policy into the arms of the sitting administration.

When the protest movement was seized by the adversary culture, it tended to mute anti-war sentiment, particularly in the
labor movement and among those within the broader public. Radical protesters did wonders for George Wallace, Richard Nixon,
and Spiro Agnew. Those who still believe that the long radical
phase of the Vietnam anti-war movement succeeded in ending
U.S. military involvement in Southeast Asia almost universally
claim that, over time, it did so by winning the hearts and minds
of the American people. They depict a gathering momentum.
They are wrong. If they were right, Richard Nixon would not have
been elected president over Hubert Humphrey in 1968 and certainly not over George McGovern in 1972.

After about 1970–1971, the less radical, more liberal elements
in the anti-war movement gained control. Thus more or less re-
united with the mainstream, the anti-war movement regained its
effectiveness. It managed to use the Democratic party to block
funds for the war in Congress, for example. It aimed at the ballot
box, not the street demonstration or the bombing of ROTC buildings. And it gained influence. Nevertheless, when all is said and
done, it is clear that the American people first followed their leaders into war, and only when those leaders lost heart, followed
them out again. The radical phase of the Vietnam anti-war movement was if anything counterproductive by its own lights, but its
overall effect was probably modest.[5]

Three conclusions may be drawn relevant to other anti-war
protest movements, in America or elsewhere. First, there is always competition among the different strains within protest
movements. Adversary culture groups alone can do little unless
they connect with a broader public in the throes of a major galva-
nizing issue, but broad sentiment rarely becomes effective without the work of the "professionals" of the adversary culture.

Second, the more radical the manifestations of protest, the
more it helps the authorities in power; the more moderate, the
more effective it is in influencing policy and the public at large.

Third, a major protest movement will always have a lasting influence on the organizations of the adversary culture and on the
organizations to their right as well as on the body politic.

THE AMERICAN WAY

A great deal of anti-war activism erupted in the United States in the recent anticipation of the Iraq War. What made this protest different from the Vietnam-era protests is that it was anticipatory. Serious protest of the Vietnam War *followed* the onset of combat. Moreover, Vietnam started out as an insurgency, while the Iraq War started with a bombing campaign. Consequently Vietnam metaphors warning against the Iraq War did not make much sense. The Vietnam War ended as a conventional war; the Iraq War, on the other hand turned into an insurgency after May 2003. As of this writing, in January 2004, it is not clear how all this will turn out, nor whether the adversary culture will find a way to append Vietnam War–era images to Iraq *post hoc*. So far they have not.

Another difference was that in the spring of 2003 the cold war has been over for more than a dozen years, and the attacks of September 11, 2001, were still fresh in mind. Vietnam-era radical protesters saw that war through the prism of a global struggle in which, in their view, the United States was on the wrong side of history. Very few radical protesters in the spring of 2003 were apologists of or ideological kin to either Al Qaeda or the Iraqi Ba'ath party. In the Vietnam era, anti-Americanism could depict itself as "progressive" and "socialist"; in the spring of 2003 anti-Americanism could not align itself with the terrorists or support the proliferation of weapons of mass destruction.[6]

Nonetheless the most radical of the winter and spring protests in 2003 had much in common with their forebears. The United States was for them still the root of all evil, and anyone who opposed the United States was thereby turned into an objective ally and given the benefit of the doubt. That included even Slobodan Milosevic and, for some, the North Korean regime. As in the 1960s, radical opposition was anti-corporate and anti-capitalist, only now the ideology was less doctrinaire Marxist and more a loose, new age "small-is-beautiful" political environmentalism. The organization ANSWER (Act Now to Stop War and End Racism), possessed of a core Trotskyite ideology, helped to shape and articulate these positions. ANSWER, headed at least nominally by former Attorney General Ramsey Clark, has argued that an American empire rooted in capitalism is despoiling the earth for the profits of the few. "Make no mistake about it," says ANSWER's manifesto, "globalization is the bulwark of empire and war is its tool."

There were many other similarities, too, between the Vietnam anti-war movement and that of the recent anti–Iraq War movement. Many were stylistic as the protesters, and especially the younger generations among them, tried to dust off and reuse sixties counterculture protest methods and symbols in 2003: guerrilla theater, teach-ins, die-ins, and other displays. Some of the same old figures—older but not necessarily wiser—returned to entertain us, among them Pete Seeger and Joan Baez.[7] Susan Sontag too reemerged, advising the graduates of Vassar College in May 2003 to "Be extremely skeptical of all claims made by your government."[8] This was a show of moderation compared to her calling the white race "the cancer of human history" some thirty-five years ago.

As in the Vietnam era, too, local radicals hijacked city councils and other local government venues to make symbolic statements.[9] As before, celebrities with no credentials whatsoever to pronounce on complex issues were unable to resist exploiting another venue for self-promotion.[10] Also as in the 1960s and '70s, the elite media was sympathetic to at least the less radical expressions of the anti-war movement, and often the radical expressions as well.[11] As was also the case decades ago, organizations and protests were funded not by small contributions but by large ones from liberal foundations: the MacArthur Foundation, the Samuel Rubin Foundation, the Solidago Foundation, the Arca Foundation, and others.[12]

There was also a new version of political tourism. Whereas Jane Fonda, Tom Hayden, Staughton Lynd, Susan Sontag, Mary McCarthy, the Reverend Sloan Coffin, and others had gone to Hanoi during the Vietnam War, some Americans of lesser reknown went to Baghdad in the winter and spring of 2002–2003.

Fonda *et al.* visited North Vietnam *during* a war, and said and did things which were not in the best interests of the American POWs, as for instance passing handwritten notes from them to

North Vietnamese officials. Nothing remotely comparable happened in Baghdad. First of all, prompted by years of bleating about the United Nations sanctions, (which was entirely the fault of the Iraqi Ba'ath party's policies), representatives of the adversary culture had been going to Iraq for years. The visitors to Baghdad in the run-up to war featured the usual suspects: opportunistic congressmen, confused celebrities like Sean Penn, and, of course, Ramsey Clark of ANSWER an unembarrassed supporter of Saddam Hussein's regime and repeat visitor since the 1991 Gulf War.

To this list were added the so-called "human shields." Hardened "peace activists" from the United States, Britain, and other countries came to Iraq in advance of the war, intent on distributing themselves around civilian targets to make it impossible for Coalition forces to bomb them. Their hopes and expectations were not met. The Iraqi authorities wanted to place them at military targets. This prompted one Australian "shield" to make the remarkable comment that "I think the Iraqi government is potentially putting us in a dangerous situation." A German actress said, "I certainly didn't come here to be a martyr." The regime also infiltrated their anti-war demonstrations with pro-Saddam elements, making it seem like they were pro-Ba'athist. "It changed the spirit of our march," said one disappointed protester, adding: "That wasn't what we expected."[13] In the end virtually all human shields left Iraq before the war began.

More important however, was the Iraq anti-war movement's political trajectory. In the Vietnam era, as already noted, the protest moved from largely liberal to radical and then back to mainly liberal attitudes. During the Iraq War the same process was telescoped into a very short period. Instead of playing out over more than a decade, as in the Vietnam War–era, it all took place in just a month or two. But the general pattern was the same, and some of the reasons for it were the same too.

With the advent of the George W. Bush administration and the terrorist attacks of September 11, 2001, those in the administration who had favored war with Iraq found themselves both well placed and their analysis seemingly vindicated by events. Opposition from within withered and was soon replaced by a radicalized opposition from without. In all the major anti-war demonstrations, held before the war started, the organizing elements were of the radical left. They were made up of some unreconstructed Stalinists but were mainly Trotskyites, with sprinklings of radical pacifists and others. Constituted as ANSWER, they were able to dominate the early street activism because they were ready and well organized.

ANSWER was able to add to its core, issue-specific radicals of environmental, anti-Zionist, anti-Semitic, feminist, and anti-globalization persuasions. In turn, the organizers then reached out to less radical groups, hoping they would swallow their distaste for the organizers' strident, anti-American views to join forces (and give financial support) for the specific cause. In February 2003 ANSWER was successful with such united-front tactics. It managed to stage large and loud protest demonstrations which were well publicized not only in the United States but in Europe and elsewhere. As intended, the association of some less radical groups diluted the radical image of the protests, leading many unsuspecting others to join the marches more or less spontaneously.[14]

But when ANSWER shut down the San Francisco financial district, and when some of its sponsored marches turned violent, some of the more moderate groups grew leery.[15] A marginally less radical group, United for Peace and Justice (itself a coalition of sixty national organizations), soon declined to join forces, or funds, with ANSWER in planning new demonstrations and "actions." In response, ANSWER resorted to the standard Communist rhetorical tactics, which is to lump all opposition with the right, even the far right. It began to attack liberals with a vengeance, singling out Todd Gitlin for special treatment.[16] This, of course, is exactly what Gitlin's Students for a Democratic Society did during the Vietnam era, with Carl Oglesby's famous November 1965 speech in Washington being the opening shot of the radical attack on liberalism.

As in the Vietnam era, not all liberals had the same attitude toward the evident anti-Americanists in the protest movement. Win Without War's leader, Eli Pariser, took a view similar to that of the liberal organizations that had supported more radical demonstrations between 1965 and 1968. He said, "I've always been a real believer that the best ideas win out if you let them happen. I'm personally against defending Slobodan Milosevic and calling North Korea a socialist heaven, *but it's just not relevant now.*"[17] So for the most part Win Without War cooperated with ANSWER.

For those who remember the Vietnam era, or those younger who have studied it, the different approaches of liberals toward the radical anti-American challenge at present are reminiscent of the distinction between Moratorium and Mobilization in 1970–1971. By then, protest against the war was moderated by liberal elements, some of whom refused to be associated with radical groups; but others did not and became effectively radical in action if not also in belief.

One of the reasons for the speed with which all this transpired during the winter and spring of 2003 apparently was due to the Internet. Protests could be large and rapidly organized because of information technology.[18] Pariser's Moveon.org became the nucleus for Win Without War.

Also new was the fact that, at many universities, an inversion of sorts went on: faculty, veterans of the sixties, protested while students looked on more skeptically.[19] When Gary Bass, an assistant professor at Princeton (and a former aide of mine) asked his class how many of them were in ROTC, two raised their hands and the rest applauded. That would not have happened in 1968 or even in 1990–1991.

What was not new was, for example, that United for Peace and Justice displayed an old characteristic of less-than-wholly-radical groups: it aped some of the tactics of radicalism. Protest groups compete with one another for "loose change," as some organizers call it—for people who aren't sure what they think ideologically but who want to express themselves through what they see as heroic gestures. Just after ANSWER disrupted downtown traffic in Washington on March 21, United for Peace and Justice praised and participated in a New York "die-in" organized by the M27 Coalition. About four hundred protesters sprawled on streets and sidewalks near Rockefeller Center during morning rush hour, snarling traffic for more than two hours.[20]

Major combat operations in the Iraq War lasted for about three weeks. Whereas in the Vietnam era the length of the war enabled the anti-war movement to evolve, in the Iraq War it overwhelmed the protests. There was not enough "bad" news to exploit. There were few body bags and, before long, the discovery of Saddam's mass graves undermined the sense of moral rectitude that animated many protesters. The steady if moderate daily casualties that followed the end of "major combat operations" have been insufficient, as of this writing, to revive major anti-war protests, though their impact on electoral politics may yet be considerable.

Everyone agreed that the Iraq War would be an important factor in the 2004 presidential election, and it may very well help elect a Democrat to the White House. The determination of Win Without War and United for Peace and Justice to focus on electoral politics, going from the streets to inside the system, mirrored the reaction of the post-Weathermen Vietnam-era peace movement's focus on the 1972 presidential and congressional elections. The movement's support for Howard Dean has had a major impact on the Democratic race, constituting a powerful insurgent force against the party's support structures. On the other hand, Howard Dean's failure to win a single state in the 2004 Democratic primaries and his withdrawal from the race in February 2004 suggest that the anti-war movement had a modest impact on mainstream politics.

What real influence did these protests have? As already suggested, they did not influence the Iraq War itself and did not change public opinion in the slightest, as best anyone could measure. About 30 percent of those Americans polled before the demonstrations began were opposed to or cautious about war, and about 30 percent remained opposed during and just after the war. Because most large demonstrations remained civil—a well-learned lesson from thirty years ago—there was little or no negative follower effect.[21]

Whether the movement will coalesce into a political force to influence the 2004 elections remains to be seen, but this is quite possible. It depends largely on evolving postwar circumstances. The administration's failure to plan well the transition from combat to reconstruction, the surprising level of violence in Iraq long after May 1, the failure to discover clear evidence of operational Iraqi WMD programs, and the flap over U.S. intelligence manipulations all auger in favor of the continued influence of the anti-war movement. Win Without War, at least, is trying hard, as its full-page ad in the *New York Times* of August 26, 2003, shows. The support that the foundations of the liberal left had poured into the demonstrations now benefited Win Without War, and, as noted, former Governor Howard Dean and others on the Democratic left.

There remains the question, what effects did the movement against the Iraq War have on the adversary culture itself? In the Vietnam era the radical phase of the anti-war movement pulled many liberals and liberal organizations to the radical side, some temporarily and some permanently. It moved the entire country toward the left, as has already been argued. Madison Avenue, as usual, captured the marketable portions of the counterculture, banalized them, and eventually helped provoke a reaction. Those today in their early twenties, for example, are a hodgepodge of skeptical attitudes. Many are still skeptical about what looks overly patriotic and conventional, but they are just as skeptical about what strikes them as stridently anti-patriotic and self-consciously countercultural.

A most entertaining and interesting example of this trend was Christopher Hitchens's theatrical support for the war policy and his scathing attacks on his old colleagues.[22] Hitchens was not the only former leftist to see things differently in 2002–2003. Michael Ignatieff, a biographer of Isaiah Berlin and human rights proponent of note, excoriated the left for its moral illiteracy.[23] Ignatieff and others called, in effect, for an American empire based on the moral obligation of ridding the world of dangerous and hateful tyrannies. For all practical purposes, Ignatieff and David Rieff now have more in common with Robert Kagan, Max Boot, and William Kristol than any of them do with, say, Henry Kissinger.[24] *Washington Post* columnist Richard Cohen, a card-carrying liberal, found himself admitting that Jeanne Kirkpatrick's old "blame America first" indictment of the Democratic party had been right all along.[25]

It is difficult to say, so soon after the event, how the Iraq War and the anti-war movement that arose against it will influence either the adversary culture, political liberalism, or the country as a whole. The war is not yet over (given continuing guerrilla actions against American troops), and neither is the war in Afghanistan. If the United States and its allies succeed in transforming Iraq into a more or less stable and democratic society while simultaneously uprooting terrorism in the area, anti-war movement will be seen by honest observers as a disgrace. But if the consequences of the war are more ambiguous or decidedly negative, the verdict will, of course, be different. An ambiguous outcome in Iraq will in all probability bolster the protest movements of 2002–2003 and reassure the adversary culture about its judgments of U.S. foreign policy and its relationship to domestic social arrangements and economic interests.

But we should not exaggerate the impact of world events on the motivations of protesters or on the ultimate health of their movements and organizations. That is because, in the final analysis, the motivation of the most committed protesters and activists may be found in various social-psychological strata, the deepest and most important of which is the same today as it was during the Vietnam War.[26] Both generations of protesters were prompted by religious impulses broadly defined.

All of us need something beyond the self in which to believe; for those who do not find such an object of belief in traditional sources of spiritual wisdom, anti-establishment activism, or activist politics associated with the pursuit of social justice becomes a secular religion. These attitudes, needless to say, have been discernible and well established in the Western world during the past century, well before Vietnam or Iraq.

Many anti-war activists seem to long for some kind of an impending apocalypse that is a proof and precondition of personal commitment: the greater and more dramatic the stakes, the more praiseworthy and more unequivocal one's dedication and commitment becomes. A Manichean moral clarity and certainty escalates personal commitment. Many members of the adversary culture— and those who choose to associate with them in heady times— express moral sentiments collectively through political protest or participation of some kind; the political goals to be achieved come to resemble objects of secular worship. Social bonds reinforce personal faith and commitment, and shared commitment in turn strengthens the social bonds. These needs and attitudes help explain why so many activists and marchers in the grip of strong and seemingly pure feelings cannot be reached by rational argument. As I wrote years ago,[27] there has never been a culture without a religion, by which I mean a set of ideas to organize our questions and thoughts about existential matters that empirical answers do not satisfy—questions about consciousness, mortality, creation, and moral logic. In societies that have become overwhelmingly secular, we have been conditioned to think of secular and religious as polar opposites. Nonetheless there remains in secular society powerful religious impulses which, when ungratified by traditional religious beliefs or institutions, migrate to other sources of gratification, the most popular of which in the twentieth century has been radical political commitment—which, as Digby Baltzell used to say, citing the secular religions of fascism and communism—hasn't done much good for either politics or religion. And that certainly seems to apply to contemporary Germany.

GERMANY IN THE SPRING

On Sunday, March 30, 2003, *Der Tagesspeigel Morgenpost*, a popular mass-circulation paper in Germany, carried a large photo of the previous day's large anti-war rally in downtown Berlin, and above it the headline read: "82% of Berliners oppose the war." Indeed, all the newspapers in Germany focused intently on anti-war rallies, speeches, and activities.

The anti-war disposition of the ruling Red-Green coalition government in Germany was everywhere in evidence, including large banners with anti-war slogans draped on public buildings throughout the country. In Dresden a quote from the poet Erich Kästner hung over the famous Dresden Opera House: "Glaubt nicht, ihr hättet Millionen Feinde, Euer einziger Feind heißt: Krieg" (Do not believe you have millions of enemies, you have only one enemy: war). A church down the street from the Wannsee Conference House bore a sign reading, "Krieg ist immer der falsche weg" (War is always the wrong way). A large sign on the local theater in Potsdam read "Kein Krieg. Nirgends" (No war. Nowhere). The performance art of the political sermon was everywhere in evidence.

These slogans accorded with majority sentiments. The government benefited politically from this confluence, which in turn helped reinforce popular anti-war opinion. Thus in Germany, unlike in the United States, anti-war protest *coincided* with the position of the political establishment and the two reinforced each other.

Opposition to government did exist but was muted. As *Die Zeit* co-editor Josef Joffe explained to me, Germans, unlike Americans, British and many other nationals, do not engage in the gloves-off public debates about public and especially foreign policy issues. Once the German government, whatever government, lays down the policy line, whatever line, most people defer to it, at least publicly. However politically incorrect the notion of national character may be, there remains something characteristically German about attitudes toward authority.

For Germans, war is particularly reprehensible because Germans started and lost two of them in the twentieth century. Thanks to two recent popular books too, most Germans tend to equate all aerial bombardment with what the U.S. and British planes did to Dresden on February 13, 1945. And most Germans do not believe that American talk about Middle Eastern democracy is sincere. Taking their cue from mass-circulation magazines like *Der Spiegel*, during the war they all "knew" that George W. Bush was a simpleminded cowboy who was elected through corruption and stealth. Much of the mass-circulation press in Germany has long been in the hands of Germany's '68 generation. It has not been charitable to most things American—except for the remnants of the counterculture and American expressions of anti-Americanism. The most oft-seen image in Germany, on T-shirts, handbags, and even on bodies as tattoos, is that of Che Guevara. His picture adorned the cover of the biggest gossip magazine in April, the German version of the American *People*, on the coming seventy-fifth anniversary of his birth.

Anti-Americanism in Europe, including Germany, is not one but three linked phenomena. One is philosophical. It has an old pedigree, as James W. Ceaser has recently shown.[28] Its romantic, anti-rationalist, racist, and anti-modern components have accumulated over the past two centuries. It has captured the imagination of many European intellectuals, and while it was originally a conservative, blue-blood reaction to a free and socially freewheeling American society, since the middle of the last century it has been taken over by the European left, thanks in part to Jean-Paul Sartre's adaptation of Martin Heidegger's anti-Americanism.

The second type of anti-Americanism is cultural; it concerns matters of taste and style and has been greatly affected by America's export of mass culture and entertainment.

The third type may be called contingent anti-Americanism, which is stimulated by the dislike of particular policies or personalities in any given U.S. administration.

In Germany in 2002-2003 these different types of anti-Americanism coalesced. The old philosophical anti-Americanism had never gone away and was absorbed by the elites of both the SPD and Green. Cultural anti-Americanism has been on the rise too, thanks to the growing penetration of American mass culture. Contingent anti-Americanism was at an all-time high, stimulated by the Bush administration's somewhat abrasive tone and policy judgments and the personality of the president.

Some observers also believe that Germany's many problems—economic stagnation, inability to assimilate Turkish guest workers, failure to maintain demographic vitality, and inability to complete the integration of the former East Germany—have led to a diffuse discontent that finds expression in animosity toward the one country that has some claim on German gratitude.[29]

This conjunction of philosophical, cultural, and contingent anti-Americanism helps to explain the dimensions and depth of German anti-war sentiment. These sentiments were also reflected in the extraordinary popularity of Michael Moore in Germany. Moore, whose politics resemble those of Noam Chomsky (shorn of the academic style and erudition), is the most popular American in Germany. The German-language version of Moore's *Stupid White Men* had sold, as of July 2003, more copies than the original English-language version in North America (about 1,300,000 versus 963,000). His film, *Bowling for Columbine*, has attracted more than 800,000 German viewers, though not all of them voluntarily, as teachers from the '68 generation took their students on mandatory field trips to see the film while others urged their junior high, high school, and college classes to attend anti-war demonstrations instead of class. Moore's book and film are understood by most young Germans (and those in other European countries) as accurate depictions of American cultural and social life.

As was true in the United States, the German anti-war movement consists of a hardcore and peripheral supporters. ANSWER's role in the United States was played in Germany by the Communist party, the residue of former West and East German factions. This was especially apparent in Berlin, where the city government is a coalition of the SPD and the PDS (Party of Democratic Socialism), the old East German Communist party. In the park area of Unter der Linden, one of Berlin's main and grandest streets, near the U.S. and Russian embassies and within sight of the Brandenburg Gate, were shantylike information booths and guerrilla theater performances. On a placard, Bush, Blair, and Hitler were equated. Also notable was a large, bright blue graffiti on the nearby train station: "Axis of Evil: US/Israel/UK." Given the Red-Green coalition government's opposition to the war, nothing has restrained these sentiments and activities.

German churches today, Protestant and Catholic alike, are also epicenters of pacifism. While Germans support such pacifism, polls show that only about 15 percent of them attend church services more than once or twice a year. In Germany, then, the church has become for most Germans a political entity—the epitome of Baltzell's reversal of religion and politics.

In the Berlin Wall Museum, next to what used to be Checkpoint Charlie, Western success in the cold war is played down. In addition to portraits of many brave and ingenious Germans who escaped from East Berlin, there are positive depictions of Mahatma Gandhi, Martin Luther King, Jr., and the demonstrators against the Pershing missile deployment in Germany in the 1980s. Also depicted are the anti-Communist mass uprisings in East Germany in 1953, Hungary in 1956, Prague in 1968, Romania in 1989, and Russia in 1991. But so are the anti-nuclear demonstrations of the 1980s. NATO is never mentioned.

There clearly are people in Germany not given to reflexive anti-American sentiments. They know that American strength in the world allows Europe's experiment in peaceful, federal unification to proceed. This minority is concerned about Transatlantic relations, notably about polls showing that only 11 percent of Germans considered the United States to be Germany's closest friend (down from 50 percent in 1995), while France ranks at 30 percent.

It may be true that the Bush administration's inner circle lives in its own closed world in which Al Qaeda and the Ba'ath party are believed to be linked. Such fantasies pale in comparison to the fantasy world of SPD-Green coalition, whose senior members of government are so deeply anti-American (anti–American government, that is) that rational arguments and questions will not receive serious consideration.

European anti-war and anti-establishment sentiments have two further stimulants. The first is a visceral and often irrational anti-Americanism, stimulated by the increasing gap between U.S. power and that of the European Union. In France, among intellectuals, this anti-Americanism is associated with a burgeoning anti-Zionism and anti-Semitism.[30] The second source of anti-Americanism, peculiar to some Western European countries, is a desire to expunge a deep sense of guilt over a European colonial past now held responsible for the terrible problems of the Middle East and other Third World areas.

And so we are once more compelled to return to the part played by unmet religious needs. In post-Christian Europe the infusion of religious energies and impulses into politics goes hand in hand with the building of a new polity: a federated European Union. As Amir Taheri, the Iranian writer observed: "Anti-Americanism plays the useful role in filling in the vacuum left by the evaporation of 19th century ideologies."[31] And as G. K. Chesterton said, "When a man stops believing in God, he doesn't believe in nothing; he'll believe in anything."

So it is that in the United States, a nation conceived from an idea and not a bloodline, anti-establishment protest fixes on the abstractions of a secular messianism; and in Germany, a nation rooted in bloodlines, such protest fixes on something far more concrete: America.

NOTES

1. Anti-American sentiment in Spain, however, is deep and long-standing, while it is not in Italy. So the fact that a bare majority of Italians opposed the war is perhaps more interesting than the fact that a larger percentage of Spaniards did. The two other NATO allies whose publics have long evinced strongly negative feeling for the United States are Turkey and especially Greece.

2. "'Drumbeat' on Iraq? A Response to Readers," *Washington Post*, February 27, 2003, p. A26.

3. "Saying No to War," *New York Times*, March 9, 2003, p. 12; Bill Keller, "Fear on the Home Front," *New York Times*, February 22, 2003, p. A35.

4. See especially in Paul Hollander, "The Resilience of the Adversary Culture," *National Interest*, No. 68 (Summer 2002).

5. I explain this line of argument in *Telltale Hearts: The Origin and Impact of the Vietnam Antiwar Movement* (New York: St. Martin's/Macmillan, 1995).

6. See the interesting essay by Edward Rothstein, "Left Has Hard Time in Era of Terrorism," *New York Times*, December 21, 2002, pp. A19, 21.

7. James Barron, "Decades Later, 60's Icons Still Live by Their Message," *New York Times*, March 30, 2003.

8. Quoted in Sam Dillon, "Reflections on War, Peace, and How to Live Vitally and Act Globally," *New York Times*, June 1, 2003.

9. See, for example, Barbara Whitaker, "Los Angeles Council Adopts Resolution Against Iraq War," *New York Times*, February 22, 2003.

10. See Rick Lyman, "Celebrities Become Pundits at Their Own Risk," *New York Times*, Week in Review, March 2, 2003.

11. See, for example, Kate Zernike's ode to Leslie Cagan, chief organizer of United for Peace and Justice, "Challenge Facing the Antiwar Movement Is Finding a Meaningful Message," *New York Times*, April 20, 2003. Michael Powell's ode to Ms. Cagan was "Hawks May Rule, but This Dove Persists," *Washington Post*, April 17, 2003. Puff pieces also inhabited the Internet. See "Protests Put Face on Anti-War Movement," an AP story datelined from Montpelier, Vt., carried by Comcast.net on April 10, 2003.

12. See Julia Duin, "Foundation Cash Funds Antiwar Movement," *Washington Times*, April 2, 2003.

13. Quoted in Neil MacFarquhar, "Human Shields, No Résumé Needed," *New York Times*, February 21, 2003.

14. Note for example, a sign with a "Socialist Workers" signature in the photo of a rally of high school students in Austin, Tex. *Washington Post*, March 31, 2003, p. C1.

15. For a description, see Evelyn Nieves, "From Sea to Sea, Rallies For, Against the War," *Washington Post*, March 22, 2003.

16. This was especially ironic it was Gitlin, whose major book on the Vietnam anti-war movement and the counterculture tried to atone for the sins of the radical left by pointing to cultural and social achievements supposedly bequeathed to America by radicalism. These achievements, however, were overwhelmingly those of liberals and liberalism. See Gitlin, *The Sixties: Years of Hope, Days of Rage* (New York: Bantam, 1987).

17. Pariser quoted (emphasis added) in George Packer, "Smart-Mobbing the War," *New York Times Magazine*, March 9, 2003, p. 49.

18. See Jennifer S. Lee, "How Protestors Mobilized So Many So Nimbly," *New York Times*, February 23, 2003.

19. See Kate Zernike, "Professors Protest as Students Debate," *New York Times*, April 5, 2003.

20. See Manny Fernandez, "Protests Disrupt Downtown Traffic," *Washington Post*, March 22, 2003, and Christine Haughney, "Protesters in New York State 'Die-Ins,'" *Washington Post*, March 28, 2003.

21. See Kate Zernike and Dean E. Murphy, "Antiwar Effort Emphasizes Civility Over Confrontation," *New York Times*, March 29, 2003.

22. See Christopher Hitchens, "So Long, Fellow Travelers," *Washington Post*, October 20, 2002.

23. Michael Ignatieff, "I Am Iraq," *New York Times*, March 23, 2003. The best such indictment by far, however, was Andrew Sullivan's "A Million Mogadishus," at Andrewsullivan.com, March 29, 2003.

24. See Max Boot's commentary arguing that anti-war protesters nearly always end up making war more, not less, likely. "Protestors with Bloody Hands," *Los Angeles Times*, February 27, 2003.

25. Richard Cohen, "Kirkpatrick Was Right," *Washington Post*, May 8, 2003.

26. Obviously there are other differences as well. During the Vietnam-era protests there was a military draft; no one except the very young or the terminally stupid thought the government would resort to a draft to fight a war in Iraq (or anywhere else).

27. *Telltale Hearts*, pp. 126–127.

28. James W. Ceaser, "The Genealogy of Anti-Americanism," *Public Interest*, No. 152 (Summer 2003).

29. See Charles Lane, "Sturm Signals," *Washington Post*, February 23, 2003.

30. Note the descriptions in Elaine Sciolino, "French Rallies Against War Shift Focus to Israel," *New York Times*, March 30, 2003.

31. Amir Taheri: "Choosing Between Friend and Foe," *Arab News*, December 1, 2002.

14

SANDRA STOTSKY

Moral Equivalence in Education: The Use of the Holcaust in Discrediting American Society

*A*bout a decade ago I gave an invited talk at a session of the New England Association of Teachers of English. In it I criticized a growing tendency by English teachers and literature anthologies to suggest similarities between Nazi concentration camps and the internment camps for Japanese Americans during World War II, ignoring profound differences. In the question-and-answer period following my talk, several teachers in the audience expressed great concern about my remarks. They believed their students should see "the essential similarities" between Nazi concentration camps and the internment camps for Japanese Americans, and felt that any discussion of differences would be "a whitewash."

Shouldn't students see a difference, I asked, between an experience in which people left a confinement alive and in good health and one in which they left in the form of smoke and ashes? More important, shouldn't they consider why there were differences and how our political principles and institutions might account for them?

Showing some irritation at my questions, these teachers professed that they did not see the differences as significant. They encouraged their students to see similarities also between Nazi concentration camps and America's "concentration camps" for Native Americans, and between the European Holocaust and the "Holocaust" perpetrated by European explorers and settlers on these peoples through the introduction of deadly contagious diseases.

These teachers had a moral perspective about Americans they were eager to transmit to their students, and they did not want their students' judgments colored by any ambiguity. We have no way of knowing how successful they have been. But the fact remains many educators, especially in the social studies, have made a concentrated effort in the past two decades to use the study of the Holocaust to encourage students to think that their country's history resembles the history of Nazi Germany, and that there is a negligible difference between most white Americans and the German Nazis. In doing so, most of them probably sincerely believe they are helping their students understand the evils of racism and intolerance. The "lessons" they seek to extract from the study of the Holocaust are among the major sources of anti-American attitudes that education stimulates today.

In an increasing number of schools in this country—and more recently in Europe—literature about the Holocaust is being used to insinuate a moral equivalence between Nazis and white Americans, and to cultivate a negative attitude toward white Americans, American citizenship, history, American society, and political institutions. Nothing could more effectively delegitimate American society than the belief that it is comparable to Nazi Germany.

Other features of current history curricula or history textbooks also contribute to this goal, as for example an emphasis on the framers of the Constitution as slaveholders, and the almost complete absence of information suggesting that racism and slavery were also widespread in non-Western civilizations. The most destructive and determined among these attempts to delegitimate the United States is the effort to use the study of the Holocaust for this purpose. These efforts, made both in this country and abroad, are not well known to the public at large.

MORAL EQUIVALENCE IN THE ENGLISH CLASS

Widely used literary anthologies published during the 1990s imply moral equivalence in a variety of ingenious ways.[1] For example, in its eighth-grade anthology, Prentice Hall's 1994 *Literature* pairs the play based on Anne Frank's diary with a play based on Virginia Hamilton's *The House of Dies Drear*. The latter centers on a mysterious old house in Ohio whose underground tunnels and caves were used by its wealthy abolitionist owner more than a hundred years ago to help runaway slaves. The two plays are implicitly linked by the central importance of the house in each play—in both cases a house that sheltered people needing protection from racist persecution. There is also explicit linkage in two pages entitled "Multicultural Connection." These pages describe the rise and fall of Adolf Hitler, explain the term "Holocaust," and provide figures on the different kinds of people who died in Eastern Europe as a result of persecution. The teaching apparatus for the plays informs the students that each reflects the theme of "The Just and the Unjust," making it reasonable for students to infer that the counterpart to the unjust in Anne Frank's story are the white racists who condoned or profited from slavery.

In another case the Anne Frank story in McDougal Littell's 1994 eighth-grade anthology is paired with a story about black Americans to link Nazi Germany to America. In a unit thematically titled "The Will to Survive," the play is offered under the title "The Invincible Spirit," followed by a group of short pieces ranging widely in mood and topic under the title "Caught in Circumstances." The first work in the group is a fictional story by Paulette Childress White about the indignities suffered by a black family that is forced to go on welfare because of the father's loss of a job; the story is narrated by the twelve-year-old daughter as she accompanies her mother to the welfare office. It is immediately followed by Langston Hughes's poem "The Dream Keeper," a poem that suggests how harsh the real world is for anyone with dreams. It is unlikely that students will miss the implied connections to Anne Frank's story.

It should be noted that the popularity of the play *The Diary of Anne Frank* in the secondary-school curriculum long antedates the current preoccupation with teaching about the dangers of intolerance. English teachers began to introduce the play, or the diary (and sometimes Elie Wiesel's semi-autobiographical *Night*), to secondary students decades ago because these works are moving personal accounts of the Holocaust presented through the eyes of sensitive adolescents. One can find the play based on Anne Frank's diary, or an excerpt from it, in the six leading literature anthologies for the eighth grade (including the two described above), in one literature anthology for the sixth grade, and in one instructional reader for the seventh grade used in the 1990s. *Night* is also taught frequently in grades 9 through 12, to judge by the presence of excerpts in two twelfth-grade anthologies and by individual trade book sales.

Four eighth-grade anthologies link the Holocaust to racism in America through an implicit comparison of Nazi concentration camps with the internment of Japanese Americans on the West Coast during World War II. Scott Foresman's 1991 anthology does so in an ingenious manner. Although it groups *The Diary of Anne Frank* with an excerpt from a play about an elderly woman in France during the occupation who pretends to be a Nazi collaborator in order to help their intended victims, the last selection in the unit directly preceding the play about Anne Frank is Yoshiko Uchida's short story "The Bracelet." This story is about a young Japanese-American girl's loss of a bracelet given by a school friend before her family is taken from their home by heavily armed soldiers to an internment camp with barbed wire strung around its grounds. The textual contiguity of "The Bracelet" and *The Diary of Anne Frank* suggests that the editors saw common elements and wanted to help students see them too. This editorial point of view is consistent across the textbooks in this series. The eleventh-grade anthology in this series, devoted to American literature, places Elie Wiesel's Nobel Prize acceptance speech directly after selections by Lorraine Hansberry and Ralph Ellison, both understandably highlighting prejudice against blacks in this country.

Contiguity of selections is not essential for linking the internment of the Japanese Americans and the Holocaust. All that is required is to have some information about the internment camps somewhere in the anthology. Two anthologies find novel ways to accomplish this. In an earlier unit in the anthology, before *The Diary of Anne Frank* appears, McDougal Littell's 1994 anthology offers a letter written by William Tsuchida to his brother and sister who were confined in an internment camp (for the Japanese) while he was serving in the U.S. army during World War II. The letter says nothing about these internment camps, but the editors make use of the letter to give students information about the camps.

Holt, Rinehart and Winston's 1993 anthology gives students the same information in a different way. It presents a short story by Yoshiko Uchida as the introduction to its eighth-grade anthology, and though the story is not about the internment experience, the biographical description at the end of the story notes that Uchida "experienced firsthand the discrimination to which many Japanese Americans were subjected during World War II," adding that she spent "a year with her family in a concentration camp for Japanese Americans in Topaz, Utah." In Holt, Rinehart and Winston's 1997 anthology, the Uchida story and biographical information no longer appear. But one follow-up activity to *The Diary of Anne Frank* suggests discussing Martin Luther King and civil rights, Eleanor Roosevelt and women's rights, or Gandhi and nonviolent protest, while another follow-up activity suggests comparing *Night* or Ruth Minsky Sender's *The Cage* with *Farewell to Manzanar*, a poorly written autobiographical piece of white-guilt literature about the experiences of a very young Japanese-American girl in one of the internment camps. The editors suggest the similarities by noting that "all three are autobiographies by people who were imprisoned during World War II because of their religious or national background."

Prentice Hall's 1994 anthology lays the groundwork for the linkage in yet another way. It includes in a poetry unit directly following *The Diary of Anne Frank* a letter in the form of a poem, conveying what a young girl might have written to a friend in response to the executive order from the U.S. government requiring the Japanese on the West Coast to report to relocation centers for internment.[2] Thus four of the six eighth-grade anthologies facilitate a linking of Nazi death camps to Japanese-American relocation camps, albeit in very different ways. Eighth-grade teachers can easily imply the analogy, if they so choose, even when they are using an anthology with a Holocaust selection that contains nothing on the internment of Japanese Americans during World War II. They may simply ask their students to read, in addition to *The Diary of Anne Frank, Farewell to Manzanar*, which is frequently recommended for eighth-grade students.

In a sourcebook for teachers published by the California State Department of Education, a study question for *Farewell to Manzanar* suggests that students "compare Manzanar with the German concentration camp in *I Am Rosemarie*" (a story about a young Dutch Jewish girl who is deported with her family to a Nazi concentration camp).[3] The sourcebook does not suggest that they discuss differences as well. Students are thus prompted to associate Nazi extermination camps with the relocation camps for Japanese Americans. Whether or not there is class discussion about the actual, historical differences between the fates of Japanese Americans as opposed to European Jews, students will likely see the internment of the Japanese Americans as an expression of anti-Japanese prejudice, because complete information is rarely given as to how the policy was formulated, by whom, and the limitations of its scope. The lack of detailed information about this historical episode reinforces the impression that the editors were disposed to create a negative image of Americans during World War II.

It is hard to avoid concluding that the editors of these four anthologies intended to lead students to see a connection between the Nazi extermination camps and the relocation camps for Japanese Americans.

There is little advice in these anthologies as to the possible moral lesson to be drawn from studying literature about the Holocaust, and how it might be discussed with the students. Lucy Dawidowicz, a historian of the Holocaust, suggested in the last article she wrote before her death that "the primary lesson of the Holocaust" is the Sixth Commandment, "Thou shalt not murder."[4] She also believed that the study of the Holocaust should lead students to see the fundamental difference between a constitutional, democratic government, ruled by law, and authoritarian or totalitarian governments that persecute specific groups for an objective characteristic (race, ethnicity, social class, etc.) rather than some form of behavior. How particular political beliefs or ideologies stimulate and legitimate such persecution would also be an appropriate question for a class discussion after reading about the Holocaust. I have yet to find such questions suggested for class discussion in the literature on the Holocaust. Meaningful cross-cultural comparisons of concentration camps may also include excerpts from *A Day in the Life of Ivan Denisovich* or *The Gulag Archipelago* as well as from the increasingly available literature about the Chinese camps under Mao. No excerpts from such works appear in the anthologies that include Holocaust literature, at least in those published in the 1990s.

MORAL EQUIVALENCE IN SOCIAL STUDIES

The strongest support in the curriculum for suggesting moral equivalence between Nazi Germany and America comes from Facing History and Ourselves (FHAO), an organization that provides materials and services to more than sixteen thousand teachers, ostensibly to help them address "racism, antisemitism, and violence."[5] Its website conveys the scope of its activities here and abroad.

Inspiration for FHAO came from courses in moral education taught by Carol Gilligan at the Harvard Graduate School of Education in the mid-1970s. Work on FHAO's resource book on the American eugenics movement was funded through the Harvard/ Facing History and Ourselves Project, with Gilligan serving as a major adviser.

Although other Holocaust curricula are taught in some schools across the country, FHAO is by far the most popular source of training and source materials on the Holocaust. Its prominence has grown since Steven Spielberg decided to provide it with funds from the revenues of *Schindler's List*. According to FHAO's website, it now reaches more than 1.5 million adolescents through its teacher network, and more than 4,500 schools through regional offices in six major cities in the United States, in addition to an office in Europe. FHAO describes itself as having an "interdisciplinary approach to citizenship education" and is supported by grants from many sources, including the Goldman Sachs Foundation and the Germenhausen Foundation, with the grant from the latter targeted to "expand outreach in Europe." The FHAO curriculum is flexible and can be taught over a long or a short period of time and at any grade level, though it most frequently takes about six to eight weeks and is usually taught in eighth or ninth grade. FHAO urges maximal interdisciplinary cooperation between English and social studies classes to help students "think deeply about issues of racism, prejudice and discrimination, and to be active participants in promoting social justice."

FHAO's goals and methods were spelled out in its first major resource book, titled *Holocaust and Human Behavior*, published in 1982.[6] This teacher manual was superseded in 1994 by a substantially revised resource book with the same title but now framed by the assumption of equivalence between Nazis and Americans. It is still in use.[7] In 2002 FHAO published an additional resource book titled *Race and Membership in American History: The Eugenics Movement*, and began to introduce this book at institutes and workshops and to develop an online course based on the book. The contents of these three resource books reveal how FHAO has evolved from laudable beginnings in the 1970s by an eighth-grade social studies teacher in the Brookline Public Schools, interested in moral education and in teaching about the Holocaust, to become a major vehicle for highly negative interpretations of American history, American citizenship, and American science. The contents of these books also provide the basis for a case study in how the social activism underlying many of the K–12 curricular trends of the 1970s and early 1980s metastacized into the manipulative and malignant anti-American moralism of the 1990s and 2000s.

The 1982 resource book seeks "to promote awareness of the history of the Holocaust and the genocide of the Armenian people, an appreciation for justice, a concern for interpersonal understanding, and a memory for the victims of those events" (p. 13). It also seeks to make comparisons and parallels with past and contemporary issues, events, and choices when appropriate, with a major goal of helping today's students prevent another Holocaust. About sixty-three of the manual's four hundred or so pages address the Armenian genocide.[8] The rest deals with the Holocaust, originally the sole focus intended by FHAO.[9] Because of FHAO's stated belief that a study of the Holocaust must have a "positive" ending,[10] the final chapter addresses political issues, including civic participation in contemporary American life.

FHAO's goal of providing "positive" civic lessons for Americans is the source of the central problem of this curriculum. In order to enable teachers to use the study of the Holocaust to stress the importance of citizen participation in America, and to urge students to speak up and act in the face of perceived social wrongs, FHAO chose to rely on a psychological explanation for the behavior of the Nazis and of the Germans who supported or acquiesced in their rise to power. FHAO portrays the Nazis as displaying "human behavior" (hence the title of the resource book) in whatever they did. Such a conceptual framework seriously downplays the deep-rooted cultural and political forces that shape human behavior and differ considerably across cultures. A neglect of cultural and political forces well serves the purposes of the 1994 resource book. Although it contains little that explicitly connects anti-Semitism and the psychology of the Nazis and their supporters to America's social problems and the psychology of Americans, the conceptual framework allows for comparisons with American society.

The purpose for studying the Holocaust is now to confront "the history of racism and antisemitism at home and abroad" (p. xiii). The preface begins with a reference to an article by Marion Wright Edelman of the Children's Defense Fund about the struggle today "for the nation's conscience and future" as "the American Dream is collapsing," pitting American against American "as economic uncertainty and downturn increase our fears, our business failures, our poverty rates, our racial divisions, and the dangers of political demagoguery" (p. xiii). In the twelve years since the appearance of the first resource book, America has become, in FHAO's eyes, a nation consumed by hatred and violence. FHAO believes that our students as having been taught to hate, and attributes "much of the violence that threatens our society" to "its roots in bigotry and hate" (p. xiii). This demonized view of American schools and American society prevails throughout the book. If this curriculum had been designed for German educators, one might understand the melodramatic statement that "we do not want yet another generation of young people influenced by propaganda to march blindly in someone else's parade" (p. xviii).

The 1994 resource book leaves no stone unturned in its efforts to make sure that students consider the task of confronting white racism in America as the chief reason for studying the Holocaust. Its first and last two chapters concentrate on racism and violence in American history and contemporary life. Such a framework enables FHAO to associate even Thomas Jefferson and Abraham Lincoln with the history of Nazism. The text points out that Lincoln regarded Africans as inferior in his early years, and notes Jefferson's status as a slaveholder and his words about Africans as a threat to "white racial purity" (pp. 76–77). Students are later asked to compare African Americans to European Jews (pp. 94–96). Questions in five other chapters also invite comparisons between events in American history (almost always with reference to black Americans) and the history of racism, anti-Semitism in Europe, and the rise of Nazi Germany.

FHAO's 1994 resource book moves back and forth from Nazis to Americans and consistently ignores the possibility that what happened in Germany might best (or at least also) be understood as a political and cultural phenomenon. It makes explicit and frequent links not only between twentieth-century America and twentieth-century Germany but also between nineteenth-century America and nineteenth-century Germany.

For example, students are asked to compare the patriotism and military service of black Americans in World War I with the patriotism and military service of German Jews in Germany in World War I (p. 113). Activities of the Ku Klux Klan in America after World War I are compared to the rise of the Nazis in Europe after World War I, in addition to other parallels between Weimar Germany and post–World War I America (pp. 125, 132, and 133); indeed, the Klan is elevated to a more prominent place in American history than the Democratic or Republican party. The text also compares American schools and school texts in the 1930s and 1940s to German schools during the Nazi era (pp. 243–244) and asks students to compare *Kristallnacht* (the highly organized orgy of mass violence against Jews throughout Germany) to an incident in Boston in which a rock was thrown through the window of a Vietnamese family (p. 267). Students are asked to discuss when the word "holocaust" is a useful metaphor for other events, after the text points out that "African Americans have labeled their experiences with slavery and dehumanization a 'holocaust'" (p. 310). The book closes with the question of whether the violence that supposedly surrounds all of us in America would lead to another Holocaust, implying that the victims of this Holocaust would be African Americans (p. 564).[11]

In the March 1995 *New Republic*, Deborah Lipstadt criticized this resource book, pointing out that "no teacher using this material can help but draw the historically fallacious parallel between Weimar Germany and contemporary America" (p. 27). Not only did she criticize FHAO's efforts to insinuate this analogy, she also questioned the usefulness of FHAO's efforts to link the Holocaust to Hiroshima, Nagasaki, the My Lai massacres, or the mass murders in Cambodia, Laos, Tibet, and Rwanda as other examples of "mass destruction." The FHAO avoids references to the Soviet gulags, or the mass murders committed by Communist regimes (excepting Cambodia and Tibet) among its examples of mass destruction.

The 1994 resource book has some clear moral injunctions for Americans. Students must help to make sure that white America ends what FHAO claims has been a denial of black American history; it must also apologize and make amends (pp. 505–513). Louis Farrakhan is singled out as one of those blacks who speaks "directly to the pain and pride" of all black people, with a quick passing remark that parts of Farrakhan's message "stereotype and demean other groups" (p. 507). There is not even a hint that the very people he stereotypes and demeans happen to be the victims of the Holocaust. It is understandable why the 1994 text refrains from discussing black anti-Semitism, especially since it uses the Holocaust to portray America's blacks as Europe's Jews.

FHAO's latest resource book, *Race and Membership in American History: The Eugenics Movement* (RMAH), is 356 pages long and consists of 76 chapters or lessons called "Readings." Its cover contains a montage of various faces, all unidentifiable except that of Adolf Hitler. The chapters contain snippets of primary source materials (excerpts from college textbooks, scholarly works, speeches, editorials, personal anecdotes, and magazine articles), strung together by explanatory narratives written chiefly, it appears, by an associate program director for FHAO, a former high school social studies teacher in the Brookline public schools. Each chapter is followed by "suggestions for independent research or group projects." According to the Foreword, RMAH was written to ask us

> to rethink what we know about our own past. While barely remembered today, the eugenics movement represents a moral fault line in our history. It was a movement that defined differences in terms of racially superior and inferior human traits. Because these ideas were promoted in the name of science and education, they had a dramatic impact on public policies and the lives of ordinary people at the time and, in turn, created legacies that are still with us today. The eugenics movement is not a historical footnote. It is a fundamental chapter in our history that ought to be examined in our classrooms.

The Overview explains the connection to the Holocaust. RMAH "focuses on a time in the early 1900s when many people believed that some 'races,' classes, and individuals were superior to others," using a "new branch of scientific inquiry known as eugenics to justify their prejudices . . .," and while "in the United States, the consequences were less extreme," in Nazi Germany "eugenics was used to shape and ultimately justify policies of mass murder." The brochure advertising RMAH also makes the connection clear, stating that "racism and eugenics had worldwide appeal. In Nazi Germany they were used to justify the Holocaust. In the United States they limited opportunities for millions of Americans." To facilitate teachers' access to the readings that explain the "connections between the American eugenics movement and its counterpart in Nazi Germany," the Overview notes that the FHAO's website now provides an instructional module with the readings that trace these connections.

Apparently FHAO seeks to suggest that Americans and American science, however indirectly, shared responsibility for Nazi Germany's extermination policies and the Holocaust. Although RMAH makes it clear that few American scientists subscribed to the eugenics movement by the time of World War II, the chapters on "The Nazi Connection" artfully quote from various sources to indicate that Hitler drew upon the ideas of many respectable German scientists for his ideas on racial "eugenics," and that these German scientists not only supported Hitler and his use of their ideas but also acknowledged the leadership of American scientists, educators, and policymakers in the eugenics movement. Karl Brandt, head of the Nazi program for the killing of the mentally disabled, is quoted as telling the court, in his defense after World War II, that the Nazi program for the sterilization and elimination of "life not worthy of living" was based on American ideas and experiences (p. 282).

FHAO also implies that the eugenics movement was the American equivalent of Soviet Lysenkoism in its effect on scientific development, although Lysenkoism is never mentioned in RMAH. On p. 274, RMAH quotes "scientist Jonathan Marks" to the effect that if biologists "did in fact widely see the abuse to which genetic knowledge was being put, but refused to criticize [the eugenics movement] out of self-interest, they paid dearly for it. As historians of genetics have noted, the eugenics movement ultimately cast human genetics in such a disreputable light that its legitimate development was retarded for decades." By using this book, social studies teachers could suggest to their students that while Stalin retarded Soviet biology for decades by his support of Lysenko's ideas, American biology was retarded during these same decades by something worse— racism and the goal of eliminating people with undesirable genetic traits. Any doubt about RMAH's ideological allegiances is dispelled by its praise of Henry Wallace as "one of the few American politicians to challenge both Nazi racism and American eugenics" (p. 283).

Despite the massive number of citations and excerpts to prop up the book's implicit thesis and explanatory narratives, FHAO fails to give a single biologist's assessment of the influence of the eugenics movement on American science. Jonathan Marks is not a geneticist; he is an anthropologist by training and an associate professor in the Department of Sociology and Anthropology at the University of North Carolina–Charlotte. Eminent scientists who *have* written about the history of evolutionary biology imply a very different judgment about the influence of eugenics on the history of American biology. For example, eugenics is mentioned in one short, four-sentence paragraph in *Evolution and the Diversity of Life*, a 722-page collection of essays by Ernst Mayr on the history of important ideas and movements in evolutionary science.[12] Moreover, from the early 1920s to the late 1940s, American biology moved from a secondary position in world biology to the forefront, as indicated not only by the size of the enterprise but by the number of Nobel Prizes won by Americans and the number of leaders of biological and medical science who came here to escape Nazism. FHAO provides no evidence that the legitimate development of American biology was "retarded for decades" by eugenics. It doesn't because it can't. All it can do is quote an anthropologist.

A curious reader might also wonder why no biologists' assessments are quoted about the influence of the eugenics movement on German science. Perhaps because they would support the judgment of Paul R. Gross:

Eugenics, positive and negative, has had no significant influence on the course of biological or biomedical science. Some of its sillier notions may have been used here and elsewhere, in the past, by racists as justification for their opinions; but there has been no visible effect on basic life science or the practice of medicine. The vast majority of biologists today, if asked to define "eugenics," would have trouble coming up with anything like a correct statement. Many would not have heard of it and most would be entirely unaware of its history. It has been forgotten, except by a few ideologues of the far left and right for whom it continues to be a *cause celebre*. . . . To connect American eugenics with the Nazi Holocaust is a monstrous exercise in special pleading.[13]

The history of the eugenics movement should be better known. The American eugenics movement at the height of its influence was responsible for the forcible sterilization of thousands of Americans and did contribute ideologically and sometimes financially to the rise of Nazism in Germany.[14] One may ask why an organization devoted to a study of the Holocaust should suggest that the eugenics movement in America was instrumental in the development of Hitler's Final Solution rather than European anti-Semitism?

In her critique of FHAO's 1982 manual (and other Holocaust curricula used in this country), Lucy Davidowicz noted that FHAO's omission of the history of anti-Semitism was its most serious failure. This omission has remained unrectified and made it easier for FHAO to use the history of the eugenics movement to discredit American society.

According to FHAO's Annual Report for 2001–2002, FHAO conducted an institute in Stockholm at the invitation of Sweden's Department of Education, with the expectation that the proceedings of the institute would be transmitted to other Swedish teachers. Although there seems to be no evidence that the Swedish government today is concerned with anti-Semitism in Sweden or in the rest of Europe, it has evinced a great interest in racism in America. FHAO has also begun to provide teacher training seminars in Berlin for German teachers in the past several years. What better way to relieve lingering German guilt over the Holocaust than by helping young Germans discover an American-dominated eugenics movement at the turn of the twentieth century as ultimately responsible for Nazi racial policies and the Holocaust?

EFFECT OF THE FHAO CURRICULUM ON TEACHERS

Although the 1994 FHAO resource book is permeated by an assumption of moral equivalence between Nazi Germany and contemporary America, it does not explicitly state that the two are equivalent. One can only speculate to what extent impressionable students who study its curriculum and read *The Diary of Anne Frank* may transfer their feelings about the Nazis to our own society.

I have been able to collect some evidence on how the FHAO's curriculum has affected teachers through the influence of workshops or with the help of graduate course work in a school of education. One example is a syllabus created in 1994 for a new course for students in grades 10, 11, and 12 in an upper-middle-class suburban high school in a Western state. Designed by two new teachers overtly seeking to address intolerance in this country, this syllabus comes close to taking for granted a moral equivalence between Nazi Germany and contemporary America. I received a copy of this syllabus from one of the two teachers as part of the application material for admission to a 1994 summer institute on civic education that I directed at that time at the Harvard Graduate School of Education. A recent graduate of a master's program at the Harvard Graduate School of Education, this teacher must have been proud of this syllabus to send it with the application.

Apparently the course description originated from a school district's decision to expand its multi-cultural education program for the 1993–1994 school year. It was also developed to "confront the growing issues associated with diversity at the high school." It claims that "hatred, prejudice, racism, and indifference" are matters that students at this high school confront daily, a claim that is implausible for an upper-middle-class high school with a high-achieving student body. Indeed, the school district's scholastic scores rate second in the state, according to information I received from the chamber of commerce. Nevertheless the course was approved by the principal, the superintendent of schools, and the school committee and began to be taught in the 1994–1995 school year.

The syllabus for "Culture, Power, and Society" explicitly connects the psychology of the Nazis and pre–World War II German culture with American cultural values and attitudes. It suggests that the psychology of the Nazis and their supporters is an inherited cultural characteristic of most of Americans. The course outline makes its thrust crystal clear. The first unit deals with "socialization and the ethos of the American psyche" and examines the "self and the individual in American society." Unit Two, which deals with racism and anti-Semitism, explains that it "will explore the roots of bias in *our* society" (emphasis mine). It goes on to state that after examining where and how racist attitudes are formed (through stereotypes, segregation, and isolation), the unit will end with the reading of *Night* and an extensive look at the Holocaust. In the fourth of the five units in the syllabus, students study homophobia in the United States. Doubtless there will be a linkage of Nazi persecution of homosexuals to the "injustice suffered by homosexual individuals" in America.

There is a convincing explanation as to why these teachers have found the study of the Holocaust so useful for addressing prejudice and bigotry in this country. It provides them with the most repellent and extreme example of the consequences of racial prejudice, and one that can be connected to the intolerance inherent in "white racist America." With the abolition of slavery and legal discrimination and the disappearance of lynching, racial prejudice has become far less visible and tangible in this country. What would better symbolize the consequences of prejudice or intolerance and make a powerful impression on young minds than images of the Nazis, the death camps, and the gas chambers? The course explicitly proposes that the "prejudiced personality" discussed in the required textbook *The Social Animal* by Elliot Aronson can be generalized to all Americans, and then harnesses this false generalization to the adolescent's emotional response to the Holocaust.

Further examples of the effects of FHAO's workshops on teachers appeared in other application materials I received. One eighth-grade teacher proudly explained how, after taking a number of Facing History workshops, she had restructured her teaching of *To Kill a Mockingbird* to "help prepare students for the Facing History unit in social studies." Her students "are now being asked to look for parallels between Nazi Germany and the U.S., looking at U.S. slavery and subsequent racism as our holocaust. . . . Excerpts from Jonathan Kozol's *Amazing Grace* [will] help them begin to see the ghettos that exist today. That's what I might like to focus on at the institute: the connection between contemporary ghettos of poor blacks in American cities with the ghettos and extermination of Jews and others in the Holocaust."

It should be noted that it is not easy for outsiders to learn what takes place in Facing History workshops. Only teachers from the schools that have arranged (and paid) for the workshop can attend, and the website that enables these teachers to exchange ideas about classroom practices and resources is password-protected.

MORAL EQUIVALENCE IN THE *ANNE FRANK JOURNAL*

The moral equivalence of America and Nazi Germany has been promoted in the teaching materials accompanying yet another effort connected with Anne Frank's diary. According to a 1991 brochure, the *Anne Frank Journal* was used as part of an educational program connected with the exhibition "Anne Frank in the World, 1929–1945," produced by the Anne Frank Centre in Amsterdam and distributed in America through the Anne Frank Center in New York City.[15] Adapted from educational material for secondary schools in Holland, the *Journal* served as preparatory material for a visit to the exhibition or for follow-up. It was also used to accompany the reading of the play based on Anne Frank's diary, the diary itself, or other reading materials on the Holocaust. Bearing a strong resemblance to the 1994 FHAO manual, the 1993 edition of the *Journal* was based on the assumption that "the study of history is

most meaningful when it has significance for present-day society."
It stressed "the need for every individual to make a choice . . . when
racial violence . . . is common." It aimed to "encourage young people to examine their own experience with racism and discrimination and to make them consider their own responsibility in racist
events they encounter." As does FHAO, it subsumed anti-Semitism under racism so that it could deal with racism against blacks
in this country. The brochure contained a few photographs showing anti-Semitic vandalism in Great Britain and Holland, but its
chief concern was the racism of "fascists" and neo-Nazis toward
"people of color" in America and Western Europe. Despite the fact
that the neo-Nazi movement in America was by the *Journal*'s own
admission rather small, students were nevertheless asked to "collect newspaper clippings about neo-nazi activities and anti-fascist
actions" and to discuss the "similarities and differences between
Berlin 1934, Paris 1986 and Neo-nazism in the USA."

The *Journal*'s ideological agenda was clearest in a section
called "A Message of Hate." It asked students: "How is the 'White
Supremacy' movement in the U.S. different from the Nazis and
neo-Nazis? How is it the same? . . . Discuss why this movement
is particularly American. Discuss the effects of a history of slavery in the United States on today's version of white supremacy?"
The *Journal* concluded its list of suggested questions for students
with: "Could today's racism lead to something like the Holocaust?" The question clearly does not have the Jews in mind as
victims of this Holocaust.

LITERATURE ON INTOLERANCE IN ENGLISH CLASSES

Pre-college students also read a great deal about the Holocaust in
their English classes at the encouragement of their teachers' professional organization. In the spring of 1994 the executive committee of the National Council of Teachers of English (NCTE)
approved a resolution urging teachers to let their students read
and discuss literature on "genocide and intolerance within an historically accurate framework with special emphasis on primary
source material." Again, genocide has been conflated with the far

broader and different concept of intolerance. Part of the rationale offered for the resolution was the need to counter the attempted denial of the "European Holocaust of the 1930s and 1940s." The NCTE also created a task force called "Committee on Teaching about Genocide and Intolerance" to compile a list of resources to assist teachers in "planning and producing instructional materials on the rhetoric and literature of genocide and intolerance." The rationale given in the announcement of the resolution stated that "continuing acts of racial, ethnic, class, and religious hostility are occurring in increasing numbers in the United States and around the world". . . and that these "destructive forces of intolerance and bigotry must be countered in every setting."

In 1999 NCTE published the work of this committee, entitled *Teaching for a Tolerant World: Essays and Resources*, for grades 9–12. As one might expect, essays and resources addressing the Holocaust appear jointly with those addressing African Americans, Asian Americans, "Chicanos/Chicanas," Native Americans, and gays and lesbians. Only two essays in the entire collection suggested that intolerance or genocide might be associated with groups other than Americans or Nazis. One essay deals with the effects of twentieth-century genocide against women, describing the experiences of Armenian and Cambodian women among others. The other essay— on the Ukraine famine—manages to indict Americans and other Westerners for not reporting the famine when it took place—a splendid example of how the left manages to cover up its own culpability by casting blame on the West in situations where it was chiefly responsible for withholding facts or misleading the public.

Last but not least, the guidelines in the National Standards for United States History proposed in 1994 by the National Center for History in the Schools at the University of California, Los Angeles, seem to reinforce the idea that the main purpose for studying the Holocaust in American schools is to indict the United States.

THE COSTS OF TURNING AMERICA INTO AMERIKA

A part of the American school curriculum today is being increasingly used not to help students learn about the social, political, or cultural history of other societies but to call attention to the deficiencies of their own society and in particular the prejudice against nonwhite people that some educators and textbook editors see as the dominant characteristic of all Americans of European descent (including the survivors of the Holocaust). One result of the effort to make America look morally equivalent to Nazi Germany is the transformation of the literature class into a pseudo–social science class. It is unlikely that Anne Frank's reflections or Elie Wiesel's spiritual and philosophical responses to the Holocaust will be at the center of student attention or be contemplated at all in classrooms where teachers are so eager to address racism, sexism, violence, alternative family structures, or homophobia in the United States.

A particularly egregious example of how Anne Frank's story is used for highlighting an array of victims of American prejudice appears in Macmillan's (1994) instructional reader for seventh grade. The editors have grouped together excerpts from Anne Frank's diary and a biography of Anne Frank by Miep Gies (a member of the Dutch family that hid the Franks) with poems by an American Indian and an African American, a story about an American Indian child, an anecdote about a Puerto Rican child, a chapter from Thurgood Marshall's biography, an excerpt from Martin Luther King's Nobel Prize speech, and an excerpt from *Beyond the Divide*, a novel by Kathryn Lasky about a brave Amish girl who survives the wilderness in the Old West of 1849 with the help of a small group of American Indians. According to the afterword in the novel, this group of Indians was in fact gradually massacred by white settlers over the next two decades and eventually obliterated as a tribe.

The thematic motifs suggested by the editors for this unit, entitled "Reach Out," are courage, faith, determination, and the need for the help of others in surviving or succeeding in attaining one's goals. Teachers can easily make these connections between Nazi racism, the prejudice directed at blacks, Hispanics, Indians, and homosexuals in this country explicit. When examples of "intolerance" range from the Final Solution to, say, parental opposition to the Rainbow curriculum in New York City, the Holocaust becomes trivialized, to say the least.

The greatest costs of these endeavors are civic and intellectual— the discrediting of our political principles, procedures, and institutions, the stimulation of interracial conflict, and the decline in the capacity to grasp and make important intellectual and moral distinctions. The latter can be illustrated by an op-ed essay by Ellen Goodman in the August 28 edition of the *Boston Globe*, on the removal of a granite block inscribed with the Ten Commandments from an Alabama courthouse. She opens with an anecdote about a Muslim who had murdered his adulterous mother because she had dishonored the family and expected an Islamic court to exonerate him on the grounds that this would be the "ruling of God." Goodman says she doesn't know how jurists using the Koran as their law book ruled in this matricide, but she sees this anecdote as an example of a struggle between democracy and theology in Iraq that is similar to "our own struggles with theocracy and democracy." Here Chief Justice Roy Moore's placement of the monument on courthouse grounds in an attempt to convey the historical fact that the American legal system is rooted in a particular moral code (the Sixth Commandment, "Thou shalt not murder") becomes analogous to the use of the Koran by Islamic judges to justify murder.

Most English or social studies teachers who use literary or non-literary materials that suggest similarities between Nazis and Americans do so, I believe, because they have been taught in schools of education (and probably in humanities courses in the arts and sciences in colleges) to see intolerance (or social injustice) as this country's enduring original sin. It is not irrelevant that well over 80 percent of K–12 teachers today are white middle-class females. Sexism has been so consistently and deliberately associated with racism, religious bigotry, and homophobia (all of them practiced by white heterosexual males) that it is not difficult for female teachers today to identify with other victims of bias and to embrace the implied or explicit extension of white male Nazi attitudes to white Americans and overlook the specifics of the discriminatory acts.

In addition, the desire to *epater le bourgeois* is as much a part of American literary and nonliterary history as is the feminist zeal to correct our moral failings—the latter being particularly characteristic of white Protestant females in the nineteenth and twentieth centuries.

While past efforts by some educators (and others) seeking to postulate a moral equivalence between the United States and the Soviet Union had to be abandoned for obvious historical reasons, the more recent trend is to conjure up such equivalence between the United States and Nazi Germany as part of the effort by pedagogical moralists and textbook publishers to address intolerance in America. The attempted reduction of America's moral status to that of Nazi Germany recalls the leftist fashion of the 1960s: spelling America as Germans would (Amerika) to suggest similarity to Nazi Germany and the moral degradation involved. Few better examples of domestic anti-Americansm are available than these attempts.

NOTES

1. Those cited were the major publishers of school anthologies during the 1990s; their anthologies are still likely in use because of the cost of replacing them. Moreover, even when state law mandates new textbook adoptions every five years, there are rarely drastic changes in content because of the cost and because teachers favor selections they want to continue using. There is no way to determine exactly what students read in these anthologies because teachers exercise their own idiosyncratic choice in the assignment of readings. Nor is it possible to obtain exact sales figures from the publishers (or other sources) in a highly competitive market to determine how many of their anthologies were sold to the schools in a given period of time.

2. A connection with discrimination against blacks and women is facilitated by the following unit, which includes a journalist's account, based on interviews with survivors, of what happened to Anne Frank, her family, and Dutch friends after they were discovered by the Gestapo. This account is directly followed by an essay by Shirley Chisholm on the prejudice that blacks and women must overcome in America.

3. Page 114 in "Literature for All Students: A Sourcebook for Teachers," a product of the California Literature Institute, published by the California State Department of Education in 1985.

4. Lucy Dawidowicz, "How They Teach the Holocaust." *Commentary*, December 1990, p. 31.

5. *Facing History and Ourselves* Annual Report 2001–2002.

6. Margot Stern Strom and William S. Parsons, *Facing History and Ourselves: Holocaust and Human Behavior.* Watertown, Mass.: Intentional Educations, 1982.

7. *Facing History and Ourselves: Holocaust and Human Behavior.* Brookline, Mass.: Facing History and Ourselves National Foundation, Inc., 1944.

8. The chapter on the Armenian genocide seems incoherently inserted into the FHAO curriculum because the manual fails to call attention to any of the

extraordinary parallels in the histories of the Armenians and the Jews, both ancient peoples of the Middle East. The chapter on the Armenian genocide provides an informative chart on the origins and history of the Armenian people, a
map of historic Armenia, information on how Armenians had considered autonomy, if not independence, during the nineteenth century as the best way for
a religious and ethnic minority to be protected. There is also a brief note on how
the Armenian response to their genocide by the Turks led to the establishment
of an Armenian republic (later taken over by the Soviet Union) and the desire of
many Armenians to regain control of their lost homeland in Turkish Armenia.

    9. Although its scholarship on the details of the Holocaust is scrupulous,
the historical framework FHAO offers for the study of the Holocaust in the
1982 (and 1994) teacher manual is crucially flawed. If the "final solution" was
about anything, it was about anti-Semitism. Yet only a twenty-two-page-long
chapter provides reading selections on the history of the European Jews and on
the causes of anti-Semitism. And it contains nothing on the origins of the Jewish people, their early history, and why so many were in Europe, Western or
Eastern. Nor are there later readings on the response to the Holocaust by what
was left of world Jewry. Because the Holocaust is so inadequately contextual-
ized in this manual, students are unlikely to learn (in this curriculum) how
much the Holocaust influenced the determination of Jews after the war to
reestablish a country of their own so that they could become a nation like
other nations, what their ancient homeland had been, and why they chose to
return there. Nor are they apt to examine the manifestations and sources of
contemporary anti-Semitism. The 1982 manual almost completely ignores contemporary anti-Semitism—its continuing virulence in some of its traditional
settings and its new sources elsewhere. Only five pages in this manual offer
short readings dealing in any way with contemporary anti-Semitism, and these
pages appear in the same twenty-two pages on the history of the European
Jews—before the manual discusses German history, the rise of Hitler, and the
Holocaust itself.

    10. Telephone conversations with Margot Strom and her associate, Steven
Cohen, April 1989.

    11. FHAO has emphasized racism and violence in American life in its work-
shops and annual conferences on human rights over the past decade. For example, of the many workshops offered for the first annual FHAO Learn-A-Thon
that took place in Brookline in May 1994, less than half dealt with the Holocaust
itself. Almost all the other workshops dealt with social issues in America.

    12. Ernst Mayr, *Evolution and Diversity in Life* (Cambridge: Harvard Uni-
versity Press, 1976, paperback reprint 1997), p 318.

    13. Personal communication from Paul R. Gross, University Professor of
Life Science, emeritus, University of Virginia, former president and director of
the Marine Biological Laboratory, Woods Hole, Massachusetts, August 14, 2003.

    14. The responsibility of the American eugenics movement for Nazi racial
policies and the Holocaust is the explicit thesis of Edwin Black's latest book,
*War Against the Weak: Eugenics and America's Campaign to Create a Master
Race* (Four Walls Eight Windows, 2003).

    15. According to the Anne Frank Center, its goals are to:
    Effectively introduce young people to Anne Frank, the Frank family's per-
sonal story, and the history of the Holocaust;

Help young people and communities explore the difficult issues of discrimination, intolerance, and bias-related violence in a positive and constructive way;

Engage young people to examine and challenge discrimination, intolerance, and bias-related violence;

Carry the Center's anti-bias message to isolated areas and underserved communities across the nation, where people seldom have opportunities to discuss the problems of racism and discrimination, and to effect community-initiated action;

Illustrate the importance of personal responsibility and tolerance by honoring those individuals who actively confront prejudice and bias-related violence.

Of late the North Korean authorities decided that they could use *The Diary of Anne Frank* in the schools as a tool of their anti-American propaganda. Reported on CBS "Sixty Minutes" on February 29, 2004.

15

BRUCE S. THORNTON

Anti-Americanism
and Popular Culture

*F*uture historians looking back on America in the decades following World War II will no doubt be puzzled by a historically
unique phenomenon: in the midst of the greatest freedom, leisure,
and material prosperity ever enjoyed in the history of mankind,
significant segments of American society have become chroni-
cally dissatisfied with the United States and its institutions.[1] This
dissatisfaction, moreover, typifies not just the usual suspects—
academics, intellectuals, and pundits—but permeates popular culture as well, the news and entertainment industries that presumably cater to the whims and beliefs of their consumers.

How do we explain this widespread disgruntled opulence? Certainly there are no empirical grounds for believing that we live in
an "air-conditioned nightmare," as the novelist Henry Miller put
it, not when more of us live longer, freer, more nutritious, less
painful, and more leisurely lives than our ancestors could ever
have imagined.[2] Perhaps part of the answer lies in the perennial human habit of being what Dostoevsky's Underground Man calls an
"ungrateful animal," prone to complaint no matter how materially
comfortable and secure he might be. Ideology no doubt lies behind
much of the complaint: those opposed on grounds of Marxist

principles to free markets, a vigorous middle class, and liberal democracy—the salient characteristics of American society—shape
their cultural products to reflect those biases.[3]

An equally significant cause for the "culture of complaint"[4] is
the status value conferred by poses of cynicism, irony, and a general suspicion about the various "illusions" that thinkers like
Marx and Freud have convinced us befuddle our collective minds
and mask the true horror of our existence. These poses have trick-
led down from those whom philosopher J. G. Merquior called the
"hysterical humanists"[5] to the purveyors of ephemeral news and
entertainment seeking to compensate for their feelings of inade-
quacy regarding their intellectual sophistication, and the tran-
sience and triviality of most of their productions.

This high status value accruing to the stance of suspicious criticism that marks the "intellectual hero" of our times is reinforced
by other cultural ideals that shape much of our popular culture.
The attitudes and ideas of romanticism have been particularly influential in the development of consumerism and popular culture
alike, since both must appeal to consumers by invoking common
cultural denominators.[6] Particularly important here is the romantic glorification of the "rebel," the lone individual of superior sensibility, sensitivity, and insight who opposes the dull conformity
of a society that worships the grubby gods of "getting and spending." Starting with Goethe's Werther (hero of the novel *The Sor-
rows of Young Werther*, 1774), generation after generation of
sensitive loners, from artists to criminals, has chastised the
bovine middle class and its philistine values. The fact that these
days this attitude of romantic rebellion is itself a conformist
cliché has not stopped well-heeled poets, rock stars, and movie actors from assuming it for both its status and cash value.

In America this idealized rebellion has found particular resonance. After all, we are a nation founded by rebels against an
unjust authority, a society whose history is filled with back-
woodsmen, fur trappers, pioneers, mountain men, explorers, Indian scouts, and cowboys—all those Natty Bumppos and Huck
Finns lighting out for the territories so they could escape the petty
rules and hypocritical protocols of shopkeepers and schoolmarms

leading settled lives. No wonder, then, that America's most enduring popular heroes are all rebels or loners of one sort of another who
march together to the rhythms of Thoreau's "different drummer."

In addition to the high value placed on rebellious individualism, romanticism also bestowed status on the sensitive soul's
conspicuous response to the suffering of his fellow man. The
eighteenth-century "Man of Feeling," prone to outbursts of weep-
ing at the slightest hint of pathos, has evolved into Sensitive and
Compassionate Man. These tender souls respond intensely and os-
tentatiously to spectacles of injustice, deprivation, and suffering,
and thus display their social and moral superiority over the self-
satisfied dullards oblivious to the pain of their fellow human beings.[7] Alan Bloom called this "conspicuous compassion," and like
Thorstein Veblen's conspicuous consumption it identifies one as a
member of a superior elite.

Critical dissatisfaction with American society, then, exploits
the status-conferring roles of the suspicious intellectual, individualistic rebel, and possessor of superior sensitivity and compassion. But what makes this discontent specifically anti-American?
"America," after all, is a capacious idea, containing not just a wide
variety of regions and peoples but also many competing versions
of what "Americanism" itself comprises. Consider the following
from *New York Times* columnist Frank Rich, on what he consid-
ers to be the un-American excesses of patriotism since 9/11: "The
most telling American fables don't come in the blacks and whites
of our current strident political and cultural discourse, which so
often divides Americans into either flag-draped heroes or abject
traitors. The great American stories, from Huckleberry Finn's to
the Dixie Chicks [sic!], have always been nuanced; they can have
poetry and they can have dark shadows. They can combine a love
of country with an implicit criticism of it."[8]

Rich here displays the received wisdom of the postmodern intellectual, the high value placed on "dark shadows" and "nuance,"
the notion that moral certainty is a Victorian relic, like chimney
sweeps and whalebone corsets, and that every ideal is mere
camouflage for a more sinister and oppressive reality. In addition
Rich defines this attitude as a more authentic "Americanism,"

a genuine patriotism besmirched by the crass manipulations of Republicans and corporations.

There is a kernel of truth in Rich's point. Railing against the injustices and snobbery of fat cats, venal politicians, and plutocrats is as American as apple pie, and reflects one of the important ways America is a product of the West. What can be called "critical consciousness," the willingness of individuals to confront and express the injustices of their own societies, lies at the heart of Western and American success.[9] After all, the ethical godfathers of Western culture, Socrates and Jesus, were both critics of their own cultures who were executed for their complaints.

But Jesus and Socrates based their criticisms on transcendent standards that their societies had fallen short of, standards validated by a spiritual and eternal reality beyond the merely material and temporal. In contrast, the current type of reflexive complaint tends to assume not a spiritual standard created and monitored by a divine power but a *material* one based on ever-escalating utopian expectations that can never be fulfilled.[10]

Since this criticism is based on unattainable standards of earthly happiness and social harmony, no matter how successful America is at delivering freedom and material prosperity to large numbers of people, it will always fall short until *every* human on the planet is well fed, secure, attractive, healthy, and brimming with self-esteem. Moreover, all this prosperity will be created with a minimal impact on the natural environment—a goal obviously impossible in the real world of flawed humans and natural limits. When coupled with a distortion of the historical evidence, this utopian standard drives much of anti-Americanism. Shorn of any practical goal, criticism of America becomes a pseudo-religion whose ritualistic critiques are, as Paul Hollander puts it, "less than fully rational and not necessarily well founded," reflecting rather a "predisposition, a free-floating hostility or aversion."[11]

Thus critiques of core attributes of American life and ideals can be fairly characterized as anti-American when they are unsupported by evidence or are based on unrealistic expectations. For example, America represents the triumph of the middle class and its values; thus to attack the *idea* of the middle class, rather than merely satirizing its shortcomings or failure to live up to its own ideals, amounts to attacking a large part of what makes America America. So too with character traits such as individualism or self-reliance—these are so ingrained in America's history and national ideals that to attack them is to undermine a key part of what Americanism entails. That's why the cowboy, the mythic image that embodies American ideals of tough self-reliance, fair play, and rugged individualism, is continually attacked and ridiculed by critics of America both at home and abroad.[12] Certainly many leftist complaints about America focus not on any particular policies, domestic or foreign, but on such general ideas associated with America. As a British journalist commented after 9/11, for leftists "it is chic to disapprove of America, not only of its rulers or those who elected them, but of the idea of America itself."[13]

Criticism of America, then, that is not based on empirical evidence, distorts the historical record, holds American behavior up to impossible utopian standards not imposed on other peoples, and attacks ideals and traits quintessentially American, will perforce be anti-American: an irrational reflex rather than constructive criticism. Under various guises, such reflexive complaints are widespread in the news media and popular entertainment.

Discussions of media bias usually get bogged down in fighting over whether the media lean right or left.[14] Part of the problem is one of definition. In his recent response to attacks on the liberal media by Ann Coulter and Bernard Goldberg, Eric Alterman writes that the liberal media "is tiny and profoundly underfunded compared to its conservative counterpart," and adds, "as a columnist for the *Nation* . . . I work in the middle of it [i.e., the liberal media]."[15] If one defines the radical leftist ideology of the *Nation* as "liberal," as Alterman does, then of course the *New York Times*, *Washington Post*, CBS, ABC, etc. will all be "conservative." But by any reasonable definition of liberalism, a news industry 89 percent of whose journalists voted for Bill Clinton in 1992 can fairly be construed as liberal.[16]

Squabbling over the media's ideological preferences, however, misses the salient point. The media are businesses that must make a profit, as the left reminds us. But contrary to the leftist vision of corporate overlords imposing ideological restrictions on cowering reporters, those who work in the media—many of whom are concerned with careerist goals and professional status—are self-motivated to pursue the most professionally lucrative stories and angles. Thus whatever serves to advance a career and earn status within the profession can occasionally trump ideology.[17] That's why political scandal is so important: it can quickly make the career of the reporter who exposes it. Many reporters during the Clinton administration who no doubt voted for him and supported his policies nonetheless pursued the Whitewater and Monica Lewinsky stories with gusto. Leftist critics saw this as proof that the media do not tilt left, but in fact all it proved was that at times careerism is more important than partisanship. But over time, partisanship influences how the media report on events, particularly when that ideology is conducive to professional rewards and approval from intellectual gatekeepers.

The most career-boosting political scandals are those involving politicians who have lied to the people in order to conceal illegal activities. Uncovering this sort of deception feeds the reporter's conception of himself as a fearless crusader taking on the powers that be. This attitude of suspicion plays as well on the notion that social and political institutions are inherently corrupt and in need of constant scrutiny, that the truth is always a sordid substratum lurking beneath the spin on the surface—one of the favorite superstitions of postmodern intellectuals. Taking this attitude helps the reporter feel as though he too is an intellectual, hip to the latest wisdom that his oafish readers can't understand.

The war in Vietnam has obviously been the crucial event legitimizing for the media the assumption that the government and the people were mired in nationalist or anti-Communist delusions. Thus Americans needed to be instructed on the true nature of the conflict, which to many in the media was not a defense of an ally threatened with Communist tyranny but *in reality* a doomed attempt to prop up an oppressive regime of capitalist lackeys trying to crush a popular socialist revolution. Thus American failure and Viet Cong success—the former predicated on American guilt, the latter on Viet Cong righteousness—formed the unspoken assumptions behind much of the media's coverage of the war.

The reporting of the Tet offensive, begun by North Vietnam in January 1968, illustrates this process of shaping the news according to an ideological script. In military terms the offensive was an utter failure for the Viet Cong and a great success for the American military. Within months after initiating Tet, the North Vietnamese forces were ejected from Saigon and Hue, their siege of Khesanh was lifted, their infrastructure of cadres in the south had been exposed and destroyed, and they had suffered enormous disparities in casualties, including some forty thousand killed. Yet as Victor Davis Hanson has written of the media coverage during the first week's fighting in Saigon, "Cameras flashed back images of a few dead Americans on the [embassy] compound grounds. Tanks and howitzers rushed through the streets of Saigon. Headlines flashed 'War Hits Saigon.'"[18] The implication back home, created out of instantaneous video footage of the carnage taken out of context, and interviews with frightened American soldiers in the heat of battle, was that Tet offensive was a success and the American effort doomed. The Viet Cong strategy of winning the public relations war in the United States, regardless of how many dead were sent back north, was validated. As Hanson summarizes Peter Braestrup's two-volume analysis of the media's coverage of Tet, "The story of a hard-fought American victory, characterized by remarkable American bravery, did not fit well with either the sensationalism that built journalistic careers or the general antiwar sentiments of the reporters themselves."[19]

After Tet, rather than capitalizing on the victory, Washington began to look for ways to escape from Vietnam, even the conservative *Wall Street Journal* warning that "the whole Vietnam effort may be doomed."[20] We all know the result of this loss of nerve abetted by the media: nearly sixty thousand Americans and millions of Vietnamese were killed, and hundreds of thousands of "boat people" renounced the privilege of living in a revolutionary, socialist society such as Vietnam was to become.

The media's assumption of the mantle of principled critic of a corrupt political establishment, which the Vietnam War helped to confer, was further confirmed by the Watergate scandal. Watergate also illustrated the many professional and financial benefits that would accrue to those who unmasked such nefarious goings-on: book contracts, movie deals, Pulitzer Prizes, and the ascension to celebrity status usually reserved for movie stars. And this lucre was sanctified by the implication of great public service on the part of lone reporters exposing the sordid reality beneath the lies of politicians and government officials. The attitude of suspicion characteristic of the modern intellectual here found its most lucrative rewards.

This reflexive suspicion on the part of the media, one frequently directed at delivering both status and professional gain as much as uncovering the truth, has at times characterized the coverage of the recent wars in Afghanistan and Iraq as well. The emphasis given to civilian casualties is a case in point. It may sound callous, but civilian casualties are an inescapable reality of modern warfare. The fact that they occur is not news, unless of course they result from deliberate policy. Yet in both Afghanistan and Iraq the print and visual media have played up civilian casualties, often devoting front-page space and grisly photos to the dead. The real story in both countries has been the extraordinarily *low* numbers of civilian deaths due to the unprecedented efforts of the American strategists and forces in combat, often at the risk of their own troops. Reporting such a truth would not suit the assumption that a corrupt government and military are unconcerned with inflicting casualties on the innocent.

The media no doubt would argue that they are merely performing their roles as "watchdogs," monitoring the government and providing the necessary information citizens need to make informed decisions. Doubtless the government needs watching, but why should we trust the media—private businesses run for profit and staffed by people some of whom are certainly principled, many of whom are careerists or biased ideologues? As soon as we had embarked on military action, we were bound to expect all the disorder and mistakes and inadvertent suffering typical of war that the media present as essential and novel information. Rubbing our faces in that suffering will not change the fundamentally brutal nature of modern warfare. What's important is that we are aware of the principles for which we are fighting and which, hopefully, justify the suffering. Absent that context, the miseries of war become an emotional media spectacle rather than useful information.

If the constant detailing of war's perennial misery often does not inform, what is such reporting supposed to accomplish? Intentionally or not, such coverage may erode our will to pursue our objectives, as Vietnam demonstrates. Feelings aroused by contemplating suffering can become too uncomfortable, particularly if Sensitive Man and Compassionate Man are made to feel guilty for the suffering. In a therapeutic culture such as ours, such feelings frequently will trump principle, national interests, and truth. It is possible that if we see enough bodies mangled by our missiles, we will feel so bad we will forget about the nearly three thousand Americans mangled in New York and Washington—and the many more likely to die in the future if we fail to take proper action now. In other words, supposedly objective coverage in fact comprises "stealth editorials" against these wars and, in effect if not in intent, represents an assault on American interests.

This interpretation of the media's coverage of civilian casualties in Iraq was confirmed by one of its (once) biggest stars, Peter Arnett of CNN, whose coverage of the first Gulf War from Baghdad earned him celebrity status and a recent television movie about his exploits. In March 2003 Arnett was interviewed by the Iraqi Information Ministry, now famous for its surreal pronouncements of Hussein's imminent victory even as American tanks were rumbling up the block. "Within the United States," Arnett helpfully informed his Iraqi listeners, "there is growing challenge to President Bush about the conduct of the war and also opposition to the war. So our reports about civilian casualties here . . . help those who oppose the war."[21] Arnett was fired by NBC, but not so much for his remarks, spectacularly false as well as ideologically driven, but for the public relations problems he created for the network.

The media's relentless accentuation of the negative, their assumption that the U.S. government and the military are untrustworthy, and their self-serving vision of themselves as superior caretakers of the truth hidden by the delusions in which their fellow citizens are mired, all may ultimately serve the ideological preferences and careers of correspondents and reporters, but they compromise America's interests and security.

A similar chronic suspicion of American society dominates the popular media as well, especially the movies and television. Despite efforts to present movies and television shows as "art," the vast majority of these productions are trivial entertainment. Hence those who create them are even more anxious than newspaper and television reporters to display their intellectual seriousness, and therefore more vulnerable to the received wisdom and intellectual fashions that trickle down from the academy.

Thus movie, television, and rock stars, and assorted celebrities who desire to project a persona more weighty than mere purveyor of entertainment ephemera, frequently ape the anti-American attitudes of leftists opposed on principle not so much to particular policies but to the very idea of America; they also convince themselves that they must be in the forefront of those who deplore the inequities of American society. When Susan Sarandon says that "The United States is a land that has raped every area of the world," she can rest assured that the gatekeepers of intellectual seriousness in the academy and the press will applaud her political sophistication and correctness.[22] The same applies to Sean Penn, who before the war in Iraq made a pilgrimage to Baghdad. Particularly ironic—given that Penn, as he later admitted, ended up being a propaganda asset for Hussein—was his statement to the BBC that he had made the trip out of a "concern" that he could be "duped by a media perspective that saturates us everyday."[23] He did not entertain the possibility of being duped by leftist ideologues or homicidal dictators.

Such moral and political myopia is all too typical of Hollywood celebrities who think that sound bite moralizing will earn them an intellectual respectability and moral stature that can outweigh the generally vulgar and forgettable entertainment they provide. More significant than the occasional absurdities of an Ed Asner, Barbara Streisand, or Martin Sheen, however, is the relentless, cumulative disparagement of traditional American values that dominates the movies, television, and popular music, not to mention the distorted view of American society that these products communicate to the rest of the world.[24]

For example, you'd never know from watching television and the movies that the average American manages to find sexual satisfaction in heterosexual marriage or describes him or herself as religious. According to one survey reported by Michael Medved, extramarital sex is nine to fourteen times more likely to be depicted on television than sex within marriage, even though married couples report a higher satisfaction with and frequency of sex than do single people. Although homosexuals make up at most 3 percent of the population, the Gay and Lesbian Alliance against Defamation recently counted more than thirty openly gay or lesbian characters on television, most of whom are depicted as charming, well adjusted, attractive, and happy, as in *Will and Grace*, one of the highest-rated shows on television. Contrast this with the complete lack of sympathetic television (or movie) characters who attend church with any regularity. The only television family in whose lives church is a regular experience is the cartoon Simpsons.[25] When religion does appear on television, it's usually in some sort of sentimental and theologically vague New Age form, as in *Touched by an Angel*.

Popular culture's hostility to the traditional nuclear family and religion, both key elements in American society and history, is part of a larger dissatisfaction with American middle-class values. Satirizing the "boobsoisie," as H. L. Mencken called the middle class early in the twentieth century, has been a staple of intellectual and artistic life since the nineteenth century, when the middle class first became dominant. Poking fun at the middle class has also been congenial with the outlook of the quirky loners and self-reliant individualists mentioned earlier, all of whom chafe at the routines and conformist values of small-town or suburban existence. Since this received wisdom dominates higher education, art, and literature, it is no wonder that popular culture is saturated with it as well.[26] By now such criticism itself has become a collection of clichéd complaints against the conformist middle class, epitomizing a new conformity. Also to be noted is that most artists and writers these days are thoroughly middle class themselves, and as much, if not more, caught up in the bourgeois pursuit of money, consumption, and status as a broker, banker, or CEO.

Again, it's important to distinguish satire directed at the middle class that nonetheless accepts the legitimacy of its basic values from a no-holds-barred attack on the middle class as intrinsically corrupt and oppressive. Making fun of the suburbs, for example, has been a staple of popular entertainment from the very beginning of suburban life. The Bob Hope movie *Bachelor in Paradise* (1961), about a sophisticated urban writer living in a suburban development to research a new book, satirizes various aspects of suburban family life such as supermarkets, electronic appliances, and commuting. But in the end the movie endorses the freedom and prosperity of such a life, once the suburbanites under Hope's tutelage have learned to add more sexual spice to their harried lives. So too with *The Simpsons*, which some may think attacks traditional American family life. In fact, as Paul Cantor argues in a perceptive essay, *The Simpsons* is one of the few popular television shows that "offers an enduring image of the nuclear family in the very act of satirizing it," celebrating concurrently the American middle class ideals of small-town life and local control versus the metropolis and rule by bureaucratic government.[27]

Such gentle satire is different from the wholesale assaults on American middle-class life found everywhere in popular culture. Even in science fiction, middle-class life is portrayed as a soulless arena of deadening conformity. Writing of the *Harry Potter, Star Wars*, and *Lord of the Rings* series, Michael Valdez Moses writes that all three speak to "a general boredom with modern bourgeois existence. The escapism of these stories is an antidote to the routine that is the special curse of safe, static middle-class life."[28] Popular culture's dissatisfaction with middle-class suburban life, however, goes beyond satire of boring routines. Such a way of life is presented as reprehensible for its alleged repression and corruption. In David Lynch's *Blue Velvet* (1986), one of the more lurid expositions of this theme, the opening sequence provides a graphic display of the suburban moral decay hidden beneath the bright and happy surface. The camera pans over an iconic house with a white picket fence, then lingers over a man with a hose who seems to have collapsed from a heart attack, then follows the water as it penetrates the lawn, finally zooming in on the many bugs and insects swarming just beneath the surface.

A more recent attack on the suburban middle class can be found in Sam Mendes's *American Beauty* (1999), which won five Academy Awards—always a reliable indication of support for received ideas. *American Beauty* tells the story of Lester Burnham, a drab suburbanite in a dead-end job, and his ultimately fatal midlife crisis that leads him to smoking pot, working out with narcissistic fervor, and lusting after his teenage daughter's fellow cheerleader. Burnham's shrewish wife, who is having an affair with a business rival, is an inauthentic real estate agent; his neighbor is a homophobic army colonel whose tyranny has literally silenced his wife, making real a stale feminist metaphor; and his daughter is a budding tart and nihilist. Every trite critique of American society is recycled in this "puerile pastiche," as Michael Medved called it.[29] In the film's universe, heterosexual marriage deadens the soul and compromises its fulfillment; the film's only positive relationship is between Burnham's gay neighbors. Business, represented by Burnham's adulteress wife, is superficial, corrupt, and inauthentic. The military, represented by the neighbor, is a hotbed of sadism and sexual repression—the film's tritest moment comes when the homophobic Colonel Pitts mouth-kisses Lester and reveals that he's *really* homosexual. American high school youth, in the person of Lester's daughter and her nubile friend Angela, are nihilistic sex fiends. The only sympathetic character beside Lester, who has awakened to the corrupt "quiet desperation" of American life preached in a thousand university seminar rooms, is the colonel's son Ricky, a drug dealer and "artist" who makes pretentious short movies. The artist and criminal, are, needless to say, two of the most worn stereotypes of resistance to bourgeoisie conformity and hypocrisy.

Despite the banality of its message, *American Beauty* was greeted with extravagant praise. Kenneth Turan in the *Los Angeles Times* called the movie "a quirky and disturbing take on modern

American life . . . a strange brooding and very accomplished film."
The *New York Times'* Janet Maslin also liked the movie's take on
"curdled suburbia," praising the movie as "full of its own brand of
corrosive novelty" and predicting approvingly, "If you don't share
the film's piercing vision of what really matters [would that be pot
and pedophilia?] someday you will." And Peter Travers in *Rolling
Stone* claimed that the movie showed "the kind of artful defiance
that Hollywood is usually too timid to deliver." I suppose that's
why a "timid" Hollywood rewarded all that "defiance" with five
Academy Awards, including Best Picture, Best Actor, Best Director, and Best Screenplay.[30]

American Beauty illustrates another technique used by those
convinced of the unworthiness of American society, namely, singling out for criticism a small segment of America and suggesting
that it represents *all* of American society and its pervasive corruption. Some of those opposed to the private ownership of guns, for
example, frequently make the gun an emblem of what they see as
the fundamental flaw in American culture and character, as well
as America's history of oppression, conquest, and lust for violence.

Another Academy Award–winning and critically acclaimed
film, Michael Moore's *Bowling for Columbine*, demonstrates how
a contested social issue such as gun control can be used to advance
an anti-American outlook. Although presented as a documentary,
the movie is very much fiction, many of its scenes cobbled together from various bits of footage shot at different times and
places. This fabrication serves the film's tendentious thesis that
the murders at Columbine High School resulted from a neurotic
and peculiarly American obsession with violence abetted by the
National Rifle Association and the weapons industry.

Thus in order to suggest that the NRA and its then president
Charlton Heston, by holding a scheduled meeting in Colorado after the killings, were callously indifferent to a tragedy that their
pro-gun policies presumably fostered, Moore spliced together the
audio from seven sentences taken from five separate parts of two
different Heston speeches (one given a year *after* Columbine),
camouflaging each splice with still or video footage to create the
illusion of one speech.[31] Moore's sleight-of-hand fooled most re-

viewers, like Philip French of England's *The Observer*, who wrote, "Within days of both events, Heston was in town at NRA rallies, speaking in a sickening patriotic rhetoric to enthusiastic audiences of gun-nuts."[32] The other "event" was the shooting of a six-year-old by a classmate in Flint, Michigan. In fact, Heston appeared in Flint eight months after the shooting at a get-out-the-vote rally, not an NRA function.[33]

Moore's disregard of fact and truthfulness, however, isn't likely to bother the intellectuals and those aping their views—they will enjoy his "hip postmodern" disregard for a "truth" most of them claim to believe doesn't exist anyway. His relentless documentation of American pathologies will flatter their anti-American disposition. Indeed, Moore's indictment of America is a constant theme of the movie and explains several sequences that have little to do with the Columbine shootings or gun control. One montage, predictably set to Louis Armstrong's version of "What a Wonderful World," details all the coups, assassinations, and revolutions allegedly fomented by the United States, each image followed by a highly suspect casualty count. The most egregious is the claim promulgated by Sadam Hussein's propaganda machine and Osama bin Laden, that UN sanctions and U.S. bombing killed 500,000 Iraqi children, a claim refuted by Matt Welch in *Reason* magazine.[34] Moore's point is obvious: the same neuroses afflicting the American character account for both Columbine and this history of imperialist oppression and murder abroad.

A recurring motif of Moore's movie is the exposure of this violent flaw in the American character. Moore dismisses the role of visual violence found in the media in helping to explain the Columbine murders by pointing to other countries where young people enjoy such entertainment without engaging in violent crime—it is the American character and the culture forming it that is responsible, thereby displaying the most stereotypical notions of anti-Americanism. Canada is continually used in these simplistic comparisons, since according to the film's dubious statistic there are seven million guns in Canada yet the Canadian murder rate is a fraction of the American. After rejecting the contribution of violent popular entertainment or the availability of guns, Moore professes ignorance concerning the answer to the question of American violence. Yet his film relentlessly suggests one: a sickness in the American soul, aided and abetted by the arms industry, racism, the Republican party, capitalism, and the NRA—the usual suspects trotted out by those who may be justifiably designated as anti-American.

Moore's diagnosis of America's sickness is given a highly dubious psychological and historical explanation in an animated sequence describing American history as one long orgy of violence against what trendy intellectuals call the "other," a violence whose origins lie in the white race's irrational fear of "people of color." We see the Puritans landing at Plymouth Rock, then slaughtering friendly Indians out of irrational fear, turning upon witches after all the Indians are gone. Then we are told how Americans kidnaped Africans and made them slaves to create American wealth. White Americans remained still neurotically fearful of rampaging black men and rebellious slaves, so Samuel Colt invented the revolver to help maintain white supremacy. The Ku Klux Klan and NRA are then presented as complementary institutions created after the Civil War to assuage white America's fears of the nonwhite "other"; thus we see an NRA member pouring gasoline on a cross next to a Klansman. The theme is continued into the present, when whites fearful of a media-manufactured hysteria about black crime keep buying the guns that end up murdering American children.[35]

This distorted version of American history—that due to some genetic deficiency peculiar to white Americans, white people are so terrified of anyone different that they resort to firearms to assuage their racist insecurities—is the standard one embraced by America's enemies at home and abroad. It is a view of American history that has become the orthodoxy reproduced in textbooks and classrooms across the land. We should not be surprised that it turns up in Moore's film.

Moore's films and books are part of a thriving popular culture catering to those who either hate America or are racked with guilt about its wealth and power or simply want to strike rebellious postures.

Another important segment of culture is the punk-rock scene, the tenor of whose ideas can be determined from the remarkable starring role that MIT linguist Noam Chomsky enjoys on the album covers and in the lyrics of many punk-rock songs, even appearing on records by Bad Religion, Propagandhi, and Chumbawumba.[36] As the historian Keith Windschuttle wrote recently, "[Chomsky] epitomized the New Left and its hatred of 'Amerika,' a country he believed, through its policies both at home and abroad, had descended into fascism."[37] Chomsky's consuming, sixties-style hatred of America typifies much of the punk-rock scene as well. Chomsky has cut his own CDs marketed to punk consumers, filled not with music but with sound bites from his speeches and books, and sporting titles such as "Free Market Fantasies: Capitalism in the Real World." As an article in *Wired* magazine put it, "Chomsky is somewhere between Kerouac and Nietzsche—carrying around one of his books is automatic countercultural cachet."[38] In other words, Chomsky and his ideas function as fashion markers for young people searching for a rebel identity.

Chomsky's vision of America is reflected in punk-rock lyrics. Propagandhi's latest album is called "Today's Empires, Tomorrow's Ashes," a phrase from a speech by convicted cop-killer and martyr of the left Mumia Abu-Jamal, and the album's liner notes recommend Chomsky's *Necessary Illusions: Thought Control in Democratic Societies* and Michael Moore's website for further reading. The following is typical of this group's juvenile-leftist thinking, from a song about an illegal alien: "It's our culture and consumption that makes [sic] her life unbearable. Fuck this country; its angry eyes, its knee-jerk hordes." Somewhat subtler, but equally reflective of the Chomskyean vision of America's awfulness, are the sentiments from Bad Religion's "Streets of America." Like their mentor, the lyricists see a country "desolate and without purpose/radiating from so many septic sources," a "spreading network of broken dreams" filled with "sparkled promises paved with pathos and hysteria." They advise "weary native sons/step back/and see the damage done," ending with a bleak vision of "false hope corridors to greener pastures." The message is clear.

This country—a land of opportunity that millions of immigrants every day risk their lives to reach, and where young men with a modicum of talent can make huge amounts of money selling shopworn angst to teenagers—is really a barren wasteland.

Such a vision of American spiritual and moral desolation prepares the ground for the political messages of those who attribute America's alleged failures to free enterprise and liberal democracy, as Chomsky does. Normal teen disgruntlement is thus channeled into a failed leftist outlook that reflexively rejects the American political order, as in the following lyric from Bad Religion's "Slaves": "Congress runs your daily life but they brainwash you so you think it's freedom." No alternatives to this bleak and oppressive U.S. social system are proposed.

It is tempting to dismiss these assaults on American society and institutions by popular culture and the media as insignificant entertainment, or we may even see them as a display of healthy self-criticism. Needless to say, we need free and open discussion of our society, government, and policies and their flaws. But true debate, the sort envisioned by the writers of the First Amendment, is reasoned, coherent, based on evidence, and clear about fundamental principles and assumptions. It is constructive in intent and focused on goals that are attainable, recognizing the limits the world imposes on human ideals and achievements. Much of the criticism of America found in popular culture and the media is none of these things. The values and principles behind the critiques are incoherent, the goals and standards of judgment are utopian, and the evidence is flawed or completely missing.

This widespread phenomenon of popularized and standardized self-doubt and suspicion may erode collective confidence in our way of life and political system. For some, this failure of nerve becomes a status symbol, a sign of superior intelligence, sensitivity, and sophistication. The problem with the trendy self-loathing is that no society, no matter how rich or militarily powerful, can survive for long if its own people do not believe that it provides a reasonably satisfactory way to live and a decent enough institutional foundation for it. By contrast, many adversaries abroad, especially the most violent ones, have no doubt about the superiority of their culture and religion and are willing to kill and die for them. Recent historical events confirm the truth of this observation. It cannot be ruled out that the terrorists of 9/11 were encouraged and felt legitimated by the messages of self-doubt, moral weakness, and corruption our media and popular culture have been sending to the world since the 1960s. This lack of self-confidence was tangibly expressed in 1975 when we abandoned an ally for whom we had spilt blood and treasure. Four years later a few students took over the American embassy in Tehran, an affront to our national sovereignty that was left unpunished by a president paralyzed by what he called "malaise." During the next twenty-five years U.S. Marines were blown up in Beirut, our embassies in Africa were bombed, and our citizens abroad slaughtered by those opposed not to any particular policy but to the very existence and nature of our society. Each failure to respond validated the Islamicist belief that our culture was morally sick and corrupt, that we were committed more to our comfort and pleasure than to our ideals.

Many have noted (and some have expressed unease over) the upsurge of patriotism since 9/11, but the real question is whether such displays are the signs of a renewed appreciation of America's virtues or merely ephemeral sentiments. The apparent disposition of popular culture to foster a corrosive, irrational criticism of our society will continue to delay the realization that, though America may not be the best country imaginable, it may very well be the best possible.

NOTES

1. Cf. Paul Hollander: "It is quite likely that never before in history have such large numbers of people, comfortable and privileged to various degrees, come to the conclusion that their society was severely flawed or thoroughly immoral," in *Anti-Americanism: Critiques at Home and Abroad, 1965–1990* (Oxford, 1992), 41.

2. For a critique of the perceived wisdom that the modern world is uniquely evil, see Raymond Tallis, *Enemies of Hope: A Critique of Contemporary Pessimism* (New York and London, 1999), 186–217. See too Hollander, op. cit., pp. 49–78.

3. On this topic, see the discussion by Daniel J. Flynn in *Why the Left Hates America* (Roseville, Calif., 2002), 39–78.

4. As Robert Hughes calls it in his book of the same name, *The Culture of Complaint: A Passionate Look into the Ailing Heart of America* (New York, 1994).

5. In "In Quest of Modern Culture: Hysterical or Historical Humanism," *Critical Review* (1991), 410.

6. For the influence of Romanticism on modern consumerism, see Colin Campbell, *The Romantic Ethic and the Spirit of Modern Consumerism* (London, 1987).

7. For a more detailed discussion of the evolution of the Man of Feeling into Sensitive Man and Compassionate Man, see my *Plagues of the Mind: The New Epidemic of False Knowledge* (Wilmington, Del., 1999), 58–75.

8. In Frank Rich, "Had Enough of the Flag Yet?" *New York Times* (July 6, 2003).

9. For a brief discussion of "critical consciousness" and Western culture, see my *Greek Ways: How the Greeks Created Western Civilization* (San Francisco, 2000), 188–198.

10. Cf. Richard Crockatt, *America Embattled* (London and New York, 2003), 51: "Projections of Americanism tend to invite all-or-nothing responses. Just as America—or rather the idea of America—has been the focus of utopian dreams and inflated expectations, it has been regarded as the stuff of nightmares too. . . . These nightmare versions of America are mirror images of the idealizations. . . . They [the impulses to idealize or demonize] may have little to do with flesh-and-blood America and everything to do with the aspirations and frustrations of the groups and individuals who promote them."

11. Hollander, op. cit., p. 7.

12 See my brief comments on the anti-cowboy phenomenon in "The Cowboy Myth," *American Spectator* (May/June 2002), 20.

13. Quoted in Crockatt, 45.

14. For anti-Americanism in the media, see Hollander, 215–235.

15. In *What Liberal Media?* (New York, 2003), 9.

16. The results of a Freedom Forum poll cited in Flynn, 109. For further evidence see S. Robert Lichter et al.: *The Media Elite* (New York, 1986), esp. Ch. 2.

17. See the remarks by Michael Schudson, *The Power of News* (Cambridge, Mass. and London, 1995), 7–9; also Hollander, 248–255.

18. In *Culture and Carnage* (New York, 2001), 392.

19. *Culture and Carnage,* 417. See too the discussion by Oscar Handlin, *The Distortion of America*, 2nd ed. (New Brunswick and London, 1996), 92–119.

20. Quoted in Hanson, *Culture and Carnage,* 406.

21 Quoted by James Bowman in "Superior to the Truth," *New Criterion* (May 2003), 59. Arnett has a long history of fabricating news. It was Arnett who reported the infamous statement by an American officer in Vietnam: "It became necessary to destroy the town in order to save it." But, as Victor Hanson discovered, "there was little evidence—other than from Arnett himself—that any

American officer said anything of the sort. . . . Arnett never identified by name the officer who was his purported source. Nor did he produce anyone—civilian or military—who could corroborate the statement. A military investigation to ferret out the guilty officer turned up nothing." In *Culture and Carnage*, 418.

22. Quote from Flynn, 85–86.

23. From the BBC website for December 16, 2002, news.bbc.co.uk/1/hi/world/middle_east/2577981.stm.

24. See Hollander, 221–255; also Michael Medved, *Hollywood vs. America* (New York, 1992), especially 216–235 and S. Robert Lichter et al.: *Watching America*, (New York, 1991).

25. Michael Medved, "That's Entertainment? Hollywood's Contribution to Anti-Americanism Abroad," *National Interest* (Summer 2002), 8–9. On the Simpsons and church, see Paul A. Cantor, "*The Simpsons*: Atomistic Politics and the Nuclear Family," in *The Simpsons and Philosophy*, ed. William Irwin, Mark T. Conrad, Aeon J. Skable (New York, 2001), 170.

26. This negative view of the middle class is so ingrained in our culture that, according to the *New Oxford American Dictionary*, one meaning of the adjective form is "attaching too much importance to convention, security, and material comfort."

27. Cantor, 165. See too his remarks on how producers of television sitcoms "set out to endorse contemporary trends away from the stable, traditional nuclear family," 164.

28. In "Back to the Future," *Reason* (July 2003), 50.

29. Medved, "That's Entertainment?" 8.

30. These reviews can be accessed online: at www.imdb.com/Turls?COM+0169547. Not all reviewers were taken in by the movie's clichés. *New Republic* critic Stanley Kaufmann wrote that all the screenwriter Alan Ball "can tell us is what many American and British and French and Italian films have already expounded. Modern urban-suburban life can be anesthetic. . . . Ball has nothing to add." *Regarding Film: Criticism and Comment* (Baltimore and London, 2001), 149. Likewise David Edelstein in *Slate* (September 18, 1999) called the movie "smug and easy," full of "stale and reactionary ideas."

31. See the detailed analysis by David Hardy at www.hardylaw.net/Truth_About_Bowling.html. See too "Michael Moore, Humbug," by Kay S. Hymowitz, *City Journal* (Summer 2003), available online at www.cityjournal.org/html/13_3_michael_moore.html.

32. *Observer* (November 17, 2002). This review and others can be accessed at http://us.imdb.com/TUrls?COM+0310793.

33. See www.hardylaw.net/Truth_About_Bowling.html.

34. See "The Politics of Dead Children," *Reason* (March 2002). Available online at www.reason.com/0203/fe.mw.the.shtml. Welch also traces the mainstream media's complicity in popularizing the flawed study that generated the false statistics: ". . . The report might well have ended up in the dustbin of bad mathematics had a CESR (Center for Economic and Social Rights) fact-finding tour of Iraq not been filmed by Lesley Stahl of *60 Minutes*. In a May 12, 1996 report that later won her an Emmy and an Alfred I. DuPont-Columbia University Journalism Award, Stahl used CESR's faulty numbers and atomic-bomb imagery to confront Madeleine Albright, then the U.S. ambassador to the United Nations. "We have heard that a half million children have died,"

Stahl said. "I mean, that's more children than died in Hiroshima . . . is the price worth it?"

35. Moore's linking of the NRA to the KKK is historically false. President Ulysses S. Grant was elected the eighth president of the NRA—an organization founded by ex-Union officers—after his vigorous prosecution of the Klan; the next president was General Philip Sheridan, who had removed the governors of Texas and Louisiana for failing to control the Klan.

36. Cf. Daniel Flynn: "Bad Religion used a Chomsky lecture as the B-side on one of their singles. When Pearl Jam set up temporary 'pirate' radio stations . . . during a mid-1990s tour, songs . . . were interspersed with clips of the MIT linguist's angry rhetoric," *Why the Left Hates America*, 88. Thanks to my sons Isaac and Cole for their help with this section.

37. In "The Hypocrisy of Noam Chomsky," *New Criterion* (May 2003), 5.

38. Quoted by Stefan Kanfer, "America's Dumbest Intellectual," *City Journal* (Summer 2002), available online at www.city-journal.org/html/12_3_urbanities-americas_dumbe.html.

A Note on the Contributors

DIGBY ANDERSON has written, edited, or contributed to some thirty books, including *Losing Friends* and *The War on Wisdom*. He has also been a regular columnist for *The Times* of London, the *Sunday Times*, the *Spectator*, the *Sunday Telegraph*, and the *National Review*.

DAVID C. BROOKS is a Foreign Service Officer with the U.S. Department of State currently in Peru. He has served in Poland, Venezuela, and Nicaragua. This article represents his personal views and not those of the State Department. All titles and quotations in his essay were translated by him.

JAMES CEASER is professor of politics at the University of Virginia, where he teaches courses in American institutions and political development. He has served as a visiting professor at Montesquieu University in Bordeaux, the University of Rennes, Oxford University, the University of Basel, and the University of Florence. He is the author, among other works, of *Reconstructing America* and *Liberal Democracy and Political Science*.

PATRICK L. CLAWSON is deputy director of the Washington Institute for Near East Policy and senior editor of *Middle East Quarterly*. He has been senior research professor at the Institute for National Strategic Studies of the National Defense University, and senior economist at the Foreign Policy Research Institute, the World Bank, and the International Monetary Fund. He has written or edited more than twenty books on the Middle East.

WALTER D. CONNOR is professor of political science, sociology, and international relations at Boston University. His books include *Deviance in Soviet Society; Socialism, Politics, Equality; Escape from Socialism: The Polish Route;* and *Tattered Banners: Labor, Conflict and Corporatism in Postcommunist Russia.*

ANTHONY DANIELS is a British physician and writer whose books include *Utopias Elsewhere: A Journey Through the Disappearing World of Communist Countries; Sweet Waist of America* (about Central America during its period of guerrilla warfare); *Zanzibar to Timbuktu;* and *Monrovia Mon Amour,* an account of a sojourn in war-torn Liberia.

MARK FALCOFF is a resident scholar at the American Enterprise Institute in Washington, D.C. He received his M.A. and Ph.D. from Princeton University and has taught at the universities of Illinois, Oregon, and California (Los Angeles) and at the Foreign Service Institute. His books include *Small Countries, Large Issues; Modern Chile, 1970–1989: A Critical History; Panama's Canal;* and *Cuba the Morning After: Confronting Castro's Legacy.*

MICHAEL FREUND is a writer and editor at the Vienna daily *Der Standard.* His publications include works on Austrian scientists, the Rothschilds, the Marienthal 1930–1980 restudy, the midtown Manhattan study, and product and design culture. He studied psychology and sociology in Vienna, Heidelberg, and New York, where he received a Ph.D. from Columbia University.

ADAM GARFINKLE is the author of *Telltale Hearts: The Origin and Impact of the Vietnam Antiwar Movement.* He spent the Iraq War in Berlin as a Bosch Fellow in Public Policy of the American Academy of Berlin. He thanks the American Academy and its executive director, Gary Smith, for the privilege.

JOHN EARL HAYNES is twentieth-century political historian at the Library of Congress. He is the author of *Red Scare or Red Menace?* and, with Harvey Klehr, *The Secret World of American Communism; Venona: Decoding Soviet Espionage in America;* and *In Denial: Historians, Communism and Espionage.*

PAUL HOLLANDER is professor emeritus of sociology at the University of Massachusetts at Amherst. In addition to *Anti-Americanism,* his books include *Soviet and American Society: A Comparison; Political Pil-*

grims; The Survival of the Adversary Culture; Political Will and Personal Belief; and *Discontents.*

ROGER KIMBALL is managing editor of *The New Criterion.* Among his recent books are *The Long March: How the Cultural Revolution of the 1960s Changed America* and *Lives of the Mind: The Use and Abuse of Intelligence from Hegel to Wodehouse.*

HARVEY KLEHR is Andrew Mellon Professor of Politics and History at Emory University, and has written widely on the American Communist movement and the radical left in the United States. His most recent book, with John Earl Haynes, is *In Denial: Historians, Communism and Espionage.*

MICHAEL MOSBACHER is director of the Social Affairs Unit, an independent social policy think tank based in London. He is the author of *Marketing the Revolution: The New Anti-Capitalism and the Attack upon Corporate Brands.*

MICHAEL RADU is co-chairman of the Center on Terrorism, Counterterrorism, and Homeland Security; senior fellow at the Foreign Policy Research Institute in Philadelphia; and contributing editor of *Orbis.* His books include *The Cuban Transition: Lessons from the Romanian Experience; Collapse or Decay? Cuba and the East European Transitions from Communism; Latin American Revolutionaries: Groups, Goals, Methods* (with Vladimir Tismaneanu); and *Violence and the Latin American Revolutionaries.*

BARRY RUBIN is director of the Global Research in International Affairs (GLORIA) Center and editor of the *Middle East Review of International Affairs (MERIA) Journal.* His books include *The Transformation of Palestinian Politics; The Tragedy of the Middle East; Anti-American Terrorism and the Middle East: A Documentary History* (edited with Judith Colp Rubin); and *Yasir Arafat: A Political Biography.*

BRUCE S. THORNTON is professor of classics and humanities at California State University in Fresno, specializing in ancient Greece. He has written *Plagues of the Mind: The New Epidemic of False Knowledge* and, most recently, *Searching for Joaquin: Myth, Murieta, and History in California.*

SANDRA STOTSKY is at present a visiting professor in the School of Education at Northeastern University in Boston. She was most recently senior associate commissioner at the Massachusetts Department of Education. She is the author of *Losing Our Language: How Multiculturalism Undermines our Children's Ability to Read, Write and Reason* and editor of *What's at Stake in the K–12 Standards Wars: A Primer for Educational Policy Makers.*

CATHY YOUNG is the author of *Ceasefire: Why Women and Men Must Join Forces to Achieve True Equality* and *Growing Up in Moscow: Memories of a Soviet Girlhood.* She is a regular columnist for the *Boston Globe* and *Reason* magazine, and has contributed to numerous publications including the *Wall Street Journal,* the *New York Times,* the *Washington Post,* the *National Review,* and the *New Republic.* A Rutgers University graduate, she immigrated to the United States from the Soviet Union in 1980.